REFERENCE

Policing and the Condition of England

CLARENDON STUDIES IN CRIMINOLOGY

Published under the auspices of the Institute of Criminology,
University of Cambridge, the Mannheim Centre, London School of
Economics, and the Centre for Criminological Research, University of Oxford.

GENERAL EDITOR: PER-OLOF WIKSTRÖM (*University of Cambridge*)

EDITORS: ALISON LIEBLING AND MANUEL EISNER
(*University of Cambridge*)

DAVID DOWNES, PAUL ROCK, and JILL PEAY
(*London School of Economics*)

ROGER HOOD, LUCIA ZEDNER, and RICHARD YOUNG
(*University of Oxford*)

Recent titles in this series:

Policing and the Condition of England

Memory, Politics, and Culture

Ian Loader
and
Aogán Mulcahy

OXFORD
UNIVERSITY PRESS

*This book has been printed digitally and produced in a standard specification
in order to ensure its continuing availability*

OXFORD
UNIVERSITY PRESS

Great Clarendon Street, Oxford OX2 6DP

Oxford University Press is a department of the University of Oxford.
It furthers the University's objective of excellence in research, scholarship,
and education by publishing worldwide in

Oxford New York

Auckland   Cape Town   Dar es Salaam   Hong Kong   Karachi
Kuala Lumpur   Madrid   Melbourne   Mexico City   Nairobi
New Delhi   Shanghai   Taipei   Toronto
With offices in
Argentina   Austria   Brazil   Chile   Czech Republic   France   Greece
Guatemala   Hungary   Italy   Japan   South Korea   Poland   Portugal
Singapore   Switzerland   Thailand   Turkey   Ukraine   Vietnam

Oxford is a registered trade mark of Oxford University Press
in the UK and in certain other countries

Published in the United States
by Oxford University Press Inc., New York

© Ian Loader and Aogán Mulcahy 2003

The moral rights of the author have been asserted

Database right Oxford University Press (maker)

Reprinted 2006

ISBN 0-19-829906-0

Contents

Preface and Acknowledgements

In his lectures on *Professional Ethics and Civic Morals*, delivered at the close of the nineteenth century, Emile Durkheim proffered the following remark:

As long as there are States, so there will be national pride, and nothing can be more warranted. But societies can have their pride, not in being the greatest or the wealthiest, but in being the most just, the best organized and in possessing the best moral constitution [Durkheim 1992/1957: 75].

Today, over a century on, this appears to ring hollow. In the face of globalizing processes that are stripping the nation-state of its capacity and legitimacy from above and below, and a rampant ethnic nationalism that mocks such civic-minded sentiment, Durkheim's pious hope—one whose conditions of possibility he himself doubted 'could ever come'—looks at best irrelevant and utopian, at worst foolhardy and dangerous.

Yet, for reasons that will become clear, it is with this broad ambition in mind that we set out in this book to address the pathologies and possibilities that attend the cultural connection between police, state, and nation. Our aim in what follows is to assess the cultural and political significance of English policing, and its place within contemporary English social relations and public life. Drawing upon a two-year study of a range of police documentary materials, and biographical and oral history interviews with various strata of the populace, senior and rank-and-file police officers, and politicians and civil servants, we have endeavoured to construct a cultural sociology of the meanings attached to the idea of policing within English memory and sensibility, one oriented to the ways in which policing has intersected with forms of social and political change in English society since 1945. Our purpose in so doing has been to arrive at a better understanding of the mutually conditioning relationship that exists between, in the words of our title, 'policing' and the 'condition of England'. But we do so in the belief that investigating the deep meanings of policing systems can tell us something important about the basic ideals of the nation, and that, by elucidating the anxieties, values, conflicts, and aspirations implicit and explicit in the stories people tell about policing, we can—as situated interpreters and social critics (Walzer 1988)—make some small contribution to that society's self-understanding and future development (Stedman Jones 2001: 45).

The narrative that follows is organized into four Parts and runs broadly thus. In Part I—'Settings and Reorientations'—we offer an exposition and critique and what has become an influential sociological account of citizens' apparent loss of *faith* in the English police since 1945—what we term the 'desacralization thesis'. In reconstructing this thesis in Chapter 1 we detail the social changes—the demise of the post-war Keynesian 'consensus', processes of detraditionalization, escalating levels of crime and public anxiety about crime, and various episodes of police malpractice and scandal—that are said to have underpinned the 'precipitous' decline of public confidence in the police in the post-war period—its transformation from a *sacred* into a *profane* social institution. As will become clear, we regard this thesis—one most readily associated with Robert Reiner—as plausible and persuasive in many respects, and much of the empirical material in this book serves in our view to deepen and extend it. But we also believe—for reasons we make clear in conclusion to Chapter 1—that it exhibits some significant lacunae as a framework for grasping the contemporary cultural and political significance of the English police, shortcomings that it is our purpose in this study to make good.

These shortcomings are brought into sharper relief in Chapter 2 when we indicate the value and significance of seeking to make better sense of the 'symbolic power' of the idea of policing. Drawing on the writings of Pierre Bourdieu and Raymond Williams and, within criminology, on the work of David Garland and others on 'penal sensibilities', we outline what is entailed in thinking about policing as a cultural institution and performance; one that remains deeply entangled with questions, not only of order and security, but of subjectivity, recognition, belonging, and collective identity. We then sketch a heuristic perspective that enables us to investigate what we term *English policing culture*—a task that requires us to attend to the formation, effects, and trajectories of *dominant, residual*, and *emergent* sensibilities towards policing, and to their intersections with other key dimensions of post-war English society and culture. We conclude Chapter 2 by delineating the reasons for our choice of documentary and oral historical/biographical methods and setting out what in research terms our efforts towards a cultural sociology of post-war English policing actually comprised.

The empirical account of these lay and official sensibilities is to be found in Parts II and III. In interpreting the materials generated by our documentary and oral historical enquiry, our aim has been to secure a grounded and detailed understanding of the competing sensibilities towards policing and social change since 1945 to be found within lay, police, and governmental memory and narrative. What consequently follows in Parts II and III is *not* any kind of 'exhaustive' account (let alone history) of post-war English policing, but, rather, a series of interventions that 'slice into' different elements of English policing culture.

In Part II (Chapters 3 to 5) we are concerned principally—though not exclusively—with the narratives that constitute *lay dispositions* towards English policing. Chapter 3 deals with the post-war fate and contemporary cultural and political force of the bobby-on-the-beat. In exploring the motifs, imagery, and silences that constitute social memories of 'the English bobby', and the ways in which this figure features in narratives of social change, we aim, in particular, to detail the outlook of those who view the bobby's presence, corporeal aura, and actions as integral to what is fondly recalled as the more disciplined, cohesive social order of the immediate post-war decades, and who take 'his' apparent disappearance to be unsettlingly symbolic of the demise of that order. In so doing, we seek to further understanding of what we suggest is a residual, but by no means insignificant, strand of contemporary public feeling towards English policing— one the desacralization thesis has tended to overlook.

We explore this sensibility—that of those we term *defenders of the faith*—further in both Chapters 4 and 5. Our concern in Chapter 4 is with the *fracturing* of the settled and deferential public orientation towards the English police that is said by proponents of the desacralization thesis to have marked the late 1940s and 1950s. In reflecting on this demise, we situate the outlook of those who cleave to this 'lost' model of police/social authority among the *diversity* of public sensibilities towards policing that have emerged in the wake of subsequent processes of detraditionalization. Drawing on our group discussions and (especially) biographical interviews with different strata of the English populace, we demonstrate the uneasy coexistence of five analytically distinct public dispositions towards policing—structures of feeling that proffer contrasting narratives of 'what has happened' to policing in the second half of the twentieth century, evince different orientations towards police authority, and project competing visions of what English policing should be or may become. Playfully extending Reiner's religious vocabulary, we term these positions *defenders of the faith*, *the disenchanted*, *atheists*, *agnostics*, and *the hopeful*.

In Chapter 5, we deepen and extend our analysis of different clusters of sentiment towards policing by considering the cultural politics of police, 'race', and nation. This chapter has two principal aims. First, we examine how the range of white orientations to the police considered in Chapter 4 respond to the post-war 'racialization' of English policing. In so doing, we consider in particular (in ways that offer a case study of our overarching analytic concern with the intersection between biography, disposition, and events) the reactions of our white respondents to the racist murder of Stephen Lawrence in April 1993 and its subsequent officially acknowledged mishandling by the Metropolitan Police. Secondly, we explore the markedly different narratives of change that constitute black and Asian sensibilities towards English policing, and appraise—using the life stories of three of our black respondents—the different senses of social possibility that pervade their memory and outlook. The Stephen Lawrence case again looms large here as an illustration of more general processes.

By so advancing our analysis of the police's 'capacity to show the nation to itself' (Gilroy 1987: 74), our purpose in Chapter 5 is to develop a grounded sociological interpretation of the mutually, if asymmetrically, conditioning relationship that exists between policing and the emergence since the late 1940s of an ethnically diverse, multicultural England. This, in turn, allows us to revisit, and in some important respects recast, the account of police authority and its post-war transformations delineated in Chapters 3 and 4. What emerges from such revisions, from the insertion into this analysis of the forms and effects of racial identification and categorization, is a more nuanced account of the diversity of lay memories and sensibilities that today struggle to determine the contours of English policing culture.

In Part III (Chapters 6 to 8) we are concerned principally—though again not exclusively—with *official* (i.e., police and governmental) *narratives*. We also set out more explicitly here to recover and interpret 'chronologically' certain selected aspects of

English policing since 1945. Our concern in Chapter 6 is with the orientation of serving and retired police officers towards 'the job' and 'the force'. In documenting and making sense of police memories and outlooks, we reconstruct the key elements of what was once a more dominant, taken-for-granted way of thinking and feeling about police work and explore the ways in which the vision of policing embedded in these memories has in recent decades been disputed, as processes of detraditionalization have come to have effects, not only upon the social world that the police are tasked with regulating, but also *within* the police organization itself. The diverse and competing public sensibilities towards police authority that emerge from Chapters 4 and 5 find, or so we contend, some equivalence here.

In developing this argument, we focus on three themes that seem to us significant in illuminating these processes: (i) the social status of 'the police officer' and its intersection with questions of police pay; (ii) the matters considered germane to learning and performing the venerated task of 'bobbying'; and (iii) the hierarchical, quasi-militaristic internal authority relations that are recalled as characterizing the English police during the initial decades of the post-war period. In the latter part of the chapter, we examine the ways in which this once seemingly settled mix of police practices, beliefs, and sentiments has been disrupted by processes of *informalization* and *diversification*, and explore the range of discordant voices that are today struggling to determine the composition, internal cultures, and organizational ethos of the English police.

In Chapter 7, the focus shifts away from questions of 'internal' police organization and culture towards some of the broader intersections that exist between policing and the social. We are concerned in this chapter with the 'police voice', its emergence and preoccupations, its meanings and effects, and its relationship to English mundane and political culture in the post-war period. Our aim is to trace the advent since 1945 of *chief constables* as prominent commentators on both 'law and order' in particular, and the 'condition of England' in general, and to grasp the extent to which they have over recent decades acquired the power to 'name', diagnose, and classify social problems. In so doing, we subdivide the post-war years using the following typology: first, a period from 1945–72 during which chief officers remained locally prominent, but nationally rather silent, figures—a stance that begins to falter towards the latter part of the 1960s. Secondly, an era—symbolically announced by then Metropolitan Police Commissioner Robert Mark's controversial Dimbleby Lecture in 1973—characterized by the advent of a number of 'political policemen', maverick 'police heroes' who for a time attained a culturally prominent place in English public life. This was to last until the late 1980s, from which time a quieter, evidently more liberal, yet arguably more effective, corporate police voice begins to emerge. In the latter half of Chapter 7 we seek to make sense of these transformations, focussing, in turn, on shifts in the working ideology of police elites, the incorporation of chief constables as a body into processes of police governance, and processes of detraditionalization that have conditioned the emergence of a humbler, more modulated police voice, one that befits the sceptical, consumerist tendencies of the present.

In Chapter 8 we offer an account of the ways in which the question 'who controls the police?' has come to cultural and political prominence since 1945. The story we narrate falls into three chronologically overlapping yet analytically distinct periods that broadly correspond to those deployed in Chapter 7. The first covers a roughly thirty-year span from the late 1940s to the late 1970s. It was a period in which questions of police governance—while not entirely free of scandal and *causes célèbres*—remained firmly the province of government officials, senior officers, and assorted constitutional specialists; one characterized by overt governmental support for the English way of 'autonomous' and 'local' policing coupled with further moves towards centralized influence and control. This came under pressure, and began to unravel, towards the latter part of the 1970s, thereby ushering in a second distinctive post-war 'moment'—one set within the backdrop of a faltering Keynesian 'consensus' and the coming of Thatcherism, and marked by a sustained radical challenge to the firmly embedded 'tradition' of constabulary independence mounted in the name of local democracy. This challenge—as we shall see—must in several respects be counted as a failure, though it is not without some significant traces and effects. It had by the late 1980s been superseded by a third key moment in the post-war history of police governance, one in which economy, efficiency, and effectiveness; performance targets, auditing, and monitoring; consumer responsiveness and customer satisfaction became the order of the day. The meanings, reception, and effects of this governmental attempt to render English policing profane form the substance of the chapter's final section.

In fleshing out the contours of the above story our aim in Chapter 8 is to chart the shifting and competing political rationalities that have shaped (or endeavoured to shape) this element of English policing culture in the latter half of the twentieth century. Many of the civil servants, national and local politicians, and senior police officers we interviewed were instrumental in the formation of these rationalities and/or protagonists in relevant struggles, and their memories and reflections thus enable us to construct a narrative certain aspects of which are familiar and amply documented, but which is less often considered in the round. But we also proffer a reading of post-war English policing that is attuned to the ways in which struggles over *police governance* are always in part contests over the cultural meanings of those two terms, one that helps us forge a better understanding of what has been—and remains—at stake in debates about police accountability.

In Part IV—'Past and Present in Contemporary Policing'—we draw the threads of our enquiry together and offer an assessment of the current condition of English policing culture. In so doing, we revisit and utilize Raymond Williams' typology of cultural forms—the *dominant*, the *residual*, and the *emergent*—that we introduce in Chapter 2 and which quietly guides our interpretative efforts in Parts II and III. We argue in Chapter 9 that English policing is today 'dominated' in Williams' terms by a culture of scrutiny and complaint. It is a culture structured around managerialism, consumerism, and multiculturalism; a culture shaped by processes of detraditionalization; one that that exhibits a deep—mutually, if asymmetrically, conditioning—affinity with what in the last several decades of the twentieth century has become a pluralistic, individualized, consumerist society. But these dominant tendencies compete, we argue, with both 'residual' and 'emergent' elements in a bid to determine the shape and future of English policing. In respect of the former, they wrestle with those forces and outlooks that yearn for an 'England' that was more orderly, disciplined, cohesive, and white—a vision of the past that is mobilized to make sense of, and to condemn, the present. This police-centred and generally reactionary cultural form—one expressing a deep emotional attachment to the authoritative social magic of policing—today assumes a marginal, oppositional place in English policing culture, albeit one that retains the capacity to shape events. In terms of the latter, the dominant culture stands in opposition to those movements and outlooks that struggle to realize, or evince sympathy towards, forms of anti-discriminatory and accountable policing in a manner that strives either to demystify the symbolic power of the police or else construct meanings and narratives that connect policing in novel ways to questions of recognition, citizenship, and political community.

The presence of these latter 'emergent' elements offers grounds, we suggest, for thinking that a more democratic understanding of English policing and its relationship to mundane and political culture lies immanent within the present—a prospect that remains, politically and culturally, open to us. With this in mind, we conclude Chapter 9 with a consideration of how the cultural connection between policing, state, and nation may be reconstituted in more inclusive, *cosmopolitan* forms, and how policing may, on this basis, offer a site for the articulation of new styles of deliberative political authority and democratic citizenship.

*   *   *

As with any piece of social enquiry, this one has benefited from the support and advice of a great many people, and several accumulated debts need to be, if not repaid, then at least acknowledged. Our sincere thanks go, first and foremost, to all those who assisted with or participated in the research upon which this book is based. These include the many individuals—citizens, serving and retired police officers, former civil servants, politicians, and government ministers—who freely gave up their time (in some cases several hours of it) to discuss questions of policing with us and from whom we learned much. Though our promises of anonymity prevent us from thanking our discussants by name, we remain immensely grateful. Thanks are also due to Peter Woods of Greater Manchester Police and Fred Worthington of Cheshire Police for their help in arranging interviews with serving police officers, and to Lesley Bailey, Carole Maloney, Anne Musgrave, and Kath Pye who accomplished the Herculean task of transcribing the countless hours of taped conversation our enquiry generated. The kindness and assistance of the library staff at Bramshill Police College (Juliet Davis and Sue King in particular), the Greater Manchester Police training school (especially Jean Titchmarsh), and the Police Federation headquarters in Surbiton were much appreciated, as were those of Duncan Brodie and the staff and volunteers at the Greater Manchester Police Museum.

The research on which this book is based was funded by the Economic and Social Research Council (grant no. R000237054) and we are grateful for its support, as we are for that of the two project consultants, Andrew Davies and Geoff Pearson. Over the course of the last several years we have delivered numerous conference and seminar presentations on our work and wish to thank all those who participated in the discussions that ensued. Such presentations were made to: the British Criminology Conference, Adelphi Hotel, Liverpool; the British Sociological Association annual conference, York University; the 'Relocating Britishness' conference, University of Central Lancashire; the 'North-west Crime Historians' day conference, Keele University, and the 'Future of Policing' conference, University of Kent; to the National Police Training College, Bramshill, and the 'Strategic Command Course' seminar, University of Cambridge; and to the Department of Sociology, Social Policy, and Social Work, University of Liverpool; the Institute of Criminal Justice Studies, University of Portsmouth; All Souls College, University of Oxford, and the Department of Sociology and Social Policy, University of Manchester.

We have, in addition, been assisted by various people whose supportive or (especially) sceptical questions and observations have done much to improve the final text. Mike Brogden, Tony Jefferson, Laurence Lustgarten, Eugene McLaughlin, Karim Murji, Richard Sennett, Roger Silverstone, Malcolm Young, and Lucia Zedner have all, though they may not realize it, helped in such ways. Neil Walker offered some incisive comments on the concluding chapter late in the day, as well as contributing much in many conversations over the last decade to our efforts to make better sociological sense of policing. We are also indebted to Robert Reiner who read a draft of almost the entire manuscript and provided some germane suggestions and welcome encouragement; as well as to three anonymous Oxford University Press reviewers for many constructive criticisms—and for persuading us to take a scythe to the 'veritable jungle of endnotes' that appeared in an earlier version. Responsibility for the 'finished' text—and the remaining notes—is, of course, entirely ours.

John Louth, Danielle Moon, and Gwen Booth at Oxford University Press offered helpful advice and support, as well as responding to several missed 'deadlines' with admirable forbearance. Our respective colleagues in the Department of Criminology, Keele University, and the Department of Sociology, University College Dublin, helped make these institutions convivial and intellectually stimulating places in which to work. Finally, we would like to express our gratitude to our friends and families who we suspect are happier than we are to see that 'the book' is, finally, done. To Penny Fraser and Alice Feldman especially, many thanks.

The authors and publisher would like to thank Taylor and Francis Ltd. for permission to reproduce in Chapter 2 material that first appeared in a much earlier form in 'Policing and the Social: Questions of Symbolic Power', *British Journal of Sociology*, 1997, 48/1: 1–18 www.tandf.co.uk, and Oxford University Press Ltd. for permission to use material in Chapter 7 that was originally published—in two parts—as 'The Power of Legitimate Naming', *British Journal of Criminology*, 2001, Part I—41/1: 41–55, Part II—41/2: 252–65.

PART I

Settings and Reorientations

1

Losing Faith?:
The Desacralization of
English Policing since 1945

It is often remarked today that citizens have lost *faith* in the English police. What though are we to make of this statement? It appears to suggest, on the one hand, a progressive diminution of public confidence in the capacity or competence of the police to accomplish the tasks expected of them. Yet it also denotes something else; namely, the coming to prominence of a secular disposition towards the social institution of policing and a corresponding attenuation of the quasi-religious aura that once enveloped the police, its officers, and its practices.

Both these possible meanings of the phrase 'losing faith' are in fact to be found in an influential sociological account of the fate of the English police since 1945 that we have termed the 'desacralization thesis'. According to this thesis—one advanced most consistently in recent years by Robert Reiner (1992, 1995*a*, 1995*b*, 1997, 2000*a*)—the 1950s represented an historical high-water mark of police legitimacy, a 'golden age' in which ' "policing by consent" had been achieved in Britain to the maximal degree it is ever attainable' (Reiner 2000*a*: 49). Police officers were, at the time, not merely looked (up) to as avatars of order, authority, discipline, and community, but venerated as totems of national pride (Reiner 1992: 761; cf. Gorer 1955). The lowly 'bobby on the beat'—a figure whose presence in post-war English life was both cemented and celebrated by the fictional *Dixon of Dock Green* (Clarke 1983; Sparks 1992*a*: 25–30)—became an archetypal English hero, the very embodiment—as Gorer (1955: 310) put it—of the 'ideal male character'. The police, it seems, like the monarchy, had become a *sacred* institution, set apart and revered as a key component of the social imaginary. They were—again like the monarchy—simply 'an aspect of being British' (Pimlott 1997: 254).

There is no suggestion in this argument that the 1950s were entirely free of either police deviance or social conflict. As Reiner (1992) notes, police memoirs of the period have subsequently shed light on the casual violence the police often inflicted upon 'suspects' (Mark 1978)—a feature of policing in this period, as we shall see, that our interviews with retired officers further attest to. The 1950s were equally marked by a litany of scandals and disputes concerning allegations of corruption or misconduct, events that were to culminate in the setting up of the 1962 Royal Commission on the Police (Critchley 1978: 270–4; Stevenson and Bottoms 1990). And the decade bore witness to 'race riots' in Nottingham and Notting Hill in 1958 (Miles 1984) and to the beginnings of what was to prove a long sustained post-war escalation in rates of recorded crime (notifiable offences rose from 438,085 in 1955 to 743,713 in 1960, a 70 per cent increase). Yet little of this, it appears, served to dent what remained unprecedentedly high levels of public approval for the police. Michael Banton (1964: vii) thus felt able to preface his pioneering sociology of police work with the observation that 'it can be instructive to analyse institutions that are working well in order to see if anything can be learned from their success'. Some three decades on, Weinberger (1995: 208) concluded her oral history of the period from the 1930s to the 1960s by observing that, while the police may not at this time have been 'the best in the world', 'they were certainly exceedingly well adapted, for much of the period and within its own terms, to the policing demands made of them'.

Numerous pieces of evidence have been marshalled in defence of these conclusions. The 1962 Royal Commission, for example, found 80 per cent of respondents to the government social survey conducted on its behalf assenting to the view that the British police *were* the best in the world. Eighty-three per cent additionally reported feeling 'great respect' for the police (with 16 per cent professing mixed feelings and only 1 per cent 'little or no respect')—a finding that varied little across social class (Home Office 1962: 102–5; Reiner 2000a: 49). Eighty-nine per cent of respondents reported that their views on these matters had not changed in the previous ten years. While the Commission recognized what it called a 'measure of antipathy' towards the police found among 18 to 25-year-olds (Home Office 1962: 103), and noted concerns about police relations with the motoring public (Home Office 1962: 114–17), it nonetheless felt able to conclude in the following laudatory terms:

The findings of the survey constitute an overwhelming vote of confidence in the police, and a striking indication of the good sense and discrimination of the bulk of the population in their assessment of the tasks that policemen have to carry out … We therefore assert confidently, on the basis of the survey, that relations between police and public are on the whole very good, and we have no reasons to suppose that they have ever, in recent times, been otherwise. This is a finding that will give great satisfaction to Your Majesty, to the police, and to the public [Home Office 1962: 102–3].[1]

Geoffrey Gorer's journalistic account of 5,000 responses by readers of *The People* to the question 'what do you think of the police?' arrived at some cognate conclusions (Gorer 1955: ch. 13; see also Almond and Verba 1963). He found 75 per cent of respondents evincing enthusiastic appreciation of the police, with any hostility that existed attaching to individual police officers rather than to the institution itself. This trait—which Gorer describes as 'peculiarly English and a most important component of the contemporary English character' (1955: 213)—is illustrated by a number of respondents' written remarks. Take this, for instance, from 'a 28-year-old higher working class woman from Formby':

I believe they [the police] stand for all we English are, maybe at first appearance slow perhaps, but reliable stout and kindly, I have the greatest admiration for our police force and I am proud they are renowned abroad.

Or this, penned by 'a 38-year-old married man from New Malden':

The finest body of men of this kind in the world. Portraying and upholding the time-tested constitution, traditions and democracy of the British Way of Life, combining humble patience with high courage and devotion to duty.

What then, almost half a century on, has happened to this, the world's 'finest body of *men*'? What fate has befallen that institutional symbol of 'the British Way of Life' (in upper case, you'll note)? It has, according to Reiner (1992: 761), been 'demystified'; robbed of its capacity to function as a unifying emblem of a common national culture, fallen from its pedestal. It has in the process been transformed into a thoroughly *profane* institution—one now increasingly subject to public scrutiny, scandal, and complaint, time and again found wanting under the resultant glare, and beset over the last three decades by what appears to have become a permanent crisis of legitimation. The police have—in short—fallen from grace.

In support of this contention Reiner points to what he describes as a 'massive haemorrhage' and 'precipitous' decline in the public standing of the English police (1992: 763; 1995a: 124; 1995b: 30; 2000a: 59). He refers, in this regard, to a 1989 MORI poll that reposed the questions first asked—almost four decades earlier—on behalf of the 1962 Royal Commission. This found only 43 per cent of citizens expressing a 'great deal of respect' for the police, as compared with 83 per cent in the early 1960s. Those expressing 'no confidence' had risen from one to 14 per cent. Reiner notes also the steady decline in public confidence recorded by the British Crime Survey over the last twenty years, with those feeling the police were doing a 'very' or 'fairly good job' falling from 92 per cent in 1982, to 79 per cent in 2000. The numbers believing the police to be performing 'very' well had more than halved in this period from 43 to 20 per cent (Sims and Myhill 2000). He points further to the array of evidence highlighting the tense relations that obtain between the police and certain economically and socially disadvantaged sections of the English populace, notably ethnic minorities and young inner-city males (e.g., Smith and Gray 1985). 'It is clear', Reiner concludes, 'that there is a crisis of public confidence in and consent to policing' (1995b: 30).

How though can we account for this apparently dramatic shift in public orientations towards the police? What factors may be mobilized to explain the English police's startling topple from grace? We want in this introductory chapter to outline some of the overlapping, mutually-reinforcing transformations that various sociological and criminological commentators (Reiner prominent among them) have viewed as contributing in varying ways, and to contrasting degrees, to the post-war 'loss of faith' in the capacities and performance of English policing. These changes have seen the emergence since the 1970s of 'a distinctive pattern of social, economic and cultural relations' (Garland 2001: p. viii) that it has become common to corral together under the term 'late' (Giddens 1990; Young 1999; Garland 2001) or 'post' (Harvey 1989; Bauman 1992; Reiner 1992) modernity. They have, it is claimed, decisively undermined the 'special historical conditions' (Reiner 1995a: 126) that made the police such revered totems of national pride in the 1950s, and given rise instead to a situation in which the police have been progressively de-centred as a source of security and identity for citizens. Our initial task then is to delineate some relevant contours of social change since 1945 and to discern the impact such changes are purported to have had on public dispositions towards the police—an analysis we advance with reference to the interplay between transformations in *political economy, culture and authority, crime and responses to crime,* and the *police organization* itself. Having done so, we briefly set out certain reasons for our dissatisfaction with the 'desacralization thesis'. This dissatisfaction—and our attendant belief that this thesis stands in need of important qualification and revision—provides a point of departure for the theorizations and interpretations that follow in the rest of the book.

Political Economy

The seemingly unprecedented levels of public consent secured by the police in the middle decades of the twentieth century rested—according to Reiner—on a specific set of economic and social relations, a particular compromise between capital and labour. As working-class movements struggled during the first half of the century to acquire some measure of collective recognition in the workplace and political representation in national and local government, and as the civil, political, and increasingly social rights of citizenship were progressively extended (Marshall 1950), so the antipathy to the police that has long marked working-class neighbourhoods began steadily to abate—or at least to become more pocketed, situational, and susceptible to negotiation (Storch 1975; cf. Cohen 1979; Brogden 1991). The *incorporation* of the working class into the institutions of political and economic life served, Reiner suggests, as an important precondition for widening levels of acceptance of, and identification with, the English police.

In the aftermath of World War II, this process of political and economic inclusion was further cemented by the emergence among governing classes—fearful of a return to inter-war depression and guided by the 1942 Beveridge Report—of a set of shared assumptions about the tasks of government and the meanings of political responsibility (Hay 1996: ch. 3). The resulting post-war settlement—one that involved a new articulation of the relationship between state, economy, and civil society—comprised two connected strands.

First, an economic strategy built around partnership between government, employers, and trade unions; Keynesian demand management to 'iron out' boom-bust economic cycles; a 'mixed economy' of public and private sectors; and an overarching commitment to the maintenance of full employment. This was coupled, secondly, with the building of a social welfare state that sought to meet the basic needs of all citizens through such mechanisms as municipal housing, state education, and universal health care, and to protect those citizens from poverty by means of state pensions, unemployment benefit, and cognate forms of social security.

There ensued—in the two decades that followed the end of rationing in the early 1950s—a period of sustained economic growth and material prosperity unparalleled in the history of capitalist production. These were—according to historian Eric Hobsbawm—'the golden years', 'an altogether exceptional phase of [capitalism's] history, perhaps a unique one' (1994: 258). From the late 1950s onwards citizens came to experience—even take for granted—sustained levels of full (male) employment, the benefits of welfare provision, and rising levels of economic prosperity. Rapid technological development diffused across classes a range of consumer goods—televisions, telephones, refrigerators, washing machines, cars—that a generation earlier had either not existed or been the preserve of a privileged few. Foreign holidays became open to 'the masses'. Prime Ministers spoke—with some confidence—of people having 'never had it so good'.[2] Sociologists detected an 'embourgeoisement' of the working class and busily set about investigating the outlooks and affiliations of the 'affluent worker' (Goldthorpe *et al.* 1969). A 'new civic narrative of inclusion' (Garland 2001: 46) appeared to have tamed, or at least institutionalized, the raw class antagonisms that marked the early decades of the twentieth century. It was this—according to Reiner (2000*a*: 49)—that provided the *economic* underpinning for the 'maximal' levels of public consent the police acquired during this period; this that enabled the crime question to assume a relatively quiet, uncontested place in English public life and popular consciousness; this that meant the problem of order was seldom conceived of—by either citizens or the governing classes—as first and foremost a matter of policing.

It was not to last. According to some observers, in fact, it came to an abrupt, decisive halt in 1973 (Harvey 1989). In the wake of the oil crisis of that year there ensued a decade of economic, social, and political turmoil. Britain in the 1970s experienced soaring inflation, rising unemployment, and—following the terms set by the International Monetary Fund for its 'bail-out' loan to the Labour government in 1976—retrenchment in public services and government demands for pay restraint. The decade witnessed, in turn, mounting levels of industrial and social conflict. A power workers' strike in the early 1970s resulted in cuts in supply and a three-day working week. The miners went on strike in 1972 and 1974, contributing on the latter occasion to the fall of the Conservative government.[3] In 1977, a bitter and protracted dispute over union recognition took place at the Grunwick film processing plant in London. And a series of strikes by low-paid public sector workers in 1978–9 (in what was dubbed 'the winter of discontent') helped bring about the demise in May 1979 of James Callaghan's minority Labour administration. By the time that government left office, the far right had come to acquire a foothold in electoral politics and violent clashes between racist and anti-racist groups—in Red Lion Square, Lewisham, Southall—had returned to the streets of Britain.

Economic prosperity had, in short, given way to recession and conflict, revealing in the process the structural weaknesses and relative decline of the British economy (Gamble 1994). The limits of the post-war political settlement also appeared to have been reached. Keynesian social democracy stood exhausted, apparently devoid of answers to pressing structural problems. Right-wing commentators spoke of Britain as 'ungovernable'. Under its new leader, Margaret Thatcher, the Conservative Party abandoned its support for the central tenets of the post-war settlement and began to 'articulate' the crisis as one of over-extended government, excessively mighty, irresponsible trade unions, and—an important conflation this—spiralling criminal and political violence (Hall *et al.* 1978; Brake and Hale 1992). Having been elected in May 1979—in the first post-war general election at which crime and policing had figured at all decisively (Downes and Morgan 1997)—the Conservatives set about remaking the economic and political landscape of Britain.

This is not the place to tell the story of 'Thatcherism', to consider the twists and turns of eighteen years of Conservative government, or to reflect upon the meanings of—and tensions inherent in—the

New Right 'project'. Such has been accomplished elsewhere by both journalists (Young 1993) and social scientists (Kavanagh 1987; Gamble 1988; Hall 1988; Jessop *et al.* 1988). Two broad features of this period of Conservative rule and its effects are, nonetheless, pertinent to present concerns. One needs to note first the New Right's fundamental abandonment of the axioms of post-war economic policy; something that saw control of the money supply (and, by this means, inflation) replace full employment as the overriding policy objective, and a radical restructuring—or 'freeing up'—of the labour market. This resulted in the loss of a quarter of British manufacturing industry (in 1980–1 alone); rising levels of unemployment; the curtailment of trade union rights; the privatization of steel, gas, electricity, telecommunications, and other public utilities; the lifting of exchange controls, and de-regulation of financial activity in the City of London. The creation of an 'enterprise culture', with its attendant valorization of 'free' market practices and values, became the governmental rallying cry of the 1980s. Similar impulses pervaded the field of social policy. Here successive Conservative administrations sought to overturn the working assumptions and institutional practices of the welfare state. Council houses were sold to their tenants (and—in the name of a 'property-owning democracy'—not replaced). Social security benefits were targeted and cut, their recipients more intensively surveilled. Local public services were put out to competitive tender. 'Internal markets' were created in the national health service. The accompanying ideological assault was on 'welfare dependency'—the aim to encourage individual responsibility, standing-on-your-own-two-feet. Under neo-liberal tutelage, citizens were encouraged to think of themselves as consumers of (once) publicly delivered goods—pensions, education, health care, even policing and security.

The upshot of these political transformations—which served, in their turn, to promote and accelerate a far-reaching, technologically-driven globalization of capitalist economic relations (Harvey 1989; Lash and Urry 1994; Castells 1996)—has been the emergence of what has variously been described as a 'market' (Taylor 1999: chs. 1–2) or 'exclusive' society (Young 1999: ch. 1); terms intended to signify an atrophying over the final three decades of the twentieth century of the bonds of social cohesion and solidarity, and their replacement by new forms of material inequality and insecurity. As Reiner (1995*a*: 125) puts it: 'since the advent of Conservative government in 1979, the effect of economic and social policy has been to reverse a century long trajectory of slow but steady reduction in social inequality'. Will Hutton (1995) speaks in this regard of the '40–30–30 society', of a society segmented into an affluent, mobile, consumer-oriented, professional, and managerial elite (cf. Bauman 1998); an employed, but economically precarious and insecure middle and working class, ever vulnerable to the next act of corporate 'down-sizing', the next relocation in pursuit of cheaper labour; and geographically concentrated pockets of low-skilled, structurally excluded individuals, some existing on poverty pay in casual dead-end jobs, others reliant on a shifting combination of residualized welfare, utilitarian crime, and 'employment' in the informal economy. Such are the structural fault-lines of late modern Britain.

What though have these transformations in political economy to do with the 'desacralization' of the English police, with what Reiner describes as the haemorrhage in levels of public confidence and approval? Let us, for now, record two such effects. The economic and social dislocations of the last three decades have, first of all, generated conflicts and disorder that the police have been called upon—often in conditions of fierce controversy—to quell; something that has made policing a much more visible and politically contentious institution of English culture and society. Think here, for instance, about the police's role in the miners' strikes of the early 1970s (including their 'failure' to prevent mass pickets from closing Saltley Gate coking plant in 1972); the confrontations between police and pickets in the crowded, residential streets around the Grunwick factory in 1977; the—now more 'paramilitary'—police's involvement in the bitterly fought 'restructuring' of the newspaper industry (encompassing, most prominently, stand-offs with pickets at Warrington in 1983 and Wapping in 1986–7); and the immense damage done to received images of English policing by the year-long miners' strike of 1984–5 (Fine and Millar 1985; McCabe *et al.* 1988). Recall the involvement of the police in the street skirmishes between racist and anti-racist organizations that marked the late 1970s; events that claimed the lives of two protestors, one—anti-racist demonstrator Blair Peach—allegedly at the hands of the Metropolitan Police Special Patrol Group (National Council for Civil Liberties 1980). And consider the disturbances that shook Britain's inner cities—St Paul's (Bristol) 1980;

Brixton (London) 1981, 1985; Toxteth (Liverpool) 1981, 1985; Moss Side (Manchester) 1981, 1985; Handsworth (Birmingham) 1981, 1985; and Tottenham (London) 1985—during the 1980s; and the peripheral housing estates of places like Newcastle, Cardiff, Salford, Luton, and Oxford in the early 1990s (Campbell 1993). The sight of police officers clad in riot gear, the first ever deployment of CS gas on mainland Britain (by Merseyside Police in Toxteth in 1981), allegations of police heavy-handedness and insensitivity (in respect of the 'Swamp 81' stop and search operation that ignited the 1981 Brixton disturbances), the murder of PC Keith Blakelock in Tottenham in 1985 (the first English police officer to be killed in a riot since 1833); these served to damage still further the received idea of the police as totems of national consensus and pride. They also helped bring to the fore—and raise critical questions about—a litany of matters ranging from the extent of police powers and emergence of paramilitary styles and technology to allegations of racial discrimination and demands for greater accountability (Cowell *et al.* 1982; Scarman 1982).

Secondly, and relatedly, one must pay attention to the tense and troubled relations that have developed in recent decades between the police and certain economically and socially marginal sections of the English populace—tensions that have exploded periodically into events of the kind just described. Policing has, of course, long been directed mainly at the poor, the powerless, the dispossessed (Lee 1981). Police contacts tend to be most frequent and adversarial with social groups which make routine use of public space—those who lack the resources needed to shield their activities from the police gaze (Stinchcombe 1963; Loader 1996). It is among those groups that policing by consent is most difficult to establish and sustain. The de-incorporation of ever larger numbers of young, inner-city, especially ethnic minority populations has, however, according to Reiner, made that task ever more intractable. As these groups have over the last three decades been structurally excluded from economic and political citizenship (Lea and Young 1984; Dahrendorf 1985), and required to exist in increasingly desperate material conditions, so their relations with the police have come to be marked by antagonism, mutual suspicion, and recurring allegations of over-control and under-protection. By such means have wider transformations in the political economy of Britain had their policing effects.

Culture and Authority

Deepening social divisions + desubordination = declining consent [Reiner 1995a: 125].

The degree of public acceptance secured by the police in the couple of decades immediately following the end of World War II rested also—Reiner suggests—on the particular structure of authority relations prevalent in British society during this period. These decades were, it is said, marked not merely by affluence and inclusion in the sphere of production and distribution, but by deference and conformity in the realm of culture (Young 1999: ch. 1). This was an era organized around certain core values pertaining to work, family, and community—one in which life-chances were largely known and accepted in advance; social identities ('husband', 'wife', 'father', 'mother', 'employer', 'worker', and so forth) were heavily pre-scripted, and the hierarchical order of things was seldom made the object of serious political questioning or challenge. It represented—according to Cas Wouters (1986: 6)—'a phase of stabilization and resignation', features of the social that served, in his view, to mediate relations (and inequalities) between men and women, parents and children, teachers and pupils, and religious/political leaders and their followers. To this list we might easily add 'police and public'. In such a climate of deference, police officers were, it seems—like teachers, doctors, and priests—accepted and respected, not so much as individuals blessed with particular virtues or renowned for specific actions, but first and foremost as holders of a socially authoritative office. They appeared somehow to embody the spirit of the age: '[t]he power of the British police was transmuted into authority primarily because they came to stand for a (largely mythical) national culture of order, harmony and restraint. Their power was legitimated by tradition' (Reiner 1992: 779).

This world has, in Reiner's view, all but disappeared. Since the 1960s especially, it has been radically undone by what he terms—borrowing a concept first formulated by Marxist political scientist Ralph Miliband (1977)—a process of desubordination (Reiner 1992: 771; 1995a: 125). Coined by Miliband in the midst of the turmoil-ridden 1970s, this term refers to:

People who find themselves in subordinate positions, and notably the people who work in factories, mines, offices, shops, schools, hospitals and

so on [doing] what they can to mitigate, resist, and transform the conditions of their subordination. The process occurs where subordination is
most evident and felt, namely at 'the point of production' and at the workplace in general; but also wherever else a condition of subordination
exists, for instance as it is experienced by women in the home, and outside
[Miliband 1977: 402].

Miliband provides here an early sighting and diagnosis of the
reconfiguration of relations between identity and authority that has
lately come to be known within social theory as 'detraditionalization' (Giddens 1994; Heelas *et al.* 1996). In both cases (though in
the latter without privileging 'the point of production'), what is
being described is a seemingly profound upheaval in the cultural
order of late twentieth-century Britain; one that has witnessed 'the
decline of traditional patterns of deference and unquestioning
acceptance of authority' (Reiner 1992: 771) and the emergence of
'pluralism, contingency, the undermining of absolutes, ambivalence
and disintegration' (Reiner 1992: 777) as prevailing cultural
motifs. Such change comprises a series of discrete transformations—in education, mass media, mobility; in gender, race, and
inter-generational relations—that have cumulatively served to generate a 'fragmented, secularized culture' (Boutellier 2000: 9) largely
devoid of socially authoritative voices. It is, moreover, a process
that 'does not easily fit into familiar ideological slots' (Miliband
1977: 403); one that has, as such, become hotly disputed territory,
the stuff of contemporary 'culture wars' about the meanings,
effects, and legacy of 'the Sixties'. We will in subsequent chapters
have cause to attend to aspects of these disputes. We shall also pay
proper heed to the counter-forces that processes of detraditionalization have in the last two decades unleashed (Garland 2001:
98–102)—indeed, these form an important ingredient of the corrective we wish to offer to Reiner's thesis. But for now, let us briefly
sketch some key elements of the detraditionalizing process and
indicate the toll they are said—or assumed—to have taken on the
legitimacy of the English police. Three such elements, in particular,
warrant further discussion.

Individualism and Pluralism

The austere, socially rigid, monochrome world of the late 1940s
and 1950s has, it is argued, been transformed in subsequent
decades by twin processes of moral individualism and cultural

pluralism (Hobsbawm 1994: chs. 10–11; Young 1999). The former term refers to the apparent withering of once disposition-forming, opportunity-determining social categories such as gender and class, and to the diminishing capacity of 'traditional' institutions (church, family, neighbourhood, schools, and so on) to legislate effectively in the realm of individual or collective morality. The entry of women into the labour market, the rise of distinctive youth subcultures, enhanced communications and mobility, the decline of (working-class) community, the impact of mass media, the 'me-decade' of Thatcherism; these have all been cited as contributors to what Hobsbawm (1994: 334) has called 'the triumph of the individual over society, the breaking of the threads which in the past had woven human beings into social textures'. To this must be added the various challenges to the nostrums of social conformity and moral absolutism presented in the 1960s, whether in the form of 'flower-power' and middle-class protest movements, or—more ambiguously—in governmental efforts to re-draw the boundaries between law and morality in respect of such matters as obscene publications, homosexuality between consenting male adults, suicide, abortion, and divorce (Hall 1980a; Newburn 1992). The combined effect of such changes has been the valorized status accorded to 'the individual' within late modern society (Giddens 1991), something that has simultaneously re-made morality as a realm of personal choice and a field of highly-charged cultural disputation.

The latter term—pluralism—points in some related ways to the character of social relations in late modern Britain. At its most banal, the term merely registers the 'diversification of lifestyles' (Young 1999: 14) that have ensued from the loosening grip of traditional authorities over individuals. But it also makes reference to the consequences of post-war Commonwealth immigration, to the transformation of Britain into a multi-cultural society, and to the formation and uneasy co-presence of 'old and new' ethnicities and 'old and new' racisms (Hall 1991). And it points to the emergence since the late 1960s of multiple forms of 'identity politics', and to the claims for recognition, rights, and resources made by social movements mobilizing around questions of gender, ethnicity, and sexuality. In a significant reversal, late modern society has—according to Jock Young (1999: 59)—become less and less willing to endure or empathize with economic 'difficulty', while increasingly demanding tolerance of, even coming to celebrate and consume, 'difference'.

These processes have, it is claimed, had at least two related effects upon the post-war standing of English policing. In a pluralistic society, the demands pressed upon the police by different social groups become both more diverse and competing, rendering it problematic for the police to sustain the fiction that they are simply responding to 'the public', and increasing the scope for conflict and de-legitimation. In an individualized society, wherein the terms and meanings of 'morality' are increasingly disputed (and commodified), it becomes ever more difficult for the police—that once paradigmatic institution of legal and social authority—to stand as the embodiment of a common moral and political community (deLint 1999: 133; Taylor 1999: 26). As Reiner (1992: 779) puts it: '[t]here can be no effective symbol of a unitary order in a pluralistic and fragmented culture'.

Mass Media

The proliferation of mass media communications must count as one of the most significant social transformations of the period since 1945. This has been most marked in relation to television, a medium that barely existed in the late 1940s but which has since come to assume a mundane, taken-for-granted place within quotidian life (Silverstone 1994). As of 1950 only 10 per cent of British households owned a television set, a figure that had spiralled to over 90 per cent by 1963 (Garland 2001: 85–7). The number and output of channels has similarly mushroomed, at first slowly with the advent of independent television (ITV) in 1955 and Channel 4 in 1981, more recently at breathtaking speed with the onset of satellite, cable, and digital technology. But the post-war period has also witnessed the expansion and diversification of radio, further consolidation of the newspaper industry, and the arrival and increasing salience of mass market 'tabloids'. Not forgetting, of course, the Internet. The mass media have, in short, become a prominent and powerful social force within late modernity (Meyrowitz 1985; Thompson 1996), something that has had far-reaching consequences for the police and public orientations towards them.

Undoubtedly most pervasive among such effects has been the social diffusion of images of, and information about, the police; and the attendant disembedding of policing from the tissue of local social relations. People today are less likely to derive such knowledge they have of the police either from purely personal experience, or from gossip, story-telling, and other forms of local knowledge. Instead, they have over the post-war years acquired widening access to information derived from fictional dramatizations of police work, from news items in which crime and policing are a staple, and, in recent years, from 'reality-television' programmes (*Crimewatch UK*, *Police-Camera-Action*, etc.) that consciously obscure the boundary between 'news' and 'entertainment'. Policing has, in short, become a highly mediated cultural form.

Now is not the time to review the voluminous literature on media representations of policing, nor to enter the debate on its effects (cf. Sparks 1992*a*; Fishman and Cavender 1998; Reiner 2000*a*: ch. 5, 2000*b*, 2002; Wilson 2000). Suffice it to note two aspects of the mass mediation of social life that are pertinent to present concerns. Consider, first, the consequences of what has become the routine fictional visualization of policing on British television. This development has in the post-war period encompassed a string of attempts to capture dramatically changing relations between policing and the social (witness the path from *Dixon*, through *Z Cars* and *The Sweeney*, to *The Bill*), not to mention the importation of numerous representations of US policing spanning *Kojak*, *Starsky and Hutch*, *Miami Vice*, *Hill Street Blues*, and *NYPD Blue*. Lately, the genre has become more internally differentiated and, as such, the purveyor of multiple, often competing, social meanings—compare, to select but a few, the uncompromising female lead in *Prime Suspect*, the contrasting nostalgic modes of *Heartbeat* and *Inspector Morse*, and the depictions of police deviance found in the likes of *Between the Lines* and *Cops* (cf. Hurd 1979; Clarke 1983, 1986; Sparks 1992*a*: ch. 5, 1994; Reiner 1994, 2000*a*: ch. 5; Eaton 1995). There are, to be sure, reasons for thinking that such drama offers its audiences forms of vicarious pleasure and reassurance (Sparks 1992*a*), thereby serving to buttress popular attachment to policing. But it has also, conversely, enabled people simply to know (or feel they know) more about policing; to fit their own encounters or demands into broader patterns of experience and possibility; to think about policing in more comparative terms (is 'my' force better? worse? more effective? more brutal? lazier? than others real and imagined). The mass mediation of policing has, in other words, generated a cultural imaginary that tends both to fuel popular fantasies of policing and to make it more difficult for people to accept the shortcomings of the 'real' thing. As McLaughlin and Murji put it, somewhat—as they admit—over stating the case:

The circulation and proliferation of hyper-real images of public policing in various media spaces means that old distinctions between the real, fictional and indeed fantasy are rapidly collapsing into a new police entertainment simulacrum. Step by step, representations of policing are flickering at such an intense rate on the television screen that the traditional organizational 'story-lines' are in danger of 'disappearing' [McLaughlin and Murji 1999a: 233].

The second point is a not unconnected one. In the early post-war years, prior to the explosion of mass media institutions, police misconduct, or abuses of power, had much more limited public exposure and circulation. Outbreaks of scandal were simply easier to prevent or, once unleashed, to contain. This is no longer the case. The subsequent mass mediation of social life has—in John Thompson's (1996) terms—transformed the *visibility* of the police, according policing a more routinely prominent place in the wider culture (Mawby 1999). In many respects, of course, this can operate—or be made to operate—to the police's advantage. There are now more channels through which the police can articulate their perspective, seek to 'name' events and problems as they see them (Hall *et al.* 1978: ch. 3). They have also since the 1970s become increasingly adept at managing and promoting their own image (Chibnall 1979; Schlesinger and Tumber 1994: ch. 4; Mawby 2002). Yet the police now also confront a mediated environment that is much more attuned to organizational scandal, misconduct, and poor performance. The proliferation of print and broadcast news, the diverse and diffuse practices of 'investigative' reporting, the TV 'talk show' ever eager to voice uncritically the experiences of crime victims or the grievances of mistreated suspects; these are the ingredients of a climate in which assorted police shortcomings—in respect of dealing with 'rowdy youths', or preventing burglary, or helping rape victims, or catching racist killers, or putting the wrong people behind bars—are routinely aired and discussed. Against a backdrop in which police malpractice is arguably now 'less flagrant and regularised' (Reiner 1992: 773) than during the middle decades of the twentieth century, this may even go some way towards explaining 'the paradox that public trust in [the police] is at its lowest ebb precisely when professional standards are at an all time high' (Reiner 1992: 773).

Reiner thus implies that media institutions have simultaneously contributed towards and reflected the post-war desacralization of English policing. In his latest research, an historical content analysis (conducted with Sonia Livingstone and Jessica Allen) of post-war representations of crime and criminal justice in cinema, fictional television crime series, and the press (The Times and Daily Mirror), some empirical support is found for this contention (Allen *et al.* 1998; Reiner *et al.* 2000*a*, 2000*b*). Reiner and his co-workers discern, for instance, an increasing tendency to represent (or report) the police in sceptical/critical terms—as unsuccessful, lacking in integrity, resorting to excessive force, internally divided, and so forth (for details, see Reiner *et al.* 2000*a*: 115–17). They demonstrate further, and more generally, a basic shift over the period from a depiction of crime as an offence against absolute collective norms to one which treats it as a matter of harm directed at an individual victim (a figure, they suggest, who has moved from a peripheral to an increasingly pivotal position in crime drama and journalism). This is accompanied by a corresponding shift in the portrayal of the police, such that their moral status as dedicated, exemplary figures is no longer conferred by their office, but has, instead, been rendered contingent, a quality to be constructed anew in the course of each particular narrative (Reiner *et al.* 2000*a*: 122; 2000*b*: 180). By such means has once revered authority been 'demystified'.

Democratization

Questions of individualism, pluralism, and mass mediation are entangled with, and inseparable from, the third post-war social and cultural development that demands consideration in this section—what we may call the democratization of everyday life. To deploy this phrase is to speak once more of the reconfigured social and authority relations that have surfaced in Britain since 1945, but to do so in ways that emphasize the effects of improved educational achievement; the coming to the fore of discourses of equality, rights, and citizenship (not least around questions of gender, ethnicity, sexuality, disability); and the heightened expectations attached to the 'quality of life', the threats posed to it, and the measures required to protect or enhance it. We are,

Jock Young (1999: 78) argues, 'increasing our level of social scrutiny and demand'. He continues:

> The very existence of a debate about the levels of risk...is *in itself* one of the great gains of late modernity. It is not so much that modernity has failed to keep its promise to provide a risk-free society as that late modernity has *taken seriously* that promise, has demanded more and realized the greater difficulty of its accomplishment [Young 1999: 78, emphases in original].

This increasing 'scrutiny and demand' can be registered in at least two ways. It can de discerned, first, in the manner in which once more taken-for-granted (one might even say 'naturalized') inequalities between individuals and groups have been called into question, subject to debate and deliberation, and recast in the lexicon of equality and justice (few today—even among free-market ideologues—explicitly defend inequality, still less injustice; the cleavages of contemporary political debate surround the *form* that equality ought properly to take). Patterns of expectation and behaviour once legitimated (spared, indeed, the need for legitimation) by dint of 'tradition' can no longer be defended as such (Giddens 1994). 'Subordinates' are now less inclined to accept their 'place' in the order of things, or to accredit that place to either fate or personal shortcomings. People have—as Wouters (1986: 4) puts it—developed 'a sharper eye' for unwarranted restrictions upon individual autonomy and 'an aversion to claims to authority that are not based upon personal merit'. The terms of engagement between men and women, employers and employees, parents and children, teachers and pupils, young and old more generally have consequently been brought into more open dispute, such that, while power imbalances persist and individuals continue to occupy, and be exploited within, positions of subordination, 'people now live in less hierarchic, less rigidly and formally regulated relations and figurations' (Wouters 1986: 11). Everyday life has, in these respects, been rendered more 'democratic'.

Cognate considerations apply, secondly, to public orientations towards institutions of social authority and expertise, whether they be the medical profession, educators, legislators, or the police. Individuals have, it is said, developed more secular, sceptical attitudes towards such bodies, while simultaneously acknowledging a wider, more diffuse array of 'authority' figures (Bauman 1999).

People today have become less willing to trust social institutions; less minded to accept their claims and heed their commands (even if—as Giddens (1990) suggests—our dependence on the expertise contained in 'abstract systems' has in fact deepened). They have, conversely, become more likely to demand 'fair' treatment, insist upon their 'entitlements', and defend their rights; more willing to voice grievances about poor performance and mobilize for a better service. This has, of course, been a complex (not to say, uneven) process. It is both the fought-for-and-over consequence of social movement politics and governmental action and the unintended outcome of developments in education, mass media, and the like. And it has encompassed enhanced legal protections (rights at work, consumer laws, the Human Rights Act etc.); new institutions of lobbying, enforcement, and redress (employment tribunals, commissions for racial equality, and equal opportunities, pressure groups, and so forth), and attendant official and popular discourses of consumerism, equality and rights. We will have more to say about the meaning and effects of these transformations as the book unfolds. For now let us merely note the emergence of a cultural climate—discernible, Reiner (1992: 771) suggests, among both 'those at the receiving end of police powers and the general public audience of policing'—in which great (often conflicting, arguably insatiable) expectations are attached to the police, and where attention is routinely and critically paid to response times, detection rates, the handling of disorder, miscarriages of justice, and so many other related shortcomings or excesses in organizational conduct. This is the environment in which the English police are today required to operate.

Crime and Responses to Crime

One does not have to concur with Jock Young's contention that 'the rapid rise in the crime rate' has since 1945 been 'the *major* motor of transformation in the development of the crime control apparatus' (1999: 17; emphasis added) to recognize that the trajectory of post-war English policing cannot adequately be grasped without due consideration being given to the 'crime question' (see also Young 1999: 35; cf. Garland 2001: 193). Three connected dimensions of this question, in particular, demand some attention.

We must have regard, first of all, to what Young accurately describes as the 'rapid rise' in levels of crime witnessed during the post-war period. Any plausible reading of the *Criminal Statistics* bears this claim out (even after one has entered all those standard caveats about how these statistics are constructed and the difficulties inherent in making meaningful sense of them). In 1950, slightly fewer than 500,000 notifiable offences were recorded by the police in England and Wales. By 1970 this figure had risen to 1.6 million, by 1980 to 2.5 million, by 1997 to 4.5 million.[4] Recorded crime thus rose from one offence per 100 of population in 1950 to ten offences per 100 in 1993. In one year alone (1991) the *level of increase* in offences was greater than the *total* number of offences recorded in 1950 (Young 1999: 122). Between 1950 and 1993, there was a twenty-eight-fold increase in thefts from motor vehicles and a forty-eight-fold escalation in robbery. Violent crime rose on average 6.4 per cent *per annum* in the half-century from 1947 to 1997. Since 1981 these rises have been borne out by repeated 'sweeps' of the British Crime Survey (BCS), albeit that the BCS has indicated lower rates of increase. Between 1981 and 1993, for crimes that can be compared, recorded crime rose by 111 per cent, BCS figures by 77 per cent. For the offence of burglary (which the General Household Survey (GHS) has investigated since 1972), police statistics record a rise of 189 per cent between 1972 and 1991, GHS/BCS findings a 61 per cent rise.[5] The proliferation since the mid-1980s of both local crime surveys (Kinsey 1984; Jones *et al.* 1986) and area-based analyses of the BCS (Hope 1997) has further revealed some marked social and spatial disparities in levels of crime and disorder, with the risk of victimization heavily concentrated among the poorest, most chronically deprived individuals and neighbourhoods. Whichever way one slices it, the rise in crime in the post-war period remains 'a massive and incontrovertible social fact' (Garland 2001: 90). Britain, in the space of fifty years, has been transformed into a 'high crime society' (Garland 2001: 90).

This is not, however, merely a matter of bare figures. We need to note, secondly, that 'crime' in the post-war period has mutated from a relatively settled social category into an object of often heated political and cultural dispute (hence the scare quotes). In part, according to Jock Young (1999: ch. 2), this has to do with the bringing to public consciousness of hitherto invisible victims of crime (e.g., women assaulted or raped by their partners; children abused by parents or residential care workers); and with the attendant revelation that crime and deviance pervade arenas and institutions they were once not readily associated with—the family, homes for the care of children or the elderly, corporations, government, even the police. But such discoveries (and the claims pressed on behalf of 'new' victims) have also served to problematize the very concept of crime itself. As debate about new manifestations of risk and danger has proliferated in recent decades, the question, not merely of where crime happens but, more fundamentally, to what behaviour the ascription 'crime' ought properly to attach, became correspondingly less clear. And as the politics of blame and censure came to infuse late modern culture (Sumner 1994: 309–15), so demands have grown for this of that 'menace' to be countered by a further extension of criminal law—to protect children from parents who 'smack' them; rivers from multinationals that pollute them; residents from 'anti-social' children; children from drug-dealers and paedophiles; employees from workplace harassment; women from 'stalkers'; ethnic minorities from racist attacks, and so on. Crime has, it seems:

Moved from the rare, the abnormal, the offence of the marginal and the stranger, to a commonplace part of the texture of everyday life: it occupies the family, the heartland of liberal democratic society as well as extending its anxiety into all areas of the city. It is revealed in the highest echelons of the economy and politics as well as in the urban impasses of the underclass. At times, it seems as frequent in the agencies set up to control crime as it does within the criminal fraternity itself [Young 1999: 30].

This has contributed, thirdly, to what Garland (2001: 163) has described as the 'institutionalization' within late modern Britain of a 'collectively raised consciousness of crime'. This, of course, is a reformulation of what has since the early 1980s come—often too unquestioningly—to be called 'fear of crime' (Hale 1996; Stanko 2000). The latter term took off in the wake of the first British Crime Survey published in 1983 (Hough and Mayhew 1983) as a shorthand for the worries and concerns expressed by citizens about the prevalence and risks of criminal victimization (on subsequent BCS findings see Hough 1995). This, in turn, prompted a stream of research attempting to account for the apparent mismatch between levels of 'fear' found among certain groups (women, the elderly) and their antecedent levels of 'objective' risk (Maxfield 1984); and the related emergence of 'fear' and 'fear reduction' as discrete objects of policy—and police—attention. These analytic and applied preoccupations have, however, attracted some stringent criticism of late, as well as numerous efforts aimed at empirical refinement and conceptual development (Sparks 1992*b*; Taylor 1995; Walkate 1998; Girling *et al.* 2000; Hollway and Jefferson 2000)—something that is reflected in Garland's analysis. Such a re-envisioning is preferable in a number of ways. In the first place, it better captures the key issue at stake here—namely, the ways in which crime and disorder have been 'woven into our common sense and the routines of our everyday life' (Garland 2001: 163) and inscribed prominently and loudly into contemporary popular and political discourse (Hope and Sparks 2000). At the same time, it usefully alerts us to the contrasting responses of ('cold') amoral, prudent actuarialism and ('hot') emotionally-charged demonization that have come to characterize the 'crime complex' of late modernity (Garland 2001: chs. 5–6; see also Young 1999).

All this, to be sure, has had some significant implications for English policing, both exerting new, more intense pressures on the police, and helping to forge new understandings of their place in managing risk and securing order. In terms of the former, it has since the 1970s served to usher the police into the foreground of English society. Rising crime and anxiety have, in particular, generated urgent—public and governmental—demands for the police to 'do something' by way of response—take resolute action, stem the tide, keep entropy at bay. For a time, in the 1970s and early 1980s, police elites tended to react to such pressures enthusiastically and in kind—often acting in ways that helped to stir the very demands they purported merely to be responding to (Hall 1980*b*). Such elites have since the mid-1980s, however, been prone to respond to cries for *more*, *visible* policing in fairly circumspect tones— emphasizing the structural limits of what the police can contribute to social ordering (Bayley 1994: ch. 1); explicitly adopting practices of call prioritization and resource targeting, striving generally to 'talk down' public expectations. The resultant perception that the police today are unable or unwilling (or both) to respond effectively to public demands for order has, it appears, generated marked dismay and disenchantment, especially among those middle- and 'respectable' working-class populations who have in Britain long tended to couple together civil peace and locally-delivered state policing (Taylor 1999: 25–6; Girling *et al.* 2000: ch. 6). One might even speak in this regard—borrowing a phrase of Ian Taylor's (1999: 232)—of a 'crisis of competence' in contemporary public policing.

We have witnessed in terms of the latter, partly in response to such perceived shortcomings, a greater readiness among citizens to resort to alternative modes of policing and security—what Taylor (1999: 26) describes as 'a general turn towards a private or tribal form of self-protection'. Since the 1980s especially, the protection of person and property has become less and less the exclusive province of the public police, and is increasingly delivered today by a plurality of state and non-state actors. Business and government organizations have come to rely heavily on either 'in-house' or 'contracted-in' security. Shopping precincts, airports, and other sites of 'mass private property' (Shearing and Stenning 1983) are policed on behalf of their owners (and users) by commercial operatives. A number of local authorities have established their own 'community forces' (I'Anson and Wiles 1995), or employed commercial firms to patrol housing estates or run CCTV operations, or have initiated city-guard and/or neighbourhood warden schemes. Individuals and communities are turning more and more to forms of security hardware (alarms, bars, gates, walls, surveillance cameras, and so on) to fortify their homes, and—in some cases—to commercial patrols to keep watch over the surrounding streets. We have, in short, witnessed the emergence of an uneven patchwork of policing and security provision, one increasingly determined by the ability and willingness of consumers to pay (Jones and Newburn 1998; Johnston 1999), and intimately tied up with the formation of 'new security communities' (Loader 1999). Against this backdrop—what Reiner (1997: 1039) describes as ' "pick'n'mix" policing for a postmodern age'—the police have been relocated as but one among an array of security options. They have, as such, come to inhabit market conditions that offer 'no site from which authoritative pronouncements [can] be made' (Bauman 1987: 167), that strip of their 'halo every occupation honoured and looked up to with reverent awe' (Marx and Engels 1975/1888: 36)—conditions that make it ever more difficult for the police to stand above the competitive fray and persuasively claim to be embodying the 'public interest'. Can one imagine a more telling indicator of the English police's contemporary desacralization?

Police Organization

Mention must finally, by way of introductory exposition, be made of the police organization itself. There were 176 police forces in England and Wales in 1945. In the main, they were small, parochial, hierarchical, rigidly disciplined organizations (Brogden 1991; Weinberger 1995). They were bodies with few specialist units or personnel, geared primarily to 'fixed-point' beat patrols and criminal investigation; these and sundry 'social service' tasks being undertaken mainly by large, working-class men of 'rudimentary educational attainment' (Reiner 1995b: 39). They were also—Weinberger (1995: 208) insists—generally well fitted to the dispositions and demands of the age. Clearly much changed during the second half of the twentieth century. 'Police forces', Reiner (1995b: 34) argues, 'have become large, complex bureaucratic organizations, with long chains of command and a network of specialist departments and roles'. What is more:

Police strength and powers have increased, public accountability and consent have declined, the police are seen as (not very successful) enforcers rather than benign helpers, the organization has become a complex bureaucracy remote from local communities, forced to rely more on force than consent [Reiner 1995b: 40].

So what has changed? What mutations in the structure, practices, and outlooks of the police have contributed to this predicament? For present purposes let us focus on three such transformations, each of which may be said to have had a close bearing on the question of desacralization.

Consider first the issue of *centralization*, or what Wall (1998: 86) terms 'the creeping, or incremental, centralized control over the police organisation'. This process—which Wall takes to be a characteristic feature of (especially) twentieth-century police history—exhibits several noteworthy dimensions. First, the post-war amalgamation of police institutions in England and Wales. From the aforementioned figure of 176, force amalgamations reduced the total number of police forces to 124 by the time of the 1962 Royal Commission. Following the Police Act 1964, this was further diminished to forty-six by the end of the 1960s, and (in the aftermath of local government reorganization in the early 1970s) to the present forty-three by 1974. Such mergers were generally defended in the name of cost-effectiveness, economies of scale, and the enhancement of career opportunities for officers. But they also, it is claimed, resulted in the administrative creation of police areas with 'little local meaning' and in the transformation of police organizations from 'small local autocracies' to 'a series of large regional bureaucracies' (Wall 1998: 84). 'On the face of it', Reiner (1995b: 37) suggests, 'contemporary police forces are fewer, larger and more remote from local communities'.

We should note, secondly, the proliferation of various 'soft' measures through which the Home Office has in the post-war period endeavoured to co-ordinate, structure, and steer police forces at a distance. These have included a cumulative strengthening—through such initiatives as the National Police College (established in 1949) and the Senior Command Course (begun in 1962)—of the Home Office's role in the selection and education of chief police officers; the part played by the Home Office in developing police training, encouraging new working practices, or securing new technology and equipment; and the role of Home Office circulars in co-ordinating and standardizing police policy across different forces. This latter tool of government, whose use became especially pronounced in the 1980s, has helped, Reiner argues, to forge a *de facto* national force (Reiner 1991: ch. 11; 1992: 769).

Thirdly, and relatedly, one may point—as Reiner has done repeatedly (1992: 769; 2000a: 188–98)—to a tilt in the balance of power within the tripartite structure of police governance that has occurred since the 1960s—a development whose meanings and effects we consider in Chapter 8. This has seen a marked accentuation in the capacities and influence of the Home Office and a corresponding erosion of local accountability; something, in Reiner's (1992: 769) view, that 'has been a major factor undermining police legitimacy in recent years'. Such a trend, it is said, has become especially apparent since the early 1980s when—against the backdrop of urban disorders and industrial strife (in the shape, notably, of the miners' dispute)—the Conservative government (together with several vocal chief constables) sought to fend off demands from a number of Labour-run local police authorities for greater democratic accountability (Jefferson and Grimshaw 1984; Lustgarten 1986; Oliver 1987; Simey 1988; Walker 2000: ch. 3). At the same time, central government became concerned to promote greater 'economy, efficiency, and effectiveness' within police forces; a process that saw the Home Office (and the police themselves) initiate a series of measures designed to make police organizations more 'business-like' and responsive to their 'customers' (Hirst 1991; Woodcock 1991; Leishman *et al.* 1996; McLaughlin and Murji 1997, 2000). This process was, in turn, deepened by the Police and Magistrates' Court Act 1994 (since subsumed into the Police Act 1996) which extended central government control over police purse-strings and enabled the Home Secretary, for the first time, to lay down national performance objectives for police forces (Walker 2000: ch. 4). A more robust regime of audit and inspection—in which bodies such as the Audit Commission and Her Majesty's Inspectorate of Constabulary now play a prominent part—has also been cemented in its wake. The performance of English police forces has, in short, become a focal concern of both Conservative and New Labour governments since the 1980s—governments which today appear less minded to consider the police a 'unique' or 'special' case, and much readier to subject them to the 'rigours' that apply elsewhere across the public—and private—sector.

The second broad issue we must address here concerns developments in police *technology* and their effects. A central aspect of this surrounds the response of police organizations to the post-war emergence of a more geographically mobile society and, in particular, the development and deployment—throughout the 1960s especially—of personal radios, computer technology, and patrol vehicles. Arguably the most significant single moment in this process was the advent in the late 1960s of 'unit beat policing' (UBP) (Weatheritt 1986). The brainchild of Home Office working parties on *Police Manpower, Equipment and Efficiency* (Home Office 1967), UBP was intended to remedy the inability of 'fixed-point' patrolling to deal effectively with increasingly mobile criminal activities. Its avowed aim was to retain the 'best' of the fixed point system (in the form of an 'area constable') and to supplement it with round-the-clock motorized patrols (cf. Bottoms and Stevenson 1992: 30–2). Initially it was met with great acclaim. But its purposes were frustrated both by a lack of the necessary resources and, Reiner (2000*a*: 61) suggests, by action-oriented police officers seduced by 'the technology of fast cars, sirens and flashing blue lights'. It has thus come to be seen—both by many police officers (Weinberger 1995) and among the public (Girling *et al.* 2000: ch. 6)—as a significant watershed in post-war policing, the point at which local, visible, service-oriented guardianship gave way to something 'more distant and less human' (Whittaker 1964: 200)—remote, technology-driven, 'fire-brigade' policing. More recent technological innovations (the coming of the police helicopter, the rise and rise of CCTV surveillance), coupled with enhanced police scepticism about the value of generic patrolling, have arguably served to buttress these impressions.

A further dimension of this issue concerns police responses— from the late 1970s onwards—to what they perceived as mounting levels of public disorder and political violence. Following a number of clashes in the late 1970s (at the 1976 Notting Hill carnival, between anti-racist groups and the National Front) at which police officers were forced to resort to dustbin lids for protection, there ensued a 'paramilitarization' of English policing; something the urban disorders and industrial conflicts of the early to mid 1980s gave further rapid impetus to (cf. Jefferson 1990; Waddington 1991). In part such 'paramilitarization' entailed providing officers with new 'protective' equipment—riot shields, helmets, public order vehicles, and, if deemed necessary, CS gas and plastic bullets. In part it involved the deployment of specialist squads—the Metropolitan Police Special Patrol Group (formed in 1965), Police Support Units (created in 1974)—co-ordinated in emergency situations by the National Reporting Centre (Kettle 1985). But it signalled above all the emergence of new governmental and police mentalities towards the problem of order; a shift that entailed the abandonment of 'minimum force' (what former Metropolitan Police Commissioner Robert Mark once termed 'winning by appearing to lose'[6]) and its replacement by a stiffer strategy more reliant on 'technology, equipment and weaponry' (Reiner 1992: 766). When one couples this—at the level of day-to-day policing— with the more frequent, if not yet routine, arming of the British police, and the onset of equipment (new 'NATO' uniforms, side-handled batons, pepper sprays) that places the contemporary 'bobby' at some practical and symbolic remove from his or her post-war forebears—one is faced, it seems, with a significant assault on received understandings and imagery of the English police. As Reiner (2000a: 70) pithily puts it: 'Dixon is out, Darth Vader is in'.

Finally, we need to examine several issues which appear to suggest that the police have in recent decades become more *out of touch* and *out of control*. Three post-war developments arise for consideration here. First, the coming to prominence of political and public concern over the unrepresentative composition of police organizations, especially in respect of gender, ethnicity, and sexuality. Some modest advances have, it should be said, been made in these domains since the 1960s, especially in terms of gender. As of March 2002, 18 per cent of police officers were female (a not inconsiderable rise on the 1963 figure of 3.5 per cent) and sixteen out of a total of 204 assistant chief constables (fourteen) and chief constables (two) are women (Smith *et al.* 2002); figures that compare with only 2.6 per cent of police establishment hailing from ethnic minorities, and a significant under-representation of black and Asian officers at senior management levels (Holdaway 1991; Holdaway and Barron 1997). Organizations representing women, ethnic minority, and gay and lesbian officers also operate today at both national level and within many individual police forces, and discrimination against members of such groups is taken more seriously than it once was by police managers. However, against the aforementioned backdrop of pluralism and democratization (a backdrop that has served to bring these questions to the fore), such shifts have largely failed to keep pace with what is now being demanded of the police in these areas, not least in the wake of the Macpherson Inquiry into the botched investigation by the Metropolitan Police of the racist murder in 1993 of black teenager Stephen Lawrence (Macpherson 1999). The police, consequently, continue to convey the impression that they remain 'far from socially representative of a much more pluralistic British society' (Reiner 1995*b*: 40).

The police, secondly, have been beset since the late 1960s by a succession of scandals that have severely undermined the idea that they are an impartial, disciplined organization bound by the rule of law. Perhaps the key event here was the exposure by the *Sunday Times* in November 1969 (with taped evidence of police wrongdoing) of a corrupt 'firm-within-a-firm' operating within the Metropolitan Police CID (Cox *et al.* 1977). An internal and external inquiry followed, both of which were obstructed and ultimately unsuccessful. Two more corruption scandals involving the Metropolitan Police's Obscene Publications and Drugs Squads were subsequently revealed, all of which culminated in the concerted efforts of Commissioner Robert Mark to clean up and, if necessary, clear out Scotland Yard (Mark 1978: chs. 7–10). Further allegations involving the Robbery Squad and another external police inquiry ('Operation Countryman') seemed only to confirm the embedded nature of corruption in the capital's police force in the 1970s. Yet we now also know that this coincided with some serious and in places systematic abuse of suspects' rights; abuses that eventually came to public light in the 1980s and 1990s with the official recognition of a litany of miscarriages of justice. The list—which spans the changes in investigative procedures introduced by the Police and Criminal Evidence Act 1984—is long, well-known, and instructive: Maxwell Confait, Judith Ward, the Maguire seven, the Guildford four, the Birmingham six, convictions quashed against many of those prosecuted by the West Midlands Serious Crime Squad (which was disbanded in 1989); four men wrongly convicted of killing newspaper boy Carl Bridgewater, the Tottenham three (wrongly convicted of murdering PC Keith Blakelock during the 1985 riots), Stephan Kiszko, and ... These cases, Reiner (1992: 765) claims, 'profoundly shook public opinion'. They also, in the short span of just over a decade, gave rise to two separate Royal Commissions into the rules governing police investigations (Home Office 1981; Home Office 1993a).[7]

We ought to take cognizance, thirdly, of the fact that the police during this period broke with their 'traditions' of public silence (or what Reiner (1992: 767) calls 'non-partisanship'), and began to take-up a more prominent stance as commentators both on matters of crime and policing, and on the 'condition of England' more generally. Early sightings of this can be detected in the mid to late 1960s with the publication by the Police Federation of a pamphlet, *The Problem*, in support of its pay claim, and the endeavours of Robert Mark (then Chief Constable of Leicester) to highlight what he saw as unduly high acquittal rates and promote certain changes in the criminal justice process (such as abolition of the right to silence). Such departures from tradition became much more pronounced, however, during the 1970s. In 1975, the Federation launched the first of two high-profile campaigns, one in support of its pay dispute with the Labour government, the other advocating 'law and order' policies that chimed closely with those of the then Conservative opposition (Reiner 1980). In 1972, Robert Mark commenced a five-year reign as Metropolitan Police Commissioner during which he became a well-known and controversial public figure, a path that was subsequently followed by his successor David McNee in his lobbying for greater police powers, and in the early 1980s by the likes of James Anderton and Kenneth Oxford in the course of disputes with 'their' police authorities over democratic accountability. As we shall see in Chapter 7, the Federation and chief officers have both of late come to adopt more modulated, lower profile and generally less confrontational stances. The genie, however, has been let out of the bottle. The police's relationship to English political culture will arguably never be quite the same again: '[t]he years of partisanship had tarnished, possibly irretrievably, the sacred aura hitherto enjoyed by the British police of being, like the Queen, above party politics' (Reiner 2000a: 74).

A Profane Institution?: Some Doubts

We have no major quarrel with the broad contours of what we have termed the 'desacralization thesis'. It clearly, for reasons we have set out, has much to commend it as an account of the central trajectories of English policing in the latter half of the twentieth century—indeed, part of our purpose in this book is to deepen and extend it. Yet for all its apparent plausibility, this is a thesis that evinces a number of explanatory shortcomings and lacunae. These derive, we believe, from the fact that its central contentions have been either largely inferred from the numerous but for the most part discrete studies of policing conducted since 1964, or else 'read off' from a series of propositions made by social theorists about the character and direction of change within contemporary society.[8] They have not, in other words, at least for the most part, emerged from dedicated investigation that takes the relationship between policing and the social as *the* object of conceptual and substantive enquiry. Two such shortcomings seem particularly germane to the focal concerns of the present study.

The first problem is that Reiner tends, if not exactly to take as given that which stands in need of fuller scrutiny, then at least too readily to presume that we are somehow locked onto a 'one-way track' (Thompson 1996: 191) from modernity to postmodernity in the realm of the social, and from the sacred to the profane in respect of the police. What results, it seems to us, is an overly one-dimensional diagnosis of the present, one that tends to efface its complexity; gloss over the uneasy coexistence of competing cultural and political forms; overlook the presence and effects of reactions and counter-tendencies to detraditionalization; and downplay the place of affectivity and 'historical allusion' (Collini 1999: 105) in contemporary English culture. In so doing, he perhaps unduly neglects the rider that Miliband (1977: 404) offered to his original thesis: '[i]f there is deep and widespread de-subordination on one side, so is there deep resentment of it on the other, which spills over onto the political system which allows it'.[9]

In pursuit of this charge, let us consider a couple of examples. Reiner marshals, as we have seen, considerable evidence to support his claim concerning the rise of more profane orientations towards the police, much of it compelling. But are there not reasons to suppose that sacred sentiments also continue to attach to this institution. If—as a number of commentators have recently suggested (Laster and O'Malley 1996; Karstedt 2002)—late modern societies are becoming increasingly 'emotionalized', should we not expect this to suffuse popular and, for that matter, official dispositions towards the police? At a moment when the problem of order is being 're-dramatized', and a new collective experience of crime is driving increasingly febrile demands for security (Garland 2001: 10, 147–8), should we not anticipate that this will have effects in the realm of policing? Can, indeed, a social institution so intimately connected with people's fears and fantasies about such matters as life, death, order, chaos, vulnerability, protection, and so forth ever be entirely free of affectively-charged sentiments, allegations, and appeal? At the very least, there appear to be tendencies within the present that continue to exempt the police 'from the ordinary realm of secular evaluation' (Banton 1964: 236).

We may, in this regard, cast a new light on Ericson and Haggerty's (1997) contention that police forces within late modern 'risk societies' are being reconfigured as 'knowledge-brokers'. Their thesis—which may plausibly be interpreted as a telling case in point of policing having become a profane instrument of governance—is that the modern police project of tackling crime and securing territorial order has increasingly been permeated by a preoccupation with generating and disseminating information that assists external agencies (insurance companies, licensing authorities, media, etc.) in the task of managing risk. But why, we may ask, is it the police who occupy the practical and symbolic hub of the new informational nexus Ericson and Haggerty describe? What aura do the police possess that enable them to create and distribute such socially authoritative knowledge, and thus contribute so centrally to the production of meaning through which populations are constituted 'in their respective risk categories' (Ericson 1994: 168)? Such questions—which are not really pressed either by Ericson and Haggerty or within the risk literature more generally—lie at the heart of the present study.

Reiner suggests, further, that under postmodern conditions characterized by individualization and pluralism, it is no longer tenable for the police to act as an 'effective symbol' of either national culture or a unitary moral order (Reiner 1992: 779). Perhaps so. But are these not also the very conditions under which some citizens will cleave to the institution of policing as *the* symbolic representation of an order, security, discipline, and authority that otherwise seem so precarious? Should we not expect, across the altered landscape that Reiner describes, to discern the persistence (or re/emergence) of particular, police-centred modes of 'state fetishism' (Taussig 1997: ch. 12). It is too early in our analysis to form judgements on these issues. But we do at least require a theoretical lens that enables questions such as these to be meaningfully posed.

The second difficulty with Reiner's account (and he is by no means alone here) is that it devotes insufficient analytic attention to clarifying the meanings and significance of such phrases as 'public attitudes', 'consent', 'confidence', and 'approval'. To be sure, Reiner's analysis possesses a nuance and sophistication that place it at some remove from those commentators on policing (whether inside or outside the police) minded to speak in banal, reductive, and often ideological terms about 'public opinion' or 'police–public relations'. He also remains more sensitive than most to the ways in which axes of social stratification such as class, age, ethnicity, and gender shape people's experiences of policing and their orientations towards the police. A couple of related difficulties nonetheless remain.

The first concerns a lack of any obvious interest (something he shares with police sociology more generally) in seeking to explain public *support* for the police—as if the absence of any pressing policy predicament means there is no explanatory puzzle to be solved. Reiner has, as we have seen, repeatedly in his recent work pointed to what he describes as a '*massive* haemorrhage' or '*precipitous* decline' in public approval for the police, and much of his explanatory effort has—by no means improperly—been aimed at trying to account for this. But hold on. Evidence from the 2000 British Crime Survey suggests that 79 per cent of people think their *local* police do either a 'very' (20 per cent) or 'fairly good' (59 per cent) job; a figure that differs little among black (74 per cent) and Asian (71 per cent) respondents, or among 16 to 29-year-old men (78 per cent) (Sims and Myhill 2000). While those thinking that the *national* police were doing a 'good' or 'excellent' job were significantly lower (54 per cent of whites, 40 per cent of blacks, 42 per cent of Asians), these assessments remained a good deal more positive than for any other criminal justice agency (Mirrlees-Black 2000). The 1989 MORI poll cited by Reiner found 43 per cent of respondents expressing 'a great deal of respect' for the police. And while one can point, with Reiner, to an overall decline in the post-war standing of the police (especially among particular social groups), this hardly amounts to a 'haemorrhage'—indeed, it is not implausible, on the basis of post-war opinion surveys, to say that approval ratings for the police have remained *relatively stable* over the period (cf. Home Office 1962; Shaw and Williamson 1972; Belson 1975). So why—in the face of corruption scandals, miscarriages of justice, paramilitarization, falling crime detection rates, the decline of visible patrols, the Stephen Lawrence affair, and so on—does confidence in the police remain in certain quarters so *high*? Surely *this* question should also form part of the sociology of policing's explanatory agenda?

Our second, and connected, point concerns the formation of what are often too unquestioningly referred to as public 'attitudes' towards the police. What is going on when an individual expresses 'respect' for the police, or ticks the 'doing a good (or bad) job' box in an opinion survey, or indicates that he or she trusts police officers, or subsequently withdraws that trust? Why is it that people come to hold these 'attitudes'? Survey methodology, for all that it has enhanced our understanding of 'police–public relations', is not well equipped to handle such questions. Yet they remain important ones; puzzles that invite us to explore more searchingly the structures of thought and feeling, the generative habits and dispositions, that give rise to specific patterns of belief about the social institution of policing. What images and associations coalesce around the idea of policing (and 'the police') within lay, professional, and governmental discourses? How is policing mobilized within competing memories and narratives of post-war social and political change? What place does it occupy within the mental and emotional repertoires of differently-situated citizens? What today do the police stand for in the English social imaginary?

If we are to develop an adequate sociological assessment of what has happened to the relationship between police legitimacy and English culture and society since 1945, then we need to supplement the emphases of the desacralization thesis by attending to these questions and others like them. This, in turn, demands that we think more fundamentally about the social meanings of policing, their sources, supports, and effects. And it requires us to develop theoretical orientations and resources with which we can better understand the cultural and political significance of this particular social institution. It is to these tasks that we now turn.

2

On Symbolic Power: Towards a Cultural Sociology of Policing

The political system performs a function of symbolic protection far beyond its specific role as an apparatus of the selective regulation of social risks...It is most of all on the symbolic level that the institutions of authority, with all their show, ritual, prescriptions, and even codes of manners and etiquette, satisfy a latent need for social protection and spread a gratifying sensation of order and security [Zolo 1990: 43].

Consider the following:

- Routine foot patrols have been shown to make a limited contribution to crime prevention and order maintenance. Most police managers have come to view such patrolling as an ill-advised use—even waste—of police resources. Targeted, 'intelligence-led' patrolling has emerged as a preferred policing strategy. Yet public demands for more 'bobbies-on-the-beat' remain widespread, prominent, and noisy. The unwillingness or incapacity of the police to satisfy these demands generates, in turn, a mixture of bewilderment, resentment, and distrust among anxious citizens. Some co-operate with neighbours, or turn to the private sector, in pursuit of alternative security provision.
- Once a month, currently on a Wednesday evening, *Crimewatch* is screened. The details of undetected crimes are described and visually reconstructed. Presenters and police officers make earnest appeals for witnesses and information—viewers are enjoined to pass on what they know, or suspect, to do their bit in the fight against crime. But questions are seldom if ever asked of the police investigation itself—what detectives are doing wrong, or might do better, or instead. The police, in short, are accorded forty-five minutes of almost completely uncritical prime-time television. *Crimewatch*, in its turn, forms but a

small part of a now diverse array of media representations of policing—a genre of cop shows and crime programmes that routinely attracts and entertains millions of viewers. What other social institutions come close to receiving this kind of—warm, supportive, even reverential—media exposure?

- In almost any London gift shop one can find, among other things, a wide assortment of police symbols—picture postcards, dolls, teddy-bears, fridge magnets, paperweights, egg-cups, bottle-stops, and so on. Sometimes, these figures are depicted in close association with other emblems of British (or should that be English?) nation/statehood—in front of 10 Downing Street, operating a red telephone box, perched on top of Big Ben. The police, in other words, are a tourist icon—a means of representing and marketing 'all that is best' about the nation to outsiders. What though does it say about British (English?) society that it elevates its police officers (rather than, say, its doctors, or teachers, or social workers...) to the status of national symbol in this way?

- Crime rates—as measured in both Home Office statistics and the British Crime Survey—have since 1993 generally been falling. But do we hear talk of a 'safety dividend'—demands for funds to be transferred away from the police towards health, or public transport, or social services, or the arts? (when crime is going up, after all, it is insistently and loudly stated that the police *must* have *more* resources). No we do not. Quite the contrary in fact. Despite plentiful evidence suggesting that the relationship between police numbers and crime levels is fairly arbitrary, politicians continue to compete feverishly with one another in promising to support increased numbers of police officers.

We could, of course, have opened this chapter with a different set of scenarios—one that would have cast the police in a much less favourable glow. There is after all—as we have seen in the previous chapter—no shortage of examples one can mobilize in such an exercise. We plumped for these, however, because they in various ways highlight and illustrate a set of sociological puzzles about contemporary policing—puzzles that we began in our critique of the 'desacralization thesis' to tease out. These puzzles—it appears from the above—concern a mismatch between what governmental and police discourse (supported by no little criminological research) says 'we' can reasonably expect policing institutions to accomplish and the hopes and expectations of the police lodged within lay mentalities and sensibilities. They take the form of a clash between the impossibility of any 'policing solution' to the problem of order and the ways in which the police—as idea and institution—loom large in contemporary culture as definers of the 'crime question' and assumed guarantors of civil peace and security. And they leave us wondering why it is that the police remain one of the principal means by which English society tells stories about itself, and about the effects this prominence entails.

The idea we want to pursue in this chapter is that these conundrums come into sharper relief if we attend more seriously to the ways in which policing is—in Unger's (1987) terms—'made and imagined'. By this we mean that policing operates within societies as a complex of institutional powers, practices, and technologies oriented to preventing crime, detecting offenders, and maintaining order. This much is familiar enough, not least because police sociology has for some four decades striven to document and understand various aspects of policing—police styles, culture, discretion, effectiveness, accountability, and so forth—thus understood. Yet policing is always also—and *this* point has registered much more dimly within police studies—a *cultural* institution and performance, producing and communicating meaning about the nature of order, authority, morality, normality, subjectivity, and the like. Policing, in other words, has to be understood as *a category of thought and affect*—a 'condensing symbol' (Turner 1974) that enables individuals and groups to make sense of their past, form judgements on the present, and project various imagined futures. As an institution intimately concerned with the viability of the state and the security of its citizens—one that is entangled with some profound hopes, fears, fantasies, and anxieties about matters such as protection/vulnerability, order/entropy, and life/death—policing remains closely tied to people's sense of ontological security and collective identity, and capable of generating high, emotionally-charged levels of identification among citizens. Through their presence, performance, and voice, police institutions are able to evoke, affirm, reinforce, or (even) undermine the social relations and belief systems of political communities, serving, in particular, as a vehicle through which 'recognition' within such communities is claimed, accorded, or denied. Policing is, in short, closely bound up with how political order and identity are represented and 'imagined' (Anderson 1991).

In elaborating on this thumbnail depiction of the relationship between policing and the social, we propose in this chapter to do three things. First, drawing principally on Bourdieu's (1991) notion of symbolic power, we outline what is entailed in thinking about policing as a cultural institution and performance and begin to develop a theoretical lens that permits better sociological sense to be made of the social meanings of policing. Secondly, we sketch out an heuristic perspective that enables us to attend, in substantive terms, to the formation, effects, and trajectories of competing sensibilities towards English policing, and to their intersections with other key dimensions of post-war English society and culture. We conclude—as a prelude to the empirical discussions that follow in Parts II and III—by delineating the methodological choices we made in this study and setting out what in research terms our efforts towards a cultural sociology of post-war English policing actually comprised.

Symbolic Power and the Idea of Policing

When collective ideas and sentiment are obscure or unconscious, when they are scattered piecemeal throughout society, they resist any change [Durkheim 1992/1957: 87].

A central dimension—we are tempted to say, the secret—of state power is the way it works within us [Corrigan and Sayer 1985: 200].

We have become accustomed to thinking about the police—and police power—in a certain way. Following Weber, though with antecedents stretching back to the political thought of Jean Bodin and Thomas Hobbes, the police have been posited as the institution through which the state 'claims *monopoly of the legitimate use of physical force* within a given territory' (Weber 1948: 78, emphasis in original). They have, as such, acquired an exclusive, ultimately non-negotiable, right to exercise a range of coercive powers—to search citizens and their property, to monitor their movements, to seize people's goods, to arrest and detain individuals. Such powers are put to use in order to protect the viability of the state and the security of its citizens—to prevent crime, detect and apprehend offenders, maintain public peace and tranquility. They are 'housed' within a specialist, hierarchical, bureaucratic institution whose members are set apart from 'civilians' by dint of their uniform, training, and an internal regime of vertical command structures and disciplinary rules and procedures. These, in turn, form part of an assemblage of organizational, legal, and political mechanisms through which the police's monopoly of coercive force can be subject to constraint, oversight, and redress, and thereby lay claim to the mantle of legitimacy.

The sociology of policing has in the years since the pioneering efforts of Banton (1964), Skolnick (1966), Westley (1970), and Cain (1973) first appeared over three decades ago been much concerned to understand and explain, and to interrogate and unsettle, these various posited dimensions of state policing. Light has, by various means, been shed on the grounded realities of the 'police/man's role'—the influences upon it, the contradictions inherent in it, the trade-offs that ineluctably accompany it (Wilson 1968; Cain 1973; Bradley *et al.* 1986). The ideal of universal—and thus impartial—law enforcement has been exposed as a myth (Jefferson and Grimshaw 1984); patrol officers' discretion—and hence extra-legal determinants of practice—found to occupy a central place in police work (Skolnick 1966; Smith and Gray 1985; Dixon 1997); organizational attention and resources shown repeatedly to fall disproportionately on the poor, the marginalized, and the powerless—those graphically described by Lee (1981) as 'police property'. Repeated studies have revealed key features of the police officer's worldview and demonstrated how 'occupational culture' shapes working priorities and practices, twists and evades legal rules, and distorts/undermines attempts at organizational reform (Punch 1979a; Holdaway 1983; cf. Waddington 1999). And, in seeking to grapple with the paradoxical effects of concentrating the power to wield coercive force in a single social institution (Walker 2000: ch. 1), legal and sociological analysts have dissected (and found wanting) extant modes of inspection, accountability, and redress, and proffered various—and variously far-reaching—proposals for making good their shortcomings (Jefferson and Grimshaw 1984; Lustgarten 1986; Loader 1996: ch. 7; Goldsmith and Lewis 2000). Police sociology has, in short, generated a host of significant and powerful insights into policing as *routine instrumental action*; insights motivated not merely by intellectual curiosity about police officers and their doings, but also, in no small measure, by (left-liberal) political concern about the deployment, distribution, and control of police *coercive* power.

It is no part of our purpose in this book to brush these rich traditions of enquiry, and the issues that quite properly vex them, aside—they will, indeed, make numerous appearances throughout the chapters that follow.[1] Yet the lacunae of the desacralization thesis and the puzzles with which we opened this chapter suggest that the police also exhibit a form of power that, while arguably parasitic upon their coercive capacities, is certainly not reducible to them. We term this, adapting a notion from Pierre Bourdieu, *symbolic power*. Such power, Bourdieu (1991: 170) maintains, is a subordinate, transfigured, and legitimated species of other modes of power (in the present case, monopolization of the instruments of violence). It is, he says, an invisible power, inculcated through instruction, habit, and routine, power 'misrecognized' as such, even exercised by those who are subject to it (Bourdieu 1991: 164). Symbolic power, Bourdieu continues, is:

A power of constituting the given through utterances, of making people see and believe, of confirming or transforming the vision of the world and, thereby, action on the world and thus the world itself, an almost magical power which enables one to obtain the equivalent of what is obtained through force (whether physical or economic), by virtue of the specific effect of mobilization [Bourdieu 1991: 170].

These highly suggestive, if somewhat elliptical, remarks on the nature of power bring to the fore, and help illuminate, several intersecting aspects of the relationship of policing to the social— aspects that speak directly to several of the questions Reiner's desacralization thesis leaves either unresolved or unaddressed. Let us, tentatively for the moment, highlight three. They indicate, first of all, the existence of a set of durable dispositions—a 'habitus' in Bourdieu's (1990: 52–65) terms—that incline a wide range of people to 'think about', and respond to, policing along some entrenched, fairly narrow tramlines. These dispositions operate at the level of what Bourdieu often refers to as 'the doxic', or at that of what Gouldner (1976) terms the 'paleo-symbolic' (see also Sparks 1992a: ch. 2). The first of these terms refers to those taken-for-granted, often pre-conscious, dispositions which *generate* and *delimit* people's attitudes, perceptions, and practices. The latter— 'paleo-symbolism'—refers also to the 'restricted communicability'

(Gouldner 1976: 224) of such beliefs and sentiment, but speaks as well (in a fashion that eludes Bourdieu) of the emotionally compelling character of that which seems to be at stake—what Bauman (1990: 43) nicely terms 'the feeling which precedes all reflection and argument'. Coupled together, these ideas enable us to speak of a set of predispositions which operate in such a way that when people think of crime and order they reach, as it were, *instinctively* for the police. Such dispositions amount—as Bourdieu might say—to an unthought category of thought that habitually and unquestioningly leads people to construe the connection between crime, social order, and policing as obvious, natural, something that 'goes without saying'.

This 'obviousness' is reinforced on a routine basis by a whole litany of police actions and mediated representations—by a regular diet of cop shows and crime news, by calls for police assistance, by the witnessing of officers at work. In order adequately to grasp the means by which dispositions towards policing are produced and reproduced, it is necessary to avoid making a hard and fast distinction between the symbols and practices of police work (cf. Garland 1990: 199). The routine activities and symbolic forms that comprise the social phenomenon of policing cannot so easily be divided. The craft skills and coercive powers that police officers deploy on a daily basis are not just goal-oriented. They serve, in addition, to communicate meaning, not only about the police and their role, but also about power and authority in society. Similarly, the symbols and signs within which police work is encoded are not merely decorative, an epiphenomenal gloss on the material practices of policing. They too have a practical effect and are mobilized for instrumental purposes. In seeking to understand how the social meanings of policing are produced, circulated, and received, one can learn as much from examining public calls for police assistance, as one can from looking at how police work is dramatized.

But it also has much to do with the fears and anxieties, and the hopes and fantasies, that the *idea* of policing evokes at a paleo-symbolic level.[2] To speak of policing is, on the one hand, to conjure a reminder of the existence of the undesirable, criminal Other. As such, it is apt to prompt, or at the very least reinforce, feelings of hostility, aggression, powerlessness, violation, and vulnerability; a sense that one's security is contingent, the social world a rather fragile and troubling place. Yet the idea of policing also brings to the fore sensations of order, authority, and protection; it makes it possible for people to believe that a powerful force for good stands between them and an anarchic world, that the state is willing and able to defend its citizens. Policing, in short, contrives simultaneously to denote both the dangerous Other and the means to deter and, if necessary, apprehend that Other. This structure of thought and feeling is, of course, conditioned by such axes of social division as class, gender, ethnicity, age, and sexuality, as well as by the extent to which police institutions are oriented to the protection of 'specific order'—the present pattern of domination within a polity and the interests of those whom that pattern favours—rather than 'general order'—the preservation of basic standards of public tranquillity in which all social groups have a stake (see Marenin 1983). Among some populations (such as young people or excluded ethnic minority communities), the symbols of policing may have precious little appeal, and the police may be as, if not more, likely to provoke feelings of anxiety and trepidation than they are 'gratifying sensations of order and security' (Zolo 1990: 43). Here, policing possesses a no less durable 'obviousness', though of a different sort.

All this provides some initial clues about to why public sentiment towards policing appears marked by a high 'fantasy content' regarding what the police can and should do (cf. Elias 1983). It offers a route to explaining why the police seem able to draw close to unconditional support from certain sections of the populace (while attracting cognate hostility from others). It indicates why people—in the face of much disconfirming evidence—stubbornly and passionately cleave to the possibility of a 'policing solution' to the problem of order. And it suggests why—in the midst of the many profaning currents discerned by Reiner and others—the idea, institutions, and practices of State (with a big 'S') Policing (with a no less mighty 'P') appear to retain at least the traces of a sacred, fetishized aura—the capacity to fascinate, enthrall, and erotically attract, as well as to unsettle, repulse, and disgust its subjects (Taussig 1992: 86; Bourdieu 1998: 40; cf. Durkheim 1915: 10).

Bourdieu's reflections alert us, secondly and relatedly, to the expressive, signifying capacities possessed by the social institution of policing. Communicating, and being invested with, meaning is of course an aspect of all social institutions, practices, and commodities (cf. Douglas and Isherwood 1979; Inglis 1998;

Willis 2000).[3] It is by no means a peculiarity of the police or of any other criminal justice institution. Yet state policing—as one of the 'active centres of the social order' (Geertz 1983: 122; cf. Shils 1975: ch. 1)—remains an especially rich site for the production and dissemination of meaning; an institution, it seems, that offers an interpretive lens through which people make sense of, and give order to, their world, the source of a set of 'plausible, feasible, useful (and satisfying) stories' (Inglis 1988: 104) about how the world is (or has become), and how it should be (or might become). In making sense of this, we can draw usefully upon anthropologist Victor Turner's (1974) notion of the 'condensation symbol'. Such symbols, Turner says, operate by bringing together under one roof an otherwise disparate set of meanings; they 'condense many references, unifying them in a single cognitive and affective field' (Turner 1974: 55). Policing, it seems to us, operates in precisely this way as a vehicle that enables individuals and groups to make sense of their past, form judgements on the present, and project various imagined futures. As an institution intimately concerned with the viability of the state and the security of its citizens—one deeply entangled with some profound hopes, fears, fantasies, and anxieties about such matters as protection/vulnerability, order/entropy, and life/death—policing remains closely tied to the maintenance of ontological security, the production of subjectivities, and the articulation of collective identities. One would hardly expect it to be otherwise.

We should take care not to overstate this point; policing may—probably does—play a modest if not insignificant part in processes of identity formation. We should equally not seek to anticipate—in advance of the patient empirical enquiry that this field properly requires—the sorts of meanings, associations, and vocabularies that policing connotes among differently situated actors. But nor, conversely, should we lose sight of the fact that policing—to put the matter in Durkheimian terms—is the source of some powerful, efficacious 'collective representations'. It exudes, for instance, the capacity to structure and shape social identities, to regulate externally *and* internally constitute the subjectivities of citizens (Corrigan and Sayer 1985: 194). And it is concerned not merely—*à la* Weber—with the protection and viability of states and statehood, but also with the formation and constitution of nations and national identities; a means by which membership and recognition within political communities are claimed, accorded, or denied (Ellison and Smyth 2000: ch. 6), a vehicle through which such communities are styled, represented, and imagined (Anderson 1991).

There exist numerous documented cases of the role played by police bodies in the formation and reproduction of both sovereign states and the national cultures with which they are intertwined. Emsley, for example, details the instrumental and symbolic part played by various gendarmes in forging the boundaries and identities of European nations in the nineteenth century, marking out 'national territory' and 'turning peasants into Frenchmen, Italians, Spaniards and Russians' (1993: 87; 2000). Walden (1982) has, in a similar vein, noted both the real and imaginary place of the Royal Canadian Mounted Police ('the Mounties') in the (violent) founding of the Canadian nation, and the part they continue to play in perpetuating the image of Canada as a 'secure and peaceable kingdom' (Taylor 1999: 25). While we are concerned in this study with the English case, it should be borne in mind that the symbolic allure of policing, and its connection to the identity of nation-states, is by no means a peculiarly English phenomenon.

Here, perhaps, lie some important clues about the *affective* character of much public identification with the police, and an indication that the attachment to policing is unlikely be shifted merely by demonstrating that it is in some sense or other 'irrational' or wrongheaded. Rendering the police symbolically less important to the production of social order may for many require a significant reorganization of self, something not easily accomplished merely by confronting people with news of scandalous events (miscarriages of justice, police racism, and the like), or disseminating up-to-the-minute research on police in/effectiveness. Policing, it seems, not unlike religion, imposes itself on the mind 'by some virtue of its own, without being accompanied by any proof' (Durkheim 1915: 17).

The notion of symbolic power alludes, thirdly, to the ways in which the police have acquired the right of legitimate pronouncement: a power to diagnose, classify, authorize, and represent both individuals and the world, and to have this power of 'legitimate naming' not just taken seriously, but taken for granted. One might point in this regard to the privileged place the police occupy—most obviously as an 'obvious' source for journalists—in fashioning public representations of crime events (Hall *et al.* 1978; Ericson *et al.* 1991; Schlesinger and Tumber 1994). The police also,

Ericson and Haggerty (1997) have argued, play an important and more diffuse role as 'knowledge workers'—producing and disseminating information that helps an array of external agencies constitute 'populations in their respective risk categories' (Ericson 1994: 168). As a body possessing an aura of authority and knowledgeability, the police are well placed to 'name' contemporary problems, diagnose their causes, and mobilize opinion behind certain preferred 'solutions'. In so doing, they are not only able, as Wilson (2000: 6) puts it, to essay 'the first drafts of a great deal of our cultural knowledge about social disorder and criminality'; they also 'communicate' a set of broader meanings about the nature of power, authority, morality, normality, personhood ('ours' and 'theirs'), and community.

To say this is not to claim that what the police say about contemporary problems remains uncontested—that is rarely the case. Nor is it to deny that, under 'mediated' political conditions, and in the face of the litany of scandals that have appeared to undermine police legitimacy in the last several decades, the police often feel compelled to engage in what Schlesinger and Tumber (1994: ch. 4) call 'promotionalism'. Indeed, various such 'promotional' efforts—the activities and imagery mobilized under the banner of community policing (Alderson 1979; Crank 1994); the proliferation of force 'mission statements'; the privileging of the police's service role; the enlisting of professional image makers (Wolff Olins 1990)—attest to the importance the police today place on seeking to 'manage' their image and secure public consent (Mawby 2002). It does appear, however, that these efforts neither succeed nor fail in a vacuum. In so far as they 'work', they do so by appealing to, resonating with, and actively cultivating, pre-existing paleo-symbolic dispositions towards policing. Police ideology depends, in other words, on the fact that when the police speak they always already occupy a place in the order of things that authorizes their entitlement to pronounce on the world.[4]

These dimensions of police *power*—those, in Wilson's (2000: 12) words, that concern 'story-making, the mobilization and differentiation of audiences, the engagement with the media, the engineering of consent'—have, relatively speaking, remained a neglected topic within the sociology of policing. One can, to be sure, identify several attempts made in recent decades to detail the place and significance of symbolism in police work. Much of that now substantial—if presently somewhat exhausted—corpus of work on 'police culture' has, for instance, drawn attention to the entrenched, narratively reproduced, and change-resistant features of the police occupational habitus (Shearing and Ericson 1991; Young 1991; Chan 1997). It has, in addition, contributed greatly to our understanding of how these habits, beliefs, and sentiments form a 'symbolic universe' (Young 1993: 14) through which a largely mythological narrative of police work—a brave, beleaguered 'us' in hot, barely understood pursuit of a dangerous 'them'—is brought into being and sustained (cf. Watson 1999).

A certain amount of attention has also been devoted to understanding how various rituals—notably, police funerals (Manning 1997: ch.1)—and symbols—such as police uniforms (Young 1991: 66–8)—are mobilized for instrumental purposes, or with how threats to the police officer's symbolic authority shape the exercise of street-level discretion, such as in the policing of juveniles (Piliavin and Briar 1964; Loader 1996: ch. 4). Peter Manning's (1997) semiotically informed attempt to theorize policing using the language and metaphors of drama—actors, roles, audiences, impression-management, and the like—has been, and remains, very much to the fore here—giving rise not only to Manning's own acute interpretations of the meanings and signifying force of control-room communications (1988), police technology (1992, 2001a), and 'zero-tolerance' policing (2001b), but also to a wider body of 'dramaturgical' work on aspects of contemporary police organization and practice. These have included accounts of the symbolic resonance of murder investigations (Innes 2002), as well as of the Royal Ulster Constabulary's ritual mobilization of its officers' bravery and sacrifice (Mulcahy 2000).

And mention must be made too—in addition to aforementioned studies of the police's role in constructing public representations of crime and order (Hall et al. 1978; Ericson et al. 1991; Schlesinger and Tumber 1994)—of that rich terrain of enquiry concerned with fictional representations of police and police work. Work in this field has paid close hermeneutic attention to the values and imagery encoded within, and put into cultural circulation by, crime novels (Knight 1980; Miller 1988; Wilson 2000), cinema (Allen et al. 1998), and various sub-genres of the 'cop show' (Clarke 1983, 1986; Sparks 1992a: ch. 5; 1994; Eaton 1995; Reiner 2000a: ch. 5). It has also begun to take seriously the emotive appeal of these fictions, and their connection with people's quotidian anxieties and unfulfilled desires *vis-à-vis* crime, order, and justice (Sparks 1992*a*). In his—oddly neglected—book on the politics of order, Robert Berki argues that this appeal does not simply stem from witnessing good triumph over evil, but lies, rather, in 'the *double* thrill of seeing morality victorious through being pushed to its very margin, to the point of embracing immorality' (Berki 1986: 57, emphasis in original). He continues (in ways that connect intimately with the concerns that animate this book):

The police are morally permitted, nay obligated, to do things (coerce, forcibly arrest, incapacitate, injure, shoot, interrogate etc.) which would be forbidden in ordinary circumstances and might in fact be morally reprehensible *per se*; yet at the same time its context elevates police work to become the highest embodiment and epitome of morality as such, the first-line defence of society at points where it is most vulnerable, its security against itself. Policing is both central and marginal to the state and to moral consciousness; hence its fascination [Berki 1986: 57].

These strands of research and reflection are valuable and suggestive, and they have in various ways informed and helped shape the orientations of the present study. Such efforts cannot, however, obscure the fact that the sociology of policing has produced few serious, sustained attempts to come to terms with the significance and appeal of policing as a cultural category. Its guiding quest to understand police work as social *action*, has, as we have said, generated many insights into contemporary policing. So too has the desire of many of its practitioners to indicate how policing today has been rendered *profane*. But these orientations are not without blind-spots and costs. They have resulted, in particular, in police sociology devoting insufficient theoretical and substantive attention to comprehending the symbolic power of the idea of policing, and left it insufficiently alive to the role that the 'sacred' might continue to play in the 'cultural constitution' of police authority (Taussig 1992: 112). As a consequence, we still know and understand relatively little about how representations of the police and policing are produced and received, or of the competing social *meanings* ascribed to policing and their various sources, supports, and effects.

Robert Reiner's work again offers a telling instance of this. Reiner is more attentive than most analysts to the 'symbolic significance' of the—especially English—police (Reiner 2000*a*: 139;

2000*b*: 52). Yet his recent writing tends to carry the implication—as much by omission as anything else—that because the police 'can no longer be totems symbolizing a cohesive social order' (2000*a*: 216) they no longer signify *very much—if anything—at all*. This—as the later works of Durkheim (Alexander 1989: chs. 4–6) or contemporary social anthropology (Geertz 1973, 1983) confirm—seems deeply implausible. As Geertz (1983: 143) puts it, '[p]olitical authority still needs a cultural frame in which to define itself and advance its claims, and so does opposition to it. A world wholly demystified is a world wholly depoliticized.'

In seeking to make good these lacunae, we may usefully turn—both for inspiration and ideas—to some recent work within the sociology of punishment. In this field, a number of writers have concerned themselves of late with aspects of the relationship between punishment and mundane and political culture. Attention here has focused on the prominent and febrile place that penal questions have come to assume within electoral politics (Beckett 1997; O'Malley 1999; Windlesham 1996, 2001), as well as on the economic, social, and cultural preconditions that have helped afford punishment its present character and place within late modern societies (Melossi 1993; Pratt 2000; Garland 2001: ch. 6). In both instances, the matter of punishment's social meanings has been much to the fore, giving rise, *inter alia*, to close readings of penal representations (Valier 2000); to socio-historical accounts of the passions animating demands for punishment and the re-emergence of penal measures that give voice and legislative effect to such passions (Simon 1995; Sarat 1997; Sparks 2000), and to situated, 'bottom-up' interpretations of how penal discourses figure within—and are reproduced, or disrupted, by—'the everyday consciousness and conversations of people in the ordinary settings of their lives' (Smith *et al.* 2000: 396; see also, Sparks *et al.* 2000). In each of these respects, the sociology of punishment's gaze has turned towards questions of 'penal culture' and its mutually conditioning intersections with the wider cultural forms within which it is embedded.[5]

Much of the impetus for this partial 'cultural turn' has derived from David Garland's *Punishment and Modern Society: A Study in Social Theory*. In this text, Garland addresses a number of important sociological questions concerning the social significance and meanings of punishment. He explores, first of all, the ways in

which cultural mentalities (systems of cognition or belief) and sensibilities (configurations of affect) condition penal institutions and
practices, establishing 'the contours and outer limits of penality as
well as shaping the detailed distinctions, hierarchies, and categories
which operate within the penal field' (1990: 196). Secondly, and
arguably more originally, Garland considers how and what punishment contributes to the creation of culture. Punishment, he maintains, is not just an instrument of social management and control, it
is also an expressive institution, a cultural performance; one whose
depictions of authority, subjectivity, and social relations help order
and give meaning to the social world. As Garland (1990: 252) puts
it, '[i]n the course of its routine activities, punishment teaches, clari-
fies, dramatizes, and authoritatively enacts some of the basic moral-
political categories which help form our symbolic universe'.

Now passion may not be 'the soul' of policing in quite the same
way as Durkheim insists it is of punishment, but many of the things
Garland asks of the penal field may also usefully be posed in
respect of policing (cf. Walker 1996).[6] Of course, policing in modern societies comprises for the most part, as we have seen, a
bureaucratic, professionalized, and goal-directed set of practices.
But this hardly entails that it is not also shaped and legitimated by
various structures of social belief and affect. Policing, like punishment, is embroiled in, and animated by, a set of cultural mentalities
and sensibilities. Policing too communicates meaning and plays its
part in the production of culture. And just as with punishment, the
way 'we' police, represent policing to 'ourselves', and position it
within an overall sense of order makes a difference both to the
formation of moral and political subjects, and to the quality and
character of social relations. Peter Manning neatly captures some
of this when he writes:

Policing remains a semisacred entity whose mysterious workings point to
the role of law, authority and power in an increasingly secularized society...Policing is an exercise in symbolic demarking of what is immoral,
wrong, and outside the boundaries of acceptable conduct. It represents the
state, morality and standards of civility and decency by which we judge
ourselves [Manning 1997: 319].

These considerations suggest that contemporary policing, like
contemporary punishment, exhibits both profane *and* sacred elements, and that it remains caught in tension—perhaps inescapably

so—between these contrasting dispositions. As Manning puts it: 'policing is poised between instrumental, efficacious action and ritual, emotional and redundant routines that affirm the certainty and value of social order' (Manning 1997: 7).[7] They offer, as such, a useful corrective to the claims and emphases of the desacralization thesis, one indicating that—in the midst of an 'increasingly secularized society'—policing continues to be deeply entangled with affect, imagination, and myth. How though are we to make adequate sociological sense of the uneasy co-presence of these 'contrasting visions'? What mode of enquiry is best able to grasp the interplay between the different strands of thought and feeling that constitute contemporary 'policing culture'?

This task, it seems to us, demands an investigation orientated to understanding both the meaningful constitution of policing as a symbolic form and the socio-historical contexts within which such meanings are generated, transmitted, and received (Thompson 1990: ch. 3). The first of these orientations directs attention towards the various producers and production processes involved in generating and putting into cultural circulation 'police-related' categories, distinctions, and hierarchies, and to the ways in which these meanings are received and appropriated by different audiences in the ordinary settings of their everyday lives (Thompson 1996: 37–43). It demands, in other words, an account of the manner in which policing is, in Stuart Hall's (1980c) terms, 'encoded/decoded'; of the seductions, valorizations, resistances, and refusals that accompany struggles over 'naming' in this field, and of how processes of meaning-building around policing intersect with 'wider' processes of individual and collective identity formation.

The latter orientation reminds us that the symbolic power of the idea of policing is not a static phenomenon, invariant across time and space, and that even when one is striving to grasp the values, beliefs, and sentiments associated with policing at a doxic/paleo-symbolic level (rather than seeking to elicit people's 'attitudes'), it is still necessary to pay heed to *competing* meanings and the relationship between them. In part this is a reminder of the importance of historical specificity and of attending to (still significant) national differences, a matter we return to shortly. It also has to do with recognizing that emotional commitments to policing are themselves structured by such axes of division as class, gender, ethnicity, sexuality, and age. And it sensitizes us to the fact that forms and patterns of identification with policing depend upon, and will vary according to, such things as the thickness of social bonds, the extent of division and inequality, and the pace and direction of social change. It highlights, in short, the vital significance of studying the meaningful constitution of policing *in situ* and in detail.

Let us then, with these considerations in mind, try to specify more fully what it means—in substantive terms—to investigate policing as culture, before considering—methodologically—how this might plausibly be done.

English Policing as Mundane Culture

Policing systems—at least once they have developed to the point at which they are no longer tools of particular political regimes (Goldsmith 2003)—take shape in response to broadly the same underlying security dilemmas, and are required to wrestle with similar sets of choices and trade-offs between competing priorities and values in pursuit of the goal of public tranquility and personal security (Marenin 1983; Walker 1999). It also remains the case that the institutional arrangements liberal democratic states put in place to deliver and govern policing exhibit a number of family resemblances (Bayley 1985). Differences in organizational styles and purposes are, moreover, under globalizing conditions, being chipped away at by the tendency of police practices (or at least policy rhetorics) to spread widely and speedily across jurisdictional frontiers in ways that open up 'local' police agencies to new forms of scrutiny and revision—witness the diffusion in recent years of such things as community policing, problem-oriented policing, and zero-tolerance (Skolnick and Bayley 1985; Goldstein 1990; Dennis 1997; see generally, Newburn and Sparks 2002). Emergent forms of cross-border co-operation between national forces—notably, but by no means only, within the European Union—are, it appears, working to flatten those differences still further (den Boer 1999; Loader 2002). In an era of globalization, there arguably remains no such thing as a hermetically sealed national police system free of exogenous influence and constraint—something that analysis of any particular regime of 'national' policing must take care not to lose sight of.

Yet none of this provides grounds for claiming that the social meanings of policing—the precise ways in which it functions as a cultural category—are invariant across territorial boundaries.

Rather, it seems safer to suppose that policing remains rooted—perhaps firmly so—in the soil of national political cultures; that its operative meanings have national genealogies that vary according to how processes of state and police formation have unfolded historically; and that they take contemporary forms that are conditioned by, and in turn condition, the particular polities of which they form part. The place that police institutions occupy in national histories, mythologies, and consciousness, their involvements in regulating social and political conflict, prevailing sentiment towards the appropriate role of state and civil society in the production of security, the narrative representations of policing that circulate in the media; these are all likely to give rise to differing levels of identification with—or distance from—the police, as well as to specific cultural constructions of the relationship between policing and the social. There is, indeed, plenty of comparative historical and sociological evidence to support just these suppositions (e.g., Walden 1982; Sheptycki 1999; Ellison and Smyth 2000; Emsley 2000).

It is—at least in part—for these reasons that we have set out in this study to produce a cultural sociology of post-war *English* policing.[8] We use the term 'English'—rather than 'British'—here quite deliberately and in full cognizance of the fact that Englishness/Britishness has lately become the subject of much heated cultural and political disputation.[9] We do so, moreover, against a backdrop—in policing as elsewhere—in which the two terms are frequently deployed in loose and interchangeable ways (cf. Holdaway 1983; Emsley 1996). There are clearly many contexts in which this does not much matter, or in which it makes perfect sense to speak of something called 'British policing'—not least because police forces in England, Wales, and Scotland are internally constituted and externally governed in broadly similar fashion.[10] But there are also occasions—of which this is one—where it *is* necessary to distinguish between the constituent nations of the multi-national British state. We do this here, in part, because Scottish policing (especially) followed a different historical trajectory from policing systems in England and Wales; because the former is located within a specific national legal/criminal justice system and distinct political culture, and because, since the Scotland Act 1998, political responsibility for all policing functions except those associated with border controls and national security has passed from Westminster to the new Scottish Parliament in Edinburgh (see Carson 1984, 1985; Walker 1999). We do so, more positively, because our concern with social meaning demands investigation, not merely of the relationship that exists between policing and the political community of the (British) state, but also, perhaps more significantly, of the connections that obtain between the idea of policing and the cultural community of the (English) nation and competing conceptions of 'Englishness'. We are, in other words, explicitly concerned with trying to document and make sense of what we term *English policing culture*, a concept (not to be confused with the more familiar and limited 'police culture') we use to refer to the amalgam of institutions, practices and policies, myths, memories, meanings, and values that, at any given time, constitute the idea of policing within English society.

What though, in substantive terms, might such an enterprise—exploring English policing as an aspect of mundane and political culture—entail? It means, first and foremost, attending to the ways in which the idea of policing is situated within what Raymond Williams calls 'structures of feeling' (Williams 1964: 64–6; 1977: 132–5; 1979: 156–74). This term—which resonates closely with Garland's (1990: 213–16) use of the notion of 'sensibilities'—serves in at least two ways as a valuable hermeneutics tool. It signals, first of all, the importance of seeking to elicit and understand, not people's propositionally stated attitudes towards policing (we must, Williams insists, 'go beyond formally held and systematic beliefs' (1977: 132)), but their actively lived and felt values, sentiments, and orientations—those untutored modes of doxic opinion that exist prior to 'ideology', and to which 'ideology' necessarily seeks to appeal, resonate with, and selectively rearticulate (Pickering 1997: 35, 45). As Williams puts it, '[w]e are talking about... specifically affective elements of consciousness and relationships: not feeling against thought, but thought as felt and feeling as thought' (1977: 132).

But it also, secondly, reminds us that these 'most delicate and least tangible' (Williams 1964: 64) elements of the social are themselves patterned by social interests—they form, that is, *structures* of feeling. This means in part recognizing that doxic/paleo-symbolic dispositions towards policing are *generated* through cultural inculcation and socialization, in specific institutional settings, in the context of deeply asymmetric power relations. And it means recognizing, in turn, that what is produced is a series of *generative* dispositions (a 'habitus', in Bourdieu's terms) that enable differently positioned individuals and groups to, within limits, engage actively with and make sense of the field of policing as *they* encounter it. If, following Williams, we take the cultural sociology of English policing to be concerned with 'clarification of the meanings and values implicit and explicit in a particular way of life' (Williams 1977: 57), this inescapably requires investigation of the substantive meanings that comprise extant structures of feeling towards policing, of the contexts in which such meanings emerge and have effect, and of the tensions, conflicts, and hierarchies that obtain between them. By such means may a better sociological understanding of the place the police occupy within contemporary English social relations be secured.

Our concern in what follows is with trying to apprehend—through a 'creative reconstruction' (Thompson 1990: ch. 6) of the meanings inscribed in various official texts and a range of oral history discussions and biographical interviews (see below)—the specific 'visions' of (English) policing that are appealed to, or projected by, different governmental authorities, police professionals, and lay constituencies. In so doing, we shall be concerned to address the following sets of topics and questions. First, the ways in which selected aspects of English policing since 1945 are remembered, reconstructed, and represented. We take as our cue here a body of recent work on 'social memory' which has—persuasively in our view—demonstrated that 'remembering' is an active, collective, and selective process that occurs in the face of, and is ineluctably shaped by, contemporary troubles and concerns. Memory is, in Raphael Samuel's nice phrase, 'stamped with the ruling passions of its time' (1994: p. x).[11] Against this backdrop, our analytic interest lies *not* first and foremost in the 'accuracy' of people's recall of specific events and processes, with trying to determine what policing 'was really like' in the 1950s, or how the 1980–1 urban disorders were 'actually' policed. Rather, we are interested in what features of post-war English policing are coded as significant by different constituencies and with the manner in which they are re-constructed. What competing variants of the English policing past are recovered (or, conversely, 'forgotten') by such constituencies, and with what effects? What characteristic vocabularies and imagery—in Bourdieu's (1990: 110) terms, what 'sayings of the tribe'—feature in these narrative reconstructions, and what is the nature of their appeal? To what uses—celebration? atonement? justification? censure?—are official and lay memories put in the present? Answers to such questions seem to us vital if we are to enhance our understanding of the persistent place of historical allusion—and of appeals to, and contests over, 'tradition'—in the constitution of English policing culture.

We are concerned, secondly, with how the conflicts, transformations, and continuities that have marked English policing since 1945 (some of which we set out in Chapter 1) are 'encoded' within official texts and representations, and 'decoded' by different public audiences. Our principal purpose here is to explore empirically the ways in which policing is situated in relation to other aspects of English society and culture, such as changing dispositions towards authority, community, and morality, and transformations in gender, generational, and race relations. How are these intersections received and represented within governmental, police, and lay mentalities and sensibilities? What key events and turning points are 'invested' in by different constituencies, and how are such events and their effects coded and assessed? What sense is made by various actors of the contrasting police styles (community policing, paramilitarism, etc.), technologies (cars, riot shields, helicopters, etc.), and discourses (democratic accountability, managerialism, etc.) that surfaced in the latter decades of the twentieth century? What connections and associations, tropes and commonplaces, fears and fantasies are embedded within the stories of historical change people assemble? If policing offers people a cultural template for rendering 'intelligible society and social relationships, serving to organise people's knowledge of the past and the present and their capacity to imagine the future' (Lukes 1975: 301), then how precisely is this template put to use in the contemporary English case? In pursuing these matters empirically in Parts II and III, we hope to arrive—in ways that remedy some of the lacunae of the desacralization thesis—at a more nuanced account of how the relationship between police legitimacy and English popular consciousness has unfolded since 1945.

Thirdly, we are interested in exploring the ways in which the idea of policing (and the particular seductive or repellent possibilities that inhere within it) contributes to the formation and sustenance of individual subjectivities, and to processes of collective identity building. In terms of the former, we are in part concerned simply with the ways in which policing features at various points in the biographical trajectory of individuals. But we shall also, more pertinently, attend to how the idea of policing figures within, resonates with, and helps to 'organize' people's sense of self and disposition towards the wider world, as well as to the various (structural *and* conjunctural) aspects of policing that are called forth and identified with, or effaced or denied, within specific subjectivities and *Weltanschauung*.[12] In relation to the latter, we are concerned with the ways in which police institutions—as potent icons of state and nation, the state 'made flesh'—serve as a token of what Billig (1995) calls 'banal nationalism'—a means by which 'the nation' and its 'qualities' are habitually and unspectacularly 'flagged' in the course of everyday life. What intersections exist between the idea of policing and prevailing (but also, perhaps, subordinate) forms of English national identity? How do different profane constructions of, and reactions to, 'Englishness' help condition public mentalities and sensibilities towards the police?[13] Along both individual and collective dimensions, however, the same important questions arise: what lines of affiliation and solidarity, and of division and exclusion, are delineated and/or reinforced by the ideas and practices of English policing? To what extent, by what means, and with what effects does policing mediate questions of 'belonging' and 'recognition' (of 'us/them', 'here/there', 'inside/outside') in late modern English society?

In posing questions such as these, and seeking to address them in ways that advance sociological understanding of contemporary English policing culture, we must retain a firm hold on the fact that what we are seeking to apprehend is not a single, uniform phenomenon, but a formation contested by different constituencies and composed of competing meanings and values. Two further sets of considerations arise here. It indicates, first, and this much has been implicit in our foregoing remarks, the importance of recognizing the multiplicity of actors (and associated discourses) variously involved in producing, circulating, and receiving police-related categories and encoding/decoding their possible meanings. In recognition of this, we have deployed the following typology to inform and give shape to our enquiry, one that distinguishes analytically between: (i) *governmental* actors—members of elected political classes (government ministers, MPs, local politicians) and permanent civil servants and their (legislative) actions, utterances, and texts; (ii) *professional* police actors—at senior management, supervisory, and 'street' levels—and their specific forms of cultural production (public utterances, annual reports, journals, period- icals, etc.); and (iii) the mentalities and sensibilities of differently situated *lay* actors who constitute the principal 'audience' for forms of police performance and representation. These 'containers' of meaning and meaning-formation are, of course, subject to various kinds of internal division and differentiation, and overlap—institutionally and discursively—in ways that analysis must be careful not to lose sight of. They nonetheless offer an important—methodological—reminder of the diverse complex of players involved in processes of meaning- production and reception around the field of English policing and, as such, of the sets of relations to which a cultural sociology of that field must attend.[14]

It signals the importance, secondly, of grasping the dynamic and hierarchical relations that exist between the elements that comprise English policing culture; something that requires judgements to be made about the trajectories and contemporary status of the mean- ings and values that struggle to give form to this field of practice. Williams here make an important and useful distinction between the 'dominant', 'residual', and 'emergent' properties of specific cul- tural formations (1977: 121–7; 1981: 204–5; cf. Taylor 1999: 54). By *dominant* he refers to those 'preferred'—often taken for granted—meanings that are operative in shaping the ways in which (in the present case) the idea of English policing is coded and ren- dered intelligible, 'ways of seeing' that invariably seek to impose closure upon political and cultural contest by 'naturalizing' a par- ticular selected reading of extant social relations and institutional arrangements (Hall 1980c). But such dominant orderings can never, Williams (1977: 125) argues, 'include or exhaust all human practice, human energy, and human intention'; something that ren- ders them destined to co-exist with alternative, always potentially oppositional, readings and practices. It is these Williams character- izes as either 'residual' or 'emergent'. *Residual* forms, he suggests, comprise values and meanings constituted in the past that cannot be verified in terms of prevailing social practice, but which nonetheless persist and remain active 'as an effective element of the present' (Williams 1997: 122)—forms that are thereby transposed, in ways that are often politically ambiguous, into a potentially oppositional relation to dominant culture. The field of

English policing offers, as we shall see, a number of wistfully recalled instances—'the local bobby', the 'clip round the ear'—of such residualized opposition. Williams also, however, refers in this context to *emergent* cultural forms—'new meanings and values, new practices, new relationships' (Williams 1997: 123); modes of apprehending the world that connect with and articulate 'that which the dominant social order neglects, excludes, represses, or simply fails to recognize' (Williams 1997: 125). By 'projecting' alternative possibilities that remain immanent within the present, these—sometimes pre-political, sometimes consciously articulated—practices 'denaturalize' what Roberto Unger (1996: 1) calls 'the basic terms of social life'; keeping open (in the present case) the possibility that English policing and its relationship to mundane and political culture can be 'made and imagined' otherwise (Unger 1987). It is with this broad—intellectual and political—purpose in mind that we set out to advance understanding of the competing cultural cross-currents that struggle to determine the contours of contemporary English policing.

In Search of English Policing Culture: Questions of Method

There seems to be abundant evidence that moderns still seek to understand the contingency of everyday life in terms of narrative traditions whose simplicity and resistance to change makes them hard to distinguish from myths [Alexander 1989: 246].

It has never been our intention in this study to write a history of post-war English policing. This is not to imply that we are uninterested in the trajectories that the English police have followed in the decades since 1945, or in the processes of economic, social, and political change with which these trajectories are entangled. Nor will it prevent us—at various points throughout the chapters that comprise Parts II and III—from seeking to 'recover' and document aspects of post-war policing that remain perhaps unknown or forgotten, or from bringing judgement to bear upon these 'discoveries' in ways that may cast modest new light on historical understanding of English policing during the latter half of the twentieth century. It is simply that these strictly historical purposes are not the animating concerns of this book.

As should by now have become clear we are concerned, first and foremost, with the ways in which particular historical events and processes are reconstructed and represented within governmental, police, and lay discourse and memory; with, that is, the competing *narratives* that constitute the social meanings of contemporary English policing. We therefore require a methodological strategy that permits us to 'access' these narratives and meanings. Such a strategy, we decided, would best comprise two complementary strands of enquiry. First, the collection and analysis of various official documentary 'representations' of policing since 1945. Secondly, a series of oral history discussions and biographical interviews with various strata of the English populace, retired and long-serving police officers, and some key governmental actors in post-war policing developments and debates.

In respect of the former, our intention is to explore—using a range of different documentary materials (the details follow shortly)—the ways in which various aspects of the police and police work have over the post-war period been encoded within official and police discourse. Given the welter of material potentially available to us, and the period (spanning more than five decades) upon which we are focussed, such an undertaking is necessarily bound to be 'partial', both in the documents that can reasonably be chosen for scrutiny and in the ways in which they are 'read'. We did not, however, select or approach these texts with a view to producing a detailed documentary study of particular moments or periods of post-war policing. Instead, we set out to examine—across a range of governmental and police discourse—the changing ways in which policing has been represented; an orientation that, methodologically, requires a focus upon such matters as the meanings of policing embedded within, and projected by, official discourse, the kinds of express or implicit associations made between policing and processes of social and political change, and official articulations of particular conjunctural controversies and events.

In terms of the latter, we selected a method capable of generating memories and representations from a relevant cross-section of lay, police, and governmental experience, sentiment, and opinion. Given our overarching interest in the way in which aspects of the past are recovered and narrated, we were not principally concerned here with seeking to produce detailed recollections of particular processes and events—as if such 'direct', unmediated access to 'how things were' was, anyway, possible. Instead, we sought to initiate dialogue—whether in individual interviews or in group settings—about the ways in which policing has featured at various moments and phases of people's lives or careers, about particular 'significant' events that respondents had 'observed' or participated in, and about how they strove to make sense of post-war policing trajectories and their intersection with other 'wider' elements of English society and culture. In so doing, we are not concerned (or at least we are concerned in very particular ways) with the historical 'accuracy' of people's recall of the past and, in *this* sense, with their 'reliability' as historical sources. Rather, our theoretical interest in policing as culture means seeking to examine sensibilities towards English policing as disclosed in the *stories* that people tell about past and present (cf. Inglis 1988: 109).[15] This, in turn, entails taking seriously—and deploying as an organizing methodological protocol—the view that 'there are no "false" oral sources', and that 'error' in oral historical accounts can offer important 'ways in' to making sense of processes of individual and collective identity formation. As Allessandro Portelli puts it, '[o]ral history tells us less about *events* than about their *meaning*...The importance of oral testimony may lie not in its adherence to fact, but rather in its departure from it, as imagination, symbolism, and desire emerge' (Portelli 1991: 50–1, emphasis in original; see also Thompson 1988; Portelli 1997: Part I).

We engaged then, with these purposes in mind, in a dedicated effort to generate a range of complementary empirical materials that would allow us to access different aspects of the relationship between English policing and culture. Our activities in this regard—which spanned a two-year period from 1997–9—comprised the following:

- A (re)reading and (re)assessment of certain 'pivotal' *governmental* inquiries into policing issues in the post-war period, including the Oaksey and Edmund-Davies Reports on police pay and conditions (Home Office 1949, 1978), the Royal Commission on the Police (Home Office 1962), the Scarman Report on the Brixton riots (Scarman 1982), the Sheehy Report on police roles and responsibilities (Sheehy 1993*a*), and the Macpherson Inquiry into the murder of Stephen Lawrence (Macpherson 1999). We also examined Parliamentary debates (as reported in *Hansard*) surrounding key selected moments during the period, including the 1962 Royal Commission, the enactment of significant police-related legislation (e.g., Police Act 1964, Police and Criminal Evidence Act 1984, Police and Magistrates' Courts Act 1994), and the urban disorders of the 1980s.

- The analysis of certain prominent sources of *police* representation. These included: (i) annual reports of the Metropolitan, (Greater) Manchester, and Cheshire Police, with special regard to how successive chief officers have since 1945 deployed their 'Forewords' to such reports;[16] (ii) reports of Her Majesty's Inspectorate of Constabulary, 1945–99; and (iii) copies of *Police* magazine (the monthly 'mouthpiece' of the Police Federation), 1968–99, and of the weekly periodical *Police Review*, 1945–99. These were again sampled and read around key events, such as the 1962 Royal Commission, the felt impact on the police of the Equal Pay Act 1970 and Sex Discrimination Act 1975, the police pay dispute of the late 1970s, conflicts over police 'accountability' of the early 1980s, the Sheehy Report, and the Stephen Lawrence Inquiry.

- A total of eighteen group discussions and twenty-three extended biographical interviews with generally middle-aged and senior *citizens* living in Cheshire and Greater Manchester.[17] The former sample comprised—on the basis of the participants' current or former occupations—nine middle-class and nine working-class groups. Three of the groups were entirely composed of ethnic minority participants and three of the (middle-class) groups were all-female. The participants in these discussions encompassed members of tenants' and/or residents' associations (eight); clubs/associations for retired professionals (three), women's organizations (three), community groups (three), and employees of a major insurance company (one). The sample of individual respondents can broadly be subdivided as follows: twenty-one men and two women; thirteen middle-class and ten working-class; sixteen white (including one man from the Republic of Ireland), five Afro-Caribbean, and two south Asian; one 'out' gay man. The individuals we interviewed were, for the most part, contacted through these kinds of organizational channels. Five of them had earlier taken part in one of the group discussions.

- Thirty-three biographical interviews with *police* officers serving, or having served, mainly in (Greater) Manchester (twenty-eight), Cheshire (four), and Staffordshire (one). The sample can be categorized as follows: twenty-nine male and four female officers; thirty white and three black officers; twenty serving and thirteen retired officers; and (at the moment of interview or retirement) five superintendents, three chief inspectors, twelve inspectors, nine sergeants, and four constables. In addition, five group discussions with police officers were undertaken, one each with groups of inspectors, sergeants, constables, retired female officers, and serving 'civilian' support staff.
- Extended interviews with six retired and four serving chief constables (including one Metropolitan Police Commissioner and two ex-Chief Inspectors of Constabulary) and with representatives of the Police Federation (two), British Association of Women Police, Black Police Association, and Lesbian and Gay Police Association.
- Interviews with four former Home Secretaries (three Conservative and one Labour), four erstwhile Ministers of State at the Home Office (three Conservative, one Labour), one Conservative ex-chairman of the Parliamentary Home Affairs Select Committee, and two former chairpersons of Metropolitan police authorities (both Labour). In addition, extended interviews were completed with five retired senior Home Office civil servants.[18]

Our aim in interpreting the perspectives generated by this combination of methods has been to secure a grounded and detailed understanding of the competing sensibilities towards policing and social change since 1945 to be found within lay and official memory and narrative. What consequently follows is *not* any kind of 'exhaustive' account of post-war English policing, but, rather, a series of interventions that 'slice into' different aspects of the relationship between contemporary English policing and culture. Each of these interventions addresses a particular substantive topic. They also differ in format and tone—some pursuing a more obviously 'chronological' line of exposition and analysis than others. Each of the six chapters that comprise Parts II and III nonetheless remains connected to, and seeks in some way to advance, the overall analytic purposes of our work.

In Part II (Chapters 3 to 5) we are concerned principally—though not exclusively—with the narratives that constitute *lay* dispositions towards English policing. Here we deal, in turn, with the fate and appeal of the 'English bobby', the 'fracturing' of police authority since 1945, and the contested cultural politics of the relationship between police, 'race', and nation. In Part III—Chapters 6 to 8—we are concerned principally—though again not exclusively—with *official* (i.e., police and governmental) narratives. Here we set out more explicitly to recover and interpret 'chronologically' certain aspects of English policing and culture since 1945, dealing, in turn, with the changing character of 'the job' and 'the force', post-war mutations in the contours and mobilization of 'the police voice', and cultural and political struggles over the question of police governance. It is with the first of our selected topics—the 'clout' of the English bobby—that we begin Part II.

PART II

Lay Narratives

3

The 'Clout' of the English Bobby

In a world where values are in apparent disorder and where social hierarchy has lost its settled nature, it is not surprising that old forms of security become alluring [Wright 1985: 22].

'The populace', George Bernard Shaw once opined, 'cannot understand the bureaucracy: it can only worship the national idols.' This intriguing remark offers, we believe, an important insight into certain strands of contemporary English sentiment towards the police. A number of commentators have noted how—perhaps uniquely—England had by the mid-twentieth century elevated the 'ordinary beat-pounding patrol officer' to totemic status—an ideal (and idealized) male character capable of representing all that was best about English society, its institutions, and its virtues (Reiner 1992: 761; Emsley 1992: 118). Ian Taylor, for instance, notes:

The important ideological influence which the image of the British police has had in the construction of a *mythological* sense of shared national community and identity, powerfully symbolized for many years in the notion of the unarmed bobby, identified by the wearing of that curious headpiece, the helmet, an icon derived from the British army in India [Taylor 1999: 25, emphasis in original].

This figure and the values (order, community, hierarchy, deference) 'he' stood for have—these very same commentators emphasize—been much undermined and eroded in subsequent decades; the police today being seemingly unable, perhaps even unwilling, to deliver the forms of local guardianship with which the bobby-on-the-beat is closely associated (Taylor 1999: 25–9). Yet the *idea* of the English bobby continues—as we shall see—to exercise a powerful, affective hold over at least some sections of the English 'populace', this emblematic and lost figure serving to signify what has 'gone wrong' with both the contemporary police 'bureaucracy' and wider English society. The following discussion between member of a tenants' association in south Manchester illustrates well the English bobby's continuing 'force':

IL: Do they [police officers nowadays] have the same qualities as the police officers you were talking about at the beginning?
Kath: No.
Ruby: They're nothing like the old ones.
Tom: The older ones?
Ruby: The old bobby with the old helmet.
IL: What was it about them that you particularly remember?
Ruby: They had authority, and you respected that authority. Like I say, they'd clip you round the ear hole, and you took it.
IL: Do you think that authority came from who they were as people, or what was it?
Kath: The uniform.
Eddie: It was the clout they had really.
AM: What kind of people were they?
Kath: Ordinary, normal people. It could have been your father, your uncle.[1]

This chapter is concerned with the place the bobby-on-the-beat has come to assume within English social memory. Against the historical backdrop of the 'withdrawal' of the patrolling officer from 'his' beat, we examine the social meanings attached to the 'local bobby' and the place this 'traditional' figure occupies within contemporary English society and culture. How is the English bobby reconstructed and remembered within lay mentalities and sensibilities? What is it that this figure symbolizes? What hopes, desires, fears, and fantasies underpin 'his' continuing allure? In exploring the motifs, imagery, and silences that constitute social memories of 'the English bobby', and the ways in which this figure features in narratives of social change, we aim, in particular, to detail and understand the outlook of those who view the bobby's presence, corporeal aura, and actions as integral to what is fondly recalled as a more disciplined, cohesive social order, and who take his apparent disappearance to be unsettlingly symbolic of the demise of that order. In so doing, we seek further understanding of what we suggest is a residual, but by no means insignificant, strand of contemporary public feeling towards English policing.

Our account of these matters is organized as follows. We begin by documenting the motifs and meanings that are attached to the bobby-on-the-beat within this particular strand of English social memory, focussing, in particular, on the forms of order, authority, and community with which this reconstructed police figure is closely identified. We then examine how people make sense of the fate that has befallen the English bobby in the latter half of the twentieth century and examine the felt social consequences of his apparent—and apparently terminal—'decline'. A final section considers the contemporary cultural force—and attendant political uses—of this official avatar of a lost, more 'disciplined' social world.

Reconstructing the English Bobby: Order, Authority, and Community

It was common among our elder, white respondents to speak of the immediate post-war decades with a wistful air of fondness and loss—often in ways suggesting that people's outlook on social history and change remains closely entangled with how they make retrospective sense of their own life-courses. They did, to be sure, welcome many of the changes of the post-war decades—such as material prosperity and consumer goods, or the national health service and educational opportunity—changes described by one woman from inner-city Manchester in the following terms:

I've watched them develop Concorde, the aeroplane. I've seen cars. I have a car. I have a washing machine, something that I thought I would never have. I have a television, I've got a video. I've just got myself a little computer. I think it's absolutely wonderful. I can switch my gas on there, I don't have to lay a fire, don't have to clean ashes out. I think I've grown up in a most wonderful, wonderful era, seeing all these developments. The only thing I regret is that I couldn't go into further education.

But such respondents were nonetheless steadfast in the view that in the late 1940s and 1950s people had been 'poorer but happier' (female, tenants' association, south Manchester). This era—time and again in our interviews and discussions—was recalled as more neighbourhood- and family-orientated, less burdened by 'freedom' and unfulfilled expectation, more replete with respect for social authority. Above all it was civil, orderly, and safe:

AM: What was social life like in 1945, the late 1940s?
Joan: It was super. Young girls could walk at night. Your mother didn't worry about where you were. You couldn't do things like that nowadays.

Ruby: You could leave the door open.
Pam: You actually knew your neighbours.
Ruby: You knew your neighbours.
Joan: There was a spirit about them, and they liked to help. There wasn't the 'couldn't care' attitude that you get now. Everyone tried to help one another, as they did during the war. There was a wonderful spirit during the war years [retired civil servants, south Manchester].

The imaginative appeal the English bobby has for many among our respondents can be adequately grasped only once this figure is situated in this remembered social milieu. For the bobby-on-the-beat is mobilized within such narratives of social order and change in post-war England as a vehicle—a significant, if not the only, organizing device—for both condensing and rendering intelligible some key properties of the period, and for understanding its transmogrification into a disordered, insecure, 'high-crime' present. The following exchange—between sheltered accommodation residents in south Manchester—makes explicit some of these connections:

IL: I wonder if I can start by just taking you back to 1945, the late 1940s, the end of the war. What was this country like then?
Gwyn: A lot nicer.
IL: How would you describe it?
Gwyn: It was a lot nicer. People were much nicer with one another. Even though we'd come through a terrible time, it still, the companionship of people, and I think you will all agree we me, it was far better then that it is today. Much, much nicer.
May: More friendlier wasn't it?
Amy: Yes.
May: You didn't have to worry about locking your doors or anything like that.
Gwyn: The police in those days were much more approachable than they are today, because you just don't see them. They're not on the streets. I was always in business, we lived on the premises, and it was lovely at night to be able to see a policeman come and try the door, the shop door. That's gone by the board now.

Let us, starting with the physical aura of this revered figure of authority, spell out some key dimensions of these reconstructions and the *Weltanschauung* they reveal.

Embodiments of Order: Reading the Police Body

One of the most striking features of lay reconstructions of the English bobby concerns the frequent references made to his—and 'he' the English bobby was and, on this view, should remain—corporeal attributes, or, more accurately, aura—something indicative of a close connection between his physical stature and moral capital. The most commonly expressed images of the local bobby denote a mature, physically imposing figure that managed simultaneously to be avuncular, friendly, and benign *and* awesome, frightening, and intimidating. Often our respondents were able to recall such figures either by name ('PC Harper', 'Bobby Fraser', 'Bobby Jacobs', 'George Hardwick', 'PC Jordan', 'PC Banks', 'Sergeant Rogers') or nickname ('PC Pigeon Chest'). But it was their sheer physical presence that is perhaps the most resonant aspect of how the local bobby is remembered. Among some, the clearest recollection was of the officer's height and stature: 'they always looked about seven foot tall, massively built, and everyone was very much respectful towards them... your brick-built, double slap-on-the-back style policeman' (retired male teacher, Cheshire). Among others, in ways suggesting that this merely reinforced their authority, the salient memory was of the bobby's amply proportioned and clearly out-of-condition body. One woman from south Manchester recalled her local officer in very much these terms: 'I can see him now, a big man, with a great big tum, but he was a lovely man'. Another respondent spoke of 'the big red-faced bobby, who used to clip you round the ear' (male, senior citizens' group, Cheshire). Another—in a manner that unusually acknowledges the location of his recollections in incidents of trouble with the police—recalled the local bobby in the following terms:

I ran with pretty tough boys, they had to be out there [on the streets of Moss Side in the 1960s]. But at the end of the day, I don't think we looked down on the police. We didn't have that, we actually respected them in a strange way, especially this one sergeant who had a great, I never knew his name, but he had a great big red face, and a big bulging neck. If you were ever unfortunate enough to be caught by this guy, you made sure you weren't caught again [53-year-old male self-defence instructor, south Manchester].

A further and often connected series of recollections points to the significance of that 'trust-inviting visual marker' (Offe 1999: 64), the police uniform. In part this concerns the way in which the uniform—and especially that 'curious headpiece' the police helmet—reinforced an officer's already robust physical presence; that 'imposing' item serving to give the bobby-on-the-beat an 'extra six inches' (male, adult education group, south Manchester). As one council tenant living in south Manchester put it, 'I always used to see bobbies that were six foot at least and their helmets made them look seven foot. You were always in awe of them, they were great big burly blokes'. But the 'very smart' (female, retired civil servants, south Manchester) uniform is also—as this recollection of the 'beautifully turned out' traffic police attests—integral to the posited link between proper, indeed impeccable, appearance and the exercise of suasive moral authority: 'they used to have white gloves on. . . . They didn't have to give any indication, they just pointed and you stopped. And I can remember thinking how impressive these men were on these little boxes' (female, tenants' association, south Manchester). It is as if the bobby was somehow able to embody *visually* the values of a civil, well-ordered, and now bygone age:

You could go out anywhere in England in my estimation. I was taken out as a child with my father, I was put on the crossbar of his old push bike and we used to go all over the place, we could go anywhere, you could talk to people, you could have conversation with people, there was people there you could trust. You could leave the bike there, you could go away, you could come back, that bike would be there. Plus the fact the difference from then and today, you could recognize a policeman, he had the proper uniform with the hat on and that is one of the biggest mistakes they have made today—you can't recognize them because these flat caps everybody is wearing them today, doormen you know. You don't see many bobbies with the old helmet [male, tenants' association, north Manchester].

Father Figures: Fear, Family, and Authority

My name is Eric and I was brought up in the slums of Hulme. I really enjoyed my life. It was always a pleasure to see a policeman walking round. And if you misbehaved yourself in those days, he'd clip you round the ear hole, and then he'd take you back home and your father would do the same [male, retired civil servants, south Manchester].

One—for the most part unspoken, unacknowledged—dimension of these fond reconstructions of the English bobby surrounds the extent to which respondents relate incidents of *trouble*, of themselves or others being spoken to, apprehended, or 'dragged' home by the police. It is in this context that people generally make reference—often in ways that run these two notions together—to the aura of 'respect' and 'fear' that they recall surrounding the local bobby. This account captures this felt disposition towards the police rather well:

We had this respect for the police. And there was a fear of the police, and think it was a healthy fear, because I think if anything it tended to give the police more authority. You would never deliberately be absolutely cheeky or foul-mouthed to a policeman. It just wasn't going to work. And you knew it wasn't going to work. And of course if you went running to mummy and daddy with the idea of that policeman has just told me off, or 'I've been arrested because', then you're back to being punished again, you got a back hander [53-year-old male self-defence instructor, south Manchester].

The English bobby may well have been—and for a number of our respondents evidently was—a 'friendly' figure one could 'always go and speak to' (male, tenants' association, north Manchester) and who 'would listen to you and that' (female, tenants association, inner-city Manchester). But he was also capable of evoking a number of (at the time) more intimidating (today, more reassuring) feelings. Among some—such as the aforementioned self-defence instructor—these took the form of a grudging recognition of police and, behind them, judicial power: 'if a police officer said do this or do that it wasn't really worth your while arguing with him, because if he arrested you for being stupid you could face a very stiff sentence'. Others spoke more warmly of an age, 'unlike today', when 'there was a lot of respect for the police' (female, tenants' association, south Manchester), one in which, 'if you saw a policeman, you knew he was watching you and you respected his authority. They had that command about them. Today they don't, it isn't there' (female, retired civil servants, south Manchester). Some—often recounting what appear to be significant disposition-forming events—describe being 'absolutely terrified' (women's organization, south Manchester) of either ambient police authority or actual reproach by a police officer—as one middle-class woman from south Manchester remarked of a lecture from a police officer she received as a child following an incident of petty theft: 'I can feel the feeling now'. For some among our respondents, such childhood memories of police authority plainly remain vivid:

My father walked us up Hyde Road and we went into the police station at Belle Vue. He marched me into the police station to let them know that we'd been found, because obviously we'd been reported missing. And he said, 'You can keep her, put her in jail, she's the one that's caused the trouble'. I can still see him to this day, picking me up and handing me over the counter to the policeman in charge. And he went and put me in a cell. My father took the other two home to let my mum know that we were alright. That was basically a lesson for me, that I don't ever do anything like that again. And, by god, I never did, did I. I can still smell those urine smells of those cells [female, tenants' association, south Manchester].

These recollections are—as this story intimates—replete with references to the ways in which police authority was in the early post-war period integrated within a broader net of informal, familial control. Indeed, for some, these connections were sufficient to blur the boundary between police and parental authority: 'the bobby on the beat was literally part of your family. He knew everybody and you knew him' (womens' organization, Manchester). The idea of policing being recalled—*but also* promoted—here is that of the police officer as *civic parent* and *moral guardian*. The local bobby represented, on the one hand, an authoritative figure that could be—and was—mobilized to buttress parental instruction and control: 'we used to get threatened as kids like. If we did wrong my mother used to say, "Bobby White will have you" ' (female, senior citizens' group, Cheshire). Yet, on the other hand, the police are recalled as deploying the fear of parental—especially paternal—discipline as a means of keeping order on local streets, either by informing parents of their children's misdeeds, or by physically marching them home: 'if the bobby said I want to see your dad, you were terrified for two or three days. You would be frightened to death of that bobby coming. He might not come, but for two or three days, you would be terrified of that bobby coming to your house' (male, tenants' association, north Manchester). In either case, the attendant 'fear' appears to have much to do with the connected willingness of these police and parental father figures to respond to misdeeds with physical punishment:

Jim: He [the local bobby] used to take you by the ear hole, and when I say that, I mean it. 'Where do you live? Right come home'. He used to take you right to your door and he used to tell the parents and then before he went away he'd give you a wallop. I've had it myself.

AM: In front of your parents?

Jim: In front of my parents...

Jean: Oh yeah...

Jim: And then when they got you in they would give you a wallop and all. It was knocked into you in a sense, it's not done me any harm, I don't suppose it has done Tony any harm, or any of us, all of the older type. But today no, there is no community, no community spirit at all [tenants' association, north Manchester].

One prominent feature of this reconstruction of the English bobby is the often impassioned support that is forthcoming for this version of police/family authority. For some among these advocates, such summary justice—what one described as the police 'belting you rather than charging you' (retired female machinist, inner-city Manchester)—was represented as a sensible, proportionate, and effective response to the misdemeanours of children and teenagers: 'the village bobby might feel your collar, and that was a terrible disgrace, but at least it was over. And it didn't criminalize things which are just often childish things which are not particularly bad' (women's organization, Manchester). More often, such chastisement is described (in stubbornly beleaguered tones that signal the disrepute and disputation that has come to encircle it) as an appropriate—indeed necessary—way of instilling the requisite 'discipline' in the young. This mode of social control has, on this view, not merely proved to be without deleterious long-term consequences ('it never done me any harm'), it also remains vital to the production of suitably socialized adults:

Sally: I had three boys, and with my boys, 'slap' and that was it.
George: It never hurt them.
Sally: They have grown up to be three good guys. They all went to university. They've all got good jobs. And none of them drink. They'd have a pint now and again. One smokes, the other two don't. They all live in the south [senior citizens' group, Cheshire].

Two further dimensions of this disposition towards the (proper) place of physical coercion in the maintenance of civic order are noteworthy. It is apparent, first, that such coercion is posited as a taken-for-granted, uncontested aspect of police–public relations during the 1950s and 1960s—something that was 'just normal' (female, retired civil servants' group, south Manchester), that one 'knew was justified' (male, insurance company employees, Manchester). At times, what appears to be present here is a moral sensibility towards violence that is happy to accept it as part and parcel of interactions between the police and rowdy citizens. In this vein, one interviewee recounted the following incident: 'there was some chap there mouthing off, a big bloke, and this police sergeant says "go home, it's Christmas". It was in the sixties. He kept mouthing and mouthing and the sergeant propped him up against the railings and really gave him what for. This guy was hanging from the railings. We just stood and gawked at him. We thought the guy had deserved it. Now they'd scream police brutality. The bloke got what he deserved' (53-year-old male self-defence instructor, south Manchester). At others, however, the prevalent sentiment is one eager to deny that a 'clip round the ear' should properly be called 'violence' at all:

Joan: They [the police] had an authority.
Eve: They had respect.
Joan: I took notice of them, and if they had give me a clip across the ear hole I wouldn't have gone home and said to me dad 'a policeman has just hit me', because my dad would say 'what for?' and I'd get another one. But they've got restrictions on them now, haven't they.
IL: Do you think the police are less violent than they used to be?
Joe: I wouldn't say they were violent before.
IL: Is that not the right word to use?
Joan: Oh no.
Mary: No.
Joe: It was a cuff behind the ear.
Hilary: A clip round the ear, we wouldn't have considered violent. Perhaps in this day and age they would [tenants' association, south Manchester].[2]

It is against a current backdrop in which 'the cuff' is more likely to be coded and officially censured in such terms—'if a policeman today clipped a little one round the ear, you can guarantee that the guy would be up on somebody's carpet the next morning' (female, tenants' association, south Manchester)—that these respondents bemoaned what they understood to be a serious undermining of the police's capacity to secure order. 'They should never', one interviewee from south Manchester declared, 'have took that authority away from them'. What one encounters here—and herein lies the second pertinent element of the *Weltanschauung* we are concerned to detail in this chapter—is a disposition towards authority that trusts the police implicitly not to exceed or abuse the power physically to chastise the unruly (young) populace, one confident that 'if a policeman is disciplined he won't step over the mark' (male, tenants' association, south Manchester). Underlying this is a vision of policing that comes close to positing unquestioned and unconditional allegiance as its preferred model of the relationship of citizens to social and legal authority. As one female respondent from north Manchester put it, 'we were bought up to respect our elders. It was drummed into us from being born. It didn't matter if they were right or wrong, you respected them'.

Civic Guardians, National Totems: The Local Bobby and the Imagined Community(ies) of England

During the course of our extended interview with him, a senior figure from the Police Federation proffered the following observation:

There were certain areas, in parts of Liverpool and Manchester, and certainly of Glasgow, where the police were hated and there was constant tension and so on. But by and large, this did not happen in the rest of the country and the police were respected. They were regarded as the uniformed embodiment of the law and of the ordered life, and people, you know, they probably didn't articulate it in that way, but they'd been brought up to respect parents and respect authority and probably teachers enjoyed the same status, doctors and professional people certainly did. And police officers were in that same category and regarded as such.

The police—along with teachers, doctors, and priests—were not merely recalled in our discussions as authority figures that were respected, even feared, *simply on the basis that they were authority*. They seem, in addition, to be integral to the material and imaginative constitution of a particular kind of local and—by extension—national community; one that is fondly remembered for its qualities of social stability and togetherness, shared lives and values.[3] The assumed connection between these 'pillars' (the police prominent among them) and that remembered community is well expressed in the following discussion:

Trishia: You trusted anybody that had a profession. They were the ones you respected.

IL: You mentioned respect of the police. What other institutions would people have valued at that time, and regarded highly?

Oliver: The doctor.

Peter: The police were valued.

Maeve: School teachers.

Trishia: They [the police] were the ones who sorted the problems out on the street. Because if they couldn't do it, nobody else could [senior citizens' group, Cheshire].

These forms of trust in the police revolved centrally around that vital neighbourhood figure and fulcrum of local social relations, the bobby-on-the-beat; a centrality made possible by the 'fixed points' patrol system that delimited the officer within defined geographical boundaries and identified him with the area within it. This at least is the prevailing memory; of an officer associated with, and responsible for, his own 'patch', a figure more likely to be summoned to his beat and called to account for what was happening on it, than—in modern police-management jargon—'abstracted' away from it. One officer—who joined in 1947—recalled in this regard 'the indignity of being dragged out of bed at about eight o'clock or nine o'clock, when it was reported, a crime on your beat that night. The police officer would drag you out of bed, "come down to the station and answer why did this happen, why did you not discover it? What were you doing? Where were you?" It made you go round on your beat with a purpose because you didn't want to [be] in that category' (retired chief constable, provincial force).

The principal beneficial effect of this organizational arrangement was to make the police officer a fixed and visible part of quotidian neighbourhood life, a person who formed 'part of the community' (womens' organization, Manchester), someone 'known to everybody' (female, tenants' association, south-east Manchester): 'he was a figure, he was part of the community because he wasn't changing and he was walking about you see. So they knew that person, perhaps not by name but by sight. They knew that person day-to-day. This is something I very much regret is missing on this estate.' Among some—as in this and the following instance—such recollections are explicitly brought to bear in judgement upon the present: 'it was very good then. You saw them walking about, you saw a policeman on the beat. There were simply much more, many more police about. But not now there isn't, you don't get that. It's very rare you see a policeman walking about, very rare. We have a community policeman, but it's very rare that you see him. But I mean years ago, you could always see a policeman' (female, tenants' association, inner-city Manchester). For others the pleasure appears to lie more in a wistful recall of the reassuring presence of the police in local social life. In terms not dissimilar to how a resident of a fishing village might describe the sight of the trawler fleet heading out to sea (or in a mining village, the miners leaving *en masse* for work) this man evokes the—for him—warming spectacle of local bobbies cycling off to report for duty:

In this particular area there were a lot of policemen. There must have been over 300 [*sic*] policemen within 300 yards of here. On the estate there must have been at least a hundred housing department houses that were allocated to the chief constable for occupation by policemen. It was funny, in the summertime, about nine o'clock, you'd see uniformed policemen on bicycles, going all over the place to their different stations. Every policeman had a bicycle because he had to get there in the morning if he was on the early shift, half past five in the morning. You'd see uniformed policemen moving in all directions. And the same when the shift had finished, the previous shift, you'd see them coming home. There was an uniformed presence all of the time [male, tenants' association, inner-city Manchester].

This rootedness in the locality also meant that even if officers could not be present 'all of the time' local people at least knew how to secure access to them. For some, this was mainly a matter of having a known and trustworthy figure to contact: 'they were friendly. You weren't afraid to go and speak to them, they would listen to you and that. If you had a complaint they would act on it. You could go and talk to them, they were friendly. But now, you wouldn't know who to approach . . . sergeant, inspector, or whatever. But then you did' (female, tenants' association, inner-city Manchester). Others made reference here to local 'police houses' (male, tenants' association, north Manchester) or to the apparently greater number of accessible police stations: 'there was more police stations about then. More local cop shops, as we used to call them. There was one in Brunswick Street, there was one at Longsight, still there. There was one in Dewhurst Street, just up the road, there was one in Piccadilly, just as you go up London Road, on the right' (male, adult education group). Taken together, these factors clearly contribute to a remembered sense that—during these years—the community could legitimately claim the local bobby as *their own*.

This felt ownership of the English bobby is intimately related to the recalled sense that this institution—in some very practical ways—*made community possible* by securing the (normative) ground upon which communal life could be enacted and enjoyed. In many of our interviews and discussion groups people expressed the view that a visible police presence not only served to uphold social order by disciplining 'unruly' elements, but that the bobby-on-the-beat also helped sustain local neighbourhoods by operating as an overt—rather than 'secret'—'social service' (cf. Punch 1979*b*). The 'clout' of the bobby derives, on this view, not merely from his legal and coercive powers but, rather, from his all-purpose problem-solving capacities, his role as a kind of *socio-moral handyman*. One retired officer describes this role in the following terms:

You weren't allowed to talk to members of the public but you did, it was the only way you found out what was going on. You had to keep your finger on what was going on and when you got to know your beat you'd be made a cup of tea, you'd have even [got] a piece of toast if you wanted, but you also knew the social lives of everybody and you became part-and-parcel of it. When I started you were the local social worker, you were the local crime prevention officer, you were the local policeman, you were the local juvenile liaison officer, what else would you be, we were everything, you were everything to everybody [retired male sergeant, Greater Manchester Police (GMP)].

Such a role received a large and supportive echo in the recollections of our respondents, many of whom recalled fondly a figure keeping an informed pastoral watch over the community. Many recalled here—it was often their earliest memory of the police—the bobby running the school crossing patrols, what one retired officer less happily referred to as 'the bane of our lives. You had to be at a particular point for like eight o'clock in the morning, till quarter past nine in the morning. From twelve to two at lunchtime, then from about three to five' (retired male inspector, GMP). Another respondent alluded to their function as 'social workers' and described (her husband was a police officer) how 'in one particular area, women used to come to the station if they were having babies, rather than going for the midwife' (female, retired civil servants, south Manchester). The following exchange encapsulates well the police's role as multi-purpose civic guardians:

Flo: They used to have police ambulances. You could run to Mayor Lane and say 'can I have an ambulance?' and an ambulance would come. You could rely on that. You could rely on them more. Like Tom said, you'd see them on crossings, you'd see them helping children across the road, and things like that. You could rely on them to help you.

Tom: I think the police station was a place of first resort for people with problems. They used to come in with problems that weren't really police matters, and they would get advice, or directed to people who could help, on things that weren't really police matters. But the police just didn't just say 'oh it's nothing to do with us, you must go elsewhere' [tenants' association, inner-city Manchester].

These recollections clearly situate the English bobby at the centre of a lost vision of community life, a community in which 'you had a feeling that the police were very much in control. There was a lot of order around' (male, adult education group, south Manchester). In this vision the bobby is not principally a member of the police bureaucracy (though the fact he is part of such a 'disciplined' organization clearly matters); he is, rather, first and foremost a servant of the locality, an omnipresent pastoral figure integral to the constitution of its way of life. This is nicely captured—and ideologically appealed to—on the front cover of *Police* magazine in January 1983, where a Christmas painting depicts a village bobby and a vicar standing on either side of a snow-covered street, each with bicycle in tow, each casting a reassuring gaze over the socio-moral well-being of his 'parishioners'.

Matters cannot however be left quite here. For if the bobby-on-the-beat serves—in these ways—as a condensing symbol of local community, he also—by extension—appears as an exemplar of English nationhood. Numerous references were made in our discussions to the English police being (then definitely, for some still now) 'the best in the world'; an element of official and popular sentiment toward English policing we take up further in the next chapter.[4] Suffice it to make two points here. First, that such warm sentiment towards the *national* police (in a state that has not, historically, possessed such a 'continental' institution—cf. Emsley 1996, 2000) has much to do with the *local* bobby, a figure imaginatively reconstructed as an organically situated representative not of the police bureaucracy or state (albeit that herein lies the source of his coercive authority), but as belonging to the English nation, a nation of local communities. The 'local', in other words, serves as the category through which 'English' policing is revered and celebrated.

Such reverence stems, secondly, from the embeddedness of this strand of English social memory—of this fading but not insignificant vision—in the immediate post-war period. This disposition towards the local bobby draws its compelling force, in other words, from its location in that brief historical period following the triumphs and sacrifices of war and prior to the fall of Empire and the—disquieting, complicating—onset of Commonwealth immigration; a period when pride in England as a 'great', and safe, and more cohesive nation, was high, and where the police occupied a prominent place among the panoply of social institutions that (had) made it so:

We weren't aware that the British Empire was about to be broken up and sold off in job lots. We still went to schools where they would paint a projection of the world on the school wall that, you'll have heard this often enough, was painted pink for the British Empire. And there we were, having emerged from a terrible war still a major power, members of the [United Nations] Security Council, of one of the five great powers of the veto, having liberated the rest of Europe. We felt superior. And we were well aware that, throughout the British Empire, the British policing pattern had been adopted. There were strong variations of it and we didn't make any distinction because the style that was being offered to the native populations was very different to the [sic] style of policing that was being offered to working-class citizens in the United Kingdom. Nonetheless, the principles of justice and of policing, the ethos of policing, had been extended throughout the Empire. So, yes, we were very, very conscious of the prestige of the British policing throughout the world, and to that extent, of course, we'd been brought up to believe that if it was British it was best. You know the jingoism and the sense what God was an Englishman [spokesperson, Police Federation].

Mourning the Lost Bobby

We always used to think that a policeman in uniform stood for law and order. Whereas today to be quite honest I just don't know what it stands for [male, tenants' association, north Manchester].

The cultural disposition towards the police and their place in postwar England set out in the last section is not only made up of recollections and reconstructions of a more ordered past. Such memories are mobilized alongside—and intimately entwined with—a tale of what has happened to the 'old bobby' and the institution and society he embodied. It is a narrative of change that mourns the disappearance of that revered figure from everyday life, and sees his loss as symbolic of both the failings of the police institution and the demise of a particular conception of, and orientation towards, social and legal authority. Let us try to distil its various elements.

Perhaps the most powerful and frequently mentioned source of grief surrounds the demise of the bobby-on-the-beat as a routine, visible presence in local social relations. This is captured in the following account, one that explicitly couples the absent policeman with another seemingly besieged icon of 'traditional' Englishness, the village:

I was brought up in a country village and we had a village constable who lived in the...the policeman had a house, which was the police station, the odd room, small room as a cell. It was a completely enclosed thing. The policeman knew everybody. And he just used to walk round, and a crime would be committed, and he would appear and he would have a look and say 'ah yes, that will be Charlie's boy'. He would just have to see what had been done and he knew who had committed the crime. Then as time went on, round about the middle 1950s, everything changed. The police house was closed down. The policeman was removed from the village, and went into the town where they had the police division, and panda cars were sent out. And as far as the villagers were concerned more crime was then committed than when they had their own village policeman who knew everyone. He just had to appear at the scene of the crime and he would virtually know who had committed the crime. He knew everyone. Once they were removed to a central police station the policeman didn't know his area, he merely went out and... [male, retired civil servants, south Manchester].

There was among some who shared this belief in the English bobby and his powers of social wizardry a reluctant, often tersely expressed, sense that the disembedding of the police from localities was a reflection of how 'life has changed' (male, retired civil servants, south Manchester) over the post-war decades. As one retired teacher living in Cheshire put it, 'in the seventies they started using more and more cars, rather than bicycles and people pounding the beat. I accept of course that technology has got to involve people in cars, but it's a fact that you didn't see a policeman walking around the streets like you did in the sixties, in this area anyway.'[5] But this development—the end of fixed-point patrolling and the advent of 'panda cars'—is nonetheless interpreted as having had overwhelmingly baleful social consequences; effects that are mainly seen to flow from the disconnection of today's police officer from locally situated feelings, problems, and demands. As one of our interviewees put it, 'we liked him [the local bobby]. He was sort of part of the village, a figure. Nowadays it's different. The police are serving a wider community, there's more crime and that. They're more mobile now. They don't always stick to the same patch. So I don't think you've got the same local knowledge that the bobby had in those days' (male local government employee, south Manchester).

The disquiet that generally accompanied this transformation was expressed in a number of ways. Among some, we encountered a matter-of-fact acceptance that one should no longer expect to find police officers patrolling suburban neighbourhoods; a view accompanied on occasions by some apparently exact recollections of the exceptional moments that serve only to prove this rule: 'we've lived in this house for thirty-five odd years, and I've only seen a police officer walk down this road three times. In fact the last time I saw a police officer, I told him so' (male, retired solicitor, south Manchester). Some explicitly contended—in opposition to officially propagated wisdoms about the limits of patrolling—that the demise of the bobby-on-the-beat had made the police more ineffective:

I thought it was all wrong. You never see them at all now. On the back streets, off main road, the only time you see them there is when there is a football match. You go up now, I bet there is somebody's house been broken into but there is no police...Police themselves might tell you we can get there quicker now, but I don't think they could. If they are on the spot, that would be enough. They would always be on street-corners, even sergeants on street-corners, and were always in the area. I am not saying they don't want cars and vans because they do. I don't think there is enough police on the beat [male, adult education group, south Manchester].

In a similar spirit, others spoke of someone now remote from local communities, one 'who doesn't want to know you' (female, tenants' federation, south-east Manchester), a figure divorced from local concerns and priorities: 'I think a lot of people today have lost contact with the police...You see them walking about down in Sale and down Manchester, and they just seem to be in a world of their own' (female, tenants' association, south Manchester). This image of a distant figure, responsible for 'too unwieldy an area' (female, retired civil servants, south Manchester), only fleetingly attuned to a neighbourhood's troubles, is well-expressed in the following exchange:

George: Eventually a policeman will come. It's probably taken him nearly an hour to get from where he is to where I am. When he arrives he's perhaps come from Bolton, the other side of Bolton, and he lives out in that direction. He hasn't a clue where he is. He's no local knowledge. Now in the old days that policeman would know his town like the back of his hand. He would know every back entry, if you went down here you'd come out there. That caught a lot of thieves, put you in touch with incidents that you could take control of. The man concerned now arriving, you have to explain to him where he is, what he can do, how best to get from here to there, and what's likely to be there at the end.

Terry: And at the end of your conversation it's how he can get back to where he came from. And that's about the only thing that he's interested in.

George: 'How can I get back to Bolton?' He used to be the man that lived down the road, now he's a man that you've never, ever seen before. He might come from Bolton, he might come from this way, that way. They've never, ever met him before [retired professionals, south Manchester].

The feeling being voiced in these accounts is one of communities having been stripped of their pastoral guardian—the English bobby, it seems, no longer forms part of 'our world', is no longer able to embody or protect its values. For some this state of affairs is further reflected in the kinds of individuals now selected to be bobbies-on-the-beat, people who no longer seem able to bring to this esteemed position the requisite qualities and commitment. As one of our respondents put it, 'it's just a job now. Before a fellow joined the police force because he wanted to do something in the community, because he cared about the area he lived in and he wanted to help the community. Now it is a job, it is just a job to bring in a salary to take home. That is what it is about now' (male, tenants association, south Manchester).

There are a number of dimensions to this complaint, most of which centre upon the incapacity of today's police officers to exude authority and secure public respect. Among some, this was felt to be a matter of the less imposing physical stature of contemporary policemen and women, of the fact that people are now confronted not with officers 'built like a brick barn' but by those who 'look like little bits of kids' (female, tenants' association, south Manchester). As one interviewee put it, 'I don't know when it all changed, but certainly pre-war a policeman in Manchester had to be six foot. And now you see them, five foot eight I think is about the lowest. I think it must make a difference. If they see this great big burly policeman, in those days, they were afraid. But now they're so small and insignificant that whenever you do see one, you don't take a great deal of notice of them' (male, retired civil servants, south Manchester). Other respondents couched the issue in terms of the changing visual appearance of police officers, as if the altered condition of the police uniform is somehow symptomatic of their waning authority: 'they don't wear any hats now. They get out of cars, they look so slovenly. Their tunics are thrown right open. They don't even look like policemen. They don't command attention and respect' (male, adult education group, south Manchester). Others conjured up an image of immature, over-qualified, and overly ambitious police recruits altogether lacking in the practical wisdom associated with the local bobby and his craft:

Donna: If they have to be graduates before they come, and then look at it as a career where they have to get as high up as they can, then to retire at this very early age, then they can't do their job. They're not in real world. They've gone through school, to university, into the police.
IL: Do you think a police officer needs to be a graduate?
Gill: No. They're not experiencing the shop floor at all.
Donna: They should have a job, some mundane job, something like that, for at least a year before they start [women's organization, south Manchester].

Common to the outlook we are describing here is the drawing of a contrast between the characteristics of today's officers and the qualities possessed by the 'old bobby'. On occasions—this is, after all, a disposition that remains passionately supportive of the *idea* of policing—such contrasts were drawn in a spirit of sympathy with those cast inappropriately—whether for reasons of age or gender—into situations of conflict. One of our interviewees explicitly compared in this regard 'the respect of a 40-year-old police officer with wisdom' capable of stopping 'some of the fracas that wind up with somebody getting arrested', with that possessed by 'a six-and-a-half stone police girl of nineteen': 'probably a kindly forty-something policeman would have said "calm it down" and it wouldn't have escalated. But I think the police are young. They have a hard job' (women's organization, Manchester). For the most part, however, the figure of the 'old bobby' is explicitly mobilized in order to highlight the apparent shortcomings of his present day counterparts. Whether by reason of age, gender, size, inexperience, career aspiration, or attitude ('I'm not sure if the police today are as interested in their work as they were then; they were very, very efficient in them days, very, very interested in all sorts of things' (male, adult education group, south Manchester)), the police officer no longer seems able to represent or stand up for the way of life with which the police were once proudly associated. Indeed, his (and now her) very diversity of significations (deLint 1997: 252), coupled with their remoteness from community life, has come instead to symbolize something else; namely, the inability of the contemporary police institution to embody successfully the promise inherent in the idea of English policing:

Unfortunately, to our mind, the police are going the wrong way. They are going right away from us and I think in a few years time we will lose complete identity as we knew it as regarding the connection between the public and the police. Change for change is no good. These people want somebody to talk to, not to pick a telephone up. A lot of people have not got telephones. A lot of people don't know how to telephone. They want somebody to identify with law and order. That is a man on the beat and this is surely being eroded away from this estate [male, tenants' association, north Manchester].

Bemoaning Lost Authority

They can't open their mouths, anybody in authority, can they, now? [women's organization, south Manchester].

This loss of local police authority is also seen as entangled with the waning of a once settled set of authority relations considered as integral to the order and cohesion that are recalled as having marked English social life during the middle decades of the twentieth century. The replacement of these relations by a greater willingness to assert individual rights and freedom, and to treat with scepticism and scrutiny the claims made by institutions of social and legal authority, is understood here as a profoundly deleterious social development. Indeed, the *Weltanschauung* we have been concerned in this chapter to document and understand is largely constituted in reaction against those processes of post-war social and cultural change that Cas Wouters (1992: 240) calls 'the individualisation of respect'; a reaction eager to register and press what are taken to be its damaging outcomes—a world less trusting, more troubled and precarious, less harmonious and safe. The contrasts and losses—and their connection to questions of police authority—are illustrated in the following discussion:

Joyce: People [then] seemed to respect each other. You had respect for one another. I mean you could go out, like I say, leave your door open, nobody would pinch anything. Either during the war, or just after-wards. If there was an accident or anything, you'd always find somebody would turn round and help. Or if there was anything wrong with a neighbour, the next door neighbour would be there. Today, it's as though you're frightened of your next door neighbour. There's no trust anywhere today. You'd trust people at one stage. You can't today.

Jim: I was robbed when I lived at the other side of Manchester. We had builders working next door. I went out at nine o'clock in the morn-ing, came back about two hours later, my TV, video, the lot went. And yet there were people working there, and nobody sees nothing.

Hazel: I blame the parents for a lot. They don't care what their kids are doing as long as they're leaving them alone.

Joyce: The police today I think...over the years, like I said, a policeman, he did give you a clip around the ears when you was a child. We were frightened of him. But today, over the years it's kind of, I don't know, to me the parents have took over and no matter what a policeman says to them...through the years, they're not frightened of the police any more. They laugh at them [tenants' association, south Manchester].

Such apparent 'laughter' in the face of police officers is considered to be the effect of a number of factors. Mention was made first here of the fact that—as one self-defence instructor from south Manchester put it—'the police haven't got the authority now to discipline anybody'. For some—those for whom discipline stands as a euphemism for physical punishment—this was seen as a matter of the police and other authority figures no longer—for fear of complaint, or reprimand, or claims for compensation—being able to exercise proper control over—especially—the young. As a member of one of our retired civil servants' groups put it, 'they can't touch them now. They daren't lay a finger on them.' Among others, it was couched in terms of the forces of bureaucracy (the illusive, invariably sinister, 'they' that recurs so often in lay discourse) and those of soft-hearted, wrong-headed liberalism conspiring—to disastrous effect—to obstruct 'our' police: 'It's absolute wanton destruction that the kids are doing and nobody can touch them. The police have got their hands completely tied' (female retired machinist, inner-city Manchester). The following account encapsulates these various elements:

Barbara: I mean the police do have an awful lot of work to do paper wise. It's unbelievable, reports. They're spending hours and hours on their paperwork. It must be soul-destroying that when they get to court, that some do-gooder then says, 'er, well he didn't have a teddy-bear when he was a little boy so we have to allow for it. We'll give him twenty hours community service'. And the young ones are laughing at them. And it's not up to the police, it's the sentencing.

Sally: But you know this community service, I'm all in favour of community service, but I think they should be made to wear, now this sounds daft, even if it's only one of these sleeveless things which says 'I'm doing community service'.

Terri: To shame them.

Sally: So that.... Yes.

Barbara: They wouldn't allow it Sal. They wouldn't allow it [tenants' association, south Manchester].

Secondly, and relatedly, it was felt that police authority had become damagingly unhinged from informal parental control. It was frequently claimed in this regard that parents today could no longer be relied upon to accept—or back up—police efforts to regulate the behaviour of the young, or even to feel the appropriate sentiments should their offspring be apprehended by the police: 'there's very few parents now that will actually be bothered about the police coming home. It was shame. If the policeman came to your door, it was shame that the police had actually visited your property. It's not now' (female, tenants' association, south Manchester). This, moreover, is considered to be something that today's generation of young people has become all too fully aware of: 'they [the police] are not as hard as they were, they can't be, they're not allowed to be. When we were brought up it was out comes the pad "what's your name, where do you live. Right, you'll be hearing from us. Now hop it. Home. I'll be round to see your parents." Now they don't go, because they know there's nothing they can do about it' (53-year-old male self-defence instructor, south Manchester). The result, it is claimed, is the emergence of a 'less subdued' population (male, adult education group, south Manchester), no longer in fear of—and more predisposed to dispute—the exercise of police authority:

You were afraid of policemen when we were young. Immediately after the war as well. I think it was about 1960 when all this changed. When it was freedom for everybody, freedom and all the rest of it. It seemed to go down from there. If a policeman tells a child off now, the child will turn round and argue with a policeman [male, retired civil servants, south Manchester].[6]

The effects of these processes are overwhelmingly interpreted—in sometimes mournful, sometimes angry, fashion—in negative terms. From this standpoint, *the* story of English social life in the post-war decades has involved the eclipse of those virtues—restraint, respect, obligation, obedience—encapsulated in 'that magic word discipline' (male, retired professional, south Manchester) and the advent of what one of our respondents tersely described as 'too much freedom' (female, tenants' association, south Manchester). Some sense of what is meant by that 'magic word'—and what, in turn, that word meant—is conveyed in this account:

It was part of our lives. From being infants starting school we were started off with a strict discipline. Carried over in a very nice manner, but meaningful. And in our homes, going back to mother again, and father, they then had the time to be interested in us, and they did the discipline. We knew no other. And the same where you worked, office, shop, wherever you worked, that discipline was there. It was just part of our lives [women's organization, Manchester].

The watershed moment in this narrative is 'the sixties', the decade when 'it all started to go wrong' (male, retired civil servants, south Manchester); the key process, it seems, a shift in relations between children and adult authority: 'between the 1970s and the 1990s, a very strange change took place. Nobody knows what caused it, but the climate of opinion changed completely about the upbringing of children. The upbringing of children was then gradually freed from all this discipline. Freedom of expression, friendliness, things like that came into the family home; informality, calling parents and other adults by their Christian names. That took place very gradually, and it resulted in a lot of the lack of respect' (women's organization, Manchester). Against this backdrop, the present inability of one of the vital exemplars of such discipline— the bobby-on-the-beat—to control young people who no longer exhibit a healthy fearfulness towards him, stands as a telling indicator of a broader process of socio-moral decline—an individual and collective erosion of the character of the nation:

I think people, on the whole, in this country are not disciplined. They don't want to be disciplined and they certainly don't respect...they are not able to apply discipline. So discipline is a factor in our make-up which is a bit thin on the ground. Discipline is thin on the ground all round because the police can't impose it, they can't clip you round the ear. You can't even tell them off too far. They're undisciplined. It's rather like having a pack of dogs that are untrained. A pack of dogs that are trained are happy dogs. You get a few undisciplined amongst them and the whole thing...It's lack of discipline which has brought on lack of respect, because respect, as you say, you look up to this person because you respect him and you accept the discipline that he has imposed. And that's how the army worked. That's how everything worked. Everything else. But when that discipline was gone, when there was a breakdown in discipline in a community, you've got problems [male, retired professionals, south Manchester].

And yet...there also exists, often at the unspoken, unacknowledged fringes of this cluster of sentiments and beliefs, evidence that these processes of cultural change have not merely affected others, but have also chipped away at the dispositions of those who so fondly recall an era in which people treated social and legal authority with due deference and close to unconditional respect. As one participant in a senior citizens' group in Cheshire put it, 'we used to think about people as pillars of society. And some television programmes made us view them differently, like ordinary people now. So where you used to think about a doctor as being, an unattainable thing perhaps for some of us. When you watch these, not just documentaries about people, but soaps that show people in another light, just to be ordinary like the rest of us really.' It appears, in other words, that those who mourn the passing of the lost authority that the English bobby once so steadfastly represented, and bemoan the advent of a world in which such authority is routinely contested and called into question, also in some manner *embody* that altered world. They are products and agents of the very process of detraditionalization they purport to find so dismaying:

Barbara: We are not afraid to take on board and challenge people in authority, whereas at one time you would probably never have dreamed of it.

IL: Does that mean that you would once have been more ready to accept that people in positions of office or power were doing the right thing?

Sally: Yes. But we know that they're not. There was also a kind of different tier. I can remember that if the priest came to visit on Sunday...Let's face it, he was only a man, but in those days he was god.

Barbara: Exactly.

Sally: But whatever he said was right. And now you see, we've got the attitude where we treat them as normal people, which is far better. But in those days, I was brought up at a convent school, and if Sister Frances said that the moon was made of green cheese, well it was made of green cheese. That's gone, because I think we've got a lot more confidence. It's sad that it's changed, but maybe it's brought confidence to a lot more people.

Hazel: But the respect has all gone [tenant's association, south Manchester].

The Cultural Presence of the Absent Bobby: Remarks on the Politics of Tradition

The sceptical orientation towards authority evident in the above exchange chimes closely with what today forms a dominant element of contemporary lay sensibilities towards the police, as we shall see in the next chapter. But it assumes here no more than a marginal, subterranean presence within a strand of English public sentiment that coalesces around altogether different motifs; foremost among them a passionately supportive belief in an idea of policing that is local, paternal, authoritarian, and not unduly burdened by bureaucracy, legal rules, or external criticism. This disposition—which we have endeavoured to document at some length in this chapter—has today, in our judgement, become a *residualized* cultural form, something that the beleaguered tone in which it is narrated itself rather suggests. It represents a worldview forged in the imperatives of another age, adhered to by a generation shaped by the privations and aftermath of war, one that stands in an oppositional relationship to the dominant detraditionalizing trajectories of the present. Indeed, its reaction against these trajectories gives this orientation towards the 'old bobby' many of the properties of a tradition, a mode of belief conceptualized by Anthony Giddens as 'an orientation to the past such that the past has a heavy influence or, more accurately put, is made to have a heavy influence, over the present' (Giddens 1994: 62). Drawing on the recent work of Giddens and John Thompson (1996: 181–8) on the place and meaning of 'tradition' in a post-traditional society, three structuring elements of this disposition towards police authority can be discerned.

This disposition acts, first of all, as a *hermeneutic* device, a means of making sense of post-war social change by telling a plausible tale about it. Within this narrative, the English bobby—as we have seen—is mobilized as an authoritative, avuncular figure deeply associated with—indeed integral to—what are recalled as the more cohesive, disciplined, and ordered decades of the mid-twentieth century. The demise of this figure and his social magic is consequently taken not merely to explain the subsequent erosion of this safer, more secure world, but also to exemplify it, as if the eclipse of the local bobby is itself a sign of social disarray. The absent guardian thus becomes a key motif to express social decline and reveal an acute anxiety about the condition of contemporary England. The bobby-on-the-beat is no longer there to monitor and admonish, and so, gradually, the order he maintained, the communities he sustained, and the nation he exemplified, become more fragile entities. As one of our respondents put it, describing the replacement of the beat officer with the panda car, 'that was the whole breakdown of civilization as it was. The youngsters on the street, they went mad, they went wild, because they weren't tamed by the police officers that walked up and down there all night' (male, adult education group, south Manchester).

Secondly, these memories of the English bobby offer material for the formation and sustenance of self and collective *identity*—an identity that often helps to constitute people's sense of ontological security: 'my brother says to me, "You can't go back Val". I said, "Well I'm sorry, I have to at times because it makes me happy when I think of those days" ' (female, tenants' association, south Manchester). This 'going-back' is made up in part of a wistful nostalgia for an inclusive, conformist, monochrome age blessed with such virtues as obedience, obligation, and constraint; one that is contrasted unfavourably with a more socially diverse, contested, and precarious present (cf. Young 1999: ch. 1). But it is also, more specifically, a police-centred subjectivity that holds uniformed authority—and, particularly, the organically situated, pastoral presence of *public* policing in everyday life—to be central to the production and reproduction of ordered social life. Indeed, these two elements are inseparably linked within this outlook, the local bobby being reconstructed as the embodiment *par excellence* of the virtues that (once) made the English nation great.

This cluster of beliefs and sentiments has, thirdly, a pronounced *normative* element to it—serving as a guide to both how the world 'should be' and what's wrong with the way 'it is'. The bobby-on-the-beat serves here as the pivotal member of a *police force of the imagination* that is routinely called upon in criticism of the 'real' thing; the latter being an increasingly distant, disenchanting, and unresponsive institution ('I look at the police, and I just feel as though I'm in a echo chamber, and I just can't get anything back' (female, tenants' association, south Manchester')) whose priorities and practices render it increasingly unable to approximate what English policing ought properly to comprise. The past, here, is actively mobilized in an effort to condemn the present and colonize the future.

To term this outlook a 'tradition', and to describe it—using Raymond Williams' terms—as a residual cultural form, is not to dismiss it as a mere historical hangover or to equate it with insignificance. Waning it may be, but this disposition towards English police authority continues to cast a shadow over the terrain of social possibility. This cluster of doxic/paleo-symbolic sentiment and belief remains capable of being articulated by political actors and mobilized into a coherent ideology. It retains, in addition, a cultural presence sufficient to help determine acceptable practices of English policing and shape the contours of professional and political debate about it. In so far as the bobby-on-the beat remains central to this *Weltanschauung*, this figure might properly be included among Ulrich Beck's (2002: 203) 'zombie categories'— 'dead' as a material presence in daily policing practice, 'still alive' as a cultural and political force.

The effects of such 'force' are registered in several ways. In respect of the police, this orientation to police authority offers a reservoir of—impassioned, instinctive—support for those committed to searching for a police-centred—or authoritarian—'solution' to the problem of order, whether by lobbying for more powers, or demanding greater police numbers, or by campaigning to enhance the pay and conditions of those officers who stand between order and chaos.[7] Such mobilizations—as we shall see in subsequent chapters—were rather more to the fore in the 1970s and 1980s than they are today. Yet the idea and image of the 'local bobby' remain valuable resources for the police. For senior officers wishing to buttress the legitimacy of the institution in adverse or hostile settings, the temptation to 'deploy' what one chief officer we interviewed called 'our brand leader, our money in the bank' is manifest indeed (chief officer, metropolitan force). Similarly, it remains possible for those—such as the Police Federation—striving to stave off either managerialist exhortations to measure and evaluate police activity, or the threat posed by the pluralization of patrol agencies (Home Office 2001), to portray themselves as defending a sacred national institution from 'out-of-touch' politicians (cf. McLaughlin and Murji 1998). As one senior representative from the Federation put it to us, 'we see ourselves, I think, as the guardians of the traditions of policing...And that's about patrolling. This is our big fight, a constant fight with the alternatives to that. The alternatives are private security, local authority security, and all that stuff. We always want that strong message about British policing about why it's good and why it's different to maybe the rest of the world.'

Conversely, the symbolic power of the English bobby stands as an impediment to those in senior policing circles whose organizational or financial logics demand greater transparency in police performance or who hold generic beat patrolling to be an ineffective use of scarce police resources (e.g., Audit Commission 1996; Blair 1998). Faced with this obstacle, such actors are often 'forced' to pay continued lip-service to the idea of the 'local bobby' while quietly taking steps to fashion an altered set of police priorities (with all that entails for the quality of public deliberation about the futures of policing), or else to embark on the occupationally risky strategy of taking on and seeking to shift some deep-rooted patterns of belief about the value of a revered symbol of order. One chief officer who has embarked on this latter path reflected on the task thus:

In the mind of the public, if we had the wherewithal to put lots of foot patrol officers out and enough officers who could pop along and sit in their front room and listen to their problems, then that would be a much better service than the one that they think they are getting now. It's going to take a huge, huge exercise, sustained effort on our part, and the government's part, and the media's part, to re-educate the public away from the notion of the patrolling officer. We are trying to hang onto this notion of policing by consent, the trusted British bobby, that policing does emanate from the local community and so on. And yet at the same time we're having to say that we can't afford to have your friendly patrolling officer wandering around just on the off-chance that something might happen, or wandering round merely to provide you with reassurance. Because that's what the public want. The public wants a sufficient number of police officers out there to be reassured, so it thinks that if there are villains out there, or vandals, or kids riding motorcycles too noisily, well that's alright because there's bound to be a police officer in a car, or on foot, round there to do something about it. And they now know that that's not true, and they would like to return to that era when they could feel reassured that there are enough police officers around. It's not going to happen, so we need to find a way of re-educating the public so that they...take greater interest in policing themselves [chief constable, shire force].

In respect of the political classes a cognate series of considerations obtains, albeit in a manner permeated by the dynamics of electoral politics. Here too the cultural embeddedness of the English bobby works to shape the field of police politics, setting limits on the moves that players can make, defining the boundaries of what may legitimately be said and done. Some of our respondents—such as one former member of the Parliamentary Home Affairs Select Committee—had little patience for the follies this entailed and seemed determined to puncture what are viewed as the myths of English policing and the institutions that sustain them. Referring to a not uncommon political promise made by then Prime Minister John Major (1990–7), our respondent remarked:

I actually believe that he said at a Conservative Party Conference 'we're going to put 5,000 more bobbies on the beat' thus reinforcing this great *Dixon of Dock Green* image that bobbies-on-the-beat would somehow stop crime. It was rubbish...Politicians say these things out of ignorance, they don't know the facts. Out of being wanting to be popular and loved, and be elected. In other words, they're trying to kid people. The media image is also going in this direction too. And the Police Federation are very adroit at stroking this image because they have a vested financial interest in having more police officers.

Others—better versed, perhaps, in what are felt to be the 'imperatives' of government—appeared more resigned to the peculiar constraints the 'clout' of the English bobby continues to impose on elected politicians, as well as attuned to 'his' continuing role as a dependable source of symbolic capital. It seems a fitting note on which to bring this chapter to a close:

HS: One of the great problems facing the police and Home Office and all the rest of it is that people like to see the bobby-on-the-beat because it's very reassuring. But the bobby-on-the-beat is a most inefficient way of coping with the prevention of crime. You will know that. But you can't tell that to the public out there. You cannot and so I fell in with that and I got an extra 1,000 police officers and made a lot of it. But I think you've got the problem of what the public perceive is effective policing and what is effective policing. That is a huge problem for the police resources in our country. Some chief constables exploit it because they say the only thing is to have more police on the beat all the time.

IL: Did you think it was suicide as a Minister to try and point out publicly that it didn't work?

HS: It's very difficult to do that. You were swimming against the tide. None of my predecessors or any of my successors were....

IL: One can see that. Politically it was very difficult....

HS: And they love to be photographed with police officers whenever they go on tour, meeting the local community all the rest of it, the bobby-on-the-beat [former Conservative Home Secretary].

4

The Fracturing of Police Authority

The central contention of what we have termed the 'desacralization thesis' is that the economic, political, and socio-cultural transformations experienced by English society since 1945 have fatally undermined the kinds of steadfastly supportive sensibilities towards police authority that we encountered in the previous chapter. This demise, it is claimed, has in large measure to do with the cavernous social divisions and individualized and pluralistic social relations that characterize late modern England. But it is also viewed as the legitimacy-eroding consequence of the police's controversial involvement since the late 1960s in what has become a regular diet of political protests, industrial disputes, and urban disorders. This view found an echo among a number of our respondents: 'sadly that [public support for the police] has gone. It's not the case now. In London at the time there was a lot of people throwing coppers in the gutter, and people calling them fuzz, pigs, the lot. It must have been the sixties I suppose' (women's organization, Manchester). One also finds it expressed in a recent historical treatise on the fate of British national identity since 1940:

The reputation of the police was sullied by the heavy-handed way they were used to contain industrial action and civil protest. Once seen as an embodiment of British fair play, they were now widely seen as the enforcement agency of an authoritarian right-wing government (much to the despair of many officers who objected to the politicization of the police). The police reputation for neutrality had been in decline since the 1960s, but it was not until the 1980s that a clear majority of the nation lost faith in them and they ceased to be part of the pantheon of Britishness [Weight 2002: 571].

One of our purposes in this chapter is to extend and develop this thesis. But we also want to qualify and revise it in certain key respects by seeking to distil the contours and substance of what we take to be a *range* of contemporary public dispositions towards English policing. In so doing, we shall not be concerned to recover in any detail the processes and events that are held by proponents of the desacralization thesis to have contributed to a marked decline in the public standing of the police. Our aim, rather, is to examine the ways in which certain key developments, conflicts, and scandals that have afflicted the police in the latter half of the twentieth century are received and appropriated within public mentalities and sensibilities. What accounts of the intersections between policing and social change are to be found within different clusters of lay experience, affect, and belief? What issues do different public audiences highlight and what significance do they attribute to them? How does policing fit into the biographical trajectories of individuals occupying different positions within the hierarchies of English society? What forms of continuity and rupture are evident in the stories they tell? And what relationships obtain between particular policing developments (changing priorities, styles, powers, resources, technologies) and police involvements (in urban riots, the miners' strike, and the like) and the relatively durable dispositions within which such happenings are rendered intelligible, but which 'real world' events are always also capable of shifting?

In addressing these questions we deploy the terms of this chapter's title—'the fracturing of police authority'—in two rather different senses. We use it first to denote, with Reiner, the *demise* of a once apparently more uniform and settled public orientation towards the English police; or what, more specifically, we contend is the residualization of a conception of police/social authority whose 'hallmark', in Hannah Arendt's (1970: 45) terms, 'is unquestioning recognition by those who are asked to obey; neither coercion nor persuasion is needed'. But we intend these terms to signify, secondly, not some simple linear shift from 'the sacred to the profane' in popular opinion (cf. Reiner 1995*a*), but the coexistence of a *diversity* of public registers that are simultaneously effects of, and responses to, processes of detraditionalization—responses that are differentially laced with 'hot' and 'cold' tempers; evince different orientations towards past and future; make different kinds of sense of key events (and possess varying degrees of 'openness' towards such events), and demonstrate contrasting levels of identification with the idea of policing in general and alternative visions of policing in particular.

Drawing on our group discussions and biographical interviews with different strata of the English populace, we have identified five such perspectives on policing and the social which we have termed—playfully extending Reiner's religious lexicon—*defenders of the faith, the disenchanted, atheists, agnostics*, and *the hopeful*.[1] Their defining components are set out schematically in Table 4.1. We will as the chapter unfolds have more to say about each disposition, as we seek both to elaborate upon and make sense of their principal elements, and to offer some initial judgement on their post-war trajectories and contemporary cultural force. We begin with those we have termed 'defenders of the faith'—something that requires us to revisit and explore further the sensibilities towards the English bobby delineated in the last chapter.

Defenders of the Faith

We'd be lost without them. We need them. We need more [women's organization, south Manchester].

Take the ropes off them altogether. We won't end up with a police state. That's to do with parliament, not the police. But if you just take these gloves off... [53-year-old male self-defence instructor, south Manchester].

Our concern here is with an outlook that Reiner and other proponents of the desacralization thesis have tended to overlook, on the apparent assumption that it has become insignificant, perhaps even withered away. It has—as we intimated in Chapter 3—become a residual disposition today. It is the stance of those fragments of the working and middle-class moulded by the imperatives of war and its aftermath who feel displaced by, and have reacted against, the erosion of authority structures that they see as having marked the last several decades of the twentieth century. It is the worldview of those who view the decline of 'respect' for social authority as having been the principal contributor not only to the advent of high crime rates as a 'normal'—if unacceptable—'social fact' (Garland 2001: 106–7), but also to a more general condition of insecurity, incivility, and precariousness. This sense of ambient malaise (and its causes) is well expressed in the following account:

Teachers, you see, were greatly respected. Doctors were respected. They were pillars of society. A local village teacher was a very important person. She or he had a small school. He knew the pupils, or she knew the pupils,

TABLE 4.1. Public sensibilities towards the English police

	Vision of policing	Narrative of change	Key issues/demands	Dominant orientations/ emotions	Orientation to policing over the life-course	Relationship of disposition to events
Defenders of the faith	Paternal local guardianship, authoritarian, central to social order	Decline since 1960s, remote, unresponsive, captured by 'vested interests'	Return of local bobby, more officers, greater powers, zero-tolerance	Strong attachment ('best in the world'), coupled with resentment, complaint, and denial	Continuity	Closed
The disenchanted	Local, visible, responsive, trustworthy, fair	Fall from grace since 1980s, awareness of fallibility	Visible policing, quality of service, fairness	Sadness, regret, support in a 'lower key'	Slow erosion of trust	Open
Atheists	Local, visible, accountable	Grudging respect undermined by experience since 1980s, sense of discrimination	Recognition, respect, justice, protection	Anger	Marked loss of faith	Once open, now closed
Agnostics	Necessary but essentially 'backstage' institution	Policing an 'increasingly difficult job', awareness of fallibility	Competence, efficiency, professional service	Indifference, pragmatism, distant sympathy	Continuity	Implicitly closed
The hopeful	Responsive to experience of minorities, accountable	History of discrimination; discernible, uneven progress since 1980s	Recognition, fair treatment, police commitment to change	Guarded expectation	Gradually more positive	Open

and probably taught the parents too. Vicars were respected. Doctors were certainly respected. You were frightened of doctors. I think in a way they are still frightened of doctors. But now and again they used to castigate you. The standing of teachers has gone now. I think a lot of that is their own fault. I think they have been taught badly by the teacher training colleges, and then they became terribly left-wing. The doctors are rather castigated as being too impersonal, people like to sue doctors when they can. I think there was much more rigidity, no, not rigidity, solidity in society. Now everyone is always having a go at the next person. Newspapers were much more informative and far less offensive [former Conservative Minister of State, Home Office].

Faced with the uncertainties of an age marked by 'a general sort of firing against all institutions', one this Conservative peer felt risked doing 'away with that that is actually precious', those we have termed 'defenders of the faith' cleave to the police or, more accurately, a particular *idea* of English policing, as a source and symbol of order and stability. In this worldview the police figure centrally, helping to organize people's sense of self and their conception of the identity and security of the English nation. It is the posture of those who feel a deep, emotive affinity with the police, one reinforced by both the mundane and mediated presence of the police in everyday life, and the abiding sense that this institution stands between 'us' and the dangers of a chaotic world. It is the disposition of those who are by 'second nature', and almost unconditionally, pro-police, people who are quick to defend this vital social institution against those who would attack and (thereby) undermine it. Yet this attachment itself coexists with some vehement criticism of police practice and performance, as we shall see. Let us then consider the constitutive elements of this structure of feeling and its meanings, supports, and effects.

Defenders of the faith believe, first and foremost, that the police are *the* source of social order, and that a policing solution to the crime question exists and can be found. This manifests itself principally, as we saw in Chapter 3, in demands for 'a return to' more visible police guardianship of local communities. But this generally coalesces with the view that the police should be accorded the resources, powers, and room for manœuvre required for them to triumph in the fight against crime. Some expressed this as a general desire for a 'stronger acting police force' (53-year-old male self-defence instructor, south Manchester). Others spoke more concretely of their wish to see the police being free to impose greater discipline: 'I would like to see them have a bit more power and move the youngsters on or give them a clip round the ear hole if they deserved it. I think they should have a bit more power in that respect. I don't think the youngsters are frightened of them' (73-year-old male retired builder, south Manchester). Such demands were often condensed into an uncritical acceptance of, and appeal for, 'zero-tolerance':

There's a place near Newcastle, which has a real bad reputation...this chief constable [sic], they're trying to get rid of him. It's a real bad place. He became chief constable and the crime rate dropped through no tolerance. He was suspended from duty and the crime rate started again as soon as they got rid of him ... There's too much political correctness about. What people want, I believe, and what people tell me, is that they want, they want to see a much tougher attitude from the law. They want to see people really lifted. Most people are asking for zero-tolerance [53-year-old male self-defence instructor, south Manchester].

The frustration and anger that routinely attend these demands have much to do with the belief that various forces and interests are today wilfully obstructing the realization of this preferred vision of policework and keeping the police in their currently enfeebled position. Some among our respondents spoke of a police force unduly bound by human rights and legal rules—'their hands are absolutely tied, they cannot take action' (retired female machinist, inner-city Manchester); or of officers being 'bogged down by paperwork' (female, senior citizens' group, Cheshire). Others referred, with no less exasperation, to insufficient resources—'in the *Manchester Evening News* last night, front-page. The police are going to lose about 400 people. People look at that and say "what's happening"' (male, tenants' association, south Manchester); to police officers who 'dare not touch' suspects (women's organization, Manchester) for fear of malicious complaint and reprimand, or to a society reluctant to give the police 'the tools to do the job' (53-year-old male self-defence instructor, south Manchester). This last respondent proceeded to detail what he saw as the perilous—and all too likely—consequences of these various refusals to bow to popular common sense:

I'm absolutely positive that something like that [the return of hanging] will actually happen, unless politicians and devotees of political correctness come to some kind of arrangement about tougher sentencing, faster sentencing, stronger policing. I think they're going to find themselves being pushed by a public to search towards some kind of, I don't know, supremo, dictator. I don't mean a political dictatorship, but something like that... I can see some kind of crime tsar. It would be a very powerful person. Such a person would have terrifying powers. And I could see some kind of move down that road. I wouldn't like to see that personally. But I could see that happening, that developing, if society believes, and it's a hysterical belief, it's not necessarily based on logical thought. I can see something very frightening, very frightening down the road.

In the face of these concerns, it should not be forgotten that defenders of the faith remain both enthusiastically pro-police ('All the dealings I've had with the police, they've been really good. I can't fault the police myself in any shape or form'—female, tenants' association, south Manchester), and inclined to sympathize with their plight: 'I think they're much maligned... We have so many expectations and they have so many more duties to fulfil these days' (women's organization, south Manchester). They are, as such, prone to gloss over or deny police misconduct (as we shall see in Chapter 5), and minded to view the police as innocent victims of those who withhold resources from them, fail to offer wholesome support, and generally render them impotent. As one woman put it: 'I feel sorry for the police, I really do, because I don't think they're getting enough support' (female, tenants' association, south Manchester). The police, on this view, are 'hamstrung', and themselves 'frustrated' and 'disheartened' (female, tenants' association, inner-city Manchester), by a host of external bodies, whether they be politicians and government officials, various 'vested interests' and 'do-gooders' (notably what one of our respondents called 'the race relations industry'), or sentencers who time and again 'let the police down' with 'just a pat on the head and "be a good boy and don't do it again"' (female, tenants' association, south Manchester). This is, in short, the worldview of those who *feel* for the police, emphasize their worth, and are strongly inclined to stick up for them.

This social inclination to support the police, one most apparent among defenders of the faith but by no means confined to them, cannot easily be separated from the police's status as *the* agency authorized to act in situations involving what Egon Bittner calls 'something-that-ought-not-to-be-happening-and-about-which-someone-had-better-do-something-now' (Bittner 1990: 246). We were struck in this context by the number of occasions in which our respondents would recount incidents of either criminal victimization (burglary, robbery, and so forth) or personal trauma (the suicide of a family member, for example) and follow this immediately and without prompting with expressions of immense gratitude for the way in which the police had handled the event. These included those who felt the police were 'super' or 'really marvellous' (women's organization, Manchester); a women with 'nothing but praise' for the police (women's organization, south Manchester), and recollections of officers having been 'very, very kind' (female, tenants' association, south Manchester).

This sense of the police performing an indispensable, unpleasant, and sometimes dangerous task—'I look at them and I think "I wouldn't have your job, I'm glad it's you and not me"'' (female, retired civil servants, south Manchester)—clearly helps to generate a capacious reservoir of doxic sympathy upon which police organizations are able to draw (see, for example, Mulcahy 2000). The related way in which the police appear to bring attributes of heroism, bravery, and sacrifice to situations of vulnerability, dread, and loss also arguably contributes to the *frisson* of pleasure that some people appear to experience when confronted with the thought or presence of police officers:

The traffic light stopped on red, and there nearest the red light, two officers of the mounted section. They were beautifully turned out. It was a sight to behold. You would have though they had come from the Horse Guards. And there was just time. I said, 'Jolly nice to see you. You make your impact here. I wish you came more often' [male retired solicitor, south Manchester].

Yet defenders of the faith are wedded first and foremost to the idea of policing rather than to the police organization itself, and while the idea and institution for many purposes overlap, the latter is susceptible to some stinging criticism on the occasions they fail to embody the former. The following discussion of the police's role in the 1989 Hillsborough stadium disaster and its aftermath illustrates well both this impulse to defend *our* police from what is considered unwarranted attack and the sense that *the* police today do not properly live up the high ideal of English policing:

AM: Is there anything that you've come across over your lives that has made you ashamed of the police?

Tony: I tell you the thing that springs to my mind, that's the Sheffield Wednesday disaster, the football. Now the police have been heavily criticized in Yorkshire. But from what I've seen on television,

I don't think it was the police to blame at all. I think it was the drunken Liverpool supporters that caused that. They were surging forward and all the rest of it, and police had to open the door that caused the flood of people, that caused the disaster. But somehow, that's been covered up. Now the police, instead of being condemned, I think they should have been admired for trying to control the situation, which got out of hand eventually of course, and a disaster happened. I still think that the Liverpool supporters, and we all know what most of them are like when they get a few drinks inside them, I blame them for that disaster to a certain extent.

Jim: The only thing I disagree with is that the police doing their job got compensation.

Tony: Yes.

Jim: Let's face it, they get paid for doing it. It's like being in the army [retired civil servants, south Manchester].

Thus it is that an often viscerally expectant pro-police sensibility can come to coexist with a catalogue of complaints about current police priorities and performance, a mix Albert Hirschman (1991) describes as 'unrealistic optimism' and 'overstated despair'. The 'despair' in the present case surrounds—as we have seen—the way in which the police have become a distant, remote, and faceless bureaucracy. Some referred here to forces covering areas that were 'too large' (female, tenants' association, south Manchester), to officers who are seldom seen, or to the lack of means to identify with any named figure of authority. As one women remarked of the police's response to a bag-snatching, 'every time we rang up to find out what was going on, it was a different person' (retired civil servants, south Manchester). Others spoke about the police having been removed to 'the end of a telephone' (male, tenants' association, north Manchester); of the difficulties of contacting the police by such already remote means—'I had to phone six times before I got through' (retired male printer, Manchester), or of their annoyance at police efforts to dissuade the public from enlisting police assistance: 'some people are very apprehensive of using the treble nine call because they think they might get into trouble for using it. There's been a blaze of publicity that you mustn't use 999... I think that has put a lot of people off' (male, tenants' association, north Manchester). In a related vein, we heard complaints of people finding police stations 'locked' (female, retired civil servants, south Manchester) or making what proved to be fruitless efforts to gain access to them: 'it was a Sunday afternoon. I went to Altrincham police station, tried to get in. They wouldn't let us in. It was broad daylight, they were there. They wouldn't let us in, pointed to a phone outside. It was an answer machine saying phone back next morning' (women's organization, south Manchester).[2] The cumulative sense of a force that is distant, unresponsive, and attending to obscure priorities is encapsulated in the following extract, as is the smouldering resentment it can imbue:

The resources that they've got now are put to good use in their own sense, but there have lost a community spirit I think. Because you see now they are flying around in the cars and all this, that, and the other, whereas at one time if you rang for a policeman he would probably jump on his bicycle and he'd come round. Now you can wait anything between two and six hours. It might only be a little trivial thing, but they always say they have an emergency on. We can't say that they have or that they haven't. We have got to take their word for it [male, tenants' association, north Manchester].

This catalogue of disquiet is interestingly—and ambiguously— entangled with the question of police technology. It is apparent first—as the above account suggests—that the word 'technology' often functions among defenders of the faith as code for distant, unresponsive policing. On this view, certain forms of police technology—'old bikes' (male, tenants' association, north Manchester), helmets, truncheons—do not properly count as technology at all, as this evocation of the 'black Maria' indicates: 'you'd find a lot of black Marias in those days [the 1960s]. There'd be one cruising up and down Princes Road...People used to behave themselves when they were around' (53-year-old male self-defence instructor, south Manchester). Rather, technology is that which clashes with, and has contributed towards the demise of, 'traditional' English policing. Such a 'clash' is most evident in the reaction of defenders of the faith to the various 'paramilitary' technologies adopted by the police over recent decades, especially such things as pepper sprays, public-order vans, and protective equipment. On the one hand, such technology holds out the promise that officers, and by extension 'the public', are being adequately protected. Yet it simultaneously speaks of a violent disorderly other that 'we', and the police, need such protection from—something that undermines the belief that English policing is a benign, intimate, family activity. For many the unacceptable limit case of such technology was the routine arming of the police, the advent of which would entail abandoning a vital ingredient of the unique policing idea of which they were so proud: 'I think the nicest thing about the British police is that they are not armed, which doesn't happen anywhere else' (male, retired professionals, south Manchester).

This orientation towards 'technology' also permeates the response to those forms of everyday police equipment—telephones, radios, cars, computers, and, most recently, helicopters—that are considered to have rendered policing more faceless and remote. Yet the last of these acquisitions—the police helicopter—illustrates well the divergent reactions technology can evoke among police enthusiasts. For some, helicopters provided the latest maddening example of what were taken to be the baffling priorities of contemporary police managers: 'they [people on the estate] like the two bobbies themselves. They are in many ways very supportive of them. But there is growing disenchantment with the senior officers who give those officers their orders. And there's also growing disenchantment with any senior officer who would rather buy a helicopter than put another constable on the beat... Anyone who likes helicopters at the expense of bobbies-on-the-beat must be an absolute raving lunatic' (53-year-old male self-defence instructor, south Manchester). For others, however, the sight of 'helicopters up here at night with their search lights on' offered a certain reassurance, a sign that the police are being fully and properly equipped 'to protect your area' (male, retired professionals, south Manchester). Some sense of these mixed feelings is evident from the following discussion:

Sally: They're not recruiting this year. They need to buy another helicopter you see. Having said that, I feel, I know I shouldn't do, but the helicopter goes up, and if they could put a helicopter over my house all night, I would not complain.

Joan: No.

Sally: People say, 'oh, the helicopter, it's really annoying'.

IL: Do you get it round a fair amount?

Sally: Oh yes.

Anne: I'm always happy when I see it.

...

Sally: We objected strongly when they were talking about buying a plane. A helicopter I can understand. We all can understand it. But what's a plane going to do for us, and our council taxes passed it, didn't they. Yes, I think the helicopter is a wonderful idea, don't get me wrong, it's brilliant. They're very rarely lose anybody with that helicopter. We've had it over our garden, we've had the spotlight on the garden. They even talk to you and say 'go in your door because there's some lunatic in your garden'.

Bill: With the thermal imaging.

Sally: It's absolutely brilliant.

IL: Would you be happy for them to patrol with the helicopter?

Sally: Yes I would, I'd love it [tenants' association, south Manchester].

We referred earlier to the confluence of affection and despair that constitutes the outlook of defenders of the faith. A further—and striking—instance of this concerned the frequency with which the litany of complaints of the kind we have just described sat alongside, and was sometimes immediately followed by, an assertion to the effect that the English—or British—police remain 'the best in the world'. The following such claim, which was preceded in the discussion by just such a catalogue of grumbles about police performance, offers some flavour of this:

IL: If you had to describe policing in this country to someone from abroad, what would you choose to say?

Jill: Wonderful.

Fiona: After being abroad where they have guns and they look really aggressive, I think it's wonderful what they do under very trying circumstances.

IL: What would you say was wonderful about it as compared with other countries?

Fiona: You just visit London, places like that, you get the impression that they're friendly. When you go to other places and go to their main cities, they've got a gun, especially in Spain. They're aggressive, whereas our policemen, the ones that are on show, don't really seem aggressive.

Jane: There doesn't appear to be much corruption. That's the good thing [retired civil servants, south Manchester].

Such utterances, it seems to us, mobilize the reputed horrors of foreign police forces—they were variously in this context described as 'violent', 'more vicious', 'corrupt', 'rude', 'government-controlled', and 'armed'—as a device enabling the English police (and, by extension, England itself) to be imaginatively resuscitated as an institution in which, despite everything, faith can still, indeed should still, be placed. As one member of a south Manchester women's organization put it, 'I lived abroad and I was so frightened when I went abroad, the police were horrendous. And I will say right now that Britain is the best country in the world to live in. It's the fairest still, and the safest. Even with all its troubles.' We will have more to say about this structure of feeling in the next chapter when we consider the place it occupies in the cultural politics of policing and 'race'. Suffice it to note here that those we have termed defenders of the faith see themselves as guardians of a prized but imperilled tradition. Having been made strangers in their own land by processes of detraditionalization that appear to have transformed 'England' into an unfamiliar, less cohesive place and its police force into a remote, unresponsive bureaucracy, they cleave ever more tightly to, and seek to defend, a vision of paternal, authoritarian English policing that they feel to be doomed. They appear, in these respects, to have succumbed to what Tom Nairn (2000: 103) calls 'national nihilism'—'the conviction of irredeemable hopelessness attaching to what is most intimately one's own'.

The Disenchanted

I would say that people didn't question their honesty and now they would do. Because of what's gone on in the past, people don't respect them [female, insurance company employees, Manchester].

Those we have termed 'the disenchanted' once arguably shared a broadly similar outlook to that possessed by defenders of the faith. But the disposition of this body of principally middle-class 'respectable' opinion—those who in the 1970s and 1980s were commonly mobilized as, and often understood themselves to be, the 'silent majority'—has in the last couple of decades been disturbed and reconfigured; undone by policing developments and detraditionalizing processes that have qualified what was a once more unconditionally pro-police sensibility. A member of our adult education group captures the ensuing complications well:

There are more checks and balances now I think than there were. I think that everything that comes forward now is checked, and is accounted to. People are willing to say, 'let's hold on, we can't accept that. Explain to me why I should do what you say'. There's that side of it, which makes society, I think, more complex and more difficult.

The disenchanted are an audience (and we are generally speaking of a constituency that has relatively little direct contact with the police) which has come to recognize the police as fallible, and which today exhibits a more sceptical, questioning, but at the same time demanding, orientation not only to the police, but to other authority figures who once stood as stable pillars of English society. The demands and disappointments that attend this process appear, on the surface at least, to overlap with those evinced by defenders of the faith, save that the disenchanted more often vocalize their unhappiness in the tones of expectant, disgruntled consumers. One thus finds among this middle-class constituency concerns with the remoteness of contemporary policing—'hey I saw a rare sight today, I saw a policeman in town' (male retired teacher, Cheshire), 'we've got a station, but there's no policemen in it' (female, sheltered accommodation residents, south Manchester); as well as demands for a more local, visible police presence. Such demands are often animated by a sense of the police having moved from the forefront to the background of English social relations, from being part of the family to being 'just part of the scenery':

AM: Do you find your views, attitudes of the police have changed?
Clive: Well they've changed since the police have moved away from the community, and their idea, the daft ideas they have, men on different styles of bikes, mountain bikes going round town, panda cars. The more remote they have got from the community, the less regard people have for them [male retired teacher, Cheshire].

One encounters, in addition, some similar orientations towards police technology, feelings characteristically expressed in terms of policework having become dominated by 'police sirens, helicopters, which you didn't have before; every day every night, police cars up and down Moston Road' (female, retired civil servants, south Manchester). Some, in this spirit, were keen to register the costs of what they saw as the tendency of technology to distance the police from localities: 'of course you've telephones, radios, you can get in touch with the police. Helicopters. It's all there. All the modern technology is used by the police. But in my view how much better it would be if more money, more resources for foot patrols. I think it would go a long way to stopping the tradition of crime. How much better if the local criminal fraternity were aware that there was a regular patrol. It does need far more police officers on foot patrol. But they're not now, they're in motor cars. It's not the same thing' (male retired solicitor, south Manchester). Others evinced a sometimes condescending bemusement towards what they saw as the misplaced professional conceit of those police managers who enjoy 'playing around with aeroplanes and helicopters' (male retired teacher, Cheshire), a sentiment that found characteristic expression in the following account:

They say there's not enough money to expand the police force, if you like. Yet it's not that long ago that the chief constable of Manchester was asking for an aeroplane, costing millions. Wasn't it? We've got a helicopter, but he was asking for a plane. What good that could do I haven't got the faintest idea [male, retired civil servants, south Manchester].

These alleged changes in police priorities and practice have—for this audience—deprived English policing of its intimate, emotionally satisfying character, thereby stripping from it much of the affection in which it was once more securely held. But this is not principally a case—as with defenders of the faith—of unrequited infatuation, of a police force failing to satisfy the heavy weight of insatiable expectation. The disenchanted have if anything fallen out of love, come to see the police as a mundane organization, one prone to commit mistakes, one no longer deserving of the public's implicit trust. This shift—which has seen this constituency place somewhat greater emphasis on questions of accountability and redress, what our opening respondent called 'checks and balances'—is not, however, mainly the product of the aforementioned complaints—important though these have been in the overall process of disenchantment. The corrosion of trust is also, and rather more, the effect of other sets of events, the appropriation and understanding of which sharply distinguish the disenchanted from defenders of the faith.

The first of these involve personal—or close family—experiences of police rudeness, excess, or abuse of power. This in some measure has to do with the slow-burning consequences of the motor-car, the spread of which in the latter half of the twentieth century has brought the middle-classes into regular unwanted contact with the police. This exchange illustrates the pertinent effects well:

Jill: I think one big difference is the motor car when you think about it, because there were hardly any after the war. And crime now,

I don't mean burglary and murders, I mean not having your own
disc, or careless driving, it takes an enormous amount of police
time. An enormous amount. And an enormous amount in the
courts. Days and days.

Sheila: The paperwork they have to do.

All: Yes.

Jill: It's made them the enemy of the middle-class people to some extent
[women's organization, Manchester].[3]

But this disenchantment has more specifically to do with what is
felt to be unwarranted police attention directed at family members—
principally our discussants' sons; incidents that had—shockingly—
brought into the lives of a middle-class audience aspects of police
power they might once have tended to deny, or dismiss as civil
libertarian bleating, or believe confined to criminal, deviant, and
therefore 'deserving' Others. One woman from south Manchester
spoke in this regard of having 'never forgiven the police' for
wrongly accusing her son of car theft. Another disrupted the
celebratory tone of one of our discussion groups by recounting the
following incident:

Jane: I think our policemen are the best in the world.

Vicky: We're talking about when they're more humane. We're not talking
about what happens when one of our children, the case of my children,
have been hauled up before the police for one thing or another. I
think there is a lot of that about youngsters wearing whatever. It
depends entirely on their clothing whether they're picked up or not.
That happened to David [her son]...What worries us, and what
worried our family when our son were badly treated and we made
a complaint, is that an earring, a ponytail, wearing black clothes,
was decided by this policeman to mean he was guilty of something
on his motorbike, and they didn't treat him as they should have
done. My husband came home very angry. There was a family
discussion, his friend calls, 'oh let me write to the chief constable
saying you're not satisfied'. What happens to the youngsters who
haven't got somebody to suggest that?

Cathy: I was going to say that. If you're a black kid and your parents
aren't literate in English [women's organization, Manchester].

The second set of relevant 'experiences' is more remote and concerns
mediated events that appear to have had an important qualifying
effect upon the once more 'hotly' pro-police outlook of this

middle-class audience. The two events highlighted most often in this context—both of which remained indicatively absent from the discourse of defenders of the faith—were the miscarriages of justice revealed in the 1990s, and the police's role in the 1984–5 miners' strike. In respect of the former, reference was made to how 'the Birmingham six, the Guildford four' had generated 'an awful lot of mistrust in the police' (male, adult education group, south Manchester). As one middle-class woman from south Manchester put it: 'I think they've lost a lot of respect in the last few years because in a lot of these cases they've brought out, they've manu-factured evidence' (women's organization, south Manchester). In the latter case, our respondents recalled 'the Conservative gov-ernment using the police force in order to kind of beat the miners with, that definitely stuck' (48-year-old male adult education teacher, Cheshire), or referred to how 'they were used to control the miners when the miners' strike was on', something in the opin-ion of this onlooker 'that left a bitter taste' (women's organization, south Manchester). This retired businessman from south Manchester reflected on the event and its consequences thus:

I think if we're going to where the police lost the faith of the public, I would put it down to the miners' strike, where ordinary working men, who were fighting for their jobs and their livelihood, were pitted against the police. Now, when working men, which policemen are, they're only working men the same... they were being used by the government to break a strike, a lengthy strike. I think that is where a lot of members of the pub-lic lost a lot of faith in them. I mean they showed it on television, they showed it on the papers, policemen driving horses at the striking miners, just to break them up.

These proximate and remote events have, it seems, been appropri-ated into this middle-class sensibility in such a way as to remove from the English police their once revered status as trustworthy upholders of Law and Order, and lend credence to stories of police misconduct that might once have been more cursorily dismissed. Such events have, in other words, helped to elevate police wrong-doing to the pantheon of 'respectable' worries, a 'respectability' that is arguably reinforced by the kind of media vehicles that now culturally circulate, and expressly or implicitly authorize, tales of police malpractice: 'all sorts of wrong things they [the police] were up to. And the public image starts to change. You only read the *Daily Mail, Sun* or whatever and they're on about police brutality' (male retired teacher, Cheshire). As for the 'wrong things' that form the subject of such concerns, these included:

High ranking officers and others in the police service who are getting to the end of their service, and as you well know, it's in the papers, if they're going to be taken to task over something, retirement. They get a damn good pension, and they get nothing as regards what's happened previously. It's just forgotten... To me there's something wrong with a system where you can just do that. Something wants doing regarding that [male, retired civil servants, south Manchester].

These movements in outlook are not however the product of such events alone. Rather, these events have become entangled with, and helped to reinforce, processes of detraditionalization that had already begun to loosen the unquestioning deference towards social authority that appears in the mid-twentieth century to have been a more settled cultural form. Some spoke of such shifts in terms of generational change: 'I think I am more sceptical than my parents were but I think that may relate to the changing times. I am more sceptical that not all policemen are good innocent and free, not all policemen are doing it for a grand design better. I think the bulk are but I mean there are others as outed in the news who do not stand up to those qualities' (male adult education teacher, Cheshire). Others, in cognate vein, spoke of how greater awareness 'of the faults' of those in power had rendered it impossible to respect people merely 'because of their office' or 'uniform': 'I mean now if you respect people, I hope we do it because we think they are worthy of respect' (women's organization, Manchester). The following conversation illustrates well this altered middle-class disposition:

Mike: All of them [the professions] have had their problems, haven't they? They've all had their problems. They've all had scandals or severe problems, you know.

Steve: I think we look at them as being ordinary people. I don't think people look up to them as they once did.

Hazel: No, and I think that the idea of you respect your betters has gone, and I think that's a good thing, because respect is something that you should earn. It doesn't matter who you are and what you do, you can still earn the respect of people.

AM: But the idea that the police will be respected as of right is...

Hazel: You don't respect somebody just because they happen to have a certain job or a certain status or whatever. That's gone and

> I think that's a good thing. It takes...you know, it changes the power balance a little bit [insurance company employees, Manchester].

This is a sensibility that has come to realize that the English police are fallible, that they get things wrong, act improperly, exceed their powers, and that mechanisms of supervision, control, and redress ought consequently to attend police practices. It remains however an essentially pro-police sentiment. The disenchanted, to be sure, today express this support more reservedly and in a lower key. They demand, as consumers, a better, more professional police service and expect poor performance and malpractice to be rectified. Yet their outlook is tinged with sadness and regret about the way this once proud national institution has been exposed and found wanting. The empirical record continues, in other words, to collide with some strongly held doxic/paleo-symbolic convictions about the police's value and social significance, as this particular strand of middle-class opinion oscillates between a recognition of police shortcomings and an impulse to support them none the less. The disenchanted still want to believe.

There can be few better indicators of this than the way some among our respondents sought out, warmly received, or clung on to reports that in someway or other confirmed that the police remain 'helpful' or 'very nice' (female, senior citizens, Cheshire); a longing perfectly illustrated by the response one middle-class women made to a member of her group, recounting how a 'very helpful' police officer had come to her aid following a car breakdown: 'that's a nice story', she said, 'when you hear so much about bent cops' (women's organization, Manchester). Yet this last remark also hints at why an unequivocal identification with the police has today become untenable. Too much is known, too much trust-depleting malpractice has been acknowledged, witnessed, or experienced, for such faith to any longer seem fitting or proper:

IL: If you had to describe policing in this country in the late 1990s to someone from abroad who didn't know anything about it, what would you choose to say?

Jane: Well I could compare it with the United States. I think generally the police are more polite. They stop you and they don't say 'what you doing lady?'

Sally: They have a little more finesse.

Jane: Yes, and the policemen are all old and fat, and fill up on dough-
nuts. They couldn't run a mile away. They're younger and fitter,
they look better. They're much more polite.

Cathy: We are trying to improve it, hopefully.

Jill: I think I'll be saying four out of ten.

Jane: No more than that?

Jill: Well I think it depends on your experiences. I know young men
who were picked up by the police on the fringe of a riot. He was
arrested, in the fracas, but he was there. The treatment that he got
in the police station... [women's organization, Manchester].

Atheists

Policemen don't shit roses [Hoggart 1988: 72].

When we speak of 'atheists' we are referring principally to a working-
class disposition, one infused with a sizeable dose of 'direct'—
though always also mediated—experience, one in which a certain
rupture in orientations towards the police is apparent. This outlook
on English policing, arising as it does out of the tense, negotiated
relationships that obtained between the police and working-class
communities in the mid-twentieth century (Cohen 1979; Brogden
1991), does not exhibit anything approaching the same enthusiasm
for the police, and the idea of policing, that one encounters among
defenders of the faith and the disenchanted. It nonetheless remains
an orientation in which the police were once viewed as undertaking valued protective tasks and accorded a degree of grudging
respect. Against this backdrop, the striking feature of the perspective we have termed atheism is how this already somewhat qualified
attachment to the symbolic power of the police has mutated into
often bitter, fatalistic forms on non-, or anti-, belief. For some this
loss of faith appears to have been born of a single enlightening
event:

The first experience I had of the police not being as good as what I thought
they were was back in 1975. On a Sunday morning the spare driver had to
get all these coaches off the garage forecourt because they weren't allowed
in the yard after eleven o'clock. There were about twenty odd coaches.
I had to do it one Sunday morning at half past six. I went in amongst these
coaches, and what should I find part hidden among the coaches, like in the

long grass kind of thing, this mini, and one copper was on the back seat sprawled out with his hand over his eyes, and other copper was on the front seat snoring his head off. I started the engine up on one of these coaches, right next to them, you should have seen them move. They just didn't want the public to see them in such disorder [male, tenants' association, south Manchester].

We propose to illuminate the elements of this working-class sensibility by focussing, principally, on the experiences of, and sensibilities towards, the police that have figured in the biographical trajectory of one of our respondents. Joan Cromwell was born in Manchester in the early 1940s and now lives alone in a high-crime, inner-city area of the city.[4] A practising Catholic and retired trade union official at a local factory, she is today active in the local tenants' association and several other voluntary organizations. The narrative she reconstructs of her post-war childhood is laced, on the one hand, with memories of conflict and non-co-operation with the police, whether in the form of local people 'hiding' an orphaned boy 'accused of stealing from the market', or what she later came to understand as look-outs blowing a whistle to alert those involved in 'pitch-and-toss' to the imminent arrival of the police. Yet at the same time she recalls 'being brought up to respect people', the police included: 'if a policeman came along and said something to you, it wasn't that my parents put the fear in me, they weren't those kind of people that say, you know, "the police will come and get you". You had respect for the police, you had respect for the police or somebody in authority...I was brought up to believe the police were people to turn to when you had trouble.' It was not, in any event, a childhood and adolescence in which the police loomed large: 'as I grew up, the police were just there and you didn't have any involvement with them. They were just around.'

Her subsequent 'disillusion' (a word she used several times during our long interview), her break from the inculcated sense that one ought to 'respect' the police, came—as it did in part for those we termed the disenchanted—during the turbulent years of the 1970s and 1980s, notably during the course of the 1984–5 miners' strike.[5] But in Joan's case, as an active trade union official, the eye-opening process was more directly experienced and keenly felt, the sense of shock more abrupt and profound. 'That', she remarked, 'is when I started to get very disillusioned with the police'. In part, this was a consequence of the attitude towards the miners that was—for her all too painfully—evident among the police officers she encountered:

I saw what went on during the miners' strike. And I saw the way that they...I used to go down to Pontefract on a Friday. I used to go down on a minibus and take money for the soup kitchens. And I watched, I used to go down to the pits, when we were going back after going to soup kitchen, and the police would be there, and the miners would be there. And they used to be shouting things like, 'keep it up lads, I'm on me second holiday, I've got a brand new car'...I thought that these are the people that, okay they're there to see to law and order and that people don't break the law, but I felt that they were trying to goad those guys into doing something so that they could then arrest them. And it was pitiful because those blokes had been out by this time maybe ten, twelve weeks and they were really finding it hard.

And, in part, it ensued from the abuses of police power that Joan either observed or heard about, abuses directed not at the 'dead-legs' who can and should expect to receive such ill treatment, but to those she viewed as decent, working men:

There was one particular occasion that stuck in my mind where there was a shop steward and he had an argument with an inspector on the picket line and that night they had word that they were coming to arrest him. And the word went round the village, and every single person came out, women, children. And the police came rolling up and they stood their ground and they said that they were witnesses that if they took this man away, that they were going to all follow. And they backed off, but came out the next day and dragged him out, and when he came back he was black and blue. But there was no proof of anything, you know there was no witnesses but this man. These are the kind of things that you hear about, what you expect to happen to the dead-legs around here, the people I'd like to see get a kicking, the drug-dealers. But when it's happening to somebody like you and I, that's just, you know, trying to get a decent deal for his family.

The altered disposition occasioned by the 'high policing' (Brodeur 1983) of the miners' strike has, in subsequent years, been deepened by a host of dissatisfactions with the way in which her local estate and its residents have come to be policed. One finds here a general sense of unmet demands for the police to do something about issues of drugs, crime, and disorder in the locality: 'I'm paying the community charge...I expect more of the police and I'm not getting it...I think that in general they don't want to know'.

There is, in the midst of this, some acknowledgement that the police 'have a hard job', as well as an evident attachment to *particular* police officers, those perceived to care about the locality and police it accordingly. Whereas as once, however, such local officers were seen to embody the English police and its virtues, they now appear only to highlight institutional shortcomings. They are good apples in a bad barrel: 'the Terry Jones' of this world—great lad, good police officer, very nice lad, does his job properly—but in general, no. I'm afraid I'm very disillusioned and I don't trust them. I sound very negative, I'm sorry, but that's the way it is. It would take an awful lot for me to get trust back in them again. I don't know how because it's very deep-rooted now.'

This disillusion arises in part—in ways that overlap with both the outlooks we addressed earlier—from the sense that the local community is being left vulnerable and unprotected. Sometimes this is expressed in terms with which we have become familiar: 'if we see a police officer we think either the Queen is coming or the Prime Minister'. But it also coalesces with the feeling that the police have been overwhelmed by the welter of crime demands they now confront—'I think a lot of them think it's too much bother, you know they spend so much time doing reports that they can't be bothered—"oh, it's another burglary", or "it's another mugging"'; and that they have, in the face of problems about which something needs urgently to be done, withdrawn from the locality:

You ask anybody, you stop anybody and ask them if they've ever seen a police officer. We want more police on patrol. I'd be quite happy to have the cameras here. You know people say it invades my civil liberties. If you're doing nothing wrong, why would it invade your civil liberties? The police are definitely not the police that they used to be. I don't feel that they are there for the community.

This sense of loss and distance is tinged further—in ways that have less correspondence with the outlook of defenders of faith and the disenchanted—with the angry feeling that this has something to do with the resentment the police feel towards *this particular* community—'whether you're black or white, they think that because you live on a council estate you are rubbish' (female, tenants' association, inner-city Manchester); and the sense that the police are consequently unwilling either to listen or respond to what residents have to tell them about local crime problems.

As Joan puts it, 'most of the experiences I have had with the police are not good. And I think that they are very arrogant, a lot of them. And because you live on a council estate, they treat you as if you are stupid. If you are a woman on your own, you're neurotic. If you phone, like I did last night, I don't think I'm either stupid or neurotic. I'm not that lonely that I'm going to ring the police and I appreciate that they have to prioritize. But half the time they don't come.' What accompanies this sentiment however, is not some blanket demand for the police to 'get tough', or exercise 'zero tolerance', but a further legitimacy-eroding complaint about the invasive or discriminatory policing that certain sub-groups within the locality are considered to receive—notably young Afro-Caribbean men (see Chapter 5), and black and white teenagers: 'a lot of the bobbies round here now they speak to the kids terribly, a lot of them do don't they' (female, tenants' association, north Manchester). The sort of angry resentment this accumulated experience can provoke is apparent in the following exchange:

Mags: My husband rang the police once and it was over someone robbing next door like. When he came he was really nasty. He said this to my husband and he was 75 years, 'You get in, and I'll speak to you later', that is what he said to Barry, 'Get in there and shut the door'. I says, 'that is my husband you are talking to, that is not a snotty-nosed kid'. He said, 'get in and shut the door'. I mean it is not nice to talk people at that age when you are only trying to do your duty for somebody robbing next door.

Dave: I think it is attitude and I think it is attitude towards the public and of the police. But I mean obviously, we are regarded as the public anyway, if we don't respect them, but there again if they don't respect us.

Mags: That's right, they are not going to get any respect from us in the first place.

Carol: You have got to give respect if you want to get it back [tenants' association, north Manchester].

One finds in Joan Cromwell's changing sensibilities towards the police a more radical loss of faith than that experienced by the disenchanted middle class. Though she began from a position of more grudging, less enthusiastic respect, she has fallen faster and further. This, as we have seen, is in large measure the consequence of certain illusion-breaking events, coupled today with a quotidian experience of the police's inability to respond effectively and equitably to the endemic crime problems of the neighbourhood she inhabits. But these events and experiences have also—as with the disenchanted—unfolded against the backdrop of a more general tide of shifting cultural orientations towards institutions and figures of authority, a change Joan's experiences have served only, in her case, to entrench. As a practising Catholic, Joan has felt this process of ambient change acutely: 'I was brought up that the people you'd respect would be the priest, the police, and your doctor. But because of the things I've seen, and I think most people, you don't have the same respect for them, because of the attitude of a lot of them...Now priests interfere with little boys and girls. It's all gone, what we were brought up to believe, that you trusted the police, you trust the doctor.' It is in this context that the lifting from the police of what she calls their 'mystique' must be understood:

Joan: I no longer have the same respect for them because I don't feel that, I don't know whether or not it's because we expect more of them, because I'm older. There's that mystique is gone, you know where you had respect for the police officer like you had respect for doctors and priests. I mean even those, it's gone a bit. I don't think they are really very interested. I don't know whether it's because they are disillusioned...

IL: What did that mystique involve? What was it...?

Joan: I think they were people that you looked up to. They were people who you felt were responsible people, they upheld the law. You felt that they were people that were, I suppose a bit naïvely, honourable people. And I don't feel that. There are some honourable police officers and women, men and women, as equally there are doctors and priests and vicars. But I think, in general, that the police are racists, I think they are racist. I think that they are very arrogant as a whole. And they feel that they are superior to you, they look down on you, and I don't think they have any right to.

Agnostics

I think we were indifferent. They do a good job, so what. We didn't have any antagonism towards them and we didn't think they were the best thing since sliced bread [male local authority employee, south Manchester].

There were among our interviewees those who did not have a great deal to say about policing—these were often our most difficult and stilted conversations. Such conversations took place with people in whose lives the police do not loom large; those who do not rely heavily upon the affective seductions of policing in the formation of their subjectivities; those who make few explicit connections between policing and the condition of England. We have termed this outlook 'agnosticism'. Agnostics are individuals who have in respect of policing lived a life marked by distant indifference. While this principally middle-class constituency forms part of the audience for policing (this constituency, after all, has few dealings with the police), they are the least interested, attentive, and discontented section of it. They appear to lack any serious, animating complaints and demands. The police, it seems, form little more than a taken-for-granted backdrop to the uneventfulness of everyday life, an institution that only registers on people's radar screens on the rare occasions they are called upon to handle criminal or disorderly events.

Agnostics possess a biographical trajectory marked above all by continuity. Just as the police do not figure prominently in the lived realities and understandings of the present, so they do not loom large in the memory. Some among our respondents—in sharp contrast to the recollections described in Chapter 3—recall a past characterized by the absent bobby: 'as a child I don't remember ever seeing a policeman. I don't. I lived in a village not very far from Warrington. You just never, ever saw a policeman about' (women's organization, south Manchester). Others similarly recall childhoods in which their parents 'didn't come into contact with the police, they went on living their lives' (women's organization, south Manchester); lives in which the police were regarded *from a distance* with what one retired teacher we interviewed called 'gentle reverence'. His parents, he recalled, viewed the police 'with mild respect. If the police wanted to be helped in any way, they would of course be helpful to them. I think they would respect the job they did. They realized that the police were one form of social discipline and had to be respected.' In ways that quietly disturb prevailing white narratives of policing and social change in England since 1945, this local authority employee from south Manchester describes his childhood recollections thus:

Paul: I've actually very few memories, because mainly, as I say, I never had any real contact with the police in those days. I suppose you look back with rose-tinted spectacles, and you've got this image of the bobby cycling around. But when I think about it, I don't know that we actually saw them any more then than we do now. I mean nowadays, the last five or six years, I've had a lot of contact with the police [in his role in the local authority]. I have a certainly better than average understanding of how they work. So now when I go to meetings with the public and they're moaning that they never see a policeman, I often think, 'did I ever actually see one?' I'm not sure. I had no contact with them. I admit I was a goody-goody, I never got into trouble. I never had the need to go to the police as a youngster. The only time I've ever had any real contact with the police was for motoring offences. And I was much older then.

IL: So you don't recall an officer being around that you would see regularly?

Paul: No. I can't recall a *Dixon of Dock Green* who used to lean on the garden fence and talk to my dad. The police were a non-event as far as I was concerned. The police weren't there on occasions we would lark around. But if somebody came out and said, 'if you don't clear off I'll phone the police' then you did, because you didn't want to be in trouble with the police. So I can't honestly remember that once a week, or once a day, the local beat bobby would come wandering around. Certainly, I don't know then that they ever wandered into residential areas, or the back streets of residential areas, any more than they do now.

Agnostics lead lives largely untouched by policing—the aforementioned professional contact and 'motoring offences' notwithstanding. The closest such individuals have come to anything approaching serious unwanted contact with the police was in the course of what one of our interviewees called 'high jinx and things' during their late teens. This respondent—now a solicitor in Manchester—described how he himself had been arrested aged 19—'charged with drunk and disorderly, pissing in the street', and how 'another couple of friends, at about 16, had a few drinks, decided that they were going to go for some cigarettes and took one of their parents' cars, were caught by the police. That was smoothed over. They were both very wealthy lads, and that I think, was basically smoothed over. Their parents went to the police station and just got a ticking off.' But, for the most part, agnostics have had very little contact with either crime or the police, and it is from this vantage point that they apprehend policing: with little expressed interest, with few articulated demands, with little cause for concern.

Certain elements of this disposition can nonetheless be teased out. This is, it should first be said, an outlook that has been permeated by, and is today in part the product of, the detraditionalizing process that has altered public orientations towards social authority in the latter half of the twentieth century. Though the structuring temper is more matter-of-fact than that evident among those we termed the disenchanted, the sentiment is broadly similar—the police, like all social institutions, should no longer treated as infallible and beyond scrutiny:

I think the present society is more questioning. You might respect them but you don't automatically assume that they know more than you. You don't automatically assume any more that they're not capable of making mistakes, because you see almost every week in the press than the police are capable of making mistakes, and they're capable of being incompetent, and they're capable of being corrupt. I'm sure you will have watched that programme about [corruption in] Liverpool police with great interest [male local authority employee, south Manchester].

Yet consider the example this respondent uses to illustrate that he no longer 'automatically assumes that they're right, that they know best': 'If I drive up to a road block and a policeman says, "you can't go down there, you're going to have to go round there", I may say, "why, what's going on?" It's more for information than questioning his right. If a policeman says, "stop, you can't go down this road, you've got to go that way" then I'll do it, because I know the police are not just going to block a road just because they happen to be inconveniencing me.' This intimates, it seems to us, that the sceptical orientation with which he now apprehends the police remains mild, polite, and limited; one that is subordinate to a second element of the agnostic outlook: namely, a passively supportive sympathy for the police. On occasions, this takes the form of a professional-to-professional solidarity of the kind that views the police as 'basically doing their job like me. I would imagine at times it's not an easy job' (male council official, south Manchester). As the aforementioned local authority employee put it, 'we often joke in the town hall that it would be a great job if it wasn't for the public. The police would be a great job if it wasn't for the public, but you've got to recognize the reality of it, it's there to serve the public.' On others, it flows from the sense that the police have a socially important and 'increasingly difficult job', one 'that by and large they still do well' (male retired teacher, Cheshire). They are, as such, for all their revealed shortcomings and rotten apples, an institution towards which decent, law-abiding people ought to retain a 'healthy respect':

I don't have problems with police. They're doing a nasty job in lots of circumstances. You get some of them who are arrogant and seem to forget that they are our police force. They think they are the law. But in general, the majority of police officers do a very nasty job, a job that I wouldn't particularly fancy doing, and they're doing it on our behalf. My view is we should support them. And since they are a cross-section of society, you're going to get your good and bad [male local authority employee, south Manchester].

This orientation is composed, thirdly, of a modest, often self-consciously pragmatic, level of expectation towards the police, an expectation that extends to little beyond the feeling that the police should be providing a competent professional service. This amounts in part to a no-nonsense assessment of what the police can do about crime, and of the reasons for mobilizing them: 'the only time we've ever had problems was when my wife had, my wife went to college one night in the car, and had it broken into and the radio stolen. We reported that to the police, but like most things it's for insurance rather than because we seriously expected them to actually achieve anything' (male local authority employee, south Manchester). But it can also result in large buckets of cold water being poured on what agnostics implicitly view as the feverish, unrealistic demands of their co-citizens:

To put more police on the beat isn't practical in this day and age. You move people around very quickly, like you've got the police helicopter. The cost of sending it up. But you can't have police here, there, and everywhere. You've got the specials. You could probably utilize those a bit more. But to me the police, fire brigade, ambulance, local government, major companies, whatever, they're all organizations, and you've got resources and you try and manage those resources to the best of your ability. But there's a level to what you can go to. I think that people in this day and age are expecting more and more. You can't have it, a bobby on every gate. It's not practical [male council official, south Manchester].

The outlook we have termed agnosticism is a pretty much contented, complacent sensibility, one inclined to be passively sympathetic towards the police and their plight, and to overlook or excuse them their faults: 'It's like society in general, there's bad ones in the police as there is in society in general' (male local authority employee, south Manchester). It is, as such, a conservative worldview, one that implicitly holds there to be little wrong with the world, or little that can be done to better it; one that is rarely roused to anger, still less activity; one that has remained unmoved by, and implicitly immune to, the conflicts and scandals that have eroded police legitimacy since the 1970s. When Colin Sumner referred, some two decades ago, to 'the apparent inability of our culture to panic over anything', he might well have had such agnosticism in mind (Sumner 1981: 282).

Yet in a late modern world marked by a collectively heightened consciousness of crime, one that is supposedly 'lived—not just by offenders but by all of us—in a mode that is more than ever defined by institutions of policing, penality and prevention' (Garland 2001: 194), there remains something gently, if inadvertently, subversive about the agnostic sensibility. It offers, at the very least, a reminder that it is possible to inhabit the world in a manner that does not make the idea of policing central.

The Hopeful

We want to consider, finally, a radically different perspective on policing and the social. Situated in the struggles of social movement politics, this is a disposition shaped by a history of conflict with the police, a history marked by tense, mutual antagonistic relations. It is also, however, an outlook that recalls those relations as having reached something of a nadir in the 1970s and early 1980s. Since then a critical engagement with the police, and re-appraisal of what policing is and might be, has taken place—albeit accompanied by some deep, continuing concerns about contemporary police practice. It is, in this sense, a disposition best characterized as 'hopeful', if guardedly so. We will have cause to consider this cluster of experience, belief, and sentiment further in the next chapter when we examine its manifestation in—at least some—black narratives towards English policing. For now, let us consider its emergence within the politics of sexuality.

We want to do this by exploring—once more—aspects of the biography of one of our respondents with whom we conducted an extended interview. Michael Wilson was born in Liverpool in the mid-1950s. A university graduate, he moved to Manchester in 1978 to work, as an 'out' gay man, for a homosexual rights group. This, for Michael, was the start of an extended involvement in equal opportunities and gay liberation/rights politics in both the voluntary and public sectors. He currently works in that capacity for a local authority. Michael's early memories of the police are not so different from those we encountered among the agnostics. He describes a 'quiet', 'suburban' childhood and adolescence in which 'there was no particular sense of being in danger'. 'I don't remember', he says, 'people particularly being burgled, or experiencing crime, or not being safe.' It was also an environment permeated by quiet support for the police: 'where I grew up, which was a very sort of law-abiding sort of centre, you know, people did sort of respect the police. There was no particular hostility to the police I don't think, looking back.' In Michael's case, at any rate, his personal experience of the police was minimal: 'I had a very quiet adolescence. I wasn't sort of a rebellious student at all. So I had no actual contact with the police at all, not until I left home.'

Leaving home entailed Michael going to university and becoming, in his words, 'much more politicised'. Suddenly, in the midst of the turbulent 1970s, he found himself running up against the police on 'picket lines, things like that, anti-racist demonstrations'. For someone hailing from his background, it came as 'quite a shock':

I think at some level, I sort of believed all those things about the police, you know, the police being there to protect you, you go to the police if you got lost, that sort of thing, and that was a shift. I mean in terms of seeing, I mean particularly on demonstrations and stuff, picket lines, the police were very aggressive, very hostile, arresting people and certain people using police horses and things like that, and it was all quite a shift.

This period of leftist political struggle coincided with Michael 'coming out' as gay in a context he describes as 'very different from now. It's much more common now, it was much more shocking then'. 'There was', as he put it, 'just no discussion or representation of sexuality. Certainly for me, growing up, and I knew I was gay from an early age, it wasn't mentioned at school, on television. There were comments but they were hostile. It was quite sort of repressive really.' Such 'repression' is certainly recalled as marking Michael's experiences of the police at this time. He speaks of operational policing characterized by 'raids on the gay scene'; 'the use of *agents provocateurs* in public toilets'; of a community that simultaneously endured—like all categories of 'police property' (Lee 1981)—over-control and under-protection: 'that was the sort of atmosphere really in terms of police. I think very much perceived as people not to be trusted, not to be approached, and if gay men in particular were victims of sort of attack, they wouldn't call the police.' He recalls, in addition, an atmosphere permeated by the 'very hostile public statements' of a Greater Manchester Police chief constable—James Anderton (1976–91)—who 'refused to meet with any lesbian and gay groups in the city, refused to meet with people.' It was, in short, a period marked by conflict, protest, and an oppositional orientation to the discriminatory operations of police power:

I would have said then, you know, the police were sort of an agent of the state, there was certainly no point in sort of talking to them, or consulting with them, or meeting with them. The nature of the people joining the police force was such that they wouldn't be, it would be a complete waste of time to talk to the police. I spend all my time talking to policemen these days.

This final aside provides a clue to how Michael's experiences of, and outlook towards, the police have shifted in subsequent years, a shift that led him to remark: 'I think if I was like twenty years younger, I think it might actually be quite interesting to think about the possibility of being a police officer.' This shift is in part a reflection—and ingredient—of the altered stances of oppositional politics and the more limited sense of political possibility that pervades the present, one that contrasts markedly with what Michael recalls as his 'real sense', in the 1970s, 'that the world was going to change very quickly around me'. In respect of the latter, Michael spoke of how, in his view, 'certainly in the gay and lesbian community, there's a real lack of young people with any sort of political interest or activism'. In terms of the former, he describes the effects of what he called a 'more individualistic' age on the once more collectivist orientations of social movement—and especially gay and lesbian—politics:

There's very few organizations that have anything more than a sort of civil rights equality perspective in them. The sense, which I had when I came out in the seventies, a sense of, like, more sort of radical sort of fundamental changes to patriarchal capitalism that I sort of grew up on in a way. It's like, you know, nobody knows what you're talking about really. Nobody talks about challenging patriarchal capitalism anymore.

But these shifts also, more specifically, have to do with a re-appraisal of relations between the police and the gay and lesbian community that followed David Wilmot succeeding James Anderton as chief constable upon the latter's retirement in 1991. Michael remembers the moment thus: 'I was very cynical, I remem-ber saying "we'll ask him but he won't turn up" and I was really, really shocked when he arrived at this meeting, and not only arrived at the meeting but made some very public and very positive statements about his commitment to fair and equitable policing. He talked specifically about lesbian and gay officers in the GMP hav-ing the right to come out and not being harassed. And he was clearly very different from Anderton, both personally and in what he was saying.' It is in the aftermath of this moment—and the pos-sibilities it was seen to create—that Michael's outlook altered from that of oppositional critique to one of critical, cautiously hopeful, engagement. He refers in this context to the new modes of dialogue that have come to infuse police relations with the gay and lesbian community in the city: 'I think the police have got the message in a whole range of ways that we actually need to be consulted.' He speaks of the very public commitment the new chief constable made to tackling discrimination inside the force and in policing the gay and lesbian community, something evident in the creation of specialist gay and lesbian liaison officers. And he notes the impact this has had on operational policing, whether in terms of ordering the city centre—'the policing of the gay village has changed quite dramatically'; or dealing with previously contentious issues: 'I think what's changed is operationally there is now a force policy, cer-tainly an informal force policy in terms of cottaging and cruising, which is around not arresting and cautioning people, not using *agents provocateurs*, not using plain-clothes officers, and if there's a problem, talking to ourselves about it.' Michael, in the course of these engagements, has clearly come to acquire a certain respect for an institution he once reviled:

What I never realised, and I think it's true, I think there's a small percentage of police officers who go into the police because they want to make the world a better place. Which I think I would never have said really. There's not very many of them. But I think there are people who are genuinely committed to sort of changing things...I've met quite a lot of police officers up and down the country. And I think there are like a small group of police officers who are actually very supportive and aware and wanting to change the police force from inside really. And I would have said, ten, 15 years ago, I would have denied their existence, really denied it.

Yet for all this Michael remains profoundly concerned about various aspects of the police organization and its outlooks and practices— concerns evident in his view that 'we're quite willing to talk to them but we also reserve the right to campaign against them'. He refers in this regard to the room that notions of 'operational autonomy' allow for 'a large core of middle managers who are sort of very much Andertonian' to circumvent stated force policies, especially in those parts of Greater Manchester where gay and lesbian communities are 'invisible'. As he put it:

I think one of the really difficult issues is in terms of getting any sort of operational consistency. So for example, the 'Bolton Seven' which happened last year, when gay men in Bolton were arrested [for committing consensual sado-masochistic acts in private]. I think there's a long way to go before there's any sort of guarantee of a lesbian or gay getting the same treatment throughout the GMP. It's almost like the GMP are seeming to be saying, 'well, you can expect to get relatively good policing in the city centre, but if you live in Wigan, well, it's going to be different'.

Michael refers further to what he calls 'the huge amount of homophobia', the 'incomprehension and lack of understanding' that, in his view, continue to pervade the police. He speaks of an organization in which officers 'don't feel safe enough to come out' and of the 'incredible hostility' that has confronted the small numbers who have; something, he feels, that contributes to the high levels of mistrust in the police that persist among the gay and lesbian community: 'I think the perception is still of many lesbians and gay men that the police are not supportive and that they wouldn't report crime to the police.' And he continues to encounter a police force that he thinks of as unduly and unhelpfully defensive: 'they're peculiar. I've never known an organization that is so, that gets so hurt so easily. The police are incredibly thin-skinned in a way, you know, they are incredibly defensive about themselves.'

This remains, however, a disposition towards the police that can accurately be termed hopeful. In part, this has to do with an orientation to the past that—in sharp contradistinction to the other sensibilities we have considered in this and the previous chapter—does not understand the trajectory of post-war English policing as a story of loss and decline. What, rather, one encounters in Michael's narrative is a sense of discernible, if uneven, change since the 1980s, change that has, if anything, increased the 'respect' that he evinces towards the police. But one also encounters here a different orientation to the future and the possibilities that may inhere within it. Realizing such possibilities requires, as Michael's own experience attests, organizational resources, political energy, and public engagement in policing debates. This disposition depends nonetheless on the express and implied claim that politics can make a difference; that it is possible to reconfigure state institutions—even those as locked into historical conflicts, and infused with discourses of morality, tradition, and 'Englishness' as the police—in order that they may contribute to a more democratic and inclusive political community. The 'hope', in short, is that the 'best' of English policing is yet to come.

5

Police, 'Race', and Nation

The amount and extent of enthusiastic appreciation of the police is peculiarly English and a most important component of contemporary English character...Increasingly during the past century, the policeman has been for his peers, not only an object of respect, but also a model of the ideal male character, self-controlled, possessing more strength than he ever has to call into use except in the gravest emergency, fair and impartial, serving the abstractions of peace and justice rather than any personal allegiance or sectional interest [Gorer 1955: 314].

The conclusions to be drawn from all the evidence in connection with Stephen Lawrence's racist murder are clear. There is no doubt but that there were fundamental errors. The investigation was marred by a combination of professional incompetence, institutional racism and a failure of leadership by senior officers. A flawed Metropolitan Police Service review failed to expose these inadequacies. The second investigation could not salvage the faults of the first investigation [Macpherson 1999: 317].

We have here two markedly different assessments of policing and—by extension—the condition of England. They stand separated in time by forty-four years. One is written by a journalist, the other by a judge. But, contrary to some expectations at least, it is the journalist who speaks of the police officer as someone 'the nation' can be proud of—a figure with 'character', 'respect', 'self-control', the impartial servant of high ideals. The judge, by contrast, strikes an altogether less exuberant note. He is reporting on the bungled Metropolitan Police investigation into the racist murder of black teenager Stephen Lawrence in April 1993. Lawrence was attacked on the streets of Eltham, south London, by a group of white youths, an attack for which no successful prosecution has to date been mounted. In the estimation of the Macpherson Inquiry, this was due in large measure to a catalogue of police errors, and London's police service was officially proclaimed to have been professionally incompetent and institutionally racist (Macpherson 1999: 317; see, further, Cathcart 1999).

The publication of the Stephen Lawrence Inquiry report in February 1999 provoked a flurry of attention and activity in various quarters. The initial media reports referred excitedly and with a sense of great moment to 'The Legacy of Stephen' (*Daily Mail*, 25 February 1999), describing a report that was going to 'confront racism' (*Guardian*, 25 February 1999) and 'change Britain' (*Daily Mail*, 25 February 1999). *The Times* spoke of a 'campaign to banish racism', while even the *Daily Telegraph*, which was subsequently to spearhead a defensive reaction to Macpherson and all it stood for, captured in its lead headline the spirit of the hour: 'we must change as a nation' (25 February 1999). Change and its rhetorics filled the air. The New Labour government immediately announced an assemblage of action plans, working parties, and targets for combating racism, not merely within the police but in respect of other public sector institutions as well (Home Office 1999*a*; see also Her Majesty's Inspectorate of Constabulary 1999). Senior Metropolitan Police officers took a series of concerted and very public steps to begin clearing up the organization's image (such as the establishment of a lay advisory panel on 'race' issues), while police forces the length and breadth of England were in effect required to digest the Lawrence Inquiry's key recommendations. Even the Police Federation—not an organization noted for being at the forefront of efforts to tackle police racism—felt compelled to embrace what in police-management parlance soon came to be called 'policing diversity'. Overwhelmingly in governmental and professional circles, the talk was of lesson-drawing, of challenges ahead and opportunities to be grasped, of a watershed having been reached. As one chief officer said of Macpherson and its aftermath in an interview with us, 'this is not wasted endeavour, this is real policing, real issues. Get it right, we survive and prosper. Get it wrong, then certainly in the London environment, we're in big trouble five years down the line.'

Yet the Stephen Lawrence affair is far from being the only contemporary instance of the pressure cooker of police–black relations having boiled over or exploded. Nor is the Macpherson Report the only such intervention to have prompted hopeful talk of 'watersheds'—remember Lord Scarman. In fact, ever since the 'race-and-crime' connection was first officially forged in the early

1970s (Hall *et al.* 1978; Gilroy 1987: ch. 3), conflicts between the police and black—especially Afro-Caribbean—communities have come increasingly to the fore; 'the struggle over signs and images' (Gilroy 1987: 109) being variously fought out between the competing codes of crime, disorder, lawlessness, and national decline on the one hand, racism, discrimination, and resistance on the other. The events, locations, and dates that make up the terrain of this struggle—the 1976 Notting Hill Carnival; the killing/ murder of anti-racist demonstrator Blair Peach at Southall in 1979; the thirteen black people killed/murdered in the Deptford fire of 1980; the urban riots/disturbances in St. Paul's (1980), Brixton (1981, 1985), Toxteth (1981, 1985), Handsworth (1981), and Broadwater Farm (1985)—have become as contested as they are commonplace. Inquiries, both official and unofficial, have ensued (Scarman 1974, 1982; National Council for Civil Liberties 1980; Independent Committee of Inquiry 1989); numerous reforms—in consultation and accountability arrangements, to police complaints procedures, in recruitment and training—have been proposed, campaigned for, enacted, or resisted. As English policing came, in the last three decades of the twentieth century to be deeply 'racial-ized', so the motifs of police, 'race', and nation were woven tightly and disputatiously together in public debate and discussion.[1]

Our purpose in this chapter is neither to offer an historical reconstruction of these processes, nor to provide detailed readings of particular conflicts or events. Numerous such accounts can be found elsewhere (Lambert 1970; Humphry 1972; Hall *et al.* 1978; Institute of Race Relations 1978; Keith 1993; Holdaway 1996; Bowling 1999; Marlow and Loveday 2000). Rather, our aim is to deepen and extend our analysis of different clusters of sentiment towards policing by examining the cultural politics of police, 'race', and nation. The chapter has two principal aims. First, we examine how the range of white orientations to the police considered in Chapter 4 respond to the post-war 'racialization' of English policing. In so doing, we consider in particular (in ways that offer a case study of our overarching analytic concern with the intersection between biography, disposition, and events) the reactions of our white respondents to Stephen Lawrence's murder and its sub-sequent officially acknowledged mishandling by the Metropolitan Police. Secondly, we explore the markedly different narratives of change that constitute black and Asian sensibilities towards English policing, and appraise—using the life stories of three of our black respondents—the different senses of social possibility that pervade their memory and outlook. The Lawrence case again looms large here as an illustration of more general processes.

By so advancing our analysis of the police's 'capacity to show the nation to itself' (Gilroy 1987: 74), our purpose is to develop a grounded sociological interpretation of the mutually, if asymmetrically, conditioning relationship that exists between policing and the emergence since the late 1940s of an ethnically diverse, multicultural England. This, in turn, requires us to revisit and in some important respects recast the account of police authority and its post-war transformations delineated in Chapters 3 and 4. What emerges from such revisions, from the insertion into this analysis of the forms and effects of racial identification and categorization, is a more nuanced account of the diversity of lay memories and sensibilities that struggle to determine the contours of English policing culture.

The Lost Nation, A Diluted Force

That England has in the post-war years been transformed by the advent of Commonwealth immigration stands beyond any reasonable doubt. Since the arrival at Tilbury docks on 22 June 1948 of the *Empire Windrush* carrying 430 Jamaican men in search of work, successive phases of immigration from the Caribbean and Indian sub-continent have altered forever the contours and shape of English society, culture, and politics. With 7 per cent of the population now belonging to a visible ethnic minority group, England has in the space of little more than half a century become a plural, ethnically diverse, multicultural nation (Phillips and Phillips 1999). How though has the diversification of what one of our respondents— a middle-class, 56-year-old man living in south Manchester— recalled as 'very much a white Anglo-Saxon country' been received and understood? And how is this process seen as having intersected with questions of policing?

One evident response to the post-war emergence of a multicultural society expresses in various, often coded, ways a sense of bewilderment, regret, and anger at what one might call 'the fall of white England'. That strand of public sentiment—discussed in Chapter 3— oriented to viewing the latter half of the twentieth century as a period of socio-cultural decline here takes a racialized turn; the demise of the English nation now being cast as coincident with the arrival and settlement of black and Asian immigrants. Consider, in this regard, the recollections of this 56-year-old man living in south Manchester:

I think society has changed from the sixties. That was a turning point, when there massive immigration into the country. And the values that people were talking about prior to that change. I mean we're not talking about race, we're talking about culture...I was at college in those days and they just started to appear, as I say, black and brown people, who were bringing them in. And I think also the attitude to violence, and the value of human life. They brought into this country a different attitude to life.

What one finds in this reaction to post-war immigration and its effects is the bringing to bear of some deeply negative emotions on an object—'England'—to which people remain profoundly attached; a process we began to make sense of in Chapter 4 using Tom Nairn's (2000: 103) evocative phrase 'national nihilism'. The particular—racialized—form this conviction takes here is one in which some kind of imagined white 'England' is stood up and measured against the current, ethnically diverse one—a diversity that is taken as both a sign of, and explanation for, the nation's 'fallen state of subjection and impotence' (Nairn 2000: 103). Some in this vein drew an explicit (and for them salient) contrast with the immediate post-war years, a world in which the—now seemingly marginalized and timid—white English voice is recalled as being able to speak proudly and without challenge: 'in those days there was pride. There was pride in ourselves, and there was pride in our country. It's not allowed now. The indigenous populations do not have a voice...We're not allowed to speak. You won't hear the indigenous population speaking about how they feel about things. For example on the radio. It's not allowed, that's the way it is. I'd better not say any more' (male, sheltered accommodation residents, south Manchester). Others—such as a group of south Manchester tenants—viewed the English nation's achievements and qualities as having contributed to its post-war 'downfall'; the passing of an 'England' that can, from this standpoint, only ever be white bringing with it a highly charged, uneasy confluence of pride and shame:

Joan: If you go to Manchester any time of the day you wouldn't know you was in England, because there's that many blacks, and that

many Chinese, that you don't know you're in England. They all
want to come here. Why?

IL: Why do you think that is? What do they like about it?

Joan: Because you've got a good health service. You've got free prescriptions.
As soon as they get off the plane they come here...

Steve: And get a handout.

Pam: And they go straight to the social and get a handout.

Steve: You know these asylum seekers. They get off the plane, say at
Manchester Airport, or Heathrow Airport, and as soon as they get
off somebody is there to meet them and say 'go to the social, tell
them you're an asylum seeker'. The first thing you get is 'I want
£168 a week'.

IL: Do you think the things that attract people to want to come and
live here are the same things that you think make this a good place
to live?

Joan: Well I've always thought it was a good place to live. To me, we've
got a Queen, we've got a good royal family. Charlie [Prince
Charles], well I wouldn't put him out if he was on fire. But that's
only my opinion. I love this country, and I think people come to live
here because, as we've just said, got a good health service. We're
struggling with that, I know that. And you can go on the dole. You
can get money without working.

Pam: I think it's one of the best countries to live in.

This imagery of the lost nation is closely entwined with the cultural
sensibility towards the police that in the last chapter we termed
'defenders of the faith', an outlook that considers the current
apparently enfeebled state of that institution to be a telling indicator of the contemporary national condition. The revision to this
sensibility that takes place here involves a racialized reworking of
the themes that organized our discussion in Chapters 3 and 4: the
eclipse of the English bobby and the fracturing of police authority.
In respect of the former, an association is forged between the fondly
remembered, locally embedded police officer and an era in which
England was white and Englishness less complicated and contested.
In terms of the latter, the questioning of police authority and the
apparent distancing of the police from what are regarded as their
'proper' concerns and constituency are viewed as consequences of
the demands and conflicts that have attended police relations with
ethnic minority—and especially black—communities.

These today constitute residual, largely oppositional, cultural
forms (Williams 1977: 121–8). They are elements of a structure of
feeling that is out of sorts with the late modern world, that lacks

significant vehicles for cultural and political expression, and which has fallen from favour, or at least become more muted, in senior police and governmental circles (we found such sentiments for the most part confined to some of the white citizens and rank-and-file police officers among our respondents). Yet this reservoir of often bitterly felt frustration and resentment retains a presence in contemporary public deliberation, and remains capable of political articulation and mobilization, of being worked into some kind of coherent ideology. Let us, with this in mind, examine further the contours, appeal, and forms of this *Weltanschauung*, considering, in particular, how its adherents respond to the questions thrown up by one recent challenge to its basic tenets—the Stephen Lawrence affair.

We begin with the question of stop and search. This practice has since at least the late 1970s been the subject of fierce public controversy, research and official data both having fairly consistently shown that young male blacks and—lately—Asians are disproportionately subjected to police stop-and-search powers (Willis 1983; Kinsey 1985; Home Office 1999*b*; Fitzgerald 2000). This much was readily acknowledged by some of the senior officers we spoke to, albeit that police discourse often continues to defend stop and search by reference to the disputedly higher involvement of blacks in street crime (see, further, Sim 1982; Lea and Young 1984: ch. 4; Gilroy 1987: ch. 3; Smith 1997). Some two decades after the issue was recognized as the principal immediate cause of the 1981 Brixton riots (Scarman 1982), it continues to serve as a litmus test of the condition of police–ethnic minority relations. For some among our white respondents, however, that fact represents an unjustified calling into question of what they plainly regard as an important, long-established, and once taken-as-read aspect of police work:

Gill: My father was in the army, he used to go out all hours of the day and night, he was stopped and searched at two and three o'clock in the morning many a time by the police...So that has been going on for years, it is not just something that has just happened recently, just started pulling blacks, whites, or anybody. That has always gone on.

Tom: I remember going to nightclubs, and they used to have an all-night bus and we used to miss that and you used to have to walk home. Used to walk and see a constable probably, who'd say, 'come here lad, where have you been, not carrying any weapons or anything like that?' But you would accept that as a norm, would accept it as a norm,' 'cause you had nothing on you anyway [tenants' association, north Manchester].

This felt contrast between a memory of consensual policing and current troubles and disputes is marked, and surfaced often in the context of debates about the impact of 'race' upon policing. One male member of our discussion group with insurance company employees made the connection explicit: 'stop and search and the colour issue. That wouldn't have happened forty years ago. Never even thought about that. If we got stopped you accepted it as part and parcel of life—you're in the wrong place at the wrong time— you wouldn't complain about it'. Against this backdrop, what is considered as black—or 'race relations industry'—lobbying around the issue occasioned particular consternation; it having apparently given rise to undue hesitancy on the part of the police in their dealings with black people (something a number of the serving officers we interviewed claimed they now felt), and contributed to a situation in which ethnic minorities are seen as making some unwarranted claims about police attention:

But you hear these guys though, these young kids—'You can't touch me because I'm black. You are only doing this to me because I'm black, you are only pulling me in because I'm black'. And they are playing on it. But a white person couldn't say 'You are only doing it because I'm white' [female, tenants' association, north Manchester].

These responses towards stop and search form part of a disposition imbued with a zero-sum conception of the racialization of English policing ('their' gains must signal 'our' losses) and eager to lay the blame for the troubles that currently afflict the police at the door of 'race'. Two particular forms of this surfaced in our discussions. It is embedded first in the idea that 'political correctness' has inhibited the police from undertaking their 'proper' task (robust law enforcement), and thereby contributed what was often felt—as we saw in Chapter 4—to be poor performance. Hence this 53-year-old male self-defence instructor's response to the suggestion that the ethnic and gender composition of the police should reflect that found within contemporary English society: 'no. They should enforce the law. Absolutely unequivocally. Absolutely, without any form of feeling of malice or whatever, they should simply enforce the law. Because if you go to live in a country you must abide by their laws. And if you don't you should be very severely punished.' Hence also this simultaneously deferential and defiant assessment of the then Greater Manchester Police (GMP) chief constable,

David Wilmot's admission—during the course of the Macpherson inquiry—that his force was 'institutionally racist':

Jim: He may be right. I don't know that he isn't. I also don't know that he is. If there's one thing I've learned, I would say he's the man who should know, he's a chief police officer. We have to accept what he says. I think that what happened over Stephen Lawrence was an absolute bloody disgrace. But the Manchester City Police Force weren't directly involved with that investigation. I also think though that the cynical side of me perhaps says 'yes, but is he jumping on the bandwagon here, is he trying to make some kind of politically correct point', because in my opinion the chief police officer of Manchester has been a bloody abject failure.

AM: Why do you say that?

Jim: Because you get crime. Violence in Manchester is on the increase. We know there are certain areas of Manchester that are no-go areas still, no matter what the senior police officers say...Lots of people are looking back to the days of [former chief constable, James] Anderton and saying 'he wouldn't have had any messing about'. People have begun looking for a strong chief police officer. To many people today, Wilmot is being looked upon, rightly or wrongly, but Wilmot is being looked upon as some kind of, the softer side of policing, and people are wanting something which is exactly in the opposite direction. Something on the lines of the Geordie police officer, senior police officer, who brought in zero-tolerance. I've forgotten his name [Ray Mallon]. I think he was suspended for an inquiry or something. People are asking for that kind of policing. They're not going to get it from Wilmot [53-year-old male self-defence instructor, south Manchester].

It surfaces, secondly, in a tendency to attribute the police's perceived failings and misplaced priorities to the undue pressures brought to bear upon them by judges, politicians, liberal elites, and, of especial importance in this context, the 'race relations industry' (a pejorative coinage that almost always functions in English public discourse as code for opposition to organized forms of anti-racism). By such means is an assessment of poor performance squared with the idea that the police are knowledgeable, socially valuable, and still capable of representing all that is best about 'England':

Joe: The police don't want these policies, they are being forced to by the government. The police want to treat everybody as equal, if they get a black kid in their police station, they want to treat me or a black kid as an equal. But they are not being allowed to, they must treat them black kids more carefully than a white kid. So the police are not allowed to be equal you know because they don't want letters going to the government, and the government would get on their back and they don't want to mess their careers up. But they might want to be fair to people all the time but they are not being allowed to. The police know what's going on and I tell you, if we got enough police and trained them properly, I think we have the best police force in the world actually in this country but just not enough of them…

IL: Do the police retain your respect then?

Joe: I mean I wouldn't do the job any way, I wouldn't do it for a gold pot. The British bobby is the best bobby in the world, they really are. It is just about being allowed to be better than he could if he was allowed to do so. I think so anyway [male, tenants' association, south Manchester]

Saving 'our' Police from Macpherson

How though does this particular articulation of the relationship between the police and the English nation stand up to the questions posed by the racist murder of Stephen Lawrence and the errors that led to the Metropolitan Police being *officially*—and unprecendently— cast as professionally incompetent and institutionally racist (Macpherson 1999).[2] There are plausible reasons to hold that this outlook finds in the Lawrence case and its aftermath a stiff and disquieting challenge—one that in many respects exceeds the shock to the received image of the English police thrown up by either recently acknowledged miscarriages of justice (the Guildford four, the Birmingham six, etc.), or—to draw a more clearly racialized comparison—the urban disorders of the 1980s. The Lawrence case presents not 'unruly' blacks engaged in mindless, unwarrantable violence, but a 'respectable', university-bound teenager set upon by a group of white racists; it permits no imagery of the 'thin blue line' bravely holding chaos at bay; only officially acknowledged police prejudice and failing; and that very acknowledgement has served to close off what has long for pro-police opinion been an established apologia and escape route at moments of 'crisis'—pin it on a few 'bad apples'.

Yet, in the face of this unwelcome knowledge, forms of what Stan Cohen (2001: 8–10) calls 'interpretive' and 'implicatory' denial' can still be found to preserve intact a received, benign image of the English police and of the malign forces that apparently confront it—a clear case of a deeply established cultural sensibility operating to subsume and nullify the impact of a potentially unsettling event. The organizing impulse here remains the idea of 'our police' having been hijacked, or at least knocked off their proper course, by social forces and movements that the Lawrence affair has served merely to fuel and encourage. Sometimes this sentiment is voiced with considerable anger and resentment:

The police have got their priorities wrong now haven't they? If it's me, they don't mind pulling me, a white person, you're easy. They can have you and there is nothing you can do about it. But I was at my mother's on Thursday and it was Stephen Lawrence's anniversary and if there wasn't thirty coppers protecting that one flag in the pavement, there was something wrong. There was police cars, motorcycles, coppers everywhere, but what was the justification, it is only a flagstone. I know it is like a memorial but they wouldn't do it for me, but this guy, one person. The police had a bit of a cock-up. But they can't do anything the police up there now, somebody shouts racism, jumps on the bandwagon. So the police have got all their priorities wrong now, it should be one law for everybody, not oh he is black leave him alone. It shouldn't work like that...

...The Lawrence thing. Ninety-nine per cent of white people it puts their backs up, to see a bobby guarding a piece of pavement for twenty-four hours in the street. Okay the boy got killed. But the way they went about it, you know, because the guy was a black kid, so much attention. It got 99 per cent of this country's backs up, because they wouldn't have done that if it was a white kid. Do you know what I mean? [male, tenants' association, south Manchester].

On other occasions it takes a more 'polite' form and follows an explicit, if grudging, somewhat casual, recognition that something has gone tragically wrong:

Joan: I shouldn't say it, but the ethnic groups are getting the upper hand in my estimation. It was terrible what happened to that black boy, but I think they've put the police in such a position now that to go to a dark boy now, they're going to be in trouble.
Norris: That's right.
Joan: That's my estimation.
Norris: I agree.
Joan: They've really put them [the police] down.
Norris: I agree with that.
Joan: They've definitely put them down [sheltered accommodation residents, south Manchester].

These extracts adopt—notwithstanding the difference of tone—the same structural form. It is not that this strand of white social memory and feeling resorts to what Cohen (2001: 8) calls 'literal denial' of a reality in which things have gone badly awry. There is clearly— in the curtly expressed references to racist violence or police mishandling—some acknowledgement that they did.[3] This is immediately followed, however, by a significant qualifying *but* whose express purpose is to confine and delimit the consequences of that recognition, and return to credibility the highly valued institution that events surrounding the Lawrence case have called sharply into doubt. What generally follows is one of two things. First, some kind of reference to the apparent inability or unwillingness of the police to take adequate steps to tackle black crime, or to the disproportionate attention that is now devoted to black victims. As one retired man from south Manchester put it, drawing what he saw as an important, neglected contrast with the 1980s riots, 'they're not allowed to do their job now, they're really not. They've got to be so careful who they apprehend, in the light of the Lawrence case and various other things. At the same time those policemen may recall an occasion, fifteen, twenty years ago, when one of their number, a certain PC Blakelock was hacked to death in Tottenham. And to the best of my knowledge no one...' There ensues, secondly, some sort of plea to the effect that things have gone far enough, that the acceptable limits of criticism have been (b)reached, that the police bashing ought now properly to stop so they can 'get on' with their job. There is, as one retired senior civil servant put it, 'a feeling that the police have been kicked around too much in the wake of the Stephen Lawrence affair. Give them a bit of a rest.'[4]

The idea of the police as exemplars and upholders of all that is best about the (white) English nation is by this assemblage of devices 'saved' from the Stephen Lawrence Inquiry's intended fall-out. Such devices have in common the mobilization of what one might call a *hierarchy of tragedy*. By this we mean that the Lawrence case is accepted precisely as such (as a tragic, unfortunate, regrettable event), only to be trumped by what would represent a bigger tragedy—that his death is blown out of proportion in such a way as to diminish the police's reputation and inhibit them from doing their job. The Lawrence case is thereby mediated through some powerfully embedded cultural sentiments about policing and 'Englishness' in ways that enable an emotionally compelling *police force of the imagination*—one doing a vital job, that most people don't care to take on, that the nation *can* still justly be proud of—to emerge unscathed from events. When all is said and done the existing order of things can remain undisturbed:

AM: You mentioned earlier the Stephen Lawrence case. What impact nationally does that have on the public's views of police? Do you think it will have a negative impact on people's views?

Mary: It won't on mine.

Sylvia: As far as those particular men. But the rest of them, you've got to have confidence in them.

Mary: You've got to have confidence in the police. Hearing that story wouldn't generally affect my view. Some try very hard [women's organization, south Manchester].

What one encounters in these reactions to the Lawrence case is a practical manifestation, or putting to use, of a structure of feeling that freezes both police and nation in imagined historical time, and thus in effect outside of time; one that comes close—in its idealized 'rejection of actual knowledge of loved ones'—to what Scheff (1994: 279) calls 'infatuation'. It is an backward-glancing, past-orientated sensibility that sees in the police (or to be more precise, a particular 'pre-vision' of the police and its intimate connection the 'white England') a kind of 'primal shelter' (Bauman 2000: 214); a secure, emotionally alluring foothold in a world its adherents otherwise feel cast adrift from (cf. Young 1999). This, as we have seen, involves a deep commitment to a set of values (order, discipline, social and ethnic uniformity) recalled from the immediate post-war past, coupled with resistance to the idea that the once settled nexus between police and nation has been disrupted, that policing and its meanings have come to be contested by other, black- and Asian-British, constituencies. It is, as such, a form of white subjectivity deeply inimical to, indeed it seeks to efface, many of the claims for recognition and resources that today attend the policing of a multicultural England. Residual and waning this identity may be but it remains a current of contemporary culture that still has to be reckoned with.

Of Course the Police are Racist, Everyone's Racist: Contextualization, Decontextualization, and Naturalization in Accounts of Police Racism

These dispositions towards police, 'race', and nation are by no means the only alignment of such terms discernible from our enquiry; nor do they exhaust the cultural sensibilities deployed to make sense of, and respond to, the issues generated by the Lawrence affair. We also encountered outlooks that appear less eager to skate over the grief and grievances occasioned by Stephen Lawrence's murder, and more willing to countenance—even propose—that *police racism* contributed manifestly to the mishandling of the subsequent investigations. These dispositions, however, take different forms, have different orientations (or non-orientations) to the past, and project divergent visions of how the connections between police, racism, and the social are presently established or may plausibly be loosened or undone. Some sense of this is neatly provided by the following exchange:

Sue: I was horrified when I saw the programme about Stephen Lawrence. It kept me awake. It was just appalling. And it was of course the police who were at fault to a large extent. I mean the awfulness of a boy being murdered just because he was standing at a bus stop and he was black, that's bad enough. But then the fact that the perpetrators got away with it. The police acted in racial way.

Pat: Well the police are a cross-section of society, and I suppose they reflect that kind of thing. To change someone's attitude, you've got to do it within yourself.

Ann: We're not going to get any group perfect, are you?

Pat: Afro-Caribbeans and the people from the Indian sub-continent and the Chinese don't actually get on. You've got it everywhere. It happens, and we are racist, unfortunately, whether we like it or not.

Ann: We're not as racist as they are amongst themselves [women's organization, Manchester].

A number of common cultural orthodoxies towards (police) racism are displayed in this account. Such ways of thinking and feeling appear widespread in both professional police discourse and public sensibilities, and we want in this section to document and consider three of them—those we term *contextualization, decontextualization*, and *naturalization*. What categories of perception and apprehension are brought to bear on police racism within these competing discourses? What economies of blame and chains of accountability are mobilized within each of them? Let us turn to these questions.

Discourses of *contextualization* seek to pinpoint—or actively forge—a connection between police racism and that present in either other social institutions or what is loosely termed 'wider society'. Such moves are, however, notably double-edged, performed with divergent ends in sight. For some, contextualization means acknowledging police racism precisely in order that it may be addressed, while also emphasizing that the police is but one among a number of British institutions whose practices are permeated by, and constitutive of, racialized relations. This is plainly the logic underpinning the Stephen Lawrence Inquiry report: the police have a problem and must do more, but let us not forget that racism is a social, not merely a police, issue. It is also arguably the spirit underpinning David Wilmot's aforementioned observation—the first such public statement by a serving English chief constable—that Greater Manchester Police was 'institutionally racist'.[5] This much at least was the opinion of one of our interviewees, a supportive witness to this little piece of police history-making:

What the chief said was that 'if we accept that there's an institutional racism in society and that we recruit from that society, then I must accept that there's institutional racism within my force'. And I thought that was the basic truth and why deny it...Under the circumstances it was the right thing to say because how can you sit there and say 'no there's no racism within my force' and lo and behold only last week we've now got two suspended [male superintendent, GMP].

Such contextualizations of police racism seem intended today to function as prompts to concerted remedial action; often coinciding in our discussions with the claim that the police 'having been hammered on this one' are 'learning pretty rapidly' about questions of discrimination (retired chief constable, provincial force); or that they were forging ahead of other public institutions in their efforts to address them: 'interestingly enough, the Bishop of Stepney, who was on the Macpherson committee, said the police service, not only is it less racist than many organizations, it's streets ahead of any other organization he knows in dealing with these issues, that it's a beacon leading the way for society' (chief constable, metropolitan force). Yet these same connections can also operate—within both police discourse and public sentiment—in a more defensive, complacent register; one that decentres *police* racism so as to mitigate the consequences of its very acknowledgement. One variant of *this* mode of contextualization—such as that expressed by one north Manchester woman—involves reacting to official claims about police racism by pointing out that racist behaviour and practices are common across institutions, of which the police are but one: 'I think it's true. Let's face it, any organization you'll get it, not just the police, any organization'. It is a claim that rests on what has become a trope about the police 'reflecting' society, one that is sometimes buttressed with the further apologia that there are features of that society all too liable to generate prejudice among officers:

I think there are racists, because the police are a cross-section of the public at large, and amongst the public at large there are people who dislike coloured people, for one reason or another. Sometimes you might think they have justification, because in Moss Side particularly, they've got a drug problem, and they have drug barons. Most of the people who are making huge profits from this turned out to be coloured people. And they have gun battles, and they kill each other, shoot each other, in the street. People who are involved, are in the main, coloured people. If you were to sort of say that the police who are dealing with that have a prejudice, it's perhaps well-founded [male, tenants' association, inner-city Manchester].

What these lay interpretations of the police–society interface display is what one might term an 'infection theory of police racism'—it is something the police 'catch' either by means of 'impurities' entering via the recruiting process, or through the daily exposure of officers to prejudice-inducing people and events. Variants of this 'theory' have in recent decades been a common feature of much police discourse, serving, from an organizational perspective, to 'explain' the continued, stubborn presence of racist officers in police ranks. At times this has taken on a stridently defensive tone. More recently, as with the remarks of this shire county chief constable, it assumes the air of baffled resignation:

The recruiting process is reasonably good. It's quite selective. We put people through training. Not enough training maybe, but not bad training. And yet still there is a succession of officers that come through, and I suppose it's inevitable, who then are uncivil and abusive, assault people on occasion, and are racist in their behaviour and attitude. And that's a constant disappointment. And I suppose it will ever be thus, because you're never going to be able to recruit over 100,000 people and run a service in a sort of society that we've got, where everybody is going to behave impeccably.

These well-meaning frustrations are clearly understandable, the sentiments, at one level, banally true. Yet that is not what is at stake here. What matters for present purposes about this mode of thought is not merely its rhetorical structure and frequency of mobilization (as Stuart Hall (1980*b*) once acerbically remarked, it is hard to imagine such comments ever so readily being made about a proportion of *criminals* from wider society 'inevitably' ending up in the police), but also its implicit take on the police relationship to the social. The 'police-as-mirror' metaphor is one that necessarily sets the police apart from 'society', the latter being posited as a (reified) entity destined only to impact upon the former and stand impossibly in the way of meaningful police reform. There is no sense here of the police as a constituent and active shaper of English culture and society, an agent playing a local but significant part in the production and reproduction of its racialized social relations. It is a failure to grasp this that renders these comforting lay and professional tropes about policing and the social ultimately so inadequate as a means of apprehending police racism.

There is, furthermore, a tendency in such discourse to *decontextualize* police racism, to wrench it from its institutional settings and relocate it in the heads and actions of discrete individual officers. This too has become an established strand of police discourse on these issues, one that surfaced particularly in our discussions in the reaction of rank and file officers to the aforementioned proclamations—issued in the wake of the Lawrence case—concerning *institutional* racism. This is not to say that such officers did not display pronounced 'abhorrence' at the murder of Stephen Lawrence and the police mishandling of it, albeit that their ire was stoked as much by incompetence ('a superintendent who stands up and doesn't know his powers of arrest? What a dickhead', one Greater Manchester superintendent exclaimed) as by racism: 'I think that was absolutely disgraceful. The fact that anybody's colour should influence a police officer's approach to the job is terrible. They are a client and entitled to your best efforts' (retired superintendent, Cheshire Police (CP)). Officers nonetheless recoiled from the lessons Macpherson and—especially—Wilmot had very publicly drawn from it ('upset', 'blazing', and 'sick as a parrot' were among many such epithets used to describe the latter's remarks). Some here explained away Wilmot's actions as those of a police politician, 'currying favour with the Home Office' (male sergeant, GMP). Others saw him as having committed what they regarded as a chief constable's cardinal sin, criticizing his officers in public: 'that man sold us down the river. He has not stood by us, not backed up his men. He said we're a lot of racists, that is basically what you lot are' (male inspector, GMP). Yet what seemed above all else to anger and bewilder our police respondents was the coupling of the terms *institution* and *racism*. Two aspects of such bewilderment are relevant here, both of which indicate how entrenched a decontextualizing mode of thought and feeling is within contemporary police sensibilities. One aspect of this was the personal affront many felt in the face of what they regarded as the suggestion that *all* officers are racist, that institutional racism was about *us*, the *individuals* who comprise the force. Some took exception to this on the grounds that it ignored their own 'colour-blind' concern to 'always try to treat people as human beings' (male sergeant, GMP), to the fact that their prejudices extended only to 'criminals, no matter what colour, nationality, or creed' (retired male sergeant, GMP). Others felt Wilmot's remarks glossed over what they considered to be decent non-racist credentials:

Society's reflected in the police, so you're going to have racialist police officers, but to say the whole structure is institutionalized racialism is a different ball game. I'm one of those officers that's very upset about it. My sister's married a coloured chap, and my niece... she's what would be termed a half-caste, a mixed-race girl. I've got nothing to be racist about, it doesn't bother me. I worked with them in Moss Side. I might have been a bit hard with those who were breaking the law, but I delivered more than one child to a coloured West Indian lady. There's a little David wandering Moss Side. This was probably in the sixties, he's probably nearly thirty now [male chief superintendent, GMP].

The flipside of this reaction concerns the ways in which the term institutionalized racism unsettles the received and powerfully felt view that police racism is about *them*, confined to a small number of prejudiced officers—the legendary 'bad apples'—who can and should be identified and dealt with. As one Manchester Police inspector put it, 'in today's multicultural society, a racist bobby is going to stick out like a sore thumb'. For some officers—such as this male inspector—Wilmot's remarks had not only muddied a

situation he took to be relatively straightforward—'you are either
a racist or you're not a racist and I don't see myself as being a
racist'—they also risked alienating public support for the police
and diverting attention away from the most obvious means of
redeeming it:

> They [the public] are actually questioning now whether we are all racists
> and fascists and I think that we've all got to really work very hard to
> recover the situation...I'm sure that they will recover it. They're going to
> have to make examples of people who are found to have done racist issues
> and nobody would...I don't think anybody would dispute that they
> shouldn't be dealt with quite vigorously and, if they need to be, sacked.
> They should be sacked and they should be out of the job.

There are various, divergent vocabularies of motive at play here,
some plainly reactionary, others sincerely baffled. They share, however, a conception of racism as something capable of manifesting
itself only in the overt, observable actions of individuals (something
our enquiry has shown to have become a less pronounced feature
of England's racialized social relations); and a decontextualizing
impulse unable to comprehend how discrimination can be located
in the police organization anywhere other than in the minds and
behaviour of individual officers. Institutions on this—reductionist—
view *are* constituted by the actions of their individual members
alone, they are marked by no other processes through which racist
subordination may occur, possess no other means by which to
think and act (cf. Douglas 1987). It is this outlook, above all, that
determines how officers respond to the admission into the official
police lexicon of the term 'institutional racism', a phrase that for
them can only shockingly mean that all are at fault, all potentially
under the spotlight. As one police inspector grumpily and revealingly put it, 'an institutionalized racist *I'm* not'.

This brings us finally, and briefly, to the third means of characterizing (police) racism that can be identified from this section's
opening exchange. It is an outlook that, again, acknowledges the
realities of police racism and, again, sets out to locate them on a
larger canvas. But it does so, this time, in order to subsume such
racism within a wider frame held to be either a universal feature of
human affairs or some hard-wired component of human nature.
Antipathy towards the Other is, on this view, a deeply embedded
social fact, something that exists—as one of our female inner-city
respondents put it—'in every culture'. It should thus come as no

surprise that these widespread cultural sentiments are found within the police:

AM: A couple of months ago, the chief constable, Wilmot, said the police, like other institutions, suffered from institutionalized racism.

Barbara: Very much so, yes.

AM: Was that a sentiment you agreed with?

Barbara: Yes, yes. You'd be a liar saying that you didn't have some form of prejudice. I've always had black friends, and Asian friends, but we've all got some prejudices, I don't care what they say.

Doreen: Do you mean against the police?

AM: Well actually the police prejudice against the community.

Barbara: They're bound to, they're human beings, they're bound to have people around who are prejudiced.

AM: This wasn't a surprise when Wilmot said this?

Barbara: Not at all. Everybody has some form of racism, whether they don't like…It's like my mother. She used to say to me 'that all Welsh people were sly'. Oh Welsh people are sly, because my mother said it. So that was a form of racism, in a way. We all have some things that we don't like. The police are just like any other person, there is a lot of racism [tenants' association, inner-city Manchester].

These *naturalizing* dispositions can of course be mobilized with different purposes in mind. On occasions, as in the above discussion, they are proffered with a certain anti-racist intent and an attendant quotient of sorrow. On others, they are deployed as defensive claims, coded attempts to explain 'our' racism by reference to that of others, a justificatory purpose that clearly animated this police constable's account of one of his colleagues: 'the most racist officer I have worked with was Asian. He was so bigoted it was unbelievable. His family came from Africa. He absolutely detested blacks. Not Asians. I'm talking about blacks. Really, really bad.' Yet such differences are, in important respects, immaterial. What all these modes of naturalization do is acknowledge shortcomings, prejudice, and discrimination in the police, only to deny that much else can be expected. It is an outlook that freezes racism outside history, one whose depiction of it as an omnipresent and unchanging cultural form has the inevitable effect—to reach for a now little-used phrase—of unbending the springs of action. For all that this outlook readily concedes—and often deeply regrets—the reality of police malpractice of the kind that occurred in the Lawrence case, these concerns are expressed within a style of thought and feeling that cannot but view the attempt to reconfigure the relationship between police, 'race', and nation as at best futile, at worst counter-productive—a doomed-to-failure meddling not so much in the national, as in the natural order of things.

Racism, Public Trust, and Police Authority: Whither the 'Silent Majority'

In order to legitimise the use of troops or armed police on the streets of Brixton or Belfast it was necessary to actively *construct* a silent majority who would support such measures as a necessary defence of the British way of life. The danger was that this majority might not remain silent, might even begin to voice other and less welcome demands, centred on some residual notion of civil liberties and the British sense of fair play— demands which, however limited, would certainly impose constraints on any policy of organised repression [Cohen 1988: 39, emphasis in original].

One central feature of the escalating conflict between the police and sections of the black community throughout the 1970s and early 1980s was the police's belief that they could depend upon the support of the white middle-classes—that section of the English populace police spokespeople used fondly to refer to as the 'silent majority' (a constituency that has since—in journalistic parlance at least—transmogrified into 'middle England'). Opinion polls showed high approval ratings for the police (Belson 1975: 7); police officers appeared poorly paid and increasingly embattled; it seemed relatively easy—at moments of social crisis—for the police to portray themselves as heroic defenders of an English way of life under threat from Irish terrorists, militant strikers, or black rioters. For all that they came to be embroiled in social conflict and increasingly politicized (Reiner 1980), the police's stock appeared—where it mattered, among governing elites and 'respectable opinion'—to remain high. In particular, such opinion could be called upon to lend support to, even demand, efforts to crackdown on 'black crime' (Hall *et al.* 1978: ch. 6). This at least is how one former head of the Home Office police department recalls it:

There were the inner-city riots in Bristol and Brixton and Toxteth and so on. And these I think rather polarized opinion and obviously those who were taking part in the riots were very hostile towards the police. Others saw the police as defending them against the rioters, again possibly not always doing enough. So I think this led to a sort of polarization...There's the basic question that no-one can ever really resolve. Is it that more black youths commit criminal offences, or is it that the police pick on black youths? This was again a major influence in the attitude of the black community to the police, particularly young men who felt, with some justification I think, that they were being picked on. Statistically the numbers who got arrested were very high, and this meant there was animosity between them and the police. But there was also, among the white population, a feeling that the blacks deserved it and the police ought to do more about it.

It is, too, the memory of this next police officer, now a superintendent in Greater Manchester Police:

Early on, there was no doubt there was great hostility to ethnic minorities coming into this country, but that was generally shared by the public at large. They weren't embraced. As long as they were kept in their place, kept in certain areas where even what you might call low-life whites didn't go, and they kept to certain occupations that we didn't want, and they didn't challenge our society—that was as far as the tolerance went. I think there was an expectation of the police that we would give them lots of stick and harassment. If they were brought in, they were to be treated differently from anybody else. When I look back at that, I cringe with embarrassment.

Today, as we documented in our discussion of 'the disenchanted' in Chapter 4, elements among the so-called 'silent majority' have lost some of their unequivocal identification with the police, and become increasingly willing to accept claims about police malpractice that might a couple of decades ago have been dismissed as hailing from the criminal or civil libertarian margins of English public life. This, we argued, is due in part to processes of detraditionalization that have loosened the grip that unquestioned social—and police—authority once held over public sentiment; a process one retired civil servant we interviewed interpreted as 'the emergence of a much more developed sense of tolerable citizenship in our society; you could say that more people have a sense of citizen identity'. Such 'loosening' has been further conditioned, however, by a number of high-profile police scandals of recent decades (notably, the miners' strike and officially acknowledged miscarriages of justice); one of whose effects has been to call into doubt the received, benign image of the English police that for much of the post-war period figured prominently in the middle-class imagination.

Included among such scandals have been a series of concerns and conflicts around 'race', of which the Stephen Lawrence case is but the latest—if, for the disenchanted, the most compelling—instance. Some of the cumulative, de-legitimating effects of this confluence of events and processes are neatly illustrated in the following exchange:

AM: How do you think the general public's attitudes towards the police have changed over the course of your lives? I mean, how did adults, when you were growing up, view the police? How do you as adults, now, view the police? Is there a difference in attitude?

Jack: We used to respect the policeman, you know what he said, that it was his word and it was true. People, because of what's gone on in the past, people don't respect them…

Fiona: The way they deal with sort of bad cases that get a lot of publicity, like the Stephen Lawrence thing. I think it's the sort of thing that really, it gives them that image which is so difficult to recover from. Because most people now, probably would say the police were racist or there is a high level of racism within the police. Even if they'd no real knowledge of it, it would be their perception from a high level case like that. And from all the evidence you have seen, you've got to think well … [insurance company employees, Manchester].

These movements of opinion, this calling into question of the police around 'race', can take a number of shapes, influenced to greater or lesser degrees by biographical experience. A notable account of the former arose from the story of one middle-aged, middle-class woman we interviewed. Born and raised in a small Derbyshire village, she went on, in 1958, to marry an Asian man she had met three years earlier at Manchester University. They are, to all intents and purposes, affluent and 'well-to-do'; he a successful businessman, she a former magistrate. Yet her once well-disposed outlook towards the police (she recalls offering cups of tea to the local 'bobby' while at university) has been transformed by the experiences of both her husband and children. She recounted one such incident thus:

I remember when, obviously my three children are coloured, and we lived [in Cheshire], in quite a big house. One day I was in the garden and Asif ran out of the gate, he was about 4, 5. He'd run out of the gate and was just playing outside the gate, the neighbours all knew him, he was safe and I was in the garden anyway. I saw a police car stop. The policeman spoke to him and he said, no he'd be about 6 or 7, he said 'where do you live?'. Asif said, 'I live here'. He said, 'now come along, tell me where you live and what are you doing here?', like he shouldn't be here. Whilst all that was going on I stood there and let it go on for a bit. I challenged him. I said, 'did you think he doesn't live here because he is coloured and a coloured person couldn't live in a house like this? Is that what your impression is?'

This kind of access to a different world, to a different order of experience, had some profound effects on the outlooks of this woman: 'I suppose I had the attitude when I was in this village of being quite respectful towards the police. When I found out what was happening to people of a different community, I lost a lot of faith in the police.' Yet this was not the only form such loosening of public trust took. We also encountered instances whose significance lies, not in any obvious shift in personal experience, but in a seeming reluctance to universalize that experience or mentally project it onto others. On one occasion this arose from some telling conversations with neighbours: 'we have Asian doctors, company directors, doctors around us. Whenever you say to them we don't like the noise from the rugby club and think about complaining they don't feel they can. They say when we come here we keep a low profile. Those people don't feel protected by our police and I think that view is illuminating' (women's organization, Manchester). On others, it entailed a recognition that one's own experiences and feelings might not be mirrored in other, more 'distant' corners of the land:

By and large I think we have a police force to be fairly proud of. Again this is the view of somebody who doesn't live in the inner-city areas of our major cities, who happens to be possibly black in the London area. Again, the news, obviously I've read and noticed about the racist element and the difficulties in their relationships with the public [48-year-old male teacher, Cheshire].

These little transitions are of some import, significant contributors to the emergence of white middle-class 'disenchantment' with the police described in the last chapter. They suggest, in particular, a certain fracturing of middle-class support for the police (a withering of the 'silent majority') and the advent of a body of 'respectable' concern about police racism. It is a strand of still generally pro-police opinion that today appears increasingly willing to offer credence to what have over recent decades been very much oppositional sentiments towards the police—outlooks more prone to interpreting events such as the Lawrence case as fitting within a broader historical pattern of police discrimination towards minority communities. Such dispositions were found—albeit as we shall see with different inflections—largely among our black and Asian discussants. There were, however, some white voices—notably among those we in the last chapter termed 'atheists'—whose experience of the police had undermined what might once have been a more supportive orientation towards the police; as in this case, where a personal history of discrimination leads this woman—reluctantly—to the following angry conclusions:

My kids are mixed race. Let me see now, my son would be about 14, 13 or 14, and going through the Arndale [shopping centre] with his friend who was white. And the Arndale was packed. He'd just gone for a pair of trainers, I can't remember what he was actually going for. And these two police officers came up to him and said 'empty your pockets', to my son, who is mixed race, not to the white lad. 'Empty your pockets'. All he had was used tissues. They made him take everything out. And my son said that by this time everybody was crowding round, and he felt that big, he was humiliated. He had nothing on him. They still didn't give a reason why they did this stop-and-search business. They were just minding their own business, walking through. As he got through the Arndale, the white lad went 'oh I'm glad they didn't search me, I've got a knife here'...
...Black kids haven't got a chance around here. The police are racist from the core. I'm telling you, I hate them. I shouldn't say it. Especially from the TA [tenants' association]. I should be able to sit here and say 'yes, I think that the police are great'. But from the experience that I've had, and the stories that I've heard from young black kids, they hate them. And they're making me feel that way now. I mean you might get one or two good ones, but it's like they're all corrupted [female, tenants' association, inner-city Manchester].

This convergence of emergent middle-class concern and oppositional white working-class memory and sensibility represents an important feature of the cultural context within which the Lawrence affair and its aftermath have been received and acted upon. The Lawrence case seems likely in its turn to contribute further to the contingency of this assemblage of contested memories and beliefs, its elements likely to buttress and stiffen the feeling of audiences far removed from black and Asian history and experience that all is not well with contemporary police responses to the problems of ethnic minority communities. This at least is the—not entirely wishful— hope of this white political activist:

I think the Lawrence enquiry has been a real sort of watershed. I think a lot of people who had never really thought about the problem said, I mean because obviously Stephen corresponded to what loads of people's ambitions for their child would be, a lot of people thought it's just outra-geous...I mean not just the non-white community but the whole community and I think it'll make people think.

This cultural backdrop has, furthermore, helped to condition the public response of police spokespeople and elites to the report of the Stephen Lawrence Inquiry—a response the ex-chairperson of one metropolitan police authority saw as containing an unusual and relatively unprecedented mix of humility and uncertainty: 'the police have learned. They're uneasy, and they're thoughtful, and they're edgy and all that. The police have moved. I don't think they've got very far. But they've undoubtedly began to move...The reaction to the Lawrence case. They've no longer attempted to say "nothing to do with us". They're admitting that things went wrong.' In part, of course, this has to do with the immediate ingredients of the Lawrence case itself, ingredients far removed from earlier episodes of controversy such as the 1980s disorders, and which effectively served to close off many of the re-legitimating appeals that have been previously available to the police in moments of racialized crisis. This much is clearly evident in the following remarks, uttered to us by a spokesman of the Police Federation:

This was a good family, this was a good kid who had been murdered. That was it. And we messed up big time in terms of the way we dealt with it. You know, there's no arguing about that. I mean people want to argue about the details of that but overall that's the truth of it. The implications of that, the cover-up which the Met conducted, and then the eventual disclosure of the detail, is the most dramatic analysis of policing incompet-ence that I think the service has ever endured.

But such responses also have much to do with the movements in outlook that we have detailed in this section, shifts that have helped constitute what has become an altered, differentiated, and appreciably more contested climate of (white) opinion around questions of policing and 'race'. Sure, as we have seen, there are elements of contemporary English society that remain more than capable of excusing 'our' police and of finding means to deny those malpractices that have in the last several decades come to public knowledge; and forces both within and outside the police will no doubt continue to pander to, or rally, such sentiments.[6] But that strand of doggedly pro-police opinion today forms but one, we have suggested 'residual', component among a number of cross-cutting strands of white memory and sensibility; an emergent fact about contemporary England that has served to narrow the space that police elites can legitimately operate in, whether around issues of 'race' or more widely. Such cultural shifts have, as such, contributed to a greater realization in police circles that 'battening down the hatches' and calling forth the 'silent majority' will no longer suffice as it once perhaps did; as well as to a dawning recognition that taking seriously the claims of Britain's ethnic minorities can no longer so easily be relegated to a peripheral, community-relations sideshow:

If the police service was not responding to that need, it would become, I guess, a remote army of occupation with 26,000 people seeking to suppress the complexity of a population of seven to eight million. Won't work. So morally right, pragmatically right, business case right, diversity should be a huge issue for the police service. And those who describe it as a sort of politically correct, bending over backwards, pandering to . . . you can see where they are coming from but get real. Get their heads out of the sand [chief constable, metropolitan force].

Other Voices, Different Stories: Black and Asian Narratives of English Policing

At the outset of one of our interviews, a Pakistani-born man now resident in north Manchester, described his arrival in Britain in the following terms:

3 July 1960 I came in this country. I reached Manchester on 5 July, I was in London, Walthamstow, for two days. I remember coming out of Piccadilly Station at that time, I was on the bus, the buses used to be electric trolley type of buses, I came out of Alexander Road, I'm in Longsight, I asked a policeman who was passing and I asked 'where is [address]?' I had one suitcase on this side, and a small bag on my left. He grabbed hold of my suitcase, and he said, 'come on Sir'. He walked with me about

five minutes in the street, turned right and left, knocked on the door, Mrs Davis was the landlord of where I was going to stay. He said, 'Mrs Davis, you've got a friend here, he looks very thirsty. Do him a pot of tea. Very good day sir.' That is how the policeman was on 5 July 1960. The policeman these days will look at you as if he is going to eat you.

This is a quaint, affectionate memoir, one that casts the police officer as the nation's butler, and bemoans his subsequent refashioning into a very different sort of animal. Yet, striking though the image is, it stands very much apart from those that generally characterized our conversations with black and Asian citizens. These narratives are themselves, as we shall illustrate below, internally differentiated and complex. Their organizing motifs nevertheless serve in some significant ways to reposition and cast fresh light on some of the themes that have pervaded discussion in this and the previous two chapters; revealing them as peculiarly white stories about the English police and its post-war trajectories. By way of introduction to this final section let us consider two instances where such light can plausibly be said to have been shed.

It is evident first that some of the idioms central to the outlook of many among our white respondents—to do with an erosion of community and the consumerism and individuation of contemporary social life; the collapse of parenting and ill-discipline among the young, the post-war fracturing of social authority—were either much less prominent or very differently present among our black and Asian respondents. Yet it is also clear that the processes brought together under the rubric 'detraditionalization' have played themselves out in particular ways within ethnic minority communities, giving rise in the policing domain to clear generational cleavages in the experiences and orientations of black and Asian people. Thus our respondents would often speak here of the respectful, nervy deference towards the police exhibited by many first-generation immigrants—a phenomenon our 'butler' story *does* illustrate. This it was felt was the product of two—rather different— factors. First, a tendency to evaluate positively the 'helpfulness' of the English police when set against what they had left behind: 'people came from a background where the police are very repressive. When they came here, they actually found it totally different. So they were very respectful of the police' (Asian male local authority employee, Manchester). Secondly, a feeling that surviving—even remaining—in an often hostile host environment meant keeping one's head down, not creating a fuss, 'making do with what they were getting':

The first immigrants that came over very much felt that they were on sufferance, they had come over to get jobs, and they didn't feel they had a right to be here as people who had been born here. That generation I think were quite frightened of authority generally and of course the police grew large in this concept of authority. So I think there was more fear of the police [female, Pakistani discussion group, Manchester].

This is contrasted (in tones that suggest a striking protectiveness towards the community's young among older black and Asian respondents) with the experiences and outlooks of subsequent—second and third—generations, those that were born and bred in Britain and had come to acquire a set of expectations consistent with that fact (as one Asian police officer said of his children: 'I know my kids are staying here. This is our home, so now you want to be an integrated part of this community and so you will now get them pushing for more. They want to be in every field now, they want to be in politics, they want to be in police, medicine, whatever'). For these generations—those who clearly feel themselves to be black- or Asian-*British*—some deteriorating relationships with the police on the ground were felt by many to have coincided with—and be partly the product of—an enhanced determination to insist on what one 35-year-old female member of our Pakistani discussion group called 'our rights', 'equality', and being 'treated fairly'. As one of our respondents put it, with particular reference to generational differences within the Asian community:

It [the loss of confidence in the police] became more evident in the younger people because they were much more likely to confront and stand firm on their own beliefs and on their own ideas, rather than the elders—the elders will actually keep quiet and put their head down and actually persevere. I think that's one of the values that people brought with them, perseverance and that life is not an easy—it's not easy, there are all kinds of difficulties and you have to persevere with those. One of those was the police and you had to persevere with that. Obviously young people have said, 'Well, you may have had to persevere with it, but we are not going to stand for it' and so you had, if you like, a cultural development within the younger people who were anti-police, in a sense [male Asian local authority employee, Manchester].

It is apparent, secondly, that wistful motifs concerning the English bobby and his post-war decline were almost entirely absent from black and Asian social memory, an absence that further indicates how intimately entangled this cultural symbol is with an image and memory of 'white England'. In its place, two themes emerge. First, a collective memory structured, not by concern about the loss of a much loved figure, but by patterns—and recalled exemplary instances—of discrimination, malpractice, and felt injustice. Numerous such instances were narrated in our discussions, both of personal and family experience, and of events from further afield (the Lawrence affair being but the latest) whose impact is clearly and strongly felt across ethnic minority communities. These ranged from 'first hand impressions of harassment and verbal aggression' (black male, inner city Manchester), through accounts of 'Asians in their twenties being stopped and asked for their passports' (male Asian council employee, Manchester), to numerous sometimes 'terrifying' instances cited to us by an Asian businessman of being stopped by the police in his car—an experience that had engendered in his case the following unsettling concern: 'when you go out to meet the police, you don't know whether he will be racist or not'. This complex of—widely circulating—experience is graphically depicted in the following metaphorical description of the black community's relations with the English police:

The first impression I got was that there's always police there up and about, up and down. It's like a hunter hunting his prey, and the prey is in abundance. Like a lion's movements. Gazelles and rhebok, they're out there in abundance, and you just have to choose. He can have his belly full any time he wants. That was the proverbial impression that I got of the police when I first came to this town—that they're not about you, you cannot rely on them to solve your problems. They're about like hunting you. You're the hunted. In other words, sooner or later you become confronted by them because they're about in abundance [black male, inner-city Manchester].

Dispositions such as these have been copiously documented in recent decades and will occasion little surprise. What has been less apparent in the midst of such historically embedded experience is a second thematic that emerged from our discussions, one that takes sharp implicit issue with white tales of loss and decline since the 1950s in favour of a post-war historical narrative that recalls police–black relations sliding towards a nadir in the late 1970s and early 1980s, before undergoing an uneven, unfinished, still reversible, but nonetheless clearly discernible turn in subsequent

years. On this—by no means universal, but widely articulated—
view, the former period is cast as a low point both in terms of
actual police actions on the ground, and in relation to the police's
remembered unwillingness to engage productively with the realities, dynamics, and consequences of an emergent multicultural
England—'they were', as one long-standing Moss Side resident put
it, 'hopeless in those days in dealing with those issues'. Subsequent
mutations in relations with the police were recognized on both
these fronts (albeit with the significant rider that there is a long way
to go, that fair and equitable policing remains some way off), with
the urban disorders of the early 1980s often serving to mark symbolically the depths of police outlook and practice, and the juncture at which some new directions began—slowly—to unfold. As
the aforementioned Moss Side resident said of police–community
relations in that troubled location: 'we've come a long way since
then. That was the beginning of the turnaround.'

But let us not run ahead of ourselves. And let us also take care
not to flatten what remains a complex and competing assemblage
of memories and dispositions towards the police; outlooks which
have different resorts to the past, connect policing to the broader
contours of English racism in contrasting fashions, and (consequently) arrive at varying assessments of the 'conjuncture' represented by the Lawrence case. To gain a better sense of this recent
history and range of contemporary social meaning and possibility,
let us then conclude this chapter with a reconstruction—drawing
mainly, albeit not exclusively, upon the biographical narratives of
some of our black respondents—of three analytical distinguishable
positions on relevant issues.

Their Nation, Their Police Force:
Oppositional (Police) Politics

Lloyd Thomas was born in Jamaica in the early 1930s, coming
to Manchester in 1962. A printer by trade, he originally came to
England 'to spend a couple of years, to get a few certificates and go
back'. Fuelled by what he now thinks of as the erroneous stories of
those who had returned—stories of the English being 'so generous',
of how they had 'got on so well', 'were earning so much money',
were 'able to provide for their families'—Lloyd's initial hopes had
been high. He was, however, to receive a 'rude awakening to the
realities of British life' in the form of what he recalls as a 'very

racist, very hostile' reaction. At work, 'the people around me were mainly white working-class people. And there was a tremendous amount of prejudice... [they] found difficulty in dealing or relating to people other than their own'. And in his search for somewhere to live:

Many homes which I personally went to, even though they had vacancies on the door, when they opened the door and they see you they just close the door and went away. We endured that kind of attitude from members of the society. Some people had on their windows 'no niggers or dogs' you know. And I think some had Irish too.

England was at that time, Lloyd suggests, a place of 'social stagnation' where black people were—far more blatantly than now—made to feel that their presence was not acceptable. Pubs, places of entertainment, these were all sites where, if you wanted to visit, 'it was a fuss, you wasn't made to feel welcome'. All this, he recalls, was hugely instrumental in black people turning inwards, forming their own organizations and groups, their own outlets for social activities and recreation. And this in turn was to create the seeds of conflict with some of the white community, and the first hostile encounters with the police:

It's no secret, West Indians like music, and the music is different from the music that English people like, and therefore some English people resented that and used to complain to the police about we keeping noise and all this kind of thing. But it wasn't so much the noise, it was because they didn't like to see black people enjoying themselves, right. And the police used to come, go into people's homes, kick in the doors, you know, break up the party, thieve the drinks, because many of them used to carry away all the drinks.

For Lloyd these experiences were vitally significant in the formation of a *black* political identity, and signalled for him the beginning of a sustained involvement in the politics of race and policing—starting in the 1960s with the Campaign Against Racial Discrimination. He was—and continues to be—spurred on by the 'indignity' he believes black people have suffered at the hands of the police, the criminal justice system, and other social institutions, and he remains—in his seventies—passionately committed to defending the black community against their racist excesses (what he insists upon calling the 1981 'disturbances' were in this context 'the voice of the unheard'). His sense of the post-war period is thus couched principally in terms of *continuity*. For Lloyd, English racism has in no significant measure abated or changed in the post-war decades, merely becoming 'a bit more clever, not as brutal, you know'. And for him, the arrest and prosecution of black people following the breaking-up of parties in the 1950s and 1960s forms the beginning of a litany of police mistreatment of blacks that continues to this day, a litany of repeated abuse, of 'dislike' and 'disrespect' towards black people, the details of which he thinks it superfluous to spell out: 'the number of black people which, you know, die in police cells and custody, and all this kind of thing. These things are well documented. I don't have to go over those cases.' For Lloyd, a few recent—albeit welcome—changes of outlook among senior officers are considered unlikely to impact greatly on this wider historical picture of institutionalized abuse:

It was a bit gratifying to hear the chief constable of Manchester say, and I think he was the first one to admit it, that there was institutionalized racism. I nearly fainted when I heard he said that. It was good to hear him say it. But as I said, I recognize, and I acknowledge, that there are a hand-ful of people who may well want to change attitudes and behaviour etc., but I'm saying that it is not enough, and they are not effective enough to deal with the majority of society that is racist. That's what I'm saying to you. But until we can change that imbalance, nothing has changed.

What Lloyd represents, stands as an exemplar of, is a strand of thought and feeling, and of oppositional black politics, which 'reads' the police as a prime instrument and symbol, manifestion and protector, of white society; an organization that 'behaves that way towards black people, because they know full well they have the support of the host community'. To this extent, he formally shares with some among our white and police respondents a view of the police as embodying and reflecting wider (racist) culture, an outlook that appears here to be given a radical political inflection— albeit that it remains, like all of the variants of this position, structurally fatalist in its effects. In Lloyd's estimation, the politics of police reform is very much epiphenomenal—a small, albeit important, cog within a far more significant struggle:

What you need to change is the whole culture, right, and the norms and values, and the expectations, right, of that society. You have to change the whole social order of that society to bring about any kind of meaningful change that will help to make or enhance the lives of the majority of people. You can't just change one institution and think the rest is alright. All of them is a load of crap. All of them are prejudiced and racist, right. The schools, the lot. The educational institutions, the lot.

This is a perspective that remains heavily committed to what John Rex (1979) has termed 'the politics of defensive confrontation'. Such politics speaks largely of a communal defence of the black community *against* the police (as Lloyd says, 'it is important to tackle the police, because they're at the forefront'); one that is unable to envisage what policing might ever positively be *for*, beyond a demand that people 'are treated and respected as human beings'. It is a position that sees no mileage in the 'very wrong, very naïve' view that policing can be altered by such means as recruiting more black officers: 'look at the States, the United States of America. Not only do they have ordinary black police, they have inspectors, they have governors, black governors. Does it change the attitude of the white police, or even some of their own black ones, against the ordinary people, or against black people in the States? No. The answer is quite clearly no.' And it is a position that sees in the events surrounding the Lawrence case only a limited amount of potential for change. For Lloyd, 'the Lawrence affair' has had the benefit of making 'a certain amount of liberals within society come out and feel ashamed of the indignity, and the brutality of the police, and the lack of humanity within the police itself'. But it plainly does not, for him, represent any kind of watershed. If anything, the case has served merely to confirm and reinforce what the long history of racism and oppositional black struggle has deeply etched into his *Weltanschauung*:

I don't think it's a bloody turning point myself. I think it has brought to light, and reconfirmed, many of the things that people like myself, and many other people, not only myself, have been saying for years, about the blatant racism within the police, and the lack of the will within the police to defend, to stand up for black people, or to any serious kind of investigation into any criminal activity against black people...

...What Stephen Lawrence has shown is not just that the police are racist, but the whole society in which we live is racist, and unless that society comes to grips with that fact and starts dealing seriously, right, with the discriminatory behaviour and attitudes, and the norms and the values, right, and the way they see other people. And disrespect, the contributions that other people have made to their own survival, etc. And unless we start understanding that, and start recognizing that they were the blood-suckers of people from other parts of the world, and their prosperity came out of that, and therefore they have an obligation to behave differently, nothing will change.

A Police Service for All?: 'Respectable' Black Concerns

Wes Richards was born in 1960 in Barbados. He came to Manchester in the late 1960s with his mother and three siblings to join his father who was here on a scholarship. Apart from a four-year return trip to Barbados, he has lived in Greater Manchester ever since. Educated at a school in the south of the city, he has spent the twenty years of his working life as a businessman. He now runs an organization helping black people start up small businesses.

Wes's initial childhood impressions of England are fond ones, and he reached his early teens thinking 'it was an advanced place compared to the Caribbean'—a view he subsequently revised upon returning from a four-year trip 'home' to find his former school contemporaries both disillusioned and disillusioning: 'I talked to people who I'd gone to school with, I looked at what they were doing and there wasn't any kind of progress. Most of them were just interested in just an ordinary regular job. They hadn't pushed ahead with any great determination, I thought that in the Caribbean there was more thrusting to get ahead. I found I'd taken on a kind of attitude to get ahead. So in that way, I thought people in the Caribbean were more advanced and the people here just got by really, did not really push themselves.'

Wes's teenage life was, on his own admission, unremarkable. 'I went to all the clubs and had friends', he says, 'it was good. I didn't have any contact or experience with the police.' And while he was aware of the mistreatment that was alleged to shape the life of many young blacks in his immediate environment, he himself 'really didn't think about them, because I don't think there are many people that go around thinking, oh the police...It is just whenever there is a problem.' He thus received something of a jolt, when in 1978, aged 18, he and his friend were pulled up by the police while canvassing for trade for the milkman on their bikes (an activity that entailed following the existing milkman in order to identify the houses he wasn't serving). The way Wes now recalls this event says much about the atmosphere that prevailed at the time:

He stopped us, and asked us what we were doing. We explained we were doing this for some extra money, and he didn't accept that, early in the morning riding round the streets looking at houses, must be up to no good. So he started to suggest that the bikes may have been stolen. We just thought, well, here we go, we'd heard it all before on television, all the rest of it, we thought this is just the beginning of it. I decided to make a run for it, but of course big mistake. I just dropped the bike and ran off and he gave chase across the fields and all my neighbours were looking seeing me running across the fields with this policeman chasing me. I thought I knew all the short cuts and all the back routes through the houses coz I knew the area and disappeared. When I got back I found him there waiting for me coz somebody must have told him. I thought well okay he is going to go through everything and at the end of the day, he'd find nothing and that would be the end of it. So okay, take me away. Got to police station, told them the bikes weren't stolen and everything else, explained what I was doing, told them I'd ran off because I thought I was going to be framed for something. But they put me in the cells anyway. When another officer came to interview me again, told him what I'd told everybody, told them and he starts to knock me about. Knocked me down, kicked me in the stomach, in the cells, and after that a few hours later they released me. Gave us the bikes back, but that was my first experience of what people had talked to me about.

Wes—perhaps unusually at the time—made a complaint, although 'lacking evidence' he felt his chances to be minimal and dropped it—'the importance had gone out of the situation. I just thought forget it'. Nor did the experience deter him—some three years on—from giving serious consideration to joining the police force (in the hope that he could 'change things'), before being talked out of it by friends and family—'they said it was a racist organization, I wouldn't survive in there'. Wes now counts himself fortunate that he did not join ('I have read and spoken to a lot of people who did join and their experience was horrendous'), although the recruitment of black officers is something he continues to view as an important social objective. Such an opening up of one of society's 'closed shops' (black male, inner-city Manchester) was expressly supported by a number of our black and Asian respondents:

There will still be racism we know that, amongst officers, so many cases have come out. But if the number increase I'm sure they will be friendlier and things will change I think. Once you get a large number of coloured policeman, mentally if you go to a station where there is thirty officers at a station and ten of them, particularly in urban areas, are coloured officers, things are bound to change [male, Pakistani discussion group, Manchester].

Wes—in a motif that, we have suggested, echoed across our interviews with black respondents—recalls the late 1970s and 1980s as
representing rock bottom in relations between the police and the
black community; something he sees reflected in both his personal
experience ('in the 1970s and 1980s you would be stopped quite
regularly... I think it was harassment basically but you just put up
with it'), and that of the wider community. It is against this backdrop that he recalls—and situates—the urban disorders of 1981: 'I
think when the riots occurred, my feeling was and I mean I remember coming down to Moss Side from Stretford, talking to people
who were milling about, all the rest of it, the feeling was it was justified. That people needed to give vent to the feeling of frustration
and humiliation they had been suffering for so long. And
I don't think I felt any sorrow or sympathy for a while for the
people who lost property, or the police. You just felt angry about
what had been going on and only wished you could get to the city
centre to destroy the whole thing. That is how I felt at that time,
just to see a lot of destruction to vent the feeling of anger.'

   In Wes's estimation, matters have since then undergone a distinct, if slow and uneven, improvement. He now describes England
as a country where 'people try to be less outwardly offensive' (they
'no longer put up notices offensive to blacks'), a 'tolerant place'
that 'compares well with other places like America or parts of
Europe'. 'I have always felt more comfortable within English society', he says, although he continues to have the 'sneaky feeling'
when among groups of white people that one is being 'tolerated'
rather than 'accepted'. And in terms of policing he detects what he
counts as some significant shifts. Sure enough, he holds some of
these to be 'cosmetic', a matter largely of impression management—
'I think the police are a bit more sensitive to the press, the media,
and their image'. He also believes these changes—in respect, for
instance, of stop and search—to vary geographically: 'I think there
has been as an improvement although you do still hear of lots of
people getting stopped in London, places like that. The impression
I get is that it's worse in London.' Yet he remains—in the wake of
David Wilmot's remarks about 'institutional racism' in Greater
Manchester Police—cautiously optimistic about what the aftermath
of the Lawrence case may bring:

[I was] very pleased and excited. I wrote, I never usually write on anything,
but it is the first time I have ever written anything to anybody in that kind

of situation. You see something on the television, on the news. You say, 'I'm going to write to this and that, congratulating him', and I did. Didn't get a response but I felt that at least now, once they have admitted the problem, how long it took to start chiselling away at it and try to make things better. And it had come from the top down. So you felt that there was a possibility that some mechanisms are in place, and accountability, that senior officers could then bring in changes that would need to be brought in. It has given me a lot of hope.

We have represented and exemplified here a markedly different sensibility towards the police from that exhibited within oppositional black discourse and politics. Despite the memory and experience of the police that it in part shares with exponents of such discourses, this outlook fits much more snugly and explicitly with established—albeit for the most part liberal—white concerns and dispositions towards the police; preoccupations that few among our black respondents actively shared. This much is apparent in Wes's felt anxieties about the police having become to 'detached from the public', 'more of a force than a service', and thus requiring 'more and more protection'. It is apparent in his particular articulation of what we have seen (in Chapter 4) are some common narratives about the withering of a once more settled police authority: 'I think there has been a general shift in terms of way people perceive authority. I think people used to think authority was infallible. In the early seventies and eighties, you used to hear about British justice being the best in the world. I mean all these high profile miscarriages of justice, you don't hear that so much any more'. And it permeates his wish to see the British police 'get back to the attitude they are there to serve the public', recognize that 'there is only so much that can be given to them in terms of police powers and police resources', and learn to be 'effective within those limits'.

A World Still to Win: An Emergent Police Politics?

Courtney Holder is in his late thirties. He was born and bred in Manchester and has never for a significant period of time left it. He loves the city, and proudly calls himself a 'Moss Sider'. Though he now lives elsewhere in Manchester he continues to work in the inner city. He remembers the area in the 1960s as being self-sufficient in shops (such that residents were spared the need to visit Manchester city centre) and close-knit; the kind of place where, if you were seen or caught doing something wrong (like 'running into Woolies and nicking things') your parents would soon know about it.

Racism—he recalls—did not figure in his experience as a child; indeed, it was not something he knew much of until white people were reluctantly moved by the local authority to the area:

White, working-class people, who were poor working-class white people, nonetheless, I think, felt themselves better, no matter how poor they were. No matter how working-class they were and the one thing they were, they were white, and as far as they were concerned that made them better than anybody, especially anybody who was black.

From that time onwards life became much more of a struggle. He recalls his first experience of racist injustice during his first day as an apprentice at a Manchester engineering firm: 'I wanted to learn, I was eager, you know, I wanted to do well, and I didn't want to sit at the back. I remember, I was the only black lad there and as I sat at the front, it was like, "Fucking move, nigger, you're sat in my seat." So, bit by bit, every seat I sat in, some white guy was always saying, I'm sat in his seat. And I moved in the room till I was at the back and I couldn't go any further. And a fight broke out in the class room, broke up when the lecturer came in...To cut a long story short, I ended up having to fight everybody in that class before they'd leave me alone. In the end, I mean, they did leave me alone, but my God, it's not something I would want other people to go through.' And he recalls what he thinks of as cognate injustices at the hands of the police. This took the form in his teens of intermittent experiences during visits to Manchester city centre— 'we were cocky, you know, we liked dancing, we pulled the girls. We bred a lot of resentment...I was a mouthy bastard as far as a lot of people were concerned, particularly people who were the forces of law and order.' As he reached his twenties—and became 'more vociferous, more articulate, more challenging'—so police attention increased, reaching a violent peak at the time of the 1981 disorders:

I've been in situations where I've been seriously beaten up by police officers...I would have brought some pictures to show you, because I could say anything, but pictures actually don't lie. It might be, if I could find them, actually, it might have to be in your book, because it's quite a horror. And there's all sorts of things that have happened to me. I've been locked up in police cells, I've...I've not committed a crime, yet. But, I don't want that to have to happen to anybody. Black or white.

Courtney now describes this as 'a painful period in my life because I went through some difficult times and it's very difficult to talk about'. The disorders also proved—on reflection—to be something of a transformative moment, both in terms of Courtney's life trajectory, and his view for the wider community. In a bid to avoid becoming 'bitter and twisted' by experience (such that one is rendered 'worse than the very thing you hate'), he threw himself into local community politics—'I made a conscious decision', he says, 'over a period of time, that I needed to do something so other people didn't go through what I went through'.

It is in the aftermath of this decision—some twenty years on—that Courtney charts, and endeavours to make sense of, the changing local contours of 'race' and policing. He speaks initially here, with some feeling, about the plight of his parents' generation (an experience and contribution he thinks are insufficiently acknowledged by younger blacks); of their 'desperate need to integrate' and of their 'no blacks, no dogs, no Irish' exclusion from all kinds of leisure outlets, community organizations, and public services: 'if they could they would have turned themselves white; I think they tried to fit in, to blend in and so on, but they weren't allowed'. He speaks of how they were forced by this rejection to establish their own community facilities and social outlets. And he observes how these responses were seen by the white community as threatening, something that invariably led to 'men in particular experienc[ing] problems with the police', who 'spent a lot of time breaking up what they saw as illegal parties'. It is against this historical backdrop that Courtney proffers the following observations:

There has always been problems with the police. I think the police reflects society and they are a microcosm of society. And where you have a society which actually views people in a particular way, then that's bound to be reflected in police. And I don't know why people make the assumption that, because they are police officers, that somehow they are imbued with some kind of special particular skill and power to rise above all the things which affects us as human beings. If you give them power, they're even more entrenched with those negatives.

For all that this formulation coheres closely with the variant of the 'police-as-mirror' metaphor that one encounters in what we earlier called oppositional black discourses towards the police, it can be distinguished from that outlook by means of its much more pronounced sense of historical contingency and political possibility. Courtney thus proceeds to detail what he sees as the dreadful state police relations with the black community had reached in the

1970s and early 1980s (see, further, McLaughlin 1994). In Moss Side, in particular, there was little 'love lost'. At the top of the organization, the then chief constable, James Anderton, was seen as standing resolutely opposed to any attempt to develop an understanding of the local black community—as one Asian male we spoke to put it, 'I think under James Anderton the whole police was very negative, we never got anything from him. That was a really dark chapter in policing and community relations in Manchester.' A local chief superintendent was remembered by one local priest we interviewed as describing the area as a 'battleground', something that was taken locally to suggest that 'you're in a war situation' and that 'the usual laws of the ordinary running of things go out of the window'. The crime and other problems of the community were in the meantime—according to Courtney—being neglected and ignored: 'there was a period in the eighties when our young people were killing each other because of drugs, because of the shootings and the City Council, nobody was interested in what was happening. We were burying our dead, organizing our funerals. I organized nearly fourteen funerals in this community. We never got any help. No sympathy. Nobody was talking about the waste in young lives.' Courtney then summed up the more general mood of the time thus:

Bad. I would say that there's no love lost between us and the police. One of the interesting things was that a lot of black people were always complaining, people like me and others were always complaining. People in London, right across the country were complaining about the police and about police abuse and abuse of powers. I think generally, a lot of people in the white community, working-class as well as other classes, considered us as anti-police. That we're always complaining, we're lawless etc. And we complained for no other reason than the fact we were being picked on. There are lots of instances whereby we'd be stopped, you know. The police would be quite derogatory about you. They would say things to actually goad you to do things. I think a lot of white working-class people experienced problems and not on the basis of colour. They certainly experienced police harassment, but not because they were white. They experience police harassment because, either they were known by the coppers to have some kind of record, but with regard to black people as far as they were concerned, you were a criminal. You were somebody who was alien to them. And so, for somebody to actually condemn you on no other basis than the colour of your skin when you have no control over that, where do you go from there?

Courtney registers, further, in a way that eludes a more strictly oppositional black discourse, what he sees as some evident shifts in the quality and character of local police–black relations. He depicts this in large measure as the outcome of a particular kind of community politics which responded to the impasses of the 1980s by seeking to build a dialogue, or 'bridge', with the police; one that proceeded on the community's—rather than police's—terms. He views such politics—which we document in more detail in Chapter 8—as having been vindicated by some notable successes (notably around issues such as rights cards and persuading the police to record 'voluntary' stops and searches), arguing that 'we shouldn't sit back and rest on our laurels, but clearly we've come a long way'. And he is aware that in the course of this process some of his own—and the local black community's—orientations to the police have shifted. It is plain that he remains sceptical of many of the 'reforms' that have in the aftermath of the Lawrence case come to attract widespread support, not least of these being the alleged benefits of recruiting more black officers (the issue, he argues, is about 'structures and systems', and he continues to fear that 'you will get people perpetuating the oppression, but instead of white officers doing it, black officers are in danger of doing it'). But Courtney has slowly come to see a *potentially positive* role for the police, an emergent disposition that has taken him—and much of the local black community—beyond a history organized principally around communal defence:

At a meeting only last week with younger people. It was an ordinary Forum meeting, but there were about forty-five people there, and I would say that about twenty of those would have been young, sort of youth age, youth club age people, that came to it. There was still concern being expressed about policing, probably because the people who were there hadn't appreciated what it was like twenty years ago. But they were prepared to accept that they need a police force. That they do need policing. Now that wouldn't have been acknowledged in the community I don't think, not so easily, twenty years ago.

In charting this unfolding, still fragile process, Courtney acknowledges the part played by the police, and especially the (now former) chief constable, David Wilmot, and local senior officers; officers whose words and deeds have—the aforementioned local priest argues—largely justified the 'step of faith' the 'community' made in the police.[7] Courtney too remains impressed with senior officers,

while reserving his judgement on just how far down the organization this revised understanding of police–black issues has reached:
'I think senior officers are working very hard. I'm not yet
convinced that the ordinary bobby on the street fully understands'.

The police's—contrasting—reactions to the Lawrence inquiry
have largely served to reinforce this assessment. There is, on the
one hand, little doubting the positive reception Wilmot's public
remarks about institutional racism have had within the local black
and Asian communities, his words being taken as a significant indicator of the police's willingness to engage seriously, discuss, and
confront discriminatory practice within the force—'he was', as one
black male from inner-city Manchester opined, '100 per cent right.
I think that he hit the nail on the head.' Yet there is equally little
doubting the weary disappointment evinced by black and Asian
people towards the kind of rank-and-file police reactions to
Wilmot's remarks detailed earlier in his chapter—a sign, as Courtney
views it, of just how great is the distance still to be travelled: 'one
thing I have been saddened about is when the chief constable actually mentioned that there is racism in the police force and wants to
get rid of that, his own officers are actually totally against him'. In
either case, it seems abundantly clear that the concept of 'institutionalized racism' has come to loom large in the contemporary
cultural politics of race and policing, serving as it does in the minds of
many blacks and Asians to symbolize what has changed, crystallize
what remains at stake, and demonstrate how the institutional and
social forces who compete over this terrain are currently aligned:

I think its significant that Wilmot, who, when he came to be chief constable, I think he had a vision. A very able senior officer, I think it took a lot
of courage for him to say what he said because it was true. I think he certainly went up in a lot of our estimations by saying it. I think that significe-
antly though, the reaction of the Police Federation and rank and file bobbies to those comments was quite interestingly significant in the sense that
they totally rejected what he was saying. And within a couple of weeks,
there was lots of incidents which actually reinforced exactly what he was
saying.

* * *

We will have cause to revisit various of the themes raised in this
and the two preceding chapters in our conclusion. In so doing, we

will reflect further upon what we think has emerged as a central motif of the previous three chapters: namely, the advent—in the wake of a once more settled police authority being called multiply into question in last several decades of the twentieth century—of a fractured English policing culture constituted through struggle between competing sensibilities, one in which questions of ethnicity and identity are today much to the fore. If—as Paul Gilroy (1987: 62) has claimed—legal institutions such as the police 'are important sites on which the limits of the nation as well as its character are routinely established', then this site has come to be fought over (even constituted), not merely by various organized social movements and political forces, but also by a wider, more diffuse complex of competing public sensibilities—sensibilities that vary enormously in their historical trajectories and contemporary force; the connections they forge between policing and the wider contours of post-war social change; the part played in their formation by the sacred and the profane, the emotionally charged and the practically mundane; and their resort to the past and projected hopes for the future. We consider these matters further in our concluding chapter. We must first however—in Part III—extend our account of English policing culture by examining more fully different modes of official memory and outlook; something that entails a shift to a more explicitly 'chronological' mode of recovery and analysis.

PART III

Official Narratives

6

'The Job' and 'The Force'

In January 2000 PC Norman Brennan, founder of a little-known organization called *Protect the Protectors*, sent a letter to—among others—the Home Secretary, the Shadow Home Secretary, the Lord Chancellor, the Lord Chief Justice, the chairperson of the Magistrates' Association, and the Chief Clerk of each magistrates' bench in England and Wales. The letter drew its eminent recipients' attention to the '1999 National Police Survey', the results of which were included.[1] This—a survey of 6,500 officers 'analysed by MORI'—purported to show the following: 69 per cent of officers dissatisfied with 'the standard of leadership within the force'; 91 per cent agreeing that 'the over-emphasis on political correctness adversely affects the way the police service is run'; 88 per cent wanting to see 'a higher budget allocation' given to 'front-line Police Officers walking the beat'; 69 per cent concurring that 'the Black Police Officers' Association represents a racial split within the Police Service'; 91 per cent believing that 'the Criminal Justice System considers the welfare of the offender more important than the victim', and 89 per cent thinking that 'tougher sentencing will reduce crime'. In his letter PC Brennan was at pains to emphasize this last point:

The poll clearly illustrates the lack of confidence that police officers have in the criminal justice system, especially when it comes to sentencing. I know I speak for all my colleagues when I say that words cannot describe adequately the frustration, time and again, at seeing offenders who have been convicted leaving the court laughing after receiving a derisory sentence.

News that police officers endure 'low morale and frustration' in 'their fight against crime' is of course scarcely news. Such has long been a staple of research on police culture (Skolnick 1966; Cain 1973; Holdaway 1983; Young 1991). Indeed, the frequency with which such a finding recurs in the literature appears to suggest that these sentiments are somehow inherent in the police condition, generated by the structural peculiarities of the job. There is, it should be said, some merit in this view. There are certain deep-seated dilemmas associated with policing modern liberal democratic societies that—at the very least—tend to condition the parameters within which police officers think and feel (Bayley 1985; Waddington 1999; Walker 1999). Yet, while acknowledging the force of this, the social analysis of police mentalities and sensibilities must remain attuned to the significance of local and national specificity, intra-organizational conflicts, and processes of temporal change. It is these dimensions of what has—perhaps now unhelpfully—come to be called 'police culture' that we aim in this chapter to address.

We want to propose that the angry, beleaguered tones in which PC Brennan makes his case arise in large measure from the ways in which the outlook on 'the Job' and 'the force' he stands for has over the last two decades been stripped of its dominant position within 'police culture' and come instead to be contested and displaced. In setting out to document and make sense of the recollections of the retired and long-serving officers we interviewed, our aim is to reconstruct certain key elements of this once more secure, unchallenged, even taken-for-granted way of thinking and feeling about the work officers do and the nature of the organization within which they undertake it, and to examine how this disposition was both shaped by, and in part constitutive of, English social relations in the early decades of the post-war period. But we want, in addition, to explore the ways in which the 'vision' of policing embedded in these memories has in recent decades been disputed, its dominance eroded, as processes of detraditionalization have come to have effects, not only upon the social world that the police are tasked with regulating, but also *within* the police organization itself. The diverse and competing public sensibilities towards police authority that emerge from Chapters 4 and 5 find, or so we contend, some equivalence here.

In approaching our task, we have opted to highlight—in a manner that is necessarily partial in its choice of topics and sketchy in its treatment of any of them—certain themes that seem to us significant in illuminating these processes. We seek, in particular, to grasp the meanings and values explicit and implicit in officers'

memories of *three* salient aspects of the job and the police organization: (i) the social status of 'the police officer' and its intersection
with what since 1945 has been the periodically quarrelsome question of police pay; (ii) the matters considered germane to learning
and performing a role that assumes a venerated place at the core of
this particular disposition towards English policing—namely, 'bobbying'; and (iii) the—hierarchical, quasi-militaristic—internal authority
relations that are recalled as characterizing the English police during the initial decades of the post-war period. In the latter part of
the chapter, we turn to consider the ways in which this once seemingly settled assemblage of police practices, beliefs, and sentiments
has been disrupted by processes of *informalization* and *diversification*, and explore the range of discordant voices that are today
struggling to determine the composition, internal cultures, and
organizational ethos of the English police.

A Good Job?: Social Status and the Meanings of Police Pay

The motives our police interviewees proffered for having initially
signed up for the Job during the middle decades of the twentieth
century fall into several overlapping categories.[2] For some, joining
was a matter of following a family tradition of either police or
military service, something that made what one retired chief
constable called 'the attractions of the uniform' appear almost self-
evident: 'my father was in the police and I joined without giving it
too much thought. My uncle had been in and I had a grandfather
way back who had been in, and it seemed to be a natural progres-
sion' (retired chief constable, metropolitan force). For others, the
'attractions' of the police lay in the almost unrivalled 'security'
offered by 'a job for life' (male inspector, Greater Manchester
Police (GMP)); a factor that was couched in terms of job-related
housing, clear 'career structure', and a generous pension. As one
retired male chief superintendent from Greater Manchester Police
put it, 'my father impressed upon me how important it was to
have a job with a pension and this was one of the considerations.
Whenever you spoke to people that I met in the services I realized
that what my father was saying made sense and that's why I joined
the police.' Such motivations co-existed, however, alongside those
pertaining to the nature of police work and its relationship to the

social. Several here spoke of 'wanting to help people' (male constable, GMP) or of wishing to join 'a really, genuine public service'
(chief constable, provincial force). Others spoke of policing as
having seemed 'a really interesting, exciting job to do' (spokesperson,
Police Federation), or of anticipating 'the excitement of testing
myself in a physical environment' (chief constable, metropolitan
force). These various vocabularies of motive are encapsulated in
the following recollections of a Manchester police inspector who,
in 1975, abandoned being a 'sales rep' to join the police (an organization, ironically, that was about to become embroiled in what
was to prove a bitter, protracted pay dispute):

Being a sales rep isn't sexy, if you know what I mean. Being a policeman
was sexy, you know it was like, 'Ooh you're a policeman. Alright.
Something to talk about there'. It's a job that's got a career structure. Being
a sales rep didn't have that at all. You either made the grade or you
didn't... There was a status to being a policeman. I'd never ever worn a
uniform in my life—apart from the cubs. And it was the discipline side of
it that appealed to me, as well as the fact that the trade unionist thing that
I explained to you before. I wasn't wanting to get into any occupation
where trade unionists' power would have anything to do with it.

An element common to many of these recollections is the felt sense
that being a police officer was during the period these officers
joined a 'steady', 'respectable' pursuit for a reasonably qualified
(and 'realistically' aspiring) working-class male. As one of our
Police Federation interviewees put it, 'it was basically a working-
class boy's job. Most of us were not graduates, were not well-
educated. I had three "O" Levels. I didn't take "A" Levels. I left
school at 16. And most of the police service was like that.' Yet it
was also, as the above account affirms, one that brought with it a
certain quotient of social esteem; something associated with being
'accepted as somebody worthy of note within the locality' (retired
male sergeant, GMP). In this respect, the social allure of the position is most often recalled as deriving not first and foremost from
money (it was, as one Manchester police inspector put it, 'poorly
paid in comparison to today') but, rather, from being thought of,
and responded to, in the same reverent terms as 'a doctor, civil
servant, or school teacher' (male inspector, GMP): 'it was a very
respectable position. It was like being a bank manager, a priest or
a vicar, or a school teacher. People turned to you. If kids were sick,
you were seen as the local man to be trusted to know what to do.

It was like being a fountainhead of authority' (retired male sergeant, GMP). It was in precisely these terms that some among our interviewees interpreted 'the Job' as a 'calling':

Oh yes, I think it's a good job, I still think it's a good job. No, that's wrong, I don't think it's a job, I personally, I'm one of these people that thinks it's a vocation, you are either going to do it or you're not. It's like being a priest, you're either going to do it or you're not, and if you want to be in the police it's certainly not the money because although he's on a lot of money compared to what I was on, so is everybody else [retired male sergeant, GMP].

These memories of the value and social authority of 'the Job' intersect closely with the matter of police pay, and it is with such connections in mind that we may usefully consider what has during the post-war decades been an often vexed public issue. The question of pay has given rise to sustained bouts of police lobbying, whether in the form of 'behind the scenes' (spokesperson, Police Federation) efforts made by then Police Federation negotiator, Jim Callaghan MP, to get pay on to the agenda of the 1960 Royal Commission, or their more vociferous, public campaigning during the 1976–8 pay dispute—what one Federation spokesperson described to us as 'the best campaign we ever run and the most successful' (cf. Reiner 1980; McLaughlin and Murji 1998). It has been deemed worthy of the attention of three official enquiries—one chaired by Lord Oaksey in 1949, the aforementioned Royal Commission, and the Edmund-Davies report of 1978 (Home Office 1949; Home Office 1961a; Home Office 1978).[3] And it has seen police officers awarded—in 1961 and again in 1979—at least two unparalleled leaps in pay.

Many among the officers we spoke to recalled 'the Job' as being poorly remunerated during the middle decades of the twentieth century. Following what one Police Federation representative referred to as the 'deliberate' efforts in the wake of the 1919 police strike to place officers 'well ahead of the average artisan wage', there existed a clear memory among our interviewees that this advantage had by the 1950s been eroded. There was, in addition, a sense among some—such as this retired shire force chief constable— that pay levels had contributed greatly to the well documented problems of recruiting during this period (Weinberger 1995: 15–25): 'it was a poor job... I was an engineer before I joined [in 1948], and the week before I joined the police, my wage was nearly £12. And when I joined the police service it was four pounds ten shillings.... They couldn't get recruits. You either wanted to be a police officer, or you wouldn't join.' Such sentiments not only informed the lobbying that attended the 1960 Royal Commission's deliberations on pay, they also appeared to motivate the Commission to rescue police officers from the company into which they had fallen:

I remember we found, myself and another PC found in another paper, an advertisement for constables for the Peterborough police, £9 something or other a week, and in the next column, and exactly level with it as it were, side by side on two columns, were refuse collectors, then called dustmen, for the local authority being paid something like half a pound, ten shillings in those days, more than a PC. We cut this out and sent it to the Royal Commission and they cited it in the Royal Commission report, policemen were paid starting rate the same as dustmen, refuse collectors, that was about it. Everybody agreed they should be paid more. You don't get a great deal of social status if the salary is as low as that. It wasn't seen to be the place to be [retired chief constable, metropolitan force].

The message plainly being promulgated here is that paying police officers too poorly undermines the status and authority of the office, in part by rendering it comparable with—less demanding, by implication more demeaning—manual jobs. Yet there is also a sense in officers' reflections that police pay has a double-edged quality, with poor (or at least modest) remuneration being recalled as an ingredient of the high(er) cultural standing in which the job was regarded in the middle decades of the twentieth century. This chief constable's memory of police–public relations in the early 1960s offers some insight into this: 'there was a lot of sympathy and a lot of empathy in the community for officers because of the poor pay and conditions that they had to work under'. So too does the attempt of the Police Federation during the 1976–8 pay dispute to articulate such sentiment using the slogan 'One way to earn £40 a week' alongside a series of advertisements depicting officers involved in assorted dangerous situations, including one officer with a dart embedded in his neck. This former chief constable's reflections on police work in the 1970s seem well attuned to this dual meaning of police pay:

Strangely enough, as the job became more difficult and policemen became assaulted more regularly, and sometimes were killed more often than they had been, there was a sympathy vote came into play and the job was seen to be very much demanding and testing. And in a sense you got this elevation of the status. 'Isn't it an important job, isn't it a difficult job', would come into the conversation which had not been present when I joined in the fifties and sixties... There was two parallel strands of the conversation. One is to do with status *vis-à-vis* your salary, your purchasing power, your worth, and the other the value of the job which you are doing, the danger of the job you are doing. The two don't always go side by side.

The aspect of this equation which has to do with the job being devalued through low pay is certainly to the fore in officers' recollections of the 1970s, as is the sheer anger and frustration felt by many officers at the time. As one officer recalled, 'you felt poor up to 1978, Edmund-Davies. I had never seen a police force nearer to striking than it was at that time. There was so much unrest and so much low morale. Pre-Edmund-Davies, there was so much anti-feeling, anti-government feeling, anti-authority feeling, within the force, I have never seen so many bobbies who were on the verge of resigning or they were talking strike' (male sergeant, GMP).

For some officers we interviewed, the prevailing memory here was of a job that was simply providing insufficient income on which to live: 'I think I actually sat down one night with the good lady and worked out if I could afford to be a policeman. It didn't pay enough' (inspectors' group, GMP). Others appeared to resent the comparison the state of police pay at the time appeared to imply—'traffic wardens were being paid more than I was' (male sergeant, GMP), or else registered its deleterious effects in terms of the quality of recruitment ('to be honest, if you had two eyes, two ears, a nose, two arms and a pulse, you were in' (male inspector, GMP)); problems of retention ('they were leaving in their droves, you couldn't keep good people' (male chief superintendent, GMP)), or the enticement to petty corruption ('the police salary up to 1978 was absolutely abysmal, so by accepting £2 for standing by a window, or £2 for being called out, they didn't see it as corrupt' (male inspector, GMP)). One Police Federation spokesperson we interviewed recalled the police temper during this period thus:

Our salary was pretty poor in '76. I mean, in London, bus drivers were earning more than five-year constables. Bus drivers, bus inspectors were certainly earning much more. And they used to come in our canteen, and there was, everyone was second-jobbing. Everyone in the police station was doing something, either fixing cars, or building extensions, electricians, or whatever their previous calling was, they were doing that. Those of us who didn't have a particular skill were doing all sorts of stuff, driving undertaker's cars, or wedding cars, or doing anything to supplement our salary...And at the same time there was a lot of corruption about as well. There was a lot of police officers taking bribes. Those of us that weren't taking bribes were doing second jobs, basically trying to earn more money.

This was the backdrop to the 1976–8 police pay dispute during which the police (in effect, successfully) strove to break the national pay ceiling that the Labour government had imposed on public sector workers. The police pay claim—the upshot of what one Police Federation spokesperson described as 'a tremendous upsurge of militancy coming right through the service'—was recalled by one retired senior civil servant we interviewed as having met with a certain 'sympathy' in the Home Office: 'crime rates were going up and they were being asked to cope with this. They were being asked to carry out public order duties and things of this sort, and yet on the other hand, they were being under-valued by a society which didn't pay them enough.' There was also an awareness that it was during this period 'very, very difficult to recruit policemen' and that 'some people [were] going into the force who in other circumstances would not have got in' (former Home Office Minister of State). Such sentiments co-existed, however, with 'the feeling that if the [pay] norm was exceeded for the police then you would have to increase it for everybody' (former Home Office Minister of State), something that gave rise to what one former Home Office civil servant described as 'quite a difficult situation': 'there was actually talk of a police strike, which was pretty well unheard of, for a very long time at any rate. And we did actually have some contacts with the Cabinet Office and the Ministry of Defence about the possibility, if there was a police strike, of deploying troops on the streets in a law and order role'. Against this backdrop, Edmund-Davies was mobilized as a means of squaring the circle, a backdoor way—as another civil servant we interviewed put it—'of singling the police out and giving them special status'.

The pay award that followed from Margaret Thatcher's decision on taking office in May 1979 to implement the Edmund-Davies Report's recommendations in full and at once had a serious beneficial impact on the standard of living of police officers. As one male sergeant from Manchester put it: 'Edmund-Davies was one of the best things to advance us. All of a sudden you felt you getting paid what you were worth, so it really improved matters, it did a lot for morale. There have been many enquiries, Royal Commissions for the police force, but that one was far more reaching. The police thought Davies and his committee was wonderful.' Among some, morale was further reinforced in the early 1980s by the government support and material rewards that accompanied the police's involvement in quelling urban disorders and industrial conflict. As one female sergeant recalled, 'the only people that benefited from the miners' strike was the police because the individuals that went got a lot more money and a lot of them bought a lot of expensive things with it, cars, washing machines, villas abroad... You speak to any police officer, male, particularly that was in around then and they'd say "oh yes, I had the 'Scargill car' or the 'Scargill washing machine'."' The effects of the boost in police remuneration in the early 1980s is well expressed in the following account:

Edmund-Davies came in and it was a damn good pay award. I think we moved then from people who wanted to do the job, to people who joined the job for the money. And there was a distinct difference. From scraping the barrel, you could afford a holiday abroad, or whatever, and a new car. You could tell when the pay rose, all you had to do was look at the car park... Like I said, in my opinion, some were joining for the money, not the job. And that was a difference, a big difference [inspectors' group, GMP].

One begins to obtain a sense from this account of how the double-edged meanings of police pay infuse officers' sensibilities towards Edmund-Davies and its aftermath. On the one hand, one encounters what might be described as a secular disposition towards the Job and its rewards, one whose basic orientation runs *this is a demanding, sometimes dangerous job for which we ought to be properly paid*. From this vantage point, the tale to be told about police pay in the two decades since Edmund-Davies is how its benefits have 'slowly been eroded' (constables' group, GMP): 'they've clawed it back in pension contributions, housing allowances, various other allowances, which have just been either taken away or eroded. I know the housing allowance was a big benefit. That's completely gone now for new recruits. Your pension contributions went up by about 3 per cent. A lot of the money has been clawed back, given with one hand and taken away again' (inspectors' group, GMP). Being a police officer has, on this view, once more become 'not a well paid job, given what they do and the dangers they face' (male sergeant, GMP); one that has begun to re-invite what for the officers concerned are some infelicitous comparisons:

PC1: We're now getting to the point now whereby if you've got a police officer who's in the job, and there's only his income coming into the family, they will struggle in this day and age. On paper, the money looks fabulous, like a really good package. In reality, it's rubbish, when you compare it, it may not be as good as other jobs. That's just my view.

PC2: The public's perception of the wages we earn is exaggerated. Compare it with a lorry driver who gets £23,000 a year. You get a bobby here on eighteen grand, something like that. They're going to fights and all sorts, working shift work, for seven grand [*sic*] a year less than lorry driving. No detriment to the lorry driver. But certainly the job we're expected to do is a lot more risky [constables' group, GMP].

On the other hand, we find among officers a wistful sense of loss that the job has come to be apprehended in these terms, as if it has somehow been sullied, its cultural worth devalued, by its association with (too much) money. On this view, *non-pecuniary notions to do with honour, obligation, duty, and sacrifice are central both to being a police officer, and to the proper relationship between policing and the social.* The story of Edmund-Davies narrated here is of the job having become much less of 'a way of life', no longer something to which—especially in the CID—you 'were expected' to devote long, often unpaid, hours (male chief inspector, Cheshire Police (CP)); one whose financial rewards have served to attract insufficiently devoted people: 'I think it was a vocation, prior to Edmund-Davies, it was a vocation, as nursing is, and still is today. We've changed now to being a salary, and that has without question attracted a number of the wrong type of people into the Job' (male inspector, GMP). For those minded to appreciate police work in this fashion, the contrast with nursing seems especially germane, a shorthand way of expressing the concern that high(er) pay had somehow atrophied the close—seemingly organic—connection that once existed between the police officer and his public:

Insp.: It was quite often in the early days that people would come up to you and say, particularly at nights or something like that, people would pass you and say goodnight. People in their, maybe forties, something like that, fifties, they would say goodnight. And a frequently heard comment was 'I wouldn't have your job for £100 a week'. Now I think that changed. Although it wasn't badly paid, it wasn't particularly well paid. The Edmund-Davies thing, the changes that came along that made police pay quite good, changed I think the public attitudes in that respect. It no longer became 'fancy doing their job, who'd do that?'

IL: Post Edmund-Davies you weren't so long suffering?

Insp.: No, we were damn well paid for it. So that was an attitude I think. If I can have a comparison say to the nursing profession, you still hear that of the nurses don't you? It's probably a problem for them, if they do have their pay boosted where they're pretty well paid some of the people will start saying, 'I know they've a bad job but they get damn well paid for it'. But you don't hear that at the moment, they've still got the public sympathy, haven't they, because people consider them poorly paid [male inspector, GMP].

Back to Basics: The Nature of 'the Job'

We want now to consider officers' reconstructions of the task that stands at the ideological core of the vision of police work embedded in their memories—namely, beat patrolling or 'bobbying'. It is striking from our interviewees' remarks just how central this activity is to the idea of police work that officers seek to nurture and publicly defend, one that appears pivotal to their occupational identity. This surfaced in our discussions in several ways—in opposition to (over-qualified) graduates and (ambitious, insufficiently committed) 'high flyers'; in evident distaste at the manner in which specialist departments have progressively devalued generic patrolling, and in some vehemently expressed hostility towards the Criminal Investigation Department (CID), an outfit variously described to us as a 'predominantly middle-class, middle-aged, male-orientated regime' (female officer, GMP) and as 'the biggest boys club in the Job' (male inspector, GMP).

This representation of 'the Job' clearly effaces the well-documented motivations and desires of a preponderance of officers and obscures certain key features of the police organization. It is evident, from our own and other enquires, that officers tend to dislike beat patrolling, have long resorted to various forms of 'easing behaviour' to avoid it (Cain 1973), and invariably take up the first opportunity to be *promoted* out of it (a career trajectory that signifies much about how the organization values such work). In this vein, some officers recalled being seduced by the CID at an early point in their careers: 'it was football, women, murders, good class thieves breaking into safes...I leaned more towards that type of person and that type of job' (male police sergeant, GMP). Even some among those who appeared to have a genuine commitment to the 'social service' aspects of beat work ('I thought it was brilliant. I actually thought it was great') found it hard to resist the allure of the CID: 'I have to confess that after a while, especially when the image of the police started to portray these crime fighters, I wanted to do something a bit more sexy than helping people' (male inspector, GMP).

Yet for all that it appears to mystify the nature of 'the Job', it is beat patrolling that remains pivotal to the idea of English policing subscribed to by the majority of those we interviewed. Some sense of its enduring significance is apparent in the following account:

It was a job that demanded a lot of you physically, because you had to be out in all weathers at all times. It was very demanding. You were always on your own. You had no pocket radios in those days. When you walked out of that police station you were on your own, and highly visible. You had to learn to survive [retired chief constable, shire force].

How though were officers prepared for this task in the early decades of the post-war period? How do they reconstruct the nature and purpose of the Job during these years? What fate do officers feel has befallen beat patrolling (and its place inside the police organization) in the latter half of the twentieth century? We want in this section—in seeking to discern the visions and values of police work implicit and explicit in officers' memories—to address each of these questions in turn.

On Police Training

The training regime the officers we interviewed were subject to was characterized by one retired chief constable who joined in 1945 as 'largely legal' and devoid of 'what I call philosophical content': 'it was just the criminal law, criminal procedure, various other things like first aid, life saving, drill, physical training, and so on and so forth. Quite a kind of military style about it'. A Greater Manchester Police inspector recalled the training he received in the early 1970s in very much the same terms: 'we did parades everyday, did self-defence training, there was attention to care of the uniform and that kind of stuff, but the bulk of it was learning the law and the procedures and physical fitness, drill, all that stuff'.

Two distinct elements can be discerned from these accounts. First, the memory of a training programme that was practically demanding: 'a very harsh, brutal, not physically, but mentally brutal regime of thirteen weeks, very tough training, which I suspect had changed little since Victorian times. Very much to test the candidate's metal. Have they got the bottle, physique, and stamina to be a cop? So attempts to break you in the first couple of weeks, mentally' (chief officer, metropolitan force). Secondly, a strong emphasis on the rote-based—or 'parrot fashion' (male inspector, GMP)—learning of criminal law, what one Manchester inspector who joined in 1978 described as 'sitting you down and pumping definitions into you'. This was often recalled as a matter of imbibing from revered texts—such as *Moriarty's Police Law*, described to us by one Police Federation spokesperson as 'the bible of the police service'—the statutory definition of a wide assortment of offences, including: 'infanticide, the crime of the destruction of child while the woman is suffering the effects of lactation', 'coinage offences, you know, counterfeiting', and 'all about abortion' (spokesperson, Police Federation). It was a regime associated with a characteristic mode of instruction:

Insp.: When I joined [in 1970], the instructor just sat at the front of the class and read from a text-book or a manual, he read the lesson, and everybody in the class religiously copied what he said. You didn't actually learn anything within the class, you just copied it, what he said, and if there was any time at the end he might ask you a few questions. Of course if you're copying word for word you're not going to be taking it in, you're not really learning it. So at the end of the day your job is to look through the day's lessons and learn it, what had been imparted to you during the day.

IL: You were learning a body of words?

Insp.: That's what it was, there was no teaching as such. That was all it was day after day, just writing in a book [male inspector, GMP].

Some officers we interviewed clearly recall things of value in the way the training they received prepared them for the job. For some this was a matter largely of having been made physically fit: 'you had drill, you had PE, cross-country running and all that jazz which nowadays seems to have gone out of the window' (chief constable, metropolitan force). Others spoke of the 'confidence' they derived as young constables from 'knowing what the law was' (retired male sergeant, GMP), a feeling sometimes accompanied by the view that today 'bobbies don't know the law. You go on a course and nobody knows if you've learnt anything, because at the end there's no exam' (male constable, GMP). This chief officer implicitly defended such training by situating it in the policing and social contexts of the mid-twentieth century:

You were coming into an operating environment where you had to be really very, very self-sufficient. As I say, no radios, you had to be able to talk your way out of trouble, and I guess what they had devised, and to some extent they were right, was a fairly demanding, testing, disciplined three months, where you either survived it and could then cope with the street, or you couldn't and it was probably best that you didn't. So I think that those who dropped out of training school, it was probably good for them and for the outfit that they did drop out of training school. They would not have coped with the streets. Policing was much simpler, I think, in terms of expectations, relationships, accountability, what you were doing. And that training seemed to produce reasonable products to cope with that environment.

Yet for most of our interviewees it is the futility of this training regime that looms largest in the memory. As one retired Manchester inspector put it: 'they spent a lot of time mis-training us really', having us 'learn really nonsensical offences'. Indeed, the strength of this sentiment is such as to invite questions about the signifying force of mid-twentieth century police training, its little contribution to the production and reproduction of *both* authority relations inside the police *and* police authority in wider English society. Such rote-based instruction appears, in other words, to project an image of the police officer as but a passive, unquestioning recipient of Law passed down from on high *and*, once moulded, as a vessel for delivering Law into the settings of everyday life, the implied relationship of the individual subject to police authority being equivalent in both cases: 'now we have this open learning style, where you're taught to question everything. But going back years ago, that wasn't the case. It was a case of shut up, watch what I do, and that was about it' (sergeants' group, GMP). It is perhaps this—the particular conception of authority implicit within the training these officers received—that underpins their reactions to what has overwhelmingly come to be interpreted as archaic:

Coinage, counterfeit coins, what to do about counterfeit coins, and the law regarding passing and producing counterfeit coins. Infanticide. Ridiculous, ridiculous offences to do with the countryside and wildlife, things like that. When I look back I never touched on those subjects since. And the vast majority of officers never did. But we spent hours learning definitions of everything—ninety-two definitions by heart. By the end of the course you had to know them. And the vast majority of them were definitions of different kinds of vehicle, definitions of a tractor, and the legal points of when a tractor can or cannot be on a road. Litter, when I was a trainer, hours teaching litter, the law regarding litter. When I think back now, absolutely useless in practical terms [male inspector, GMP].

On Beat Work

It is also apparent from officers' recollections that as novice constables they experienced a yawning gap between the instruction in law that dominated their training and the practical exigencies of the job; something that prompted certain well-worn clichés about police training ('you can forget all that bloody rubbish you learned at Brusch [training centre]' (spokesperson, Police Federation)) and about how and where the job was *really* learned: 'you just picked it up', one retired police inspector we interviewed observed, 'you just literally picked it up'. This discrepancy has much to do with a memory—and practical conception—of beat work as a job in which law enforcement did not figure prominently. Rather, officers recall being 'tied to the ground' (retired chief constable, metropolitan force) and tasked with deploying a range of resources—of which law was but one—in the ordering of territory, what one member of our constables' discussion group characterized as being 'responsible for eight hours for that patch of land' (cf. Holdaway 1983). As such, the job is remembered as coalescing around two related practices: *pastoral care* and *informal social control*.

In respect of the former, one retired officer we interviewed recalled the job in the following terms: 'I've never been a thief taker or anything like that. I suppose the term I've always used is that I look upon myself as a glorified boy scout, that's the sort of thing that I've enjoyed doing, I've enjoyed my contact with people' (retired male sergeant, GMP). Another recounted in similar terms, and with evident pride, some of the responsibilities that attended working his beat:

We used to go out of our way if somebody was ill, we used to go out to houses where there were people who were infirm, and the regular job of the beat was to go in and make the person a cup of tea, turn them over in bed to stop them getting bed sores. I am not making this up. It was a regular part of the beat. My main job on a beat, apart from looking after schoolchildren, was looking after the elderly, calling on people seeing if they are all right. On nights trying door handles seeing if property was okay. It wasn't about catching baddies... You'd get phone calls in the middle of the night from elderly folk that had fallen out of bed, the first people they called were the police. The police would go and lift them and pull them back in, not the ambulance people. Policing was a lot about servicing in those days [male inspector, GMP].

'Bobbying' is reconstructed here as not merely providing a routine visible presence on the beat, but as a series of recurring activities oriented to maintaining the social fabric of urban neighbourhoods. Several instances of such work were cited in this regard. Some registered the enduring significance of 'showing the mums and the children across the road': 'you would build up a relationship, you would see the grown-up, you'd know the families. So you'd know that a young lad that you were perhaps dealing with a few years later as a teenager was the little so-and-so that you used to show across the road when he was five or six' (retired male sergeant, GMP). Others recalled daily visits to the properties of those who were 'away from home' (retired male inspector, GMP), or spoke of the police officer's role in activating others to govern urban territory: 'in my day as a bobby you put reports in on public clocks that were slow, pavements that were cracked or flags loose, holes in roads. When you went round your beat, you saw them, you fell over the bloody things, so you put a report in' (retired male inspector, GMP). Many described the routine practice of checking the properties (and, by implication, the protective habits) of local denizens: 'we used to check door handles, and make sure the shops were shut up at night. We'd walk along in the early hours of the morning, four and five o'clock, and we'd go religiously from one end of the street to the other, if there was a row of shops, and try the door handle at the front. And if we found one open occasionally we would ring the shopkeeper up and say "you've left your shop open, there was a light on upstairs". It was a waste of time. But it showed a certain relationship, a certain job profile that is different now' (male inspector, GMP). In what is a clear echo of the lay memories discussed in Chapter 3, the job is plainly recalled by officers as having been integral to the constitution of local social relations:

You were part of the community. You weren't just a separate thing there like a bottle of medicine, take it when you need it. We were there all the time whether it was good, bad or indifferent. You were there and you were sharing it with them, you suffered when they suffered, and you tried to make life easier where you could help and where you had the authority or the know-how [retired male sergeant, CP].

The care of the flock entailed in this role also encompassed the social regulation of its errant or wayward members. This again however was not recalled as a matter principally of law enforcement—'domestic violence, drunk in pubs, pub fights, that sort of thing, you wouldn't have locked anybody up unless they persisted' (retired male chief inspector, CP); but, rather, as requiring officers to deploy their symbolic and physical authority in an effort to quell unruly citizens or neighbourhood conflicts. As one retired Greater Manchester Police sergeant put it:

Many a time, I'm sure a lot of bobbies like me, they've clipped somebody's ear or, I would not clip anybody, but they've told them off or frightened the life out of them and left it at that because it wasn't worth going to court really. Just trying to put the lad back on the line—'if you do that again you'll be inside', and it worked, it worked in those days...I mean I didn't want to blacken a lad, fourteen or twelve, who had just made one slip. A good dressing down with a policeman usually does the trick.

For the most part, it is the symbolic dimension of police authority that is recalled as pivotal to the task of local ordering; something that is seen to have depended on people responding with little or no complaint to the express or implied threat of legal sanction (and officers' presumed knowledge of Law), and on the capacity of officers to make constructive use of the in-the-dark deference of those with whom they dealt: 'they [the public] thought the police had more powers than they actually had...We used to use what we termed the "Ways and Means Act". You used ignorance of people to a large extent to achieve the ends you wanted' (male sergeant, GMP). It was in respect of such situated 'bluffing' that some among our interviewees insisted upon the significance for police order maintenance of an *imposing physical stature*—'those people were feared by the public, they were respected, so they never actually had to use violence' (retired male sergeant, GMP)—and *the uniform*: 'you command more respect if you're in uniform and you can hold that uniform. Fifty per cent of the job is done before you start and that's without overacting. In fact the more you underplay it the more effective you are' (retired male sergeant, CP). It was also in this context that we were repeatedly told of the importance—in assisting officers' 'survival' in hostile settings in days prior to the advent of radio communications—of *'walking* to a fight', and of the cognate need to 'get the crowd on your side' by 'not winning' any ensuing confrontations 'too well' (retired male chief superintendent, CP).

But officers also recounted ways in which physical violence was brought to bear on this task. Some here remembered 'big sergeants [who] always carried what was called a night stick, and they weren't against poking people with it, or hitting them with it either, if the need arose' (support staff group, CP); while others spoke of the sometimes 'vicious retribution' that ensued in the event of assaults against police officers: 'if they battered a policeman, they got a bit of a thump in the cells to put them in order. If they came back to the police station to complain, nobody would take the complaint' (male sergeant, GMP). This retired chief superintendent proffered the following reflections on the summary justice that marked his early years in the job during the 1950s:

In an area where there's a lot of crime and drunkenness and bawdy behaviour, they would expect rough treatment from the police and they get it, if it was required. If it was more a civilized area, well they wouldn't expect rough treatment and they wouldn't get it, because one of the things you learn quickly in the police force is how to assess character. You can assess a person's character within a very short time of talking to him or her. If they're f'ing and blinding to you right away, you know damn well that they don't expect to be treated in a reasonable way and in those days they weren't. If they were rough with policemen, they got manhandled, and nobody complained about it. There's many a fellow stood up in the dock, the next morning, he'd got a black eye and nobody complained. If he did the magistrate would have no sympathy at all...The days of instant justice went a long time ago, but that system worked.

The Demise of 'Bobbying'

The dominant sentiment of our police interviewees is that 'the Job' understood in these terms has in the latter decades of the twentieth century been significantly eroded. This was not, to be sure, the outlook of all. Some recalled policing in the 1950s and 1960s as a shambolic operation that has come to be viewed through inappropriately rose-tinted spectacles: 'the old beat system was not all that great shape. There was not all that many men about and they could not be readily contacted...I can remember hearing in the fifties a uniform sergeant saying to our CID sergeant, "Are your lads about tonight?". He said "Why?". He said, "Well I've only got one policeman out and one inside"—and that was for a city like Chester. It's mythical all these policemen that have suddenly disappeared' (retired male chief superintendent, CP). Others recalled what one Manchester inspector described as the 'endemic' petty corruption that used to attend relations between officers and local people, practices that included 'discounts in local shops' (retired male inspector, CP), 'getting two quid for calling out the window company to board up a plate glass window' (male inspector, GMP), and receiving 'brown envelopes' from garages for passing road traffic accident repairs their way. 'Everybody knew it went on', one male sergeant remarked of such 'envelopes', 'I defy anybody who was in Manchester and Salford Police at that time to say they didn't do it.'

Yet the prevailing disposition remains that this revered job—the task that lies at the ideological core of many officers preferred idea of policing—has been radically and detrimentally undermined. Several factors are mobilized to account for this. This demise is seen, first, as a prime indicator of the distance that today stands between the police and the public, something attributed by many to the advent of Unit Beat Policing (UBP): '1ˢᵗ April 1968. That's when the English police service went down the tubes and I blame Lancashire County [Council] and the Labour Party, because that was the marking point. There's dozens of examples, factually stated, that prove the 1ˢᵗ April was a disaster in policing terms, historical policing terms' (male chief superintendent, GMP). Many recognized that this outcome was an unintended consequence of UBP, something that flowed from the sheer number of calls mobile officers were required—fire brigade fashion—to respond to, or from the tendency of officers to treat the patrol car as what one police constable we interviewed called 'your own little world': 'in your car it's warm. You aren't going to get out of your car. It's human nature' (male constable, GMP). This did little to detract, however, from the felt sense that the disembedding of officers from everyday life—'now if you see a policeman on foot it's practically flag-day, isn't it' (retired male sergeant, CP)—had opened up a de-legitimating chasm between the organization and a law-abiding populace that feels the police are no longer 'part of us' (retired male sergeant, CP):

The public's perceptions of a police officer in my day was helmet, smart tunic, pressed trousers, clean shoes who strolled about his beat, and was everybody's friend. The perception now is that this officer is totally aggressive—everything about him looks aggressive. He doesn't walk about the streets, he rides about in a car or a van, and on that van there is a riot windscreen. That doesn't give the impression of policing as I know it [retired male sergeant, GMP].

Secondly, officers bemoan the ways in which generic patrolling has been devalued *by* and *within* the contemporary police organization. Some referred here to the manner in which specialist departments 'encourag[e] people to get away from grass roots policing' (male sergeant, CP) and routinely assume precedence over uniformed patrolling. As one member of our constables discussion group put it, 'you go into specialized departments, and you do something wrong, they put you back on the streets. If you're on the streets and you've done something wrong, they never say they'll put you into a specialist department. So what does that say? Whenever they're short the first thing they do is take somebody out of uniform and put them into a specialist department.' In a related vein, others decried the capacity of the organization to 'generate paper for the sake of generating paper', something that is seen as contributing hugely to 'officers spending an inordinate amount of time in the police station' (male constable, GMP). One recently retired Greater Manchester Police sergeant voiced this complaint in the following terms:

When I arrested somebody I had four forms to fill in, I had a fingerprint form to fill in, a descriptive form to fill in, five foot ten, beard, glasses, curly hair, tattoos, you know, all this sort of, you know a descriptive, brief summary of offence and charge sheet that's it. Forty-eight separate foolscap forms now and who's come up with all that lot? So you go in there, I could be out on the streets half and hour later going and doing something else, locking somebody else up, or whatever, or there in uniform walking around or driving around. Now, if you arrest somebody at the start of your tour of duty, you're off the streets for eight hours—that's why there's nobody around. Too many specialist departments and too much paperwork.

We encountered, thirdly, a felt sense that the status and authority of 'the Job' had in various ways atrophied in the past several decades. For some, this had much to do with a literal decline in the size and presence (and, to this extent, effectiveness) of the people now recruited to undertake what is considered as necessarily a man's task: 'this is a potentially violent job. The policeman to me is six-foot, he's athletic, he's an imposing character. Now you've got five-foot two-inch policewomen with long hair. The only aggressive thing about them is this big belt they wear with all their things hanging down, and people don't have the same respect for something like that' (retired male sergeant, GMP). For others, the crucial factor is the altered social context of police work, the coming of a world in which people are more rights-conscious and less compliant, a world in which a police officer's authority is no longer taken as given:

You used to be able to bluff a lot more is perhaps the best word. You could bluff people a lot more because they were not as *au fait* as to their rights as they are now. Nowadays they know a lot more, more street-wise than they used to be. If you try to bluff them they are far more likely to call your bluff now than they used to. One time the bobby was the bobby. If he said something you did it. Nowadays it is just a young lad in uniform. It goes back again to what I was saying, natural authority, uniform, national service. People respected a uniform. The uniform said do something, you did it [male inspector, GMP].

A Disciplined Body of Men

The policeman is expected to have a mind of his own, at all times. Police Service discipline is geared to this fact. It is not only necessary discipline; it is also a type of discipline that the policeman himself recognises, and accepts, as being necessary. It is, therefore, no drawback [Wainwright 1967: 15].

One striking memory of the character of the police organization during the middle decades of the twentieth century surfaced during our interviews with officers: that of a 'disciplined' institution structured around a hierarchical, quasi-militaristic set of authority relations. Some sense of this is to be gleaned from this former senior officer's response to having been asked to describe the organization he joined in 1956.

Inevitably very different. National Service was still on. The war was still in recent memory. People were used to authority. It was an authoritative and authoritarian organization. A lot of that was reflected in society as well. I joined Peterborough which was tiny by today's standards, about 120 or thereabouts, officers, civilians. Extremely proud of itself, very smart, physically very smart, actually did quite a good job I think, probably a very good job by the standards of the day, but minute. Ran a very tight ship...People accepted the status quo, with sergeants, inspectors, and so on. There was a family atmosphere with a strict structure.

This 'atmosphere' was in part the product of a police force modelled on 'military traditions' (chief constable, shire force)—'the internal discipline was much akin to being in the armed services. The obedience, I'm not saying this is a good thing, the obedience was tremendous' (retired chief constable, provincial force); something reinforced by the number of supervisory officers during this period who hailed from military backgrounds. As one Police Federation spokesperson remarked of the force he joined, 'most of the hierarchy, people who'd been in longer than me, had all been in the military, had all done National Service, so it was a very—it was a much more militaristic culture.' But it also—as the above account of Peterborough Police suggests—formed part of a wider assemblage of authority relations prevalent in English society during the immediate post-war decades. As one retired Manchester police sergeant recalled, 'discipline was very hard. If you were late for duty by more than five minutes you were reported to the chief superintendent and fined...It was oppressive really. You see most of life then was like that. Factories, schools, there was harsh discipline in all aspects of life.'[4] The following recollection—of a serving inspector who joined Manchester Police in 1964—captures well the occupational culture and associated dispositions in force at the time:

When you joined you knew you were joining a disciplined service. You are joining a uniformed organization and you were told from day one if you were told to jump, you jumped. You obeyed your Sergeant, Inspector whatever. The type of person in my opinion who could not take that shouldn't be in the job anyway. Now I had no difficulty, if a sergeant says 'do that', you did it. If the inspector says 'do that', you did it. You might feel a bit peeved sometimes, because like in any organization, there was some people in rank who abused you, you know were really nasty at times. It is an extremely macho organization the police is, as you have probably gathered by all your research. You didn't complain because it would have been wrong to complain.

What then are the key properties of this particular set of organizational relations? First, a memory of superior officers as powerful, awe-inducing creatures—characteristics that are encapsulated in the following account: 'supervisors in those days, Inspectors in the mid-sixties, all had National Service backgrounds. They were to a certain extent tyrants. If somebody said to me as a PC, in fact it happened to me, "You've got to go and see the Inspector for your annual appraisal", it was polished shoes, pressed trousers. They were like God in those days. You were frightened to death of an Inspector, you were frightened to death of a Sergeant. Inspector was God, if he said "jump", you jumped' (male inspector, GMP). Supervisory ranks were in this regard recalled as distant figures—'they didn't fraternise then. They kept themselves a little bit away from staff' (male inspector, GMP)—with whom lowly constables would maintain at best fleeting, formal relations. As one serving chief superintendent from Greater Manchester Police put it, 'they would never refer to me while I was on probation by my first name. I was never referred to by my first name'. But such ranks were also reconstructed—using, revealingly, religious terminology—as objects of what one retired Manchester officer called 'fear and trembling': 'certainly of an Inspector who was God, and possibly even the Sergeants'. Several officers described the habits and practices that served to constitute this relationship, whether in respect of 'shitting yourself' if the Inspector requested one's presence (male inspector, GMP), or 'standing to attention' (male inspector, GMP), or otherwise being humbled by the presence of revered senior figures. As one respondent—who was subsequently to climb to these exalted heights—recalled, 'the Assistant Chief Constables and the Chief Constable were God. If I met the Chief Constable as I went up the stairs and he was coming down, I would squeeze myself up against the wall to let him by' (retired chief constable, metropolitan force).[5] Such hierarchies were also the subject, however, of more formalized ritual enactment, practices that encompassed collectively 'standing when senior officers entered the room'; 'saluting Inspectors on the street' (male inspector, GMP), and lining up for morning parade:

We used to parade properly, used to have to stand to attention, full uniform, helmet on and produce your appointments, and then they'd examine it and you put them down and you'd make notes of all the stolen cars, and it was all done to attention, you know stood up. Now you go in and you're lucky if they're wearing ties, and they have a very informal brief, don't even call it a parade. Strange thing was the parade always took place fifteen minutes before the start of your tour of duty, we weren't paid for it, that fifteen minutes you gave to the job. Your pay started from seven o'clock if you're on mornings, so quarter to seven you had to be there, if you were there at fourteen minutes to seven you were done for being late in your own time. It was hard discipline really [retired male sergeant, GMP].

We encountered, secondly, memories of what—on the surface at least—was a culture of compliance, one in which supervisory officers were treated as being always—in effect—'right': 'I remember the first day I went to Hyde, there was a constable who said to me, he said "there's only one person you have to worry about here and that's Sergeant Bird, he's not always right but he's never wrong", and I think that summed up a lot of the Sergeants. But he was a fearsome man, he was a huge man, he had a huge shaven head and the biggest hands I've ever seen' (retired male chief inspector, CP). What flowed from this, it seems, was an ethos of unquestioning obedience—'if your Sergeant said go and stand on that flag for three hours, you actually stood on that flag for three hours' (constables' group, GMP); coupled with a lack of any serious expectation—it was simply unthinkable—that individual decisions and organizational practices were open for discussion: 'you did as you were told as you would do in the military. And you didn't negotiate shift changes or anything like that. You got a shift change because you were told. There was no consultation basically. You were told when you have your leave. You weren't consulted on policies, you weren't consulted on process changes or anything like that' (male chief superintendent, GMP). It appears, in short, to have been a culture in which 'what would be termed bullying today, you accepted it as discipline' (male sergeant, GMP).

The principal manifestation of this set of vertical authority relations surrounded supervisors' efforts to monitor and regulate patrol work. Our interviewees narrated several tales of how sergeants 'would appear like a ghost' on their beat (retired male constable, GMP), or 'go out in plain clothes at night, checking up officers were doing their job' (female constable, GMP), or even lay traps for unsuspecting constables: 'when I first started, at night, all you're doing is shaking hands with doorknobs, it wouldn't happen now. You'd find that some sergeants would stick a matchstick in the door so that if you tried the door it would fall out, so they could tell whether you were doing the job properly or not' (retired chief constable, shire force). In this vein, we also heard recollections of capricious or 'vindictive' supervisors—those who 'treated people like dirt, made their lives a misery by petty persecution'; or 'spent more time hunting the poor bloody [probationers] for their misdeeds than they actually did in policing the borough' (spokesperson, Police Federation), or who delighted in hauling constables in to account for their apparently sloppy work. One provincial chief constable recalled in this regard, 'being dragged down to the police station to explain to the inspector why I hadn't found three break-ins on my beat. They'd all been through skylights. I remember, a bit cheekily, saying to him, "what do you expect me to do, walk along the roof tops?". I got a bollocking for being cheeky, and I should have found them. I wasn't told how I should, but I should have.' Yet for all such recalled 'excesses', this remains a culture of discipline that at least some among our interviewees could appreciate given the occupational 'realities' of the time:

There was a definite militaristic thing, because a lot of the supervisors had either returned from, you are talking about the 1960s here, and they had either done military service as a conscript, or had actually served in the war and were still young enough to be active within the police service itself. It was only, what, seventeen years previously that the war had ended. So some would still be in middle life. But it was disciplined with a purpose because you got to remember there were no personal radios, there was very little transport for the supervisors. So there was a need for, in my opinion, there was a need for that type of discipline to prevail because, by and large, and even today, you are trusted to get on with the job. That's the uniqueness of being a police officer. You can be given directives and obviously you have the law to comply with. But nevertheless there is that central core of self-discipline that's absolutely essential. That still applies in today's world. But in those days, from a supervisor's point of view, I would think, I wasn't a supervisor then, but I would think that the disciplinary side of it, that semi-militaristic approach, ensured that there was a certain code of conduct that prevailed [chief constable, metropolitan force].

This institutional ethos—or 'code of conduct'—is also remembered as intruding in various ways into officers' lives beyond the force. Some referred to this in terms of being 'owned' by the organization, a relationship, they remember, that made it especially difficult to shield family life from the demands of the Job. One officer described here being asked to work the day of her father's funeral—'I had only had one day off for my dad's funeral and I thought "how can you phone me up on the day of his funeral and ask me to work a three-to-eleven?"' (female officer, GMP). Others—such as this retired Cheshire chief superintendent—recalled the frustration attendant upon being moved frequently from job to job and, thus, from house to house: 'whilst you had a job for life, they took so much for granted of you. They literally thought they owned you. They would move you willy-nilly.' The disadvantages that attended living in 'penal settlements' of police housing—'they owned the roof over your head. If I'd have been killed or died on duty, my wife would have been out of the house' (retired male chief superintendent, CP)—were deemed particularly worthy of comment in this regard:

They moved you round every year or two. It was a tradition of the time with the county police forces that you were moved round every two or three years so you didn't become over-friendly with the natives. Of course if you fell out with somebody, one of your bosses, you were on your way [retired male chief superintendent, CP].

We used to call them colonies and to some extent we were nannied in the sense that it was rent-free accommodation. It was decorated for us, we were inspected. The house had to be inspected every week where they kind of checked for dust and all that. It's incredible really [male chief superintendent, GMP].

This last account begins to allude to some of the further restrictions on personal freedom that the organization was recalled as imposing upon officers' lives. While such constraints—seeking permission to marry for instance—began to dissipate in the immediate post-war period, there remained a host of ways in which the organization strove to ensure that officers were—and were seen to be—avatars of social and moral 'respectability'. Some sense of what this entailed is provided by this account: 'in your social life, you were expected to go to the police club. It would be frowned on being a regular in a bar. Anything you did that could expose you to criticism was either banned or frowned on. Getting into debt, that was a hanging offence' (retired male sergeant, GMP). In this vein, officers spoke of 'it being frowned upon if your wife had a business' (retired male constable, GMP); of having 'to show you lived in a clean, tidy, respectable house' (male inspector, GMP); of 'two officers [in the 1960s] having to leave because they had separated from their wives' (male chief superintendent, GMP), of a detective sacked for 'putting a telephone operator up the shoot' (retired male chief superintendent, GMP), and of being 'locked up' at night in single-sex dorms at training school during the early 1980s. The female officer who recounted this last practice described her reactions to it in the following terms:

Ten weeks at [training school] I found awful. I hated it because you were locked in, you weren't trusted, you know. I had been out in the world so to speak, I was 28 years old, I had worked, I had not come straight from school or college. So I had got a bit of experience and I was, the women were kind of you go in this, at night, and they lock you in. You know you couldn't get out. They did not trust like other officers coming to your hostel, with it being mixed, and that I found it very difficult. You know there was no trust [female constable, GMP].

As this, and the following recollection, demonstrate, the restrictions entailed by these organizational efforts to shore up the 'respectability' of police officers became—as the post-war years unfolded—increasingly archaic and untenable—made so by the socio-cultural transformations that English society began during the Sixties to undergo:

I found it very frustrating joining at 19, I came in and I found it incredibly restrictive. I knew that it would be restricting to a degree, wearing a uniform, following the shift pattern, and obviously having to implement the law. It wasn't the operational side of policing, it was the institution of policing itself, where there was distinct lack of trust in you as an individual. It's a funny mixture actually, because you were given a huge responsibility for a young lad of 19. You'd gone through a relatively brief training course, you're then put out on the street on your own, no radio, no telephone. You're supposed to be dealing with anything that you come across, or that you actually find. So there's a huge responsibility, huge discretion. But at the same time, you were obviously being checked by the sergeant and the inspector to find out where you were and what you were doing. That was fine, because that was partly to do with support as well as making sure that you were still on your beat and doing your job. That was proper supervision. I think it was the internal side, the pettiness of the arrangements internally, right the way through to where you could or couldn't live. Here we were in the mid-sixties, I was 19 years old, we were not allowed to go and live in a flat [chief constable, shire force].

An Altered Force in a Diverse World?: Discordant Voices, New Contestations

It is a whole cocktail of changes in terms of our attitudes, our culture, our attitudes to discipline and welfare, ethnic minorities, grievances towards female officers... The way I behave. I don't swear any more... I don't shout any more. Part of it is self-protection, but part of it is I am more compelled to do it in a more professional way [male chief superintendent, GMP].

The police memories we have documented in this chapter simultaneously do two things: they seek to *reconstruct* the nature and social significance of police work during the middle decades of the twentieth century, and—very often—they *project* a particular vision of how that job should be performed today. They stand in this sense as efforts to mobilize the past (or, more accurately, a selectively remembered account of that past) in a bid to judge and reshape the present. Such efforts are required because the idea of policing explicit and implicit in these accounts—of a white, masculine, rigidly ordered organization administering firm pastoral authority over a compliant populace—has over the last two to three decades come to be disputed and disturbed. This process—one mutually, if asymmetrically, conditioned by the currents of social and cultural change outlined in Chapter 1—remains uneven and resisted, a transformation whose future trajectory remains uncertain. The police dispositions set out above retain a significant, if currently somewhat muted, presence within the thicket of beliefs and sentiments that compose what has—often too unquestioningly— become known as 'police culture'. But these sentiments no longer go unchallenged, or stand dominant, and they compete today with new voices and alternative meanings in struggles to determine the working cultures and institutional ethos of the English police. We want in the remainder of this chapter to indicate some of the ways in which this once more settled police outlook has unravelled in the latter part of the twentieth century, and to consider briefly its likely ramifications. The discussion is organized around two broad themes—informalization and diversification.[6]

Informalization

We use this term to signify a quiet transformation in authority relations inside the English police, one that has seen the demise of supervisors schooled in military discipline, and some attendant shifts in the dispositions and constraints governing the routine internal supervision of police work. Several of our respondents described signs of the police having become what one female officer from Manchester called 'less hierarchical', or, as she put it, 'you have actually seen this rigid pyramid with its very defined size turning into a more sort of jelly like, softer organization'. In a similar vein, others spoke of an institution that had become 'much more open' (inspectors' group, GMP), the named indicators of which included officers of different ranks being 'on first name terms'—'it is not like Sergeant Bolton, it is hello Alan can you do this? (sergeants' group, GMP), and the advent of generally more 'informal' working relations. As one serving Manchester inspector commented, 'I can go to my chief inspector, superintendent, no matter, on a more informal footing than when I joined. I remember when I still called them Sir. But we have a much more open relationship— he is my boss but we are closer. So it is much more relaxed than what it was, very much more so on a divisional level. The modern sergeant, inspector are much more closer to the PCs than they were when I joined.' For some, generational—and, by implication, wider social—change is of no little importance in accounting for this turn:

When I look back, it was a strange relationship, because it was very us and them, you are the constable, I am the sergeant. Very often these sergeants were older, they weren't younger people like they are now. They were older, you noticed them as being particularly older. A lot of them were ex-service. Their life was a service background. They tried to carry that tradition into the police service. But of course they were coming up against young people like myself all the time. We were not children of the war as such, we were sixties children and things like that. So there was a conflict in that respect. There were two very different generations of supervisor and recruit, new people coming in [male inspector, GMP].[7]

As this account suggests, this shift is viewed in part as the product of 'new'—post-military—cohorts of recruits who have today come to occupy senior managerial positions with the police. Many of these officers—among them several chief constables—took up their positions with little time for what they saw as 'out-of-date, old-fashioned', 'lagging' institutional practices (chief constable, shire force), and coupled this with what was sometimes a highly self-conscious, publicly articulated desire to re-make police organizations.[8] As one such chief officer said of the provincial force he inherited,

'for the last six years of so [under the old chief], things had ossi-
fied...So the force was ready and ripe for change. It was crying
out for change and was frustrated because he would not allow
change to occur.' The ensuing managerial agendas tended to
involve, on the one hand, a determination to sweep away 'old'
habits and ways of doing things and replace them with 'new' organizational procedures and priorities. For one such chief officer this
encompassed 'getting equal opportunities really to work, introducing tenure policies in specialist branches and introducing openness within the organization in reporting terms. New systems for
selection and for promotion, opening up the organization, making
it transparent. Replacing subjective interview styles for selection
for promotion by assessment centres which have some form of
objectivity, criteria which are common. Introducing competency
requirements, identifying the competencies required for particular
posts or particular ranks; devising tests that enable you to measure
those and work it up. That was a hell of a cultural shock to the
organization' (chief constable, provincial force). On the other hand,
it entailed an institutional push both to involve staff in decision-
making and to encourage among them a greater readiness to take
decisions: 'the organization was also extremely hierarchical and
authoritarian. Everything came up to the top, which is very comfortable for people in between, because you never had to take any
responsibility. A report that landed on your desk that was too hard
to know what you do with; initial it and pass it up to the next one
and eventually somebody will make a decision. Then when it
comes down you can't be blamed if things go wrong because you
were only doing as you were told, it wasn't your decision. We'd to
cut through all the nonsense of that' (chief constable, provincial
force). The emergent organizational form created by this 'new
breed of worldly-wise, educated' senior officers (male inspector,
GMP) was described to us by one black officer in the following
terms:

The police organization itself has become...more human. I mean we've
gone away from the days of the old type, the old military types that was in
charge of the police service—that was one of the old criteria of chief
constable, and the old big boys' networks—to an organization that really
is more human. The staff are treated more humanely, more civilly. It's
no longer the tack you know, do what you're told, because I'm senior to
you. Do it. Do this. Do that. Today you actually do have a say in

policy-making decisions. You have a say now, politically, because we actually go out and sit down and listen and talk to the staff. Not always
reflected in satisfaction surveys, but I mean it is a way...

Processes of informalization have been fuelled, secondly, by what
was felt to be an altered disposition among contemporary constables, a mood that is habitually more sceptical, questioning, and
minded to complain. Some expressed this shifting temper in a tone
of frustrated incredulity ('If I said to an officer your job today is
seven beat, I want you to do this that and the other, the first thing
out of his mouth is "why, do I need to? What sort of job is it?".
I've known officers refuse to do things and there's been no disciplinary action' (male chief superintendent, GMP)); or else spoke
of the open disputation that has, it seems, become part and parcel
of the police force today. As one Greater Manchester Police sergeant reflected, 'if they said you are working one shift next week
and they've changed it to do another shift, you'd never question
that. You might mumble but you never questioned it. With discipline like that I thought things got on better. No moaning and
groaning. Nowadays trying to move somebody from one shift to
another is tremendous. They've all got kid's birthday parties, half
term. Things like that. There's more whinging now.' Others—such
as this serving Manchester inspector—registered the same shifts
in generally more positive terms: 'at one time you accepted far
worse conditions. But of course the vast majority of the public did,
didn't they? You accepted a shift system that was appalling as
the norm. And you didn't complain because that's the job you
wanted to do. But there is a lot more discontent in that respect. If
they're not happy with the shift system, or something like that,
they want to get it changed and do something about it, for personal reasons, for welfare reasons, and health and safety reasons,
things like that.'

These clearly represent competing judgements on the merits or
otherwise of this more questioning police temper, a point to which
we return shortly. Implicit within them, however, is a conclusion to
which they commonly allude—namely, that the processes of
detraditionalization that have refigured lay sentiments towards
police authority find some equivalence in the altered dispositions
of contemporary police officers. The point was registered by
one member of our sergeants' discussion group using the

following—for him telling—analogy:

When we go back to when I joined in 1974, they wouldn't dream of questioning other senior officers at all. You would not even question other constables who'd had five or six years' service, and you were very much speak when you were spoken too. But that was also true of society as a whole, particularly say the ten or fifteen years before it. I look at my own family, they are all under twenty. They won't ever agree with me, I am just there to be criticized and slapped down. But again going back thirty or forty years ago, it was the old thing 'wait 'til your father gets home'. Now my family wouldn't 'wait 'til your father gets home' unless he is coming in with a wallet.[9]

Finally, this process is seen as arising from certain shifts in the cultural and legal environment within which police organizations operate—shifts that have both filtered into the consciousness of their members and come significantly to shape policy and practice. Particular mention was made here of a set of issues pertaining to such matters as stress, welfare, and health and safety (and their attendant grievance procedures)—issues recalled as having few parallels in police forces of the 1950s and 1960s, an era when 'debriefing' and 'counselling' would have 'taken place down the pub' (sergeants' group, GMP). For some, such preoccupations were matters largely of window-dressing, 'put in place' more to 'pander to the political need' than as part of any genuine effort to 'look after staff' (inspectors' group, GMP). Others—from a rather different standpoint—spoke of what they saw as the half-hearted, intermittently concerned attempts to take seriously the impact 'the Job' can have on the well-being of those who do it. One female officer from Manchester recalled the following incident in this regard: 'I had seen this girl die there in front of my eyes, I was so helpless and I just found that very difficult to cope. Not only had I seen this girl die and I could not do anything, I had to tell her mother as well. You know and after that there is no welfare for you, you just go on to the next job. That is the other thing. There is a welfare officer but no one ever says, "Are you okay Rach?". We are supposed to be a caring organization but to our own we are not. I really feel strongly about that we are not. You go to all these jobs and are expected to deal with it, and to think it doesn't effect you.'

For all the cynicism, and disappointment, and suggestions of patchy performance that pervade these accounts, they nonetheless offer further testimony to the fact that issues such as these have permeated police organizations in ways that have made their own small contribution to the informalization of their working cultures. At the very least, as this heated discussion of the news that police officers involved in the 1989 Hillsborough football stadium tragedy had been awarded compensation demonstrates, they have become part of an unfinished contest about the contemporary meanings—and responsibilities—of 'the Job' and 'the force':

Sgt1:   I thought it was obscene on the grounds, like you said, that you know when you join the police service how exposed you are going to be, and the police have responsibility towards you, by training you adequately, by making sure you've got the right equipment, by making sure you can deal with situations. Having said that, Hillsborough was exceptional. I don't know what I'm trying to say. My first reaction, I was horrified that officers should get compensation, or even think about getting it. The more I have thought about it, particularly with the three female officers, they did not get the counselling, we do have a responsibility to the welfare of our staff. If we haven't provided them with something like that, then we have failed and we are at fault. So it is that. I think they are quite right to make a point of it. Now whether they should get fifty quid or £50,000 is a different matter.

Sgt2:   The issue is not the counselling, the issue is money. That is my view anyway. If you are looking at £400,000 compensation, and you look at, you know…I remember going back to '77 I was working on Christmas Day, and had to go to report on somebody being knocked down on a railway line. I only had three years service in…We had to go and search the railway line for a body on Christmas Day. We found the body—what was left of it—on this railway line. The effect that that had on me on Christmas Day, having to go home then and have your Christmas Day lunch and your family say, 'what sort of a day have you had?'. That is how it was. You just had to be quite tough then, this is the kind of thing you deal with.

Sgt3:   If you took it seriously you wouldn't be able to deal with this. You got to apply a sense of humour or a sick sense of humour to get you through it afterwards. Like when you are in a chase, you laugh about going round the roundabouts the wrong way and the silly things you do. It is only afterwards you think…

Sgt2:   I had a cot death once with a baby who was only eight weeks old. I had a child of myself at that time, my son who was ten weeks, and it was a little boy. When you go round, you know to get all the stuff out of the cot, and all the clothes. I was absolutely

> heartbroken over that. It affected me that for months after, every time I picked my son up I could burst into tears. But, again, I couldn't turn around and sue somebody saying, 'why wasn't I dealt with, you know because I had to deal with a traumatic incident'. You have to cope.

Sgt1:   But you shouldn't have to cope. That is what I am saying. You shouldn't have to cope. We have got a responsibility to you [sergeants' group, GMP].

Diversification

The second phenomenon we are concerned with—a diversification in the social composition of the police and its effects—drew comment of competing kinds from a number of our respondents.[10] Such comments alluded—from different standpoints—to the challenge that such diversity posed to the once dominant police dispositions documented earlier in this chapter and hinted at the emergence within the police of new cultures and a revised organizational ethos. This is not to say that the female, black and Asian, or gay officers we interviewed described working lives that were somehow free of difficulty and discrimination. Far from it. Nor, conversely, is it to deny the documented fact that female and minority officers can often, *as* police officers, share similar outlooks on 'the Job' and the wider world with their male, white, or heterosexual colleagues. It is however to record the sense many of our interviewees had of how over the last couple of decades things have changed in the police for those who occupy these subject positions and, in turn, how the presence of female, ethnic minority, and gay officers has, slowly and unevenly, begun to refigure the practices and meanings of English policing. Let us consider these matters a little further, taking gender, ethnicity, and sexuality in turn.

Prior to the Sex Discrimination Act 1975, *female officers* were restricted to separate departments and performed work that differed from that of their male 'colleagues' in terms of both their responsibilities (they were confined to matters involving juveniles, women, missing persons, and other problems that fell under the rubric 'women's work') and conditions of service (women typically worked day shifts, had longer work-breaks, and were paid 90 per cent of what men earned). As a Home Office Minister in post at the time of the Act reflected, 'women officers at that stage were very largely, though not exclusively, involved in offences involving children and other sort of sexual cases. But they were not seen as people who were entitled to be regarded as fully-fledged police officers.'

The immediate effect of the Sex Discrimination Act—legislation essentially forced upon the police in the face of opposition from the Police Federation and senior officers alike—was the closure of women's police departments; something recalled by one female officer in the following terms: 'I think the constables were probably alright, but the women who were already sergeants and inspectors and what have you—they'd been in their own little department if you like, in their own little world, just got thrown in at the deep end. You know, one day they were in their own department doing their own jobs that they knew and were very competent at, and then the next day they were meant to be looking after this shift of men and women doing jobs in some cases they really didn't know anything about' (spokeswomen, British Association of Women Police (BAWP)). But the Act also, in bringing down such formal barriers, issued a direct challenge to an organizational culture in which—in the words of one provincial chief constable—'sexism was very rife, very rife indeed'. The memories of the following two officers—who joined in 1973 and 1972 respectively—offer further testimony to this:

It was sexist, yeah. I suppose very sexist. It was no different, or it was in line with, sexist views in society. Women were not seen as proper coppers. They had a different role. When I joined they were a policeman's partner [male Asian officer, GMP].

When I joined, you were either a nymphomaniac or a dyke, you couldn't be normal [female inspector, GMP].

Numerous examples of this culture of discrimination were cited to us during the course of our work. Some remembered the persistent, seemingly entrenched hostility to female officers expressed by supervisory officers: 'you kept coming across senior officers who just didn't want to know policewomen. Didn't want them on special groups or anything like that' (retired male inspector, CP). One female inspector from Staffordshire described the difficulties created by 'higher police officers behind your back colluding to keep you down', noting successive requests for postings being rejected on the basis that, 'no, you're wrong here, we wanted men', or 'although we take woman constables, we don't take woman sergeants'. Others referred to instances of the organization continuing to treat women as best suited to specific kinds of work: 'even as a sergeant and inspector, because we were still rare in the 1980s, if there was a missing person, a missing child or a rape, they still used to call upon me, they never called upon my male colleagues' (female inspector, Staffordshire Police). 'If there was a job with a baby' another officer recalled, 'you would call a policewoman to hold the baby, for God's sake!' (female constable, GMP).

Officers would similarly describe the 'banter' and 'sexual harassment' that are recalled as routinely attending life as a female officer in the 1970s and 1980s. One recounted how—as an inspector—she only managed to get her male colleagues to remove a 'girlie calendar' by physically moving offices and threatening to 'tell senior officers why' (female inspector, GMP), while another spoke of how—in the face of such incidents—'a lot of women could not handle it and were very upset and suicidal, and nothing ever happened' (female constable, GMP). The entrenched nature of these practices, and the outlooks that underpin them, was described by one chief constable thus:

If you take the debate back twenty-five years ago when people were blowing the whistle and saying 'sexism', you know, you are not treating females the same. And I can remember bosses standing up and saying, we treat females exactly the same as males. And they didn't. There were glass ceilings on recruitment and all this business, you know. Very subtle, around 10 per cent of the force would be female because that was the considered wisdom of the day. In the macho world of policing if you got more than one in ten, then you would have a disaster if it came to the heavy situations, and it's not proven to be the case. Even now we've not fully resolved that and there are still members of my organization who think there is no place for women [chief constable, metropolitan force].

In the course of our interviews we encountered officers who remained passionately committed to this latter position. Such officers were eager to detail the apparently numerous reasons why women could not (and should not) be accepted fully into the force, including: women's incapacity to deliver or withstand physical violence— 'I'm not so sure a squad of women tooled up for public order is going to sort the public order out' (male chief superintendent, GMP); their inability to exert 'authority' over the public (male constable, GMP), and the related need for male officers to look after them: 'they can say all they like about equal ops, your natural instinct is to protect the woman' (inspectors' group, GMP). But these reactions—which almost always privilege, indeed essentialize, the ever-present possibilities of violence that attend policing—stand today as precisely that, *reactions* to a shift in gender relations that has occurred over the last two decades in the wake of the greater integration and numerical presence of female officers within the contemporary English police (Smith *et al.* 2002). As one female sergeant remarked of women police officers today, 'it's quite interesting because most of them are fairly, they're young, they've been brought up in the environment where we all train together, work together, do the same job and I think this is it, again, they don't see it as a problem being female and therefore nobody else does. They feel it's, "well that's their problem and not mine", you know?' (spokesperson, BAWP).

We must take care not to overstate the extent of this 'shift'. Successive surveys of police forces have found that deployment patterns of policewomen routinely ignore the Sex Discrimination Act. Women are restricted from many 'specialist' positions, and their greatest visibility was in relation to the activities they had been involved with prior to the 1975 legislation: the 'women's work' of dealing with children, rape inquiries, domestic violence, and the burgeoning field of 'community relations' (Young 1991; ch. 4; Brown 1997). As recently as 1993, Her Majesty's Inspectorate of Constabulary reported 'blatant breaches' of equal opportunities legislation within the police, and in 1996—despite noting some general improvements—it still found 'scepticism, tokenism and indifference' (quoted in Brown 1997: 29).

But we must also pay heed to our respondents' sense of how the working environment in the police has altered for female officers in the last couple of decades. Some spoke here of what they saw as the lead given on these issues by a 'new generation of managers' who, it was felt, are 'not just paying lip service to equality and all the rest of it. They actually see it's important, and the fact that they do need to reflect society and they need more women, they need more ethnic minorities and all the rest of it, and they need to be seen to be doing the right thing. As I say, it isn't just lip service, that's what they feel, that's their attitude' (spokesperson, BAWP). Others, in a similar vein, noted the significance of managers who 'are prepared to readily recognize the benefits that females can actually bring to their management teams, the differing style, which comes out of your experiences' (female inspector, GMP); or referred to female officers with the confidence now to challenge what might once have been accepted as the norm (such as what one female sergeant described as the 'diabolical' view she encountered in the 1980s that the CID could contain no more than one female detective) and raise issues that would once have remained buried in organizational silence. As a spokesperson from the British Association of Women Police we interviewed put it, 'I'm sure that's why a lot of these harassment cases have come out, because people felt empowered if you like to actually complain'. At the very least, it was felt, these shifts have served to keep quiet those who might once have been tempted to make the working lives of female officers a misery:

It [sexism] is still there but it is changing. So yeah, that is a lot better. What they've stopped is the banter. Everyone is careful what they are saying, taking things a lot more seriously, and everyone has just stopped that. Everyone is just so careful what they do and say now, in case someone complains about them. But it is better for the workers, sure. It has got to be [female constable, GMP].

Questions of *'race' and ethnicity* within the police organization first came to public prominence during the 1960s. Prior to that, as the 1962 Royal Commission on the Police discovered, there were no (recorded) black and ethnic minority police officers in England and Wales. In the years following the Commission, the recruitment of ethnic minority officers slowly began to surface as a necessary step towards improving police relations with minority communities. The exercise, however, remained an intrinsically limited, and not especially urgent, one. As one former Conservative Home Secretary reflected, 'you had to make a compromise between efficiency and acceptability I think, and that was more or less the conclusion that we came to in the Home Office back in those days. But it wasn't anything like the problem it is today. We certainly never thought for one moment of compelling forces to recruit so as to ensure a certain proportion of the force was black. That would have been complete heresy.'

This was 'heresy' in part because the very idea of a black police officer seemed at the time inimical to dominant conceptions of the 'English bobby'. One 'Jedd' cartoon in *Police* magazine intimates how remote the possibility was that ethnic minorities would—or should—become established within the police. The 1969 cartoon depicts a scene from policing in 2019 showing a giant computer and a black police sergeant—each, it seems, as ridiculously far-fetched as the other (*Police*, June 1969: 9). The Police Federation's outlook on black officers during the period took as read what it assumed to be the bigotry of the white populace, something that gave rise to the following rationale for failing to take up the issue of ethnic minority recruitment:

Around about 1959, following the race riots, it was suggested that one solution to this problem might be to have black police officers, and our attitude was expressed as, 'No, the time is not right. Yes, there are areas in this country where black police officers would be employed safely and would be accepted by the predominantly white liberal communities. But how would they get on outside the *Mother Redcap* [pub] in Camden Town on Saturday night?'. That was the test we applied. And that was our policy for a while. It was certainly our view that the public did not like the idea, would not like the idea of a black or Asian person in a police uniform either arresting them or telling them what to do. And the first black officers met a great deal of hostility and antipathy and provocation on the streets. What we didn't recognize was the extent to which they were being discriminated against and subject to racial harassment in the workplace [spokesperson, Police Federation].[11]

This mention of workplace discrimination finds a clear echo in the memories of the black and Asian officers we interviewed, with our respondents recollecting, in particular, the isolation experienced by ethnic minority officers recruited during the 1960s and 1970s: 'when I joined it was very difficult, there was no campaigns to recruit members from the ethnic minority. If anything you were breaking down barriers to come into an institution which was predominantly white. There were no Asian officers, it was purely white' (male Asian officer, GMP).[12] These respondents remember how, in this context, the job involved a daily struggle for acceptance and recognition. This was generally experienced as a pressure to 'maintain standards', 'to work harder than my other colleagues' (male Asian officer, GMP); either because black and Asian officers felt 'we were path finding for other people' (male Asian officer, GMP), or because they worked under a spotlight that was seldom shone upon their white counterparts. As one black officer from Manchester recalled, 'it wasn't such a political hot potato. You knew that all the time people were watching you to see what you did right and what you did wrong, and you knew, I mean I knew, that I had to be twice as good as my peers to be seen as being their equal, yet I had to do half a thing less than them to be sacked.' Relatedly, these officers spoke of how acceptance—even daily survival—involved trying to accommodate oneself to the police's racist culture: 'you start to acquiesce, in order to get by on a day-to-day basis. Because in those days, I mean, police officers were not politically correct, so you would "get" the racial jokes, you would "get" the sexist jokes' (male black officer, GMP). Acceptance, if and when it came, was often felt to have been conditional and grudging:

Alright, you're on board, but you know really, there's still this white domin-ated male society and you know, blacks and females were a thing apart, because they didn't really want much of either [male black officer, GMP].

Since the 1960s, the numbers of black and Asian officers within the police have slowly increased to the point where, in 2002, 2.6 per cent of police officers in England and Wales hailed from ethnic minori-ties backgrounds (Smith *et al.* 2002). Questions of racial discrimi-nation within the force have however—in response to, and as part of, the conflicts and controversies discussed in Chapter 5—assumed a far greater prominence within English policing—often, it was considered, in ways that had altered the experience of black and Asian officers today. A number of factors were mobilized to account for this. Some attributed this, first, to the altered social contexts from which today's recruits are drawn ('they've had a broader, more liberal education and they've had a wider experience of a multi-racial society. They are less likely to regard this country as a white, Anglo-Saxon, Protestant preserve' (spokesperson, Police Federation)); and to the environment in which they are now trained and socialized. As one black Manchester officer put it, 'I suppose that's the big difference for a black person joining the service today; that we're all political, we're all educated, we're all doing diversity training. We all know what's going on, whereas we didn't have it in those days.' Some alluded, secondly, to a shift in senior manage-ment culture that has seen questions of racism inside the force treated more seriously—not least because of the pressure now exerted on this issue by Her Majesty's Inspectorate of Constabulary (1997, 1999). One effect of this, it was felt, is that ethnic minority officers today rarely experience 'anything overtly negative' (male black officer, GMP); something that has made 'being switched on' to forms of 'subtle and covert' discrimination (male black officer, GMP) a more pressing supervisory task. As one provincial chief constable commented, 'people who are clearly prejudiced, bigoted, racist, sexist, I think in many instances are more crafty, more subtle about the way in which they allow manifestations to show. That makes it more difficult to deal with.' One member of our police inspectors' group summed up the shifting dispositions found among both supervisors and constables towards expressions of racism in the following terms:

I must say it's a long, long time since I've ever heard any racist comments by any officers or colleagues. It just doesn't happen. It's not tolerated either. At one time if you ever picked somebody up on that in a group situation, they'd think 'what's wrong with him?'. Now, it's acceptable. They'd be looking at you as if to say, 'why aren't you doing something to stop it'. It's a thing you don't tolerate. It just is not tolerated under any circumstances.

Reference is made, thirdly, to the emergence within the police of a more articulated black and Asian voice and, in particular, to the formation in 1994 of the Black Police Association (BPA). For some officers, the value of such a body was the recognition it accorded to their dual identities—to the fact that 'we're members of the black and Asian community first, who happen to be police officers' (spokesperson, BPA). As one Asian officer we interviewed reflected, 'I don't differentiate between white community, black community or whatever, but deep inside, I have been an ambassador for my community, my people, yeah.' Others—such as this BPA spokesperson— articulated its purposes in the following terms: 'as long as you've got that chill factor around the police service, you are not going to get recruitment and you are not going to get legitimacy that you want in the black community. And the aim of the National Black Police Association is to challenge this disparity, and we are fortunate to have our power base in the black community. We have a link to those communities that the high echelons of the police service don't. We have a link to that community which the Police Federation doesn't.' The impact the BPA's emergence will have on what this spokesperson called 'the dynamics of the organization' remains to be seen. But its presence signals nonetheless a certain fracturing of police culture, serving to communicate the message that there is no single identity that goes with being a police officer, no uniform, monochrome outlook that the English police stands for. This, perhaps, is what animates the consternation its existence appears to prompt among many in the service:

We also have a very delicate problem with the Black Police Association. They are sending out messages to quotes 'the black community' more or less saying, 'we hate the police just as much as you do.' It is quite frightening. They are alienating themselves from the main body of the police service and making their own assimilation into the police service and integration on terms of full equality all that more difficult... There is deep resentment that they need to have a Black Police Association anyway. We do accept that there needs to be support groups, but they don't see themselves as a support group, they see themselves as a campaigning group and part of the black agenda, not the police agenda [spokesperson, Police Federation].

Further evidence of cultural fragmentation inside the police is provided by the Lesbian and Gay Police Association (LAGPA). Formed in 1989, in the teeth of much unease and opposition inside the organization, LAGPA aims to offer 'advice and support' to *gay and lesbian officers* and 'provide a bridge, a link, between the community and the police' (spokesperson, LAGPA). In so doing, the Association signals a sharp break from the social world of policing that characterized the middle decades of the twentieth century. Recollecting this period, one respondent described how, 'in the 1950s any police officer found to be homosexual would be seen off the premises immediately', adding, 'and we were of course detailed to keep observation in public lavatories to arrest homosexuals. It was regarded as one of the most deadly sins' (spokesperson, Police Federation). As recently as 1992, an editorial in the *Police Journal* introduced an article about homosexuality by noting that it should be debated even though it was a topic 'most police officers, as with heterosexual members of society generally, have no sympathy with' (*Police Journal*, January 1992: 1). And the LAGPA representative we interviewed recalled how 'up until about the mid-1970s it was never discussed at all', and spoke of 'closet' gay officers feeling it prudent to 'invent non-existent girlfriends, or boyfriends in the case of women'.

It would be inaccurate to suggest that matters have in this regard changed radically—continued police hostility to homosexuality is well documented (Young 1991: 142; Burke 1993). But here, as the emergence of the LAGPA attests, our respondents detected (uneven) signs of a police force in the midst of (uncertain) transition, of a force conditioned by—and making small contributions to—processes of cultural change and the demands of social movement politics (see Parris 1995). Some spoke here of 'policemen who live with their partners, homosexual police officers of both sexes, all that kind of thing. Absolutely unthought of and certainly not tolerated in the police force of the fifties, sixties, or even the seventies' (spokesperson, Police Federation). One gay officer we interviewed recalled 'coming out' to colleagues as having given rise to 'absolutely no problems' and described the attitude of his senior officers to gay and lesbian officers as 'very, very protective' (spokesperson, LAGPA). He also echoed the remarks of female and black officers regarding the prohibitions on hate speech: 'there is a blame culture within the police. A lot of people are physically checking what they say before they actually say...It [homophobic insults] is one of the things they could instantly lose their job over'. In this context, one provincial chief constable—noting both the persistence of anti-gay attitudes within the police and certain signs of what he saw as progressive change—opined that the politics of sexuality has today become firmly situated as part of a wider equality agenda:

Culturally we've shifted incredibly. I see a number of these issues as being inter-linked because they're all about challenging old prejudices. We now have openly gay, male gay officers, who go about their job without any problem. It was...I remember far more prejudice as a young officer being expressed against homosexuals ever than against black people. Remembering the debates about the time of the legalisation of homosexual acts between consenting male adults in private, I can remember people that I thought were urbane and quite civilized talking about a 'bum boys charter'. The level of antagonism was quite tremendous. Homophobia hasn't disappeared. But not only has the public attitude changed, the attitudes within policing have changed, so that it's fine for an officer to come out and say that he's gay. People no longer recoil, they won't refuse to shake hands or whatever.

* * *

It seems apparent from these interpretative sketches of what we have termed 'informalization' and 'diversification' that the received idea of policing ('the Job') and the English police ('the force') fondly recalled by many of our respondents—one whose tenets we set out at some length in the earlier part of this chapter—has in the latter years of the twentieth century been undone—radically and perhaps fatally so. It is an outlook—like the residualized public dispositions discussed in Part II—that has been disrupted and displaced by both active political struggles and institutional reconfigurations around questions of 'race', gender, and sexuality, and by the effects on English society and culture of processes of individualization, social and moral pluralism, and quotidian democratization.

These changes—and the fragmentation of 'police culture' they are entangled with—met among our police interviewees with competing responses, a number of which we have detailed already. Some officers spoke matter-of-factly, sometimes with a hint of ambivalence, of the police being swept along by tides of change they have little choice but to accept: 'I mean the police today, it does reflect society. What are society's influences? The educational system, attitudes with and towards authority. You can't expect young men and women to come into the police who are suddenly a differently animal. I reflected my era, the people today reflect their influences and family' (male chief superintendent, GMP). A common theme here was the emergence of a more educated, challenging society—children will argue with parents, parents with teachers...constables with sergeants—that the police had, as best they are able, to accommodate themselves to. 'You can't', as one retired chief constable put it, 'just bang the table and say, "this is what we'll do". You just can't do that anymore. Society is on the whole infinitely more intelligent. They are much more aware and human rights are much more to the fore.' There is, on this view, simply no turning back the clock:

IL: If someone tried to reintroduce the kinds of relationships between sergeants and bobbies that you described to me when you joined, how would that go down?
PC: There would be mass exit of bobbies [constables' group, GMP].

Yet this is precisely what those among our respondents who actively bemoan the 'decline' of 'the Job' and 'the force' at least implicitly envisage or yearn for—often in tones suggesting some realization that the outlooks they cleave to are no longer culturally or politically dominant. We have proffered ample evidence of this disposition at various points throughout this chapter, not only in warm reconstructions of how 'bobbying' used to be done, but in often angry, emotive denunciations of such things as the declining status of beat officers; political correctness; women police; the eclipse of unfettered, unquestioned authority; civilians; the end of the devotion denoted by a willingness to work long, unpaid hours, and the advent of what officers were fond of calling 'compensationitus' (male chief superintendent, GMP).[13] It is an outlook symbolically condensed in the felt demise of the attribute that all police forces *qua* police forces demand—'discipline':

That's died out now. We don't salute anybody nowadays. We don't seem to be as disciplined as we could be and I think that's a bad thing because very often—the discipline of doing the job—someone's life might depend on it. Unless you are disciplined and you are drilled. We're in situations sometimes where the wheel could easily come off. If people aren't drilled and disciplined in those things then it isn't going to work [male inspector, GMP].

Finally, we encountered those who not only believed strongly that the police had changed markedly and for the better in recent decades (much more so, some claimed, than other public sector bodies), but also evinced a certain pride in what had been effected. As one Manchester female officer put it, 'I think the police service, because of the focus it has got on it both politically and socially, actually is aeons ahead of other organizations in how they do try and deal with shedding the discriminatory processes and policies'. Some spoke, in this vein, of how a 'plural, multi-racial society' demands 'a response from the police which the traditional police didn't have' (retired chief constable, shire force) and welcomed the fact that officers 'could no longer' so readily, or without challenge, 'use the Ways and Means Act' (chief constable, provincial force). The good police officer, it seems, cannot in contemporary English society survive equipped only with the 'virtues exemplified by *Dixon of Dock Green*' (retired chief constable, shire force). 'Nowadays', as one of our black police respondents put it, 'the good bobbies are officers who are educated, aware, and politically correct.'

7

The Power of the Police Voice

We who alone see the reality and the whole of recorded crime should not be reluctant to speak about it. We who are the anvil on which society beats out its problems and abrasions of social inequality, racial prejudice, weak laws and ineffective legislation should not be inhibited from expressing our views, whether critical or constructive [Mark 1977: 118].

The choice of images to appeal to and identify with can tell us much about the values of both actor and audience [Weiner 1981: 99].

It is time now to shift our focus away from questions of 'internal' police organization and culture towards some of the broader intersections that exist between policing and the social. We are concerned in this chapter with the 'police voice', its emergence and preoccupations, its meanings and effects, and its relationship to English mundane and political culture in the post-war period. Our aim is to trace the advent since 1945 of the English police as prominent commentators on both 'law and order' in particular, and the 'state of the nation' in general, and to grasp the extent to which they have over recent decades acquired the power to 'name', diagnose, and classify social problems. In so doing we ask: what are the political, organizational, and cultural conditions of possibility for the emergence and subsequent transformation of the police as social commentators since 1945? What narratives—about the police and policing; criminal justice and 'law and order'; politics and government; community, morality, and authority; in short, about 'the condition of England'— have surfaced in police discourse, and which are ascendant (or waning, or residual) today? What does the coming to prominence of the police voice tell us about the changing character of English culture and society in the latter half of the twentieth century?

Our particular substantive concern is with the stances and utterances of *chief constables*—though we will, as the chapter unfolds, make reference where pertinent to the Police Federation and other staff associations. In part this choice is dictated simply by constraints of time and space—a single chapter does not offer sufficient room to make adequate sense of the different strands that compose the 'police voice' today. But it also reflects the fact that the post-war postures and campaigns of the Federation have in recent years been both fondly documented in an extensive 'insider' account (Judge 1994), and subjected to some searching external scrutiny (McLaughlin and Murji 1998; see also Reiner 1978, 1980). There did not, in short, seem much to be gained from trampling once more over this already well-trodden terrain. We therefore decided at a fairly early stage in our enquiry to seek to generate—through a reading of the published autobiographies and associated writings of senior officers; analysis of how respective chief officers of the Metropolitan, (Greater) Manchester, and Cheshire Police have since 1945 deployed the 'Foreword' to their annual reports; and in-depth interviews with (six) retired and (four) serving chief constables—empirical material that might cast light on one particular aspect of post-war police mobilization—what we ought more accurately to term the *elite* police voice.

Our interest does not, however, lie in chief police officers as an occupational group *per se*. Nor is our principal goal to contribute to the small but burgeoning 'chief constables studies' literature that has surfaced in recent years—valuable though that work undoubtedly is (Reiner 1991; Wall 1998; Savage *et al.* 2000). Rather, our purpose is to treat the role of chief constables as *legitimate namers*—their power, that is, of 'authorized, public, official speech which is spoken in the name of and to everyone' (Bourdieu 1987: 838)—as a vehicle for illustrating, and furthering an understanding of, our central theme—namely, the cultural and political significance of the English police. This demands that we pay historical and sociological heed to the ways in which the contours and conflicts of English society and culture—what Robert Mark selectively opts to call 'social inequality, racial prejudice, weak laws and ineffective legislation'—enable and constrain the police's capacity to mobilize and proselytize on behalf of particular visions of policing and nation. But it requires also that we think about and analyse chief officers as producers and regulators of social meaning; that is, as cultural agents with a significant symbolic power to authorize, categorize, evoke, represent, reinforce, and undermine elements of the wider culture, whose presence as interpreters of social institutions, conflicts, and hierarchies presupposes something significant about the ownership and framing of relevant issues, and whose individual and collective utterances contribute in small but potentially telling ways to the formation of opinion and belief.

The argument that ensues runs broadly thus. We begin by constructing and elaborating upon a typology of police commentary during the post-war period, and recovering the themes, preoccupations, imagery, and rhetoric that have characterized the senior police voice during what for analytical purposes we distinguish as three distinct periods of intervention—1945–72, 1973–86, and 1987–present. We then proceed to develop an account of these shifts by seeking to grasp: (i) contemporary transformations in the professional ideology of police elites; (ii) the relation of those elites to the architecture and programmes of government, and (iii) the changing social and cultural conditions within which the police voice—with all its authoritative 'social magic'—has since 1945 been called forth, transmitted, and received.

Making a Mark: The Emergence of Chief Constables as Social Commentators

How then are we recover the emergence and subsequent transformations of chief officers as commentators on matters of social and political controversy? When did the elite police voice begin to surface in England as a cultural force? How might we best characterize its (changing) contours, substance, and tone? In addressing these questions, we believe it fruitful to subdivide the post-war years roughly as follows: first, a period from 1945–72 during which chief officers remained locally prominent, but nationally rather silent, figures—a stance, as we shall see, that begins to falter towards the latter part of the 1960s. Secondly, an era—symbolically announced by Robert Mark's controversial Dimbleby Lecture in 1973 (Mark 1977: ch. 5)—characterized by the advent of a number of 'political policemen' (Kettle 1979), maverick 'police heroes' who for a time attained a culturally prominent place in English public life. This was to last until the late 1980s (the signifier of its demise we take to be the Association of Chief Police Officers' (ACPO) attempt—from 1986 onwards—to bind chiefs to collective decisions by means of what Savage and Charman (1996) call 'presumption

in favour of compliance'), from which time a quieter, generally
more liberal, yet arguably more effective, corporate police voice
began to emerge. Let us now sketch the main contours of each of
these periods.[1]

1945–72: Local Influence, National Silence

In the two decades following the end of World War II, a period of
relative social consensus, wherein crime, though rising, had not yet
become a prominent bone of electoral contention, the English police
remained for the most part what David McNee (Metropolitan Police
Commissioner 1977–83) was later to call a 'silent service' (McNee
1983: 71). While often colourful and controversial figures on their
own 'patch' (e.g., Sillitoe 1955; Chadwick 1974; and, generally, Wall
1998), rarely during this period did chief constables enter the
national political fray, or (certain *causes célèbres* of the 1950s
notwithstanding (Critchley 1978: 270–4)) assume significant repute
beyond either their own force—or professional police—boundaries.
The reminiscences of the few who did acquire such prominence (and
it is noteworthy that senior police writing of this period falls squarely
within the genre of 'personal memoir') clearly attest to this, commenting on the social merely *en passant*, and evoking a sense of
proud satisfaction with career, police, and nation (see Scott 1954;
St. Johnston 1978). Thus, Harold Scott (Metropolitan Police
Commissioner 1945–53) in his *Scotland Yard* (a book encompassing
chapters on such matters as 'The Fingerprint Department' and 'The
Mounted Police and the Dogs', and replete with fond recollections of
the 1953 Coronation and all it stood for) evinces a certain pride at
the problems experienced meeting Marshall Tito's requirement for a
bullet-proof car during his state visit in 1953:

> It was a tribute to the peacefulness of English political life that no such car
> was available in this country. The car used was placed at our disposal by
> the Government of Northern Ireland [Scott 1954: 139].

A firm focus on the local—and a relative absence of (social)
commentary—was thus the order of the day for most chief officers
during at least the first two decades of this period; something that
is clearly evident from our analysis of the—generally brief—
'Forewords' to chief constables' annual reports from London,
Manchester, and Cheshire.[2] Here two themes are particularly
apparent. First one detects an ongoing concern about rising levels

of crime in general, and certain types of offenders in particular. In 1951, Manchester's chief constable reported 'the highest number of crimes in Manchester ever recorded' (Manchester Police annual report (MAR) 1951: 3); by 1961 he was warning that rising crime levels constituted 'a threat to society which cannot be ignored' (MAR 1961: 7). The Metropolitan Commissioner similarly noted that '1964 has proved to be the worst year of the century for crime' (Metropolitan Police annual report (MPAR) 1964: 7). Against this backdrop, youth crime emerges as a particular worry, not least in the years immediately following the end of World War II, with the Metropolitan Police Commissioner noting of 9 and 10-year-olds in 1949: 'these are the children of the war years and they present an urgent problem that should not be neglected. Too young to be admitted to most existing clubs, unable to remain in overcrowded homes, they run wild in the streets and inevitably get into trouble' (MPAR 1949: 9). So too does a certain level of senior police puzzlement about why all this may be happening:

Perhaps the most disturbing feature of the rise in crime today lies in the fact that neither the absence of real poverty nor the more progressive methods employed in dealing with delinquents appear to have done anything to reduce the volume of crime [MPAR 1958: 7].

Rising levels of crime—coupled with the oft-noted problems of congestion, motoring offences, road safety, and hostile contact with 'those who are by nature law abiding' (MPAR 1954: 15) ensuing from the post-war escalation in car ownership and use—contributed in no small measure to a second much vocalized elite police concern during this period: the ongoing shortfall in authorized police establishment. Although, as we saw in Chapter 6, the Oaksey Committee (Home Office 1949) and the Royal Commission on the Police (Home Office 1961a) had both improved pay and conditions, the inability of forces to recruit and retain sufficient numbers of officers represented an abiding worry among chiefs during this period. In 1950, the Metropolitan Police Commissioner warned of the 'the very grave position' on force strength, something that had, he felt, resulted in 'the standard of policing of the Metropolis fall[ing] far short of what we all desire and what could be achieved if more were available' (MPAR 1950: 6). As successive Commissioners noted, an under-strength force impacted seriously on the police's capacity to meet rising demands and expectations:

Whole new towns have grown up and over 1,000 extra miles of road have to be patrolled. It is not surprising, therefore, that the complaint is often heard, especially in the outer suburbs, that 'we never see a constable'. Much police work goes on unseen, but it is certainly true that the number of men available is insufficient to deal adequately either with crime or traffic [MPAR 1952: 7].[3]

From around the mid-1960s, however, it is possible to discern a shift in the scope, content, and tone of chief constables' commentaries.[4] In the first place one finds an increasing emphasis on—and attempts to account for—what is viewed as an increase in violence. One dimension of this concerned street robbery—or what by the early 1970s had come to be known as 'mugging' (Hall *et al.* 1978). In his 1970 report, the Metropolitan Police Commissioner stated that 'robberies and assaults with intent to rob are still our greatest problem' (MPAR 1970:7); while the chief constable of Manchester wrote of 'vicious behaviour' by 'spineless creatures' in 'dimly-lit streets' (MAR 1971: 3), and described such attacks as 'symptomatic of a malaise which is affecting virtually the whole country' (MAR 1969: 4). This in turn was coupled by an increasing preoccupation with collective—often 'political'—violence, as is evidenced in the references of the Metropolitan Commissioner to 'mods and rockers' (1964), football hooligans (1967), 'radicals' demonstrating against authority (1968), and 'the use of bombs for political ideologies' (1971). England—from the perspective of senior officers—had entered 'an age of violence' (MAR 1970: 7).

Thus it was that chief constables began to use their annual reports as a means both to document what they judged to be a rising tide of disorder and to situate the apparent increase in lawlessness within broader changes in the prevailing socio-moral climate. As early as 1964, under the heading 'Social Behaviour', the chief constable of Manchester complained of a 'mushroom growth of clubs' that depended 'for their attraction on appealing to the lower instincts of humanity' (MAR 1964: 4–5). In cognate—if more sweeping—terms the Metropolitan Police Commissioner noted 'the general tendency for members of the public to be more articulate regarding their rights—though not always about their obligations—and more militant in their actions', and bemoaned 'our permissive society, the lack of parental influence on young people and the lowering of moral values' (MPAR 1969: 11, 8). Manchester's chief constable even mused in this context on the apparent failings of the post-war 'welfare settlement':

It is disappointing to have to record at a time of near full employment with better housing, the welfare state and improved social services which make conditions generally much better, increases in crime particularly those offences of violence to the person and property, which cause much distress and alarm to law abiding citizens [MAR 1968: 3].

What we are witnessing here are the stirrings of senior police unease about the 'state of the nation' and the advent of a more strident articulation of the police perspective. Further evidence to this effect can be found in the changing posture of the long since *nationally* organized Police Federation. With the publication of a pamphlet, *The Problem*, in 1965, the Federation broke with its traditional silence on 'law and order' issues and began both to warn of the risks of an under-resourced police force losing the 'battle' against crime, and lobby more actively for 'higher wages, better equipment, and a change in managerial style' (Savage *et al.* 2000: 46).[5] For one of its former presidents this changing temper was encapsulated in a notable shift in the reception accorded to the Home Secretary at the Federation's annual conference:

He'd come along in all his pomp, like the viceroy, to tell us what splendid chaps we were and that the government was on our side and then depart to a load of 'Hear, Hears!' and polite applause. From the 1960s, we started writing speeches which told them he was falling down on the job, letting down the public, and betraying the police service, and they used to get very, very angry about it.

At a senior level this altered register was perhaps most evident in chief officers' orientations to the criminal law and criminal justice process. For much of the period up until the late 1960s, such comments as chief constables expressed on the content and operation of criminal legislation (and they were few) tended to be cautious and generally appreciative—see, for instance, the positive reception accorded to the Street Offences Act 1959 (MPAR 1959: 10) and the Metropolitan Police Commissioner's description of the Betting and Gaming Act 1960 (which de-criminalized gambling) as 'welcome legislation which removed from the police a distasteful duty which tended to strain relations with the general public' (MPAR 1961: 20). During the 1960s, however, the characterization of legislation as a solution and resource was increasingly super-seded by an approach that was far more critical of both the legislative process and the criminal justice system (albeit that a concern with 'do-gooders and their like' has long formed part of the chief officer's outlook (St. Johnston 1978: 194)). One of the first references of this kind is to be found in the Metropolitan Police annual report of 1963:

They [the CID] have worked long hours conscientiously and loyally despite a growing feeling that the odds are against them and that the bar-riers protecting the suspected or accused person are being steadily rein-forced in a way which hampers the detection of crime and the conviction of criminals whilst the latter prey upon their more deserving fellow citizens with greater confidence [MPAR 1963: 12].

What ensued in the remaining decade of this period was an increas-ing flurry of comment oriented to suggesting that the scales of justice were being tipped in favour of the accused to the detriment of society at large. For the most part, this was confined to the pages of chief constables' annual reports, whether in respect of the failure of the bail system 'to provide adequate protection for society' (MPAR 1970: 9); the efforts made by 'well meaning bodies to find means whereby offenders, particularly those in the younger age group, are dealt with outside the purview of the criminal courts' (MAR 1968: 3); or demands 'for sentences which will be more effective in deterring these villains from coming into our hands again' (MPAR 1970: 8). However, not all chief officers felt so constrained. In 1965, Robert Mark, the then Chief Constable of Leicester, gave a public lecture at Nuffield College, Oxford, urging four specific changes in the criminal law—the introduction of majority verdicts in jury trials and the pre-trial disclosure of defence alibis, abolition of the caution against self-incrimination, and a requirement for the accused to enter the witness box (Mark 1978: 72). Mark also took to the pages of the *Guardian* to public-ize research he had commissioned which found what for him were unacceptably high numbers of contested trials culminating in acquittal (Mark 1965). The then Labour Home Secretary Roy Jenkins was, according to Eric St. Johnston (1978: 289), 'impressed'.[6] By 1972 Mark had been appointed to what was to be a turbulent five-year term as Metropolitan Police Commissioner. The political policemen were about to enter the national stage.

1973–86: The Policeman as Hero

It is not sufficient for us unilaterally to tune in to public needs; the public is entitled to be aware, too, of the police perspective [MPAR 1984: 8].

It was against—yet also very much as part of—the backdrop of the economic and political convulsions that appeared to engulf Britain from the early 1970s onwards (see Chapter 1) that certain chief officers broke radically with the 'tradition' of police silence (and—for some—behind-closed-doors influence) and came to assume a prominent cultural presence in English public life. Robert Mark (Metropolitan Police Commissioner 1972–7) was clearly the trail-blazer—and watershed figure—here, but it was a path soon followed by David McNee (1977–82) and Kenneth Newman (1982–7) in London, by the—contrasting—figures of James Anderton in Manchester (1976–91) and John Alderson in Devon and Cornwall (1973–82), and to a (perhaps) lesser extent elsewhere by the likes of Kenneth Oxford (Merseyside, 1976–89) and Geoffrey Dear (West Midlands, 1985–90). These visible, high-profile chief officers—dubbed by Alderson (1984: 127) the 'hero chiefs'—became for a time almost household names; parading the national political stage, putting the police perspective on events, proselytizing author-itatively, energetically, and in largely unprecedented ways, for particular visions of police and nation. Never before, the historian E. P. Thompson (1980: 201) was stirred to remark, had the police assumed 'such a loud and didactic public presence'.

This can be registered in a number of ways. One may note first the tendency among (some) chief constables to write more lengthy and expansive 'Forewords' to their annual reports. It is revealed, secondly, in the increasingly adept manner in which chief officers made use of the media (Mark, one of our interviewees noted, was 'quite sparing with the occasions he chose to go public, but when he did he made it count' (retired chief constable, metropolitan force)), or took to the lecture podium (see Mark 1977). In one year alone Anderton delivered sixty-four speeches, attended 134 civic func-tions and a further seventy-one police gatherings (Prince 1989: 81). Alderson recalled in an interview with us that he was engaged 'in an ideological struggle for about seven years', during which time 'I lectured, I wrote, I publicised' (Alderson 1984: 112). And in his autobiography McNee (1983: 235) records, 'I established a personal relationship with all the editors of major newspapers. I gave hundreds of speeches and lectures; some were serious, some light-hearted, but each made a point or two about some aspect of policing and its social impact.' Such presence is discernible, thirdly, in the changing genres and content of senior police writing. One aspect of this concerns the shift in the police autobiography from *personal memoir* to *social commentary*; something demonstrated by both the range of topics—and targets—discussed (compare Scott's cosy aforementioned tome with McNee's reflections on 'Order and Disorder', 'Race and Riots', and 'Terrorism and the Siege of the Iranian Embassy') and by their sharper critical edge—Mark, for instance, unleashes a number of passing blows on 'the race relations industry', the National Council for Civil Liberties ('a small, self-appointed political pressure group with a misleading title'), and the then Labour government (a 'mediocre crew', 'maintained in office only by the support of the extremist and authoritarian left') (Mark 1978: 150, 139, 244, 259, 303, 317). But the autobiography is also joined by a new genre of police chiefs' writing, the academic tract, one most closely associated with what one of our interviewees called the 'cerebral' John Alderson (Alderson and Stead 1973; Alderson 1979, 1984), but which also encompassed influential contributions from others (e.g., Jones 1980; Oliver 1987).

Yet for all that the police came—by this complex of means—to assume a prominence in matters of social controversy during the 1970s and 1980s no single coherent senior police voice emerged during this period. This in part is because the aforementioned figures spoke, wrote, and lobbied as *individual* chief officers. For all that the persuasive force of their utterances may have depended largely—as Bourdieu (1991) might say—on the social authority of their office, the 'police heroes' of this time were to a large degree mavericks, promoting a police outlook outwith the umbrella of the Association of Chief Police Officers (ACPO) and by no means always with the (public) support of their senior peers. But it flows also from the fact that they were proselytizing on behalf of different (and in some respects competing) visions; something that came prominently to the fore when John Alderson opted to submit independent evidence to Lord Scarman's enquiry into the 1981 Brixton disorders, in clear opposition to that proffered by both David McNee and ACPO. As Alderson later remarked during an interview with us, such action 'didn't help my relationships with my colleagues, as you can imagine, but I had to put up with that'.

Thus it was that a multiplicity of senior police outlooks entered public discourse from the mid-1970s onwards, outlooks that shared little in common save for a distinctly police-centred perspective on social problems.[7] One finds John Alderson's tireless campaigning on behalf of his particular—police-led—conception of 'community policing', a vision his colleagues were often publicly wont to dismiss as inapplicable to the realities of policing tense inner cities (McNee 1983; Prince 1989) or other hostile communities (Hermon 1997). One encounters—in sharp contradistinction—James Anderton's very public attempts to 'protect' his operational independence from what he declared to be a Marxist-inspired plot on the part of 'his' police authority to gain political control of the police, and his all-too-frequent—and frequently fundamentalist—proclamations on the 'decline' of the nation's morals (Kettle 1979; Prince 1989; McLaughlin 1994). And one has Robert Mark's diagnosis of what he chose to call 'a perplexed society'—a kind of technocratic authoritarianism which valorizes 'professional' expertise and its avatars (e.g. civil servants, senior police officers) while bemoaning 'amateurs' meddling ignorantly in public affairs (e.g. politicians, trade unionists, the Police Federation, juries, the civil liberties lobby); stands tellingly preoccupied with threats to state security rather than 'ordinary crime'; and presents the police—following his attempt to rid the Metropolitan CID of corrupt officers—as the English nation's most important 'guardians of freedom' (1978: 171), hamstrung in their task by a combination of legal technicalities and what Mark in his Dimbleby lecture called the 'cancer' of 'bent lawyers'.

This latter aspect of Mark's *Weltanschauung* was to inform what came closest to being a dominant senior police message during this period—the pursuit of police powers.[8] From slow, principally local, beginnings in the 1960s, the 'campaign' for a less fettered police and a more stringent criminal justice response to crime and public disorder came to the fore in the 1970s and early 1980s. Three aspects of this mobilization are noteworthy here. First, a heightened attack on what Mark called the 'inexplicable leniency of the courts' (MPAR 1975: 10) and demands for a more robust penal regime: 'the only possible remedy for this level of violence in society is the imposition by the courts of the toughest possible forms of punishment' (MAR 1985: 6). Secondly, vocal opposition to certain pieces of legislation, notably the Police Act 1976 which introduced for the first time—in the form of a Police Complaints Board (PCB)—an independent element into the police discipline system (all forty-three chief constables in England and Wales opposed this measure). James Anderton—who went on to describe the Police and Criminal Evidence Act 1984 as 'unduly restrictive and complex' and express 'grave doubts' about the newly-formed Crown Prosecution Service (MAR 1985: 5)—described the PCB as 'one of the most expensive pieces of relatively unproductive bureaucratic machinery ever devised in this country' (MAR 1978: p. x). Mark—who clearly thought his professional autonomy was being undermined, and that the PCB would hinder his efforts to 'clean up' the Metropolitan Police (Mark 1978: ch. 16)—launched a fierce assault on the proposals, describing them as 'unwieldy and impracticable' (MPAR 1974: 29) and—two years on—as 'largely unworkable' (MPAR 1976: 22). Having reached the heights of rhetorical excess in his characterization of the PCB—to an audience of Metropolitan Police Federation members—as 'unnecessary, cumbersome, expensive and potentially sinister machinery' (1978: 241), Mark finally resigned over the issue.

Thirdly, Mark and, in his turn, McNee spearheaded a more wide-ranging attack on the operation of the criminal justice system, arguing that the scales of justice were skewed in favour of the defendant and against the police (and, hence, against society in general):

I am firmly of the opinion that the task of the police is being made unwarrantably difficult by certain restraints of criminal procedure. More than ever a system of justice is required which, for the protection of society from the criminal, is as effective in securing the conviction of the guilty as it is in securing the acquittal of the innocent . . . An excess of liberty which makes ordinary people fear to leave their homes is not freedom under the law as we know it [MPAR 1977: 8–9].

In this spirit, Mark sought to rein in what he viewed as the excessive concessions made to the accused and advance instead a reform agenda which highlighted longstanding police criticisms of the criminal justice system. These included: a right to silence that 'might have been designed by the criminals for their especial benefit and that of their professional advisers' (Mark 1977: 39); a trial acquittal rate 'too high to be acceptable' (Mark 1977: 63); and a minority of criminal defence lawyers 'who are more harmful to society than the clients they represent' (Mark 1977: 65). Mark's advocacy clearly set the tone for others and McNee's succession saw no let up in the volley of complaints. Particularly prominent here was the Bail Act 1976 and its 'dispiriting' (MPAR 1979: 11) effect on police morale: 'I am greatly concerned about the frequency with which active criminals, particularly those who are prone to violence, are being given bail under the provisions of the Act' (MPAR 1978: 10). More broadly, McNee used the opportunity of the Royal Commission on Criminal Procedure (Home Office 1981) to present the police's 'shopping list' of proposed changes to the criminal process (foremost among them increasing police powers of stop and search and other means of obtaining evidence); suggesting in so doing that he was asking the Commission merely to recommend legalizing what had already become *de facto* police practice (McNee 1983: ch. 8).

By the mid-1980s, however, this strident campaigning tone was beginning to recede. In the wake of the Brixton riots and the ensuing Scarman Report (Scarman 1982), and in the midst of escalating levels of recorded crime (despite greater police powers and resources), a more modulated, low-key police approach starts to emerge. This in fact becomes apparent towards the latter part of McNee's reign, before taking a much more discernible shape under his successor. Following his appointment in 1982, Kenneth Newman devoted several capacious forewords to explaining his philosophy of post-Scarman, partnership policing and outlining the changes he wished to instil within the Metropolitan force. In his 1984 report, he proceeded to outline at length his views on 'police professionalism', while also situating what senior officers had hitherto presented as restrictive pieces of legislation in the context of (suspected) police malpractice. While the elite police voice was not about to fade into some kind of pre-1972 silence, it was in the process of adopting a less culturally noisy, yet arguably more politically sophisticated, tone:

On occasions [police officers] have, quite wrongly, behaved in ways suggesting they were anticipating—and pre-empting—failures of the judicial process to deliver what they would have viewed as justice . . . Greater professionalism in the observance of the rule of law and commitment to changing bad law or bad practice by consultation and informing the Parliamentary process will draw less criticism and will avoid some of the less helpful changes in law [MPAR 1984: 14].

1987–Present: A Corporate, More Liberal Voice

During the course of the late 1980s the didactic elite police presence that had been such a feature of English public life for nearly two decades began, in important respects, to dissipate. With the advent of what Reiner *et al.* (1998) call a 'post-critical' era, whereupon the 'crises' of the 1970s and early 1980s began to subside (note, to take but one instance, the end of the open warfare between (some) chief officers and local police authorities following the abolition of the Metropolitan County Councils in 1986—see Chapter 8), the wilder reaches of senior police social commentary came to be reined in, and chief officers became markedly less inclined to participate in open political dispute, either among one another or with other institutions of governance. And as a particular generation of maverick 'police heroes' came—one by one—to be replaced, so a more corporate, less activist, and in some ways more liberal senior police voice assumed greater prominence.

This did not of course prevent chief constables from continuing to articulate—in the pages of their annual reports and beyond—a number of preoccupying concerns about crime and the social. Worries about violence—and particularly violence against police officers—came, for instance, much to the fore in the late 1980s and early 1990s. In 1988, Anderton expressed unease about 'an escalation in the use of gratuitous violence in the commission of crime' and wondered 'just how long it will be before police officers on routine patrol are permanently armed' (MAR 1988: p. v). Cheshire's chief constable wrote of 1994 as the year 'in which the issue of officer safety rose, quite rightly, to the top of the policing agenda' (CAR 1994: 9), while the Greater Manchester and Metropolitan forces reported more officers carrying holstered side-arms while responding to emergency situations (Manchester) and an increase in the number of armed response vehicles on patrol (London). As Paul Condon (Metropolitan Police Commissioner 1993–2000) put it, commenting on what he called the 'tragic' death of WPC Nina McKay in 1997: 'I shall continue to provide my officers with the best equipment available to make their working lives as safe as they can be' (MPAR 1997: 3).

Anxieties about drugs also surface as a major preoccupation of senior officers during this period—and not merely in metropolitan areas. In 1993 the chief constable of Cheshire called for the establishment of a Royal Commission on the issue, before proceeding in the following year to describe drugs as 'probably the greatest menace to our society' (CAR 1994: 9). The issue also prompted him to make what in the 1990s was a relatively rare diagnosis of the prevailing social climate. Expressing further concern about the drugs (and youth crime) problem, Cheshire's senior policeman observed that it:

clearly raises questions about parental responsibilities and one wonders if the values and standards of past generations are being eroded to such an extent that an increasing number of young people are left drifting helplessly to determine their own values and standards in an increasingly materialistic society [CAR 1992: 7].

Yet a number of clearly discernible shifts are also apparent in the substance and temper of elite police discourse during this period. One might note first here an increasingly pronounced (and, in comparison with the 1970s and 1980s, distinctly introspective) concern with the functioning and performance of the police organization itself. In part this has to do with the advent of managerialism and enhanced governmental concerns from the mid-1980s onwards with financial accountability and value for money (Leishman *et al.* 1996; McLaughlin and Murji 1997); something that finds clear expression in the increasingly prominent references to budgetary considerations in force annual reports (see, for example, Cheshire Police Annual Report (CAR) 1988–92; MAR 1989, 1991; MPAR 1996–8). In this vein, Cheshire's chief officer wrote of 'efficiency, effectiveness and economy' as 'buzz words which condition much of the thinking and decisions taken by police senior managers' (CAR 1989: 8), before going on to bemoan 'a background of escalating operational demands and an economic climate that demands optimum use be made of all police resources' (CAR 1990: 7). He continued in much the same spirit in the following year: 'I experienced more difficulty and frustration in 1991 than in any of my eight years as Chief Constable in attempting to match demands on the Force against the level of financial provision provided within the Police budget' (CAR 1991: 5).

   This introspection has relatedly to do, however, with the attempt on the part of senior officers (again, in part, under pressure from central government) to reconfigure the working culture of the police so as to improve the 'quality' of the service it offers. The

'Plus Programme', launched by Metropolitan Police Commissioner Peter Imbert (1987–93) following the publication of a report he commissioned on the force's 'corporate identity' in 1990 (Wolff Olins 1990) clearly figures highly here. So too does David Wilmot (who in 1991 succeeded Anderton in Greater Manchester) committing his force—despite what he called a huge increase in workload and a chronic shortage in manpower—to provide the best possible service in the most acceptable manner, to improve the public consultation process, and to make the most efficient use of resources (MAR 1991). Wilmot's inaugural foreword also sets out a new force philosophy (Wilmot was—in political outlook—a very different animal from Anderton), as well as new procedures for race relations investigations, steps to address equal opportunities, and enhanced management skills training. In the ensuing few years, Greater Manchester Police's annual reports (which—mirroring the national trend—have since the late 1980s become glossy promotional documents) reinforced this revised force image, encompassing such things as the new chief's 'statement of intent' and the force's 'common purpose and values'; and a regular 'force balance sheet' outlining the 'resources', 'demands', and 'results' for the year. In 1995—in a clear signal of the altered times—the chief constable wrote confidently of the force's new-found 'corporate identity and mission' (MAR 1995: 2).[9]

A second key theme of this period is the eclipse of the moderate authoritarianism that had prevailed in senior police discourse throughout the 1970s and early 1980s, and the emergence of what one might call a professional and pragmatic liberalism (Reiner speaks relatedly here of the 'dominant ideology' of 'post-Scarmanism' (Reiner 1991: 346–7)). One dimension of this is an acceptance among senior officers of the main contours of the investigative process post-Police and Criminal Evidence Act 1984; something evident in both the marked decline in senior police commentary on the shortcomings of the criminal justice system and the demise of open lobbying for greater police powers (though it is worth noting that ACPO took advantage of what Rose (1996: 327) claims was an invitation 'to draft government policy' in the run up to the Criminal Justice and Public Order Act 1994 in order to secure their longstanding aim of—effectively—abolishing the suspect's right of silence). It is demonstrated by the fact that chief officers came more and more—at the level of public rhetoric and force initiative—to take seriously the fight against racism and sexism both within and outside of the force, and increasingly committed themselves to speaking *against* rather than *with* the grain of the more reactionary aspects of rank-and-file police opinion (see, for example, 'Police Chief: This Can't Go On', *Guardian*, 19 February 1999). And it is notable that those among the 1990s cohort of chief officers who attained national prominence (Charles Pollard in Thames Valley, Keith Hellawell in West Yorkshire and then as 'drugs tsar', Wilmot in Greater Manchester) did so through their association with left-liberal causes—Pollard with the active promotion of restorative justice; Hellawell with (once) advocating a more 'mature' debate on drugs; and Wilmot with a very active and public campaign to improve police relations with the gay and lesbian community in Manchester, and with being the first chief officer to state—in the course of the Macpherson enquiry into the racist murder of Stephen Lawrence—that his force was 'institutionally racist'.

Some cognate shifts in respect of the rank-and-file police voice also occurred in the course of the late 1980s and 1990s. Potentially the most significant of these was the aforementioned advent of the Black Police Association (in 1994) and Lesbian and Gay Police Association (in 1989), organizations whose presence has served to undermine the Police Federation's claim to be the sole 'voice of the service'. The Federation has—as we saw in Chapter 6—long viewed these organizations with a certain suspicion. Their presence, however, has not only fragmented and pluralized the 'police voice' on certain social issues; it has also arguably contributed to the Federation beginning to make some uncharacteristically positive utterances—especially in the wake of the Macpherson Inquiry—about questions of diversity and discrimination. As one of the Federation's senior representatives claimed, 'we've changed, we've changed. We now realize that this problem [racism] is so great that we in our organization are going to address it and every police officer is going to address it.'

Taken together, these represent significant—albeit not uncontested, hegemonic—changes in police opinion, ones that, in particular, served to make chief officers in the 1990s something of a moderating influence on the more populist, authoritarian leanings of national politicians. One recently retired provincial chief constable reflected on this altered relationship of senior police 'expertise' to government thus:

What I will never do is comment on a major political controversy, unless I can address it from a purely professional viewpoint. And even if I'm being critical I make very clear that I am not criticizing the right of the government to make decisions, or policy, or whatever. I'm merely saying that from a professional viewpoint this could be better, or that could be better, or this won't achieve what people think it's going to achieve. I tried to do that with the last government, and with Michael Howard in particular, because I wrote a couple of quite critical articles in magazines about criminal justice policy which got picked up by the media. While never challenging the Home Secretary's right, I'm not challenging the democratic process, but if the Home Secretary says, for example, 'prison works', I actually think he's wrong [retired chief constable, provincial force].

This extract also serves to illustrate what we ought to register as two important continuities in the senior police outlook during the post-war period. First, the deeply-held belief that when chief officers enter debate on matters of social controversy, they are able to do so—in a manner that is somehow *above* politics—on the basis of, or in order to defend, their *professional* expertise and judgement. This connects, secondly, to the view that chief officers possess an intimate—almost mystical—connection with 'the public'. This sense of being 'in touch with' and 'accountable to' the law-abiding English populace has long been entrenched within the senior police habitus. It pervades Mark's belief that the police can and should define and represent the 'public interest'. It is implicit in Alderson's 'social contract' theories of policing. And it is to be found in one 1980s chief constable's feeling that 'what is important is that level below the police authority. What about the population?' It is a view of the chief constable as a wise, organically-situated translator of popular sentiment, one that finds an idiosyncratically English expression in the following account:

I suppose we tried to take into account what we thought were the views of everybody concerned. When I was in South Yorkshire my wife's home was in Hull and we were constantly travelling backwards and forwards to see her parents. On a road into Hull, there was a village called Fishlake which I spotted on the sign post on many occasions I travelled down that road. That particular area was coming into South Yorkshire. When we were sitting down at some of our planning meetings, deciding the policy, what we were going to put in standing orders, that sort of thing, I used to say 'what do you think they'll think about this at Fishlake?' [retired chief constable, metropolitan force].

Making Sense of the Police Voice: Ideology, Governance, and Culture

How may we make sociological sense of the emergence and subsequent mutation of the senior police voice within English public life since 1945? What are its conditions of possibility, its meanings, and effects? What does it tell us about policing as a social institution and about the culture and society of which policing is a part? An adequate account of these issues must, we think, encompass at least the following three factors and the intersections between them: (i) the professional ideology of police elites; (ii) the relationship of chief officers to the institutions of government and the impact of this on the social organization of police mobilization; and (iii) the (changing) social and cultural conditions within which the police voice is promulgated and received. Let us consider each in turn.

Police Ideology: The Making of the 'Post Mark-sist' Chief Constable

The emergence of chief constables from their locally-oriented, traditionally silent posture during the course of the 1970s was in part the—unintended—consequence of two important (legislative) changes initiated in the early 1960s. The first—a reduction in the number of forces from 117 in the early 1960s to the present forty-three by 1974—had the effect of enhancing both the relative status of each of the forty-three surviving chief constables, and creating a stronger institutional platform from which any one of them might speak (although such a base has, of course, long existed in London). The second, a line of judicial interpretation—both before and after the Police Act 1964—that robustly defended the doctrine of 'constabulary independence', conferred on chief constables an 'almost divine status' (Reiner 1991: 10) as holders of an unique, independent office, answerable to the law and law alone (Lustgarten 1986); a legal power that has long found cultural expression in the working ideology of senior officers (Savage *et al.* 2000: 193–208):

When you're appointed chief constable you are in a very privileged position. You're not a government servant, and you don't have to take orders from politicians, either local or central. You don't have to take orders. You have to listen to advice, and respond to it. There is nobody above you [retired chief constable, shire force].

Yet while these aspects of the legal and constitutional apparatus clearly served as institutional preconditions for the emergence from the body of hitherto 'local' chief constables of a number of vocal 'cosmopolitans' (to borrow Castells' (1983) terminology), they go but a short way in explaining why this transformation occurred. What was still required was the formation of a professional ideology that could legitimate (if only in the eyes of senior officers themselves) the rise of 'political policemen' (Kettle 1979) capable of assuming a prominent place in English public life. This (historic) task fell to Robert Mark. His enduring significance lies not, in our judgement, in his tirades against juries or 'bent lawyers', nor in his efforts to rid the Metropolitan Police of corrupt detectives—important though these appeared at the time. Rather, it lies in his attempt to overhaul the relationship of the English police—and senior officers in particular—to the wider (media) culture. In general terms, this saw Mark consciously strive to 'open up' a profoundly wary organization to the willing overtures of the print and broadcast media (Mark 1978: 146–51); a change whose ramifications—for both police and culture—continue to resonate today (Schlesinger and Tumbler 1994; Mawby 2002). More specifically, and of greater relevance to present concerns, he endeavoured to mobilize his peers around what one might call *an explicit theory of the chief constable as social commentator*. Two aspects of this are noteworthy here. Mark argues, first, that on the basis of their unrivalled front-line experience and their resulting knowledge of problems of crime, justice, and order, senior officers are ideally placed to enter, and contribute to, public debates on 'law and order', either on behalf of their forces or in defence of the broader 'public interest' (Mark 1978: 153–4). In a message clearly intended for his traditionally unforthcoming colleagues, Mark then forcefully urges them to mobilize as the agents best placed to serve in practical terms as what he calls 'guardians of freedom':

Are chief officers of the police in future likely to contribute from evidence and experience to public debate on law and order issues before legislation is passed, or are they, as in the past, to remain silent and sole possessors of relevant information from a mistaken belief that they have no right or duty to speak? If the latter, the public interest will be ill-served.

. . . The biggest disadvantage under which the police labour is the unnatural and harmful reticence of their leaders, some of whom, indeed, do not seem to understand the extent of their moral responsibility [Mark 1978: 170–1; 260].

These vitally important passages enable us to cast a more distanced historical eye over the—at the time—much debated emergence of the likes of Mark, McNee, Anderton, Alderson, and Oxford. They suggest that, for all their substantive differences, their contrasting visions of policing, order, and authority, these 'police heroes' held in common a *shared* ideology of the chief constable as a prominent cultural presence, a vocal participant in public affairs, an active agent in the making and remaking of opinion. It was this, above all else, that signalled a break with the past; a break that led historian E. P. Thompson to arrive at the following—characteristically caustic—judgement on the late 1970s: 'there is nothing new about Sir Robert Mark's or Sir David McNee's illiberal and impatient notions. What is new is the very powerful public relations operation which disseminates these notions as an authorized, consensual view—an operation which presses its spokesmen forward on every occasion. This is new. This is formidable' (Thompson 1980: 200; cf. Hall 1980b: 16).

Matters, as we have shown, have altered somewhat since Thompson's gloomy diagnosis was penned—the police voice has become quieter, its tones and demands discernibly less 'illiberal'. What *has* endured, however, and this we suggest is the abiding legacy of Mark's reign, his *fundamental* break from 'outdated customs', is the taken-for-granted, almost banal, acceptance among contemporary police chiefs of their role as social commentators. For all that Mark and his path-breaking fellow travellers made their contemporaries uncomfortable at the time (and there is much evidence to suggest that they did), it is Mark's vision of the police chief that has come to predominate in senior police circles, and his heirs generally recognize that contributing the police voice to public debate is today part and parcel of the job.[10] As one retired provincial chief officer put it, 'if you are sort of in the public arena, fighting for your force, it does have an effect. I don't think in this day and age that you can keep your head down.' This is not to deny that 'local' chief constables continue to exist. Far from it. It is to point out, however, that even those who have no wish to stoke controversy, or to parade the national stage, have come to realize the importance—if only on their own patch—of promoting one's force and seeking to shape (local) opinion. As one current chief of a shire force remarked, 'I think it's important to do that. It's not just getting the message back to your own staff, but it's getting the message through to the public'.

This is of course in no small measure a product of the deeply mediated arena in which chief constables operate today—a context that bears almost no comparison to that faced by their forebears of the immediate post-war period. In an age of 'informational politics' (Castells 1997: 311), where authority has been stripped of its settled character and is endlessly fought over, and where access to the media has become a precondition of successful 'political' mobilization and governance, the option of silence has—sociologically speaking—been closed off (cf. Thompson 1996: ch. 4). 'Outside the media sphere', Castells (1997: 312) observes, 'there is only political marginality', and there is little reason to suppose that a mute police would be spared entirely from such an outcome. The contemporary chief has thus—as this recently retired provincial chief noted—become required to perform in, and be adept at using, the institutions of the wider public sphere: 'I think there is a larger degree of sophistication and understanding of the larger political system by chief officers today. Most of us are much happier in those environments. We're probably better at handling the media than they used to be'. In these altered conditions, Mark's contribution is to have offered *avant la lettre* a strident—and for many in the police world deeply appealing—image of what an authoritative articulator of the police outlook could look like:

People at the bottom, at the sharp end so to speak, they loved it. Here was somebody that was saying things that needed saying, who was sorting out corruption which nobody in their right mind wanted to see. He was taking on, not tilting windmills, he was taking on big power blocks and winning. He was very good news [retired chief constable, metropolitan force].

If this image has been embedded in the working common sense of contemporary senior police officers, then they have not taken from it merely a gunslinging preoccupation with 'taking on big power blocks and winning', but have forged, instead, a more modulated, reflexive, and politically astute conception of the chief constable's public role—what one might call a 'post Mark-sist' police ideology. This term signifies a number of evident continuities between the 'police heroes' of the 1970s and early 1980s and the current cohort of (otherwise more liberal) chief officers, not least a preference for legitimating (and to this extent self-censoring) their power to name on the basis of 'autonomous' professional judgement, and a tendency to believe they can speak to and on behalf of the 'public interest'. Yet it also signals some clear departures from the received Mark-sist inheritance, notably in respect of its more tempered sense of 'when it is best to speak', and a seemingly greater reluctance to become embroiled in public and political controversy.[11]

Thus one finds contemporary police elites evincing relatively little interest in seeking through their pedagogic efforts to 'mould' the social in the police's preferred image, a project that had been close to the heart of a number of prominent chief officers in the preceding two decades. One detects further a strongly felt desire among contemporary police chiefs to avoid acquiring a reputation for what was variously described to us—in respect of almost all the 'police heroes' of the previous generation—as 'crusading' or 'posturing'. This has to do in large measure with respecting both the limits of the chief constable's office ('I thought Alderson grossly misused his position for the last two years he was in office'), as well as its dignity ('I don't think he influenced many people, Jim Anderton, he was more of a figure of fun').[12] It stems also from the realization that 'if you become rent-a-gob you lose credibility anyway'; that 'in a democracy' the police should not 'seek to lead on big social issues' or act as 'the arbiters of moral standards'; and that there are certain issues about which it is too occupationally risky to speak:

There are some issues, which really as chief officer, you shouldn't talk about. That's a matter for politics, politicians, and Parliament. I mean I would like to think I have made an impression of where I stand on homosexuality and lesbianism and that kind of issue, but I will not get drawn into debate about the age of consent. That has nothing to do with me as a chief officer. And if I were to talk about it and the debate went one way or t'other, I'm compromised as chief. In some ways it's as simple as that [chief constable, metropolitan force].

The post Mark-sist police ideology differs then from that evinced by—or at least implicit in the actions of—both the silent and idiosyncratically outspoken chief constables of the post-war period. It is a worldview that recognizes the occupational requirement to ensure the presence of the police voice within the wider culture (mainly, though by no means only, through media channels), while also understanding the distracting ephemerality of much late modern media discourse. As one chief constable put it, 'some issues, they're just not worth talking about, it's a lot of hot air and it will blow away. Let somebody else do the spouting, we will just get on with delivering a proper policing service in [force area]'. More significantly, it is an ideology that has learned from the experience of Mark's generation the pitfalls of mistaking voice for influence; one that has, in so doing, come to acquire a less culturally prominent but perhaps more politically effective presence in contemporary English society:

You have to be able to work within the political system, at local and national level. And if you don't understand how politics works you will fail. And you don't succeed, by and large, by taking things to the newspapers. Any pressure group that has to go public means that it's failed. You try and influence in other ways [retired chief constable, provincial force].

Organizing for Governance: The Eclipse of the Maverick and the Collectivization of the Police Voice

The rise and fall of the police 'maverick' and the adoption of a less strident public tone by contemporary chief constables cannot fully be accounted for without due regard to the professional socialization of different generations of police leaders, their social organization, and their connections to the apparatus of government. The 'political policeman' of the 1970s occupied a very particular moment in the history of chief constables' recruitment and socialization (Wall 1998: ch. 10 and *passim*). They formed a cohort that surfaced after the era of ex-military men and Trenchard's Hendon-trained 'officer class', but before the levelling effects of the Senior Command Course (which commenced in 1962) had started fully to kick in. These were individuals who—as Dave Wall (Wall 1998: 301) puts it—'had literally to carve out their own careers'; something he rightly views as forging the kind of fierce independence (over and above that which has routinely been part of the elite police habitus) that underpinned their coming to prominence as national figures. The experience of ensuing generations was to be markedly different. Identified and 'fast-tracked' early in their careers, required to pass through the rigours of an extended interview, and then schooled together on the Senior Command Course (for details of which, see Whittaker 1964: 137–40; Wall 1998: 226–8), the contemporary generation of chiefs has come to be 'welded together' as 'an increasingly unitary cohesive elite'

(Reiner 1991: 86; see also Savage *et al.* 2000: ch. 4).[13] One former chief constable we spoke to reflected on these mutations thus:

I am one where you had to make your own career. And now there's a generation where they're selected as sergeants, and they're clones. They're all alike. They come from the same sector, the same situation. They've got a rule that they won't say rude things about each other, or they won't rock the boat.

A further important component of this change surrounds the police elite's representative organization, the Association of Chief Police Officers (ACPO). Launched in 1948, ACPO was created as a means for the 'collective bargaining' of senior police pay and conditions, a forum for informal socializing, and a vehicle for forming and proffering 'advice' on matters of interest to the police (Reiner 1991: 362–7; Savage *et al.* 2000: ch. 2). However, while its 'policy-making' functions have cumulatively come to assume prominence over its 'trade union' role, and while critics have long suspected it of being a murky and somewhat sinister power in the land (Thompson 1980), there is evidence to suggest that ACPO has for much of the post-war period been a loosely assembled and rather ineffective organization (Reiner 1991: ch. 11; Savage *et al.* 2000: 62–9). This at least is the view that prevailed among the (retired) chiefs we interviewed. Their overriding recollection is of a body functioning as little more than an 'informal' and 'pretty cordial club'; one whose 'main players [were] often from small county forces', and whose capacity to arrive at binding collective decisions on matters of policy was severely hamstrung by the 'petty jealousies' of individuals deeply committed to their own (operational) independence and 'fiefdoms'. As one erstwhile Chief Inspector of Constabulary reflected, 'ACPO will not properly function because you get forty-three chief constables and they seem to be totally unable to agree. There is no coercion, there's no force in any policy they make.' It was also the judgement of one retired Home Office civil servant we interviewed. In his view, ACPO during the 1970s and for much of the 1980s was 'able to form a common view only with great difficulty and very slowly. And so for policy-making it had not nearly the influence it deserved or should have exerted. Its heartbeat, its pulse, simply wasn't geared to government.'

Thus it was that at the moment in the 1970s when the police voice appeared—to some chief officers at least—urgently required to address what they perceived as a mounting crisis of authority, ACPO seemed singularly unable to act. And thus it was that such individuals were forced to go it alone, advancing what they judged to be the 'police case' beyond—and at times in open opposition to—their representative body. From the mid-1980s onwards, however, this confluence of factors began to dissipate. As a generation of police leaders came to be superseded by one that was less individualistic and more consensus-oriented, so ACPO began to turn itself into what one serving chief constable we spoke to called 'a much better organized, more cohesive, more influential body'. In the aftermath of the 1984–5 miners' dispute, when, under the auspices of the National Reporting Centre (Kettle 1985a), it played a key role in co-ordinating mutual aid arrangements, ACPO came over the ensuing decade to: (i) acquire a Home Office-funded permanent secretariat; (ii) enhance its policy-making capacity by requiring dissenting chiefs to 'opt out' of collective decisions in writing (what Savage and Charman (1996) call 'presumption in favour of compliance'); and (iii) divest its 'trade union' functions to a separate organization (the Chief Police Officers' Staff Association), thus enabling it to advise government without appearing to be 'feathering our own nests' (retired chief constable, provincial force). ACPO has, in short, developed under its umbrella what one current chief constable we spoke to called 'a much more corporate way of making the overall policy of the police service', a situation the current cohort of chief constables are generally predisposed to accept: 'a decision made at ACPO Council now carries a lot more weight than it may have done ten or fifteen years ago. Chief constables are less likely to diverge from those decisions than they used to' (chief constable, shire force).[14]

How though do these organizational shifts relate to the temper, circulation, and effects of the senior police voice, to chief constables' role as social commentators? Some such effects can clearly be discerned. They have served to reduce the presence in political and public debate of 'rogue' chief constables pursuing their own personal agendas.[15] They have minimized the likelihood of public disputes breaking out between chief officers—an aspect of the 1970s and 1980s that one serving chief described to us as 'in police cultural terms, bad news'. And they have enabled senior police spokespeople to enter public conversation with the weight of their colleagues behind them, thus allowing ACPO to compete more effectively for attention and influence with the voice of the police rank and file (cf. McLaughlin and Murji 1998):

We've become much more professional in lots of ways. And that is where I think we have recaptured in the public mind the leadership of the police service, which we'd abdicated almost in one sense almost to the Police Federation, who would be trotted out as the police spokesman [retired chief constable, provincial force].

Yet these organizational changes have also—ironically—served in many ways to lower the cultural prominence of the elite police voice. ACPO's reconfiguration has in large measure been fuelled by both the direct enticement of national government, which has long worried about and wanted to improve the 'quality' of police leadership, and which in the late 1980s urged ACPO to organize itself as the government's principal point of contact on policing-related matters (Savage and Charman 1996); and the looming threat of further force amalgamations and the formation of a national police force. Against this backdrop, the greater orientation of ACPO towards Home Office agendas, and the strengthening of its capacity to formulate policies that impact *across* forces on the ground, is considered by many chief officers as the most viable means to protect the 'tradition' of local policing; something that is reflected in both their collective explanation of ACPO's role in the miners' strike (Reiner 1991: 188–9), and the more general view of one recently retired chief that 'ACPO is the price that you pay for a decentralized police'.

This 'internal' perspective on ACPO's reconfiguration during the 1980s and 1990s has recently been endorsed by Steven Savage and his co-workers, whose research on the organization has done much to illuminate these changes (Savage *et al.* 2000). In the face of such centralizing measures as Home Office circulars, national performance objectives, and more robust trans-force regimes of audit and inspection, they argue that ACPO has acted in recent years as 'an effective counter-centralizing agency' (Savage *et al.* 1996: 103; 2000: 204), seeking to standardize police practice across forces in a bid to stave off further central government intervention. ACPO has in this way, they suggest, come to be incorporated within a multi-tiered, overlapping network of institutions—Home Office, Her Majesty's Inspectorate of Constabulary, the Audit Commission, the Association of Police Authorities, and so forth—within which policing policy is today being deliberated upon, enacted, and revised. As Savage *et al.* put it: '[ACPO] has been increasingly incorporated into government, perhaps to a point where it has become part of government' (2000: 38).

Viewed in this light, the discernible reduction in the cultural prominence of the police voice since the mid-1980s appears as the product of ACPO's *ongoing transformation into an institution of governance*—one whose purpose is to act as a mover of, and responder to, policy initiatives on the one hand, and as an agency striving to shape and co-ordinate police practice across forces on the other. Chief constables have, in other words, traded visibility for (greater) effectiveness, *cultural* prominence for *political* influence. As they have come to assume a corporate presence within the relatively closed communities of national policy-making (Wall 1998: 310), so their need to lobby, to shape opinion, to occupy a vocal place in the wider culture, has, if not entirely diminished, then at least been considerably reduced.

Culture and Authority: The Rise and Fall of the Secular Priests

We documented in Chapter 3 the presence of a widespread social memory that reconstructs and represents the two decades from 1945 to the mid-1960s as orderly, cohesive, and deferential; an era when religious, medical, pedagogic, and police authority was respected, even feared, simply on the basis that it *was* authority. Such recollections also resonated with, and found expression among, the (retired) chief officers we spoke to. One ex-provincial chief constable referred to the 'unbelievable' aura of 'compliance' that characterized the Lancashire mining village in which he spent the early part of his police career, something that meant 'when you walked your beat, you were a power in the community'. Another former chief spoke—in a cognate vein—of a:

rich seam of unexpressed understanding between people and policemen, and [of] how the police could do something to help them, as well as to lock them up when they needed to be locked up. It was a relationship that was of its time, and it didn't last more than, I would have thought, about ten years, and then it began to change, society began to change. The halcyon days, for the policeman on the beat, in my view, would be about 1948 to 1958.

In so far as these reflections tell us something important for present purposes about policing in the immediate post-war period, it is that the cultural conditions required in order for the police to exercise effectively what we have called their 'power of legitimate naming' were—sociologically speaking—in place. They suggest these were times when the police could function as 'secular priests' (Young 1991: 14–15) and have their pontifications on 'good and evil' taken seriously. Yet the presence of such conditions also alerts us to the fact that the preconditions of social order lay elsewhere, beyond the police; and that (notwithstanding the 'violence' that the police might deploy to retain order on Friday nights, and the pedagogic homilies immortalized in *Dixon of Dock Green*) they consequently had little need to activate this power, to make themselves a prominent cultural presence. The very conditions that would have enabled chief constables to mobilize their symbolic power of representation during this period simultaneously help to account for its absence.

It was not until the mid-1970s—following increasingly levels of material prosperity and the advent of mass consumption in the 1950s, and the revolts against settled authority (and for individual autonomy) that ensued in the late 1960s—that, in the midst of a sustained economic and political crisis, the police voice felt compelled to bring itself to the fore in defence of a political and social order it adjudged to be threatened—hence, for instance, Mark's abiding concern with violence and industrial unrest, preoccupation with what he supposed to be the failings of the justice system, and impatient asides about 'extremist' politicians and 'weak government'. We have recounted the economic and social context of this mobilization, and the ensuing 'drift' into what Stuart Hall (1980*b*) called the 'law and order society', in Chapter 1, and there is little to be gained from revisiting this territory here. Two issues do arise, however, that are germane to our present concerns, each of which will repay some further attention.

The first addresses the fact that—in addition to the enhanced instrumental position they assumed in English society in the late 1970s and early 1980s (the extra pay, the greater powers, the increase in numbers, and so on)—the police also took up a prominent symbolic presence as *interpreters of the crisis*—secular priests whose authoritative preaching possessed a powerful (emotive) appeal for large numbers of besieged and anxious ('respectable') citizens, condensing a welter of concerns about 'the condition of England' into some convincingly simple narratives and appealingly 'tough' solutions—more powers, more order, the restoration of authority.[16] In this regard, various police leaders presented themselves both as having been stirred reluctantly into action by the shortcomings or excesses of others (politicians, lawyers, journalists, religious leaders, and the like), and as being able to speak in a non-partisan fashion in defence of the ordinary, decent, law-abiding 'public'. In a period of great turmoil, the police were—in Robert Mark's words (1977: 20)—'a bastion to which people at every level look for reassurance and comfort'.[17]

The capacity of the police to proffer this sort of reassurance, with all its authoritative social magic, is clearly central, secondly, to both the visible prominence of 'police heroes' in the troubled politics of the 1970s and early 1980s, and their success in securing public and political support, and thus resources, during moments of social crisis. Yet it has now become possible to view this prominence, not merely as instrumental in Britain's turn in the early 1980s towards a more 'authoritarian populist' mode of rule (cf. Hall et al. 1978), but—culturally—as a last futile throw of the dice in defence of the crumbling order of post-war authority, deference, and social rigidity. The attempt by Thatcherism to respond to the unravelling of this order by buttressing some of its beleaguered institutions (the nation, the family, 'our police') could not disguise the fact that the underpinnings of the post-war social order were undergoing profound change; indeed, in another part of the woods, the New Right's free market fundamentalism was helping to hasten this very collapse (Gray 1995). From around the mid-1960s onwards, the post-war (more affluent, consumerist, but also in some cases alienated) generation indicated its desire to challenge established authority, to argue with it rather than merely accept its word, to make the moral and cultural crisis permanent and hence no longer a crisis (Bauman 1999: 140–53). It was against all this that the police voice entered the breach in what now appears to have been a final—*superficially confident*—attempt to put the pieces back together and keep an emergent, necessarily more open and contested, moral order at bay. No wonder the 'police heroes' of the 1970s had such a short shelf-life; the cultural—as well as organizational—preconditions of their reproduction were, even as they spoke, being pulled from under their feet.

This cultural undermining of the police's power of legitimate naming has in part to do with a series of transformations that social theorists have termed 'detraditionalization' (Heelas *et al.* 1996). The decline of the sacred and the emergence of multiple (secular) authorities; the withering of deference and emergence of citizenship rights and entitlements; the replacement of rigid hierarchy with greater mobility, individual freedom, and (hence) uncertainty; the emergence of mass (and increasingly niche) media communications, the incapacity of 'tradition' to be defended as such (Giddens 1994)—all this has served to erode the foundations upon which police legitimacy once more securely rested, and helped create a climate of scrutiny which has both heightened people's expectations and sharpened their reactions to poor performance. Against the further backdrop of escalating post-war crime rates, and the coming to cultural prominence of hitherto concealed abuses of police power, the police by the late 1980s could no longer so boldly assert their symbolic authorizing power.

To this must be added the more contingent—and to some degree unintended—consequences of the managerialist project launched by the Conservative government in 1983 (Leishman *et al.* 1996; McLaughlin and Murji 1997). In its drive for economy, efficiency, effectiveness; preoccupation with auditing, measurement, and *financial* accountability; and valorization of private sector values and ways of doing things, this project has not merely had all kinds of effects on the internal workings and thinking of police organizations—as we shall see in Chapter 8. It has also more broadly served to erode—if not yet entirely erase—some hitherto significant cultural differences between the police and other public and private bureaucracies (and between the police and commercial suppliers of security 'products' (Loader 1999)); as well as prompting chief officers to conceive of themselves as 'managers' (Reiner 1991: 333–40)—a role, it needs hardly to be said, that is not so readily associated with persuasive social commentary. The cumulative effect of these collapsed distinctions and raised 'consumer' expectations is summed up nicely in the words of this retired chief:

I think they [the public] are much more critical. They demand of us as they demand of the gas board, and hospitals and doctors and everybody else. They demand much more, are less forgiving. Doctor friends of mine they will say the job is not worth a light compared to what it was twenty years ago. Nobody quarrelled with a doctor. The doctor said something and you accepted it. You didn't even subconsciously criticize him, now you criticize him quite openly and complain about him. Same with solicitors, same with accountants. Everybody who was in a privileged position is now being held to account much more. There's no use bleating about it, it is a fact of life [retired chief constable, metropolitan force].

The net result of these post-war transitions is that the police's power of legitimate naming has come to acquire an *embedded yet contested* place within contemporary English culture and society. Such power has been embedded to the extent that chief officers' *entitlement to speak* on matters of crime, justice, and social order has come to be taken for granted, accepted largely without challenge as an unspectacular feature of English political life. Chief constables have in other words become—locally and nationally— one of the 'cast of regulars...whose appearance on the media enables them to function as accredited representatives of public experience' (Keane 1998: 166); and to this extent have established themselves as 'owners' of (or at least major shareholders in) a wide range of—crime-related—social problems. Such is the contemporary basis of the police's symbolic power: 'they can make claims and assertions. They are looked at and reported to by others anxious for definitions and solutions to the problem. They possess authority in the field. Even if opposed by other groups, they are among those who can gain the public ear' (Gusfield 1981: 10).

This capacity continues to be buttressed in some measure both by the police's close—and seemingly obvious—association with often deeply-held public anxieties and desires concerning matters of order and chaos, life and death, liberty and security, and the like; and, more contingently, by the revered status as symbols of law, order, and nation that the police retain (often, as we have shown, in a nostalgic mode) among at least some sections of the English populace. Notwithstanding the fact that these cultural supports have atrophied and been greatly residualized in the post-war years (cf. Reiner 1992), they continue, it seems to us, to offer some kind of basis from which the police could potentially reassume a more prominent and pedagogic presence in the public affairs of the nation.[18] Despite his recognition of the altered cultural conditions in which the police now operate, the aforementioned ex-chief constable clearly remains enticed by this possibility:

I think in a sense society badly wants to feel anchor points within it. It has looked to the church. Even people who didn't go to church, look to the church to form leadership of sorts and is disappointed that it has not.

I don't think it is too far fetched that they still do look and will continue to look at the police to give themselves a fulcrum perhaps to operate against. And if the police leadership can find itself able to give that in a sort of way, a caring position that is defensible, positions which are articulated sensibly, in which people can play up to, then I think it is quite a service. At the moment it does not do that nearly enough, it is terribly careful you do not go too far, don't be seen to be moralistic, don't to be seen to be doctrinaire. But there is a role somewhere in there for leadership of the positive sort, the police standing up for what is right and good [retired chief constable, metropolitan force].

It is our judgement that this has—sociologically speaking—become an implausible project for the police to pursue, something the cautious tone in which the prospect is mooted itself rather suggests. For while the police have over the second half of the twentieth century come to lodge themselves firmly in the wider (media) culture, and assume a normalized presence in public debate, their substantive claims have come during that period to be *routinely challenged* by a plethora of competing voices over which the police seem to exercise less and less symbolic authority. The police voice today is mobilized and put to work within a culture composed of 'numerous authorities' that 'tend to cancel each other out', such that 'the sole effective authority in the field is one who must chose between them' (Bauman 2000: 64). Against this backdrop, the kind of conservative, moderately authoritarian, anti-permissive, middle-English worldview that many police leaders (of whom Mark was the predominant and most influential example) were eager in the 1970s and 1980s to articulate has, quite simply, lost its cultural purchase, and, if not disappeared, become something of a residual, almost subterranean element within English culture (cf. Hitchens 1999). It is the view that dare not speak its name.[19]

There is of course no guarantee that this state of affairs will persist, or that the current cohort of liberal chiefs will—culturally and organizationally—reproduce themselves, or that the police power to name, classify, authorize, and diagnose will not once more seek to assume a more didactic, fundamentalist presence within English society. It is hard, however, to escape the conclusion that a quieter, more modulated, apologetic, and for the most part liberal, disposition prevails among senior officers today at least in part because its coheres with the dominant, consumerist tendencies of the age.

8

Cultures of Police Governance

We want in this chapter to develop further our cultural sociology of English policing by means of an analysis of police governance. In so doing, we are concerned with a question—*quis custodiet ipsos custodes?*—that clearly predates the formation of modern police systems, one whose wider significance and paradoxes have long been the subject of reflection in both political and constitutional theory (Berki 1986; Walker 2000). This question has also—in its delimited *police* form—been pressed under specific conditions, by various agents, in different registers, and with contrasting degrees of urgency and success within the territorial boundaries of modern nation-states (Bayley 1985: ch. 7). But what of the contemporary English case? How are we to make adequate sense of what is commonly understood as the coming to political and cultural prominence in the years since 1945 of the question who controls the police? What events and controversies have prompted that question to be posed? What forms has it assumed and with what effects?

The story we wish to reconstruct falls into three chronologically overlapping, yet analytically distinct, periods that broadly correspond with those deployed in the last chapter. The *first* covers a roughly thirty-year span from the late 1940s to the late 1970s. It was a period in which questions of police governance—while not entirely free of scandal and *causes célèbres*—remained firmly the province of government officials, senior officers, and assorted constitutional specialists (Hart 1951; Marshall 1965), rather than circulating with any great force within the wider culture. It was also a period—following the 1962 Royal Commission and the Police Act 1964—when the institutional architecture of contemporary police governance was legally enshrined; one characterized—we shall suggest—by overt governmental support for the English way of 'autonomous' and 'local' policing coupled with further moves towards centralized influence and control—some (such as force amalgamations) explicit and up-front, others opaque and more 'backstage'. This settled configuration of elements came under pressure, and began to unravel, towards the latter part of the 1970s, thereby ushering in a *second* distinctive post-war 'moment'—one set within the backdrop of a faltering post-war 'consensus' and the coming of Thatcherism and characterized by a sustained radical challenge to the firmly embedded 'tradition' of constabulary independence mounted in the name of local democracy. This challenge—as we shall see—must in several respects be counted as a failure (though it is not without some significant traces and effects); an early and prescient signal of which came in 1983 in the form of a Home Office circular to police forces entitled *Financial Management Initiative*. This was to herald the onset of a *third* key moment in the post-war history of police governance, one in which economy, efficiency, and effectiveness; performance targets, auditing, and monitoring; consumer responsiveness and customer satisfaction became the order of the day. The meanings, reception, and effects of this governmental attempt to render English policing profane form the substance of our final section.

In constructing an account of these developments, our aim is twofold. We want first—drawing both on various of the documents we outlined in Chapter 2 and on interviews with civil servants, national and local politicians, and senior and rank and file police officers—to flesh out the contours of the above story and to chart, in particular, the shifting and competing political rationalities that have shaped (or endeavoured to shape) the English police in the latter half of the twentieth century. Many of our interviewees were instrumental in the formation of these rationalities and/or protagonists in relevant struggles, and their memories and reflections thus enable us to construct a narrative certain aspects of which are familiar and amply documented but which is less often considered in the round (cf. Jefferson and Grimshaw 1984; Lustgarten 1986; Jones and Newburn 1997; Reiner 2000*a*; Walker 2000). But we want also, in so doing, to proffer a reading of post-war English policing that is attuned to the ways in which struggles over *police governance* are always in part contests over the cultural meanings of those two terms—meanings that have emerged out of, and been conditioned by, the broader social and political landscape of post-war England, and which have, in turn, competed over and left their traces upon that wider context. What visions of policing—and of its connections to government, to democracy, to citizenship—have been inscribed within different mentalities of English police governance? How may we assess the post-war trajectories and contemporary cultural and political force of each of them? Answers to these questions are, we hope to demonstrate, central to an adequate understanding of what has been—and remains—at stake in debates about police accountability.

Autonomous and Local?: The Imaginative and Institutional Architecture of English Police Governance

The basic soundness of our present police system is not due merely to the fact that reasonable people operate it successfully—though that is certainly true. Nor, again, is the system sound merely because it follows a tradition of local policing which is traceable back for many centuries—though that is also true. In our opinion the present police system is sound because it is based upon, and reflects, a political idea of immense practical value which has gained wide acceptance in this country, namely, the idea of partnership between central and local government in the administration of public services. This idea...admirably suits the British temperament [Home Office 1962: 47].

During the course of the 1950s, against a backdrop of steadily escalating crime rates, the police were beset by a number of public conflicts and scandals—some entailing disputes between chief constables and local watch committees, others involving criminal activities by police officers (including in one case a chief constable), still more centring on alleged police misconduct towards members of the public (Home Office 1959; Critchley 1978: 270–4; Stevenson and Bottoms 1990). They were—when set against the controversies that were later to subsume the police—pretty small fry, and *Police Review* remained confident enough to dismiss them as 'unrelated incidents'. Yet they were sufficient to raise concerns among governing elites about aspects of the relationship between 'police and public', while also indicating certain ambiguities and deficiencies in extant arrangements for supervising policing and bringing police officers to account for their actions. One retired senior Home Office official we interviewed recalled the moment

thus: 'accountability really took off in the 1960s and it had plenty
to base itself on....I think the pattern of abuse of power, miscarriages of justice, had started and it was well under way by 1960.'

The response of the then Conservative government was, in 1959,
to establish a Royal Commission on the Police under the steward-
ship of academic lawyer and former Minister of Health Sir Henry
Willink. The first such enquiry into the police since 1929, the
Willink commission was tasked with the job of reviewing 'the
constitutional position of the police throughout Great Britain',
with particular reference to the composition and function of police
authorities, the status and accountability of police officers
(including chief constables), and matters relating to the relationship
between police and public and the effective handling of complaints.
The Commission reported in 1962, and having considered and
rejected the case for radical reform (something that prompted one
of its members, Professor Goodhart, to pen a sharply-worded
memorandum of dissent advancing the case for a national police
force), it opted instead for 'tidying up what had been messy and
inefficiently applied' (retired Home Office civil servant)—namely,
the tripartite allocation of responsibility for the police between the
Home Secretary, chief constables, and local police authorities. This
in turn formed the basis of the Police Act 1964, a measure that was
'for thirty years'—in the words of another retired Home Office
official—to serve as a 'brilliant means of holding the position' between
the competing claims of central and local government, professional
autonomy, and democratic governance. This, at least, was the spirit
in which the then Home Secretary, R. A. Butler, laid the legislation
before Parliament:

This Bill modernises the law. It strips away those remnants of a nineteenth
century police system which impede progress in modern days. It preserves
those features, notably the role of the local police authority, which are of
proved value. It opens the ways for the adaptation of the system, under
firm central guidance, to meet the requirements of the second half of the
twentieth century. I present it to the House as a businesslike, balanced,
fearless, forward-looking Bill [*Hansard*, vol. 634, col. 102, 29 November
1963].

The Royal Commission's endeavours resulted in set of institutional
arrangements under which roles and responsibilities were demarc-
ated broadly as follows: chief constables were given statutory

responsibility for the 'direction and control' of their force; local police authorities (now composed of two-thirds elected councillors, one-third appointed magistrates) were to maintain an 'adequate and efficient' force to which end they were—among other things—able to appoint, discipline, and retire senior ranks and receive from chief officers an annual report; the Home Secretary was placed under a duty 'to promote the efficiency of the police', and was accorded various powers to assist in the fulfilment of this, including requiring force amalgamations, calling for reports, instigating local inquiries, and ratifying appointments of senior officers. The details of this 'very delicate' (retired Home Office civil servant) and radically under-specified 'balance' need not detain us further for the moment, though we will have reason to revisit them in due course (cf. Marshall 1965; Jefferson and Grimshaw 1984: ch. 2; Lustgarten 1986: chs. 6–7; Walker 2000: chs. 2–3). Instead, the following questions lie immediately before us: upon what governmental rationalities and ideologies did this particular 'holding operation' rest? What were its economic, political, and cultural conditions of possibility? Why and when did these begin to unravel?

The 'Royal Commission model' (Walker 2000: ch. 3) is organized around *two* connected ideologies, both deeply embedded in English sentiment towards and representations of policing, both consequently pivotal in shaping the contours of post-war disputes about police governance. The first of these—police autonomy or *constabulary independence*—came in the decades both before and after the 'landmark' legal judgment in *Fisher v. Oldham Corporation* [1930] 2 KB 364 to assume an almost canonical place in official proclamations about how policing ought properly to be governed.

Though the historical origins (and precise legal status) of this murky doctrine remain disputed—some commentators holding that it can be traced back to the formation of the English police system in the nineteenth century (Brogden 1982: ch. 2; Jefferson and Grimshaw 1984: ch. 2)—there is little doubt that it began to be taken much more seriously by governing and police elites in the early decades of the twentieth century—according to Lustgarten (1986: 43–8) as a means of insulating the police from local watch committees that had begun to fall under the control of Labour Party representatives (cf. Walker 2000: 45–9). Among other things, this manœuvre entailed such elites treating *Fisher v. Oldham* (which held that police authorities were not liable in tort for the actions of *individual* police constables) *as if* it offered legal authority for protecting the general decisions of *chief* constables from the interference of such authorities. This extended version of the doctrine was thus enshrined and disseminated as orthodoxy by government and senior police officers *before* it received ambiguous statutory backing in the Police Act 1964 (the Act gave chief constables 'direction and control' of their forces, while making police authorities responsible for maintaining that force as 'adequate and efficient') and ringing judicial endorsement from the Court of Appeal in *R. v. Commissioner of the Police of the Metropolis, ex parte Blackburn (No. 1)* [1968] 2 WLR 893 (see, on this, Walker 2000: 49–52).

The Royal Commission—having engaged in what Walker (2000: 70) calls an 'oddly fatalistic discussion' of the doctrine—effectively treated it as an unquestionable premise from which to proceed, rather than as an object of enquiry and scrutiny, something that helps explain the narrow conceptual boundaries within which the Commission framed its deliberations and recommendations. It was also by the mid-twentieth century a nostrum that 'ran very deep' in the Home Office ('in some ways deeper than now', as one retired official put it)—a feature of the governmental outlook that is nicely encapsulated in the words of this former senior civil servant:

We were all, everyone was terribly concerned that the police should not be seen as an agency of the government. The tradition was immensely strong. I was brought up on the case of *Fisher v. Oldham Corporation*, 1933 [*sic*]—that has always been at the heart of the Home Office attitude.

The active promotion of constabulary independence was—as this account indicates—animated principally by the fear of (illegitimate) political involvement in police affairs—a fear which has deep roots in both 'the soil of conventional wisdom' and the then prevailing mindsets of English political culture (Walker 2000: 53).[1] In its extended form the doctrine assuages this fear by making two claims: first, and negatively, that police decisions must not (and should not) be determined by any external political authority; secondly, and in a more positive spirit, that the police are to be rendered accountable to and through law (and law alone). By these means—separation from politics, subservience to law—had English policing (and, by extension, English parliamentary democracy) come by the mid-twentieth century to be officially represented; by these means also have they been marked out as different from, and superior to, the policing and political institutions of other nations (e.g., Mark 1978: 56). A particular social imaginary is, of course, mobilized here—one that projects the police as a bedrock, national institution (clearly set apart from such mundane public authorities as education or housing, much more akin—in terms of its of its significance to the social fabric—to a body like the monarchy); an institution belonging to 'the people' rather than government, and accountable to them (mysteriously one is bound to say) through the majestic splendour of Law rather than the dirty, meddling, dangerous business of politics.[2] Seen in this light—as a *cultural* as much as a legal doctrine, one deeply entangled with a certain English conception of good governance—it is unsurprising that constabulary independence came to figure so dominantly, not only in the deliberations of the 1962 Royal Commission and the ensuing Police Act, but also—as we shall see—in subsequent struggles over the democratic governance of police. The robust formulation of this former Conservative Minister of State at the Home Office encapsulates what many among the governing classes consider to be at stake:

I fully understand and will attempt to uphold the doctrine of operational independence. The tripartite system by which the police are governed in this country, the police authority, and the Home Secretary, and the chief constable, that is the way to do it. It is untidy, but it has built-in safeguards, which are unique, I believe, to our country, and are the best safeguards we have against the police becoming a kind of elite above the law. They've got to be within the law, under the law, as they serve the law. I think our arrangements are the envy of most people who look for a non-authoritarian and democratic, but efficient means of resolving these issues, of how a democratic society is to be policed. It's very difficult, very complex, and it calls for a lot of understanding of human nature, both on the part of the police, and those who legislate for them, and supervise them.

The second nostrum that structured much of the Royal Commission's thought—*local policing*—assumed nothing like the same degree of hegemonic dominance—and its contest with the competing claims (and alleged dangers) of centralization was at the time—more so than today—a lively and open one. That such was so is demonstrated by the number of powerful voices in senior police and legal circles—the Association of Conservative and

Unionist Lawyers, Chief Constable of Lancashire Eric St Johnston, most prominently Professor Goodhart in his 'memorandum of dissent'—who were actively promoting the case for a national police force, and provoking some serious political and professional discussion of its merits. Yet local policing was—still is—an entrenched cultural sensibility within English society, and it clearly played a key part in conditioning both the work of the Royal Commission and its effects. This is most clearly apparent in the veneration the Commission accorded to what it called the 'long tradition of local responsibility for the maintenance of law and order', a tradition whose modern survival 'helps to explain why there are still so many separate police forces, each identified with its own particular locality' (Home Office 1962: 10). But it helps to account, also, for the political reception accorded to Goodhart's dissenting memorandum. For all the plaudits heaped upon him for what was commonly regarded as a logical, clear-sighted demolition of his co-Commissioners' muddled thinking, 'the nationalisation of the Police Force never', a *Police Review* editorial commented, 'came within the realm of practical politics' (*Police Review*, 6 July 1962). As one senior Home Office official recalled during an interview with us, 'it [Goodhart's memorandum] clashed with some core values—operational independence and the threat to local control'. The importance of 'local affiliations and loyalties' (Home Office 1962: 9) thus assumed its proud place in shaping both 'the idea of partnership between central and local government in the administration of public services' (Home Office 1962: 47) that the Commission took to be so central to the 'British way' of doing things, and the architecture of the resulting Police Act.

Yet it is also clear that localism—'knowing how to adjust to the community, and to their standards, to their principles, to their hopes and aspirations', as one retired chief constable approvingly put it to us—has for much of the post-war period been both somewhat grudgingly accepted, and considered rather bothersome, by many—'reasonable people'—within government circles. As an official who served in the Home Office for much of this period opined, 'I know they [police authorities] look better, more democratic... but I can't say the cities have been any better policed because of them'. While centralization was to become for some three decades after the 1962 Commission the practice (or virtue) that dared not speak its name, the economic, cultural, and political conditions that obtained in the decade or so immediately before and after the Police Act 1964 permitted localism to be (further) chipped away at by those who remained luke-warm about its merits and unsettled by its potential consequences:

I think that there are some arguments for having a national police force. It would make it easier to deploy troops around the place, police officers to work where they're needed. It would probably make it easier to have consistent policies and standards, and training would become more consistent too. But it has...I've always thought that it was an overriding objection that it would cut the police away from the local connection which they have now. The Warwickshire Constabulary is the police force for Warwickshire and this fuses local loyalties and enables local people through the police authority to exercise a degree of control over the police...

...I toyed from time to time with the idea of a national police force as being more efficient than forty-one [sic] local ones, but came back to believe that although you had to pay a price in some loss of efficiency by keeping your forty-one local forces, nevertheless, the importance of having a local say in the control of the police was of sufficient importance to make that loss of efficiency worthwhile, provided you could have the sort of co-ordination through the Inspectorate of Constabulary and the last word really rests with the Home Office [retired Home Office civil servant].

In the three decades spanning 1945 to the mid-1970s, this outlook—which couples warm official rhetoric about the traditions of localism with efforts to extend long-leash central controls over policing—quietly and relatively uncontroversially held sway. This of course involved no fundamental break from the pre-World War II past—the history of English policing, especially in the twentieth century, has been characterized by 'creeping, or incremental, centralised control over policing' (Wall 1998: 86). Nor—as we shall see—did this governing impulse suddenly give way during the 1980s and 1990s. Two things are nonetheless striking about the mid-twentieth-century period: first, what one retired senior civil servant we interviewed called the Home Office's 'wish to exert more influence' over the police (something he referred to as a 'very significant change'); and, secondly, the dominance that this culture of governance (with its quiet, melioristic interest in steering policing from the centre) came to acquire—a pre-eminence the under-specified tripartite relationships introduced by the Police Act 1964 did little to hinder and much by omission to facilitate. One thus sees in this period the high watermark of what one might call *centralization, English style*—not an open, deliberated-upon, legally enshrined decision to reconfigure the police along national lines (*à là* Goodhart); but, rather, an undramatic, behind-the scenes, and generally opaque accumulation of central control and influence (Wall 1998: 86). It is—one might say—the management of the policing system by those who feel they have been trained and placed to 'know best':

The Home Office has always mistrusted police authorities. Police authorities were the people who might get it wrong either by promoting the wrong people, because they are part of promotion, or by withholding money for the proper development of police. I think the Home Office over the years played a very skilful hand in developing national standards without ever running into the criticism of a national police force. There was the emergence of the Inspectorate of Constabulary, the development of the scientific and technological bits of the Home Office, it all made the Home Office an agency for nationalizing the police [retired Home Office civil servant].

Some elements of this process—force amalgamations foremost among them—were, it should be noted, both overt and to some degree contested. Responding to a perceived sense that the policing system was 'ragged and out of date' (retired Home Office civil servant), and that the remaining small forces (often with an establishment of fewer than 200) were inefficient, barriers to the development of police careers, unable to take advantage of new technology, and unsuited to an increasingly mobile society, the then Labour Home Secretary, Roy Jenkins, announced in May 1966 an amalgamation programme aimed at reducing the number of forces from 117 to forty-nine (Jenkins 1991: 187).[3] There followed— under the provisions of the Police Act 1964—a number of quasi-judicial local inquiries into particular force mergers (those in Lancashire and Cardiff proving the most disputed) during which the assorted claims of localism were pitted against these 'modernizing' proposals. For at least one of the protagonists involved, these objections were motivated by little other than complacent, if well-meaning, sentiment:

They thought that they were close to the people, which I think they were. But in terms of dealing with serious crime, it was just a joke. A case in South Wales for instance. I remember this with great clarity. There was a meeting at the Home Office, and Cardiff wanted not to go into South

Wales, a new force called South Wales. And the town clerk then, he was asked why they felt very strongly that there should be a separate Cardiff City police force, to which his answer was, 'for reasons of civic ceremonia'. Well that was the end of the Cardiff City police force [former Labour Minister of State, Home Office].

For the most part, though, the steady accumulation of central influence over the police during this period was accomplished by 'softer', less transparent instruments of governance. Prominent among these were efforts to shape the means by which senior officers were trained and selected. These included general measures such as the establishment of the Police Staff College (eventually, at Bramshill) in 1949 and the introduction of the Senior Command Course in 1962, and, more particularly, 'using key appointments as a means of intervening in the policing system' (retired Home Office civil servant).[4] But they also encompassed: the progressive standardization of police training following the report of the Police Post-War Committee in 1947 (Home Office 1947; 1961b); the provision of 'intellectual leadership' (retired Home Office official) through courses at Bramshill; and the taking of an active lead—through the deployment of civil service and financial resources—in developing new technology (police radios, command-and-control computer systems, the police national computer) and policing styles (panda cars and unit beat policing). One former Home Office official reflected on these latter initiatives thus:

One doesn't normally associate this concept with Roy Jenkins, but he was the chap, as Home Secretary in his first innings, who really made the police develop their radio communications, and made sure that each constable had his radio communication. He also put in train the procedures which led up to the setting up of the police national computer. I put a chap, a fairly senior chap, full-time on developing the national computer. The police themselves weren't terribly interested until they realized what happened, what results it produced. We more or less thrust it upon them.

This 'application of intelligence, in the broadest sense, to policing problems and challenges' (retired Home Office civil servant), was for the most part undramatic stuff—the mundane adjustments of 'the gardening state' (Bauman 1987). It was also—compared with the regulatory regimes that were later to unfold—somewhat loosely formed and ad hoc.[5] Yet for all its apparent hesitancy, the culture of police governance that had formed by the mid-twentieth century was still able to leave its mark on English policing's progressive centralization:

There was quite a lot of sporadic debate within the Home Office about what the actual instruments of government were. Yes, you could pass a law, but Parliament was even more reluctant then than now to make time and actually do it. At the other end, weak instruments like police training, the support for the academic community, feeding back into attitudes, and all of that. And then in the middle, secondary instruments like money, approvals for appointments, stuff like that. I don't think, either the politicians, or the official machine, often, if at all, consciously registered the use or the exertion of governmental power. A careful analysis of the particular problem would be addressed and a selection of instruments used in the bit of surgery concerned. It was much more muddled, or woolly. Much more semi-conscious, as I think the process of government was in this country. I think it has become much sharper, much cleaner in the nineties. For good or for ill [retired Home Office civil servant].

That this particular culture of governance managed to acquire such ascendancy during this period was due in large part to the presence of a particular complex of economic, social, and cultural conditions—full employment, the welfare state, and associated components of the 'post-war settlement'; coupled with much more rigid and deferential social relations (see Chapter 1). These combined to produce what one former senior civil servant called 'a very stable situation' in respect of relations between police and the social—something he reconstructed in the following terms: 'the ethnic minorities had not appeared, the poor were tired and lacking in spirit to complain. Car owning middle-classes had not yet been hit by traffic laws...It was not a great concern of government. It was not an issue, policing, it happened. It was settled.' At the local level, this lack of wider social tension and conflict goes some way towards explaining what Lustgarten (1986: 52) called the 'remarkable self-abnegation' of police authorities for much of the 1960s and 1970s (see Brogden 1977). At a national level, it helps to account for the relative lack of overt party-political disputation aroused by police matters during this period, and for the pivotal part that a small coterie of Home Office civil servants was—for a time—able to play in managing the policing question:

Looking back, the odd thing is how little we involved ministers in those days. I don't think it would happen now. We did most of this work, setting up training centres, the police college, really without very, very much reference to ministers...It's a long tradition in the Home Office. The Police Department particularly used to function more or less on its own without very much change of personnel...Don't forget there wasn't the proliferation of ministers that we've got now. At one time the Home Office managed with one minister, and one junior minister. The old Home Office was built on that basis. There were three grand rooms, one for the minister, one for the junior minister, one for the Permanent Secretary. In my time they got more and more. We had to have one for the Lords and such like. There are doing, frankly, some of the things that they were always quite happy for officials to do [retired Home Office civil servant].

These conditions, and the culture of police governance they coalesced with, began to unravel towards the latter part of the 1960s and early 1970s—as this account itself hints at. Early sightings of this—and accompanying shocks to many prevailing governmental assumptions *vis-à-vis* policing—were to be found in such symptomatic events as the anti-Vietnam demonstrations at the US embassy in March 1968—'Grosvenor Square was', one Home Office official recalled, received as 'a distinct threat to the order of the body politic, exposing a vulnerability in policing which had to be mended, and pretty fast' (cf. Callaghan 1987: 257–61). A year later, in 1969, the exposure by *The Times* of entrenched corruption in parts of the Metropolitan Police CID was to provide a further—in some ways more unsettling—challenge to received official outlooks on the English police:

Police corruption was a major shock to the system. A part of the Queen's Government was found to be, inexcusably, not merely deficient but rotten. A lot of people, especially most crime journalists, have known forever, ever since Robert Peel, that people who spend their working life in the CID in contact with criminals are exposed to temptation, and some fall for it. That is how it is. You have to expect it. But I think there had been a lot of eyes turned away in Government. And it was a painful and difficult, not least I was going to say for Conservatives, but in a funny way just as hard, or harder, for [then Home Secretary] Callaghan, who typified the Labour Party, because these were their folk [retired Home Office civil servant].

By the early 1970s, the 'oil crisis' and economic retrenchment had resulted in escalating levels of social and industrial strife, the most telling single instance of which—for those in government at least— was the mass-picket induced closure of a coking plant near Birmingham during the 1972 coal strike: 'the nature of the threats coming from society was mounting, and daunting, and required a lot of adjustment. Do you remember the Saltley coke works?' (retired Home Office official). As industrial and political violence, street battles between racists and anti-racists, and other assorted ingredients of social crisis continued throughout the 1970s to deepen, so did the anger felt by many fragments of the English populace and the sense of disquiet in elite circles about government 'under siege' (retired Home Office civil servant) and a nation 'out of control' (former Conservative Minister of State, Home Office). In the midst of all this questions of policing came increasingly to the fore; the police the subject of intensifying cultural dispute and political controversy. An era characterized by the 'absence of a sustained critical discourse about policing within British society and politics' (Walker 2000: 81) was drawing abruptly to a close. Its termination was to bring the imaginative and institutional architecture that had been enshrined within the Police Act 1964— 'a creature of the forties and fifties and early sixties [that] didn't look forward to the problems of the late sixties and seventies' (retired Home Office civil servant)—under some radical and ultimately fateful scrutiny.

Small Acts of Treachery: Struggling for Democracy in a Moment of High Policing

With growing incredulity we began to sense that policing was a sacred cow of huge and totally unsuspected dimensions. It was taboo even to ask for information as to the nature of the beast, let alone what purpose it served or who was in charge of it [Simey 1988: 31].

While the election of a New Right Conservative government under Margaret Thatcher in May 1979 may not have initiated the politicization of the English police, it heralded the onset of a spell of troubled politics in which policing—and questions of police accountability in particular—were destined to loom large. The Thatcher government had, as noted in Chapter 1, been returned on a platform which promised to overhaul the 'welfare consensus' that had structured the governance of British economic and social life during the post-war years, and to make the restoration of 'law and order' an utmost government priority. These aspirations were neatly condensed in a Conservative manifesto pledge to 'spend more on fighting crime while we economise elsewhere'. They were to result in the police assuming a pre-eminent place—instrumentally and symbolically—in the practical affairs of the nation.

In seeming contrast to the ambivalence of its Labour predecessor, the Conservative administration in the early 1980s articulated a stridently pro-police line. 'Margaret Thatcher was', one former Home Office civil servant reflected, 'rather sympathetic towards people in uniform, and was very sympathetic towards the police, and there was a substantial increase in police numbers and a big increase in police pay'. Meeting in full the pay settlement recommended by Lord Edmund-Davies (Home Office 1978) was in fact one of the government's first actions in office—and a highly politically symbolic one at that (the previous Labour administration had committed itself merely to phasing in the award). One former Home Office official we interviewed recalled the moment thus: 'I've never forgotten. He [incoming Home Secretary, Willie Whitelaw] said on arriving on the doorstep of the Home Office, was it 5th May, or 4th or something: "Right, we've got one thing to do, we've got to get the police their money before the Ministry of Defence give the army theirs. We've got to do it by next Tuesday." And he did.'

There ensued a period of several years in which the police were located at the forefront of the 'fight against crime' and provided with the officers, equipment, and powers that were deemed necessary for the task. This former Home Office civil servant nicely captures the mood—and priorities—of the times:

The police, generally speaking, got what they wanted. I remember within the Home Office this caused a certain amount of difficulty because there were other parts of the Home Office, the criminal justice system, the prisons perhaps most of all, immigration and so forth, who felt that they weren't getting their share of the cake. But whenever it came to a political decision I could win, not because of any merit on my part in putting the case, but simply because Margaret Thatcher and her government were favourably inclined towards the police. They saw the police as preserving law and order in the riots and so on and having a difficult time. Which was true, I mean they were having things thrown at them and policemen being injured and so on. And they were, in the Thatcher view, to be given more or less whatever they asked for.

The police were also at this juncture—as this account intimates— being prevailed upon to handle the violent disorders that resulted from the economic restructuring and welfare retrenchment introduced by the Conservative government in the early 1980s. Inner-city disturbances in Bristol in 1980 and Brixton, Moss Side, Handsworth, and Toxteth in 1981 (and again in 1985); industrial flashpoints at Warrington (1983), Wapping (1986), and during the year-long miners' strike of 1984–5; the continuing threat posed by IRA violence; these all brought the police into the heart of political and social conflict. The early 1980s was, in short, a moment of 'high policing' (Brodeur 1983); a time when some basic questions of social order and state security appeared to governing elites to be at issue; a point at which the police came to be thought of by many in government as 'semi-heroic' (retired Home Office civil servant). At the very least, these circumstances gave a new, politically urgent twist to the long-established official view of the English police as unique, a social institution whose sacred importance was sufficient to exempt them from the rules, constraints, and regulatory mechanisms that applied elsewhere across the public sector. It was against this backdrop that the imaginative and institutional architecture enshrined in the Police Act 1964 came under sustained, critical challenge—one that called into question the hallowed doctrine of constabulary independence and sought to reconfigure the relationship of the police to institutions and processes of local government. So what forms and orientations did this 'movement' for democratic policing take? How can we best make sense of the intense, bitterly fought contest over the meanings of policing that unfolded in the early 1980s and of the failure of the campaign for democratic accountability to achieve its goals? What legacies—if any—has it bequeathed to the present?

The challenge to the tripartite arrangements set in place by the Police Act 1964 assumed two—very closely connected—forms. It resulted *first* from a number of Labour-controlled metropolitan police authorities—notably those in Greater Manchester and Merseyside, but also to some extent others such as West Midlands, South Yorkshire, and Humberside—breaking with their hitherto supine posture and adopting instead a more expansive conception of a police authority's role and responsibilities. These authorities, in various ways, began to call into question what had for much of the period since 1945 largely been taken as given. They disputed the ways in which particular events—such as the riots and the miners' strike—were being policed—as the ex-chairperson of one metropolitan police authority said of the former: 'the [police] said that the situation called for the enforcement of the law. We argued that you would never make people good by force.' They began to demand information, query how money was being allocated and spent, even on occasions to activate and test the limits of their powers to set police budgets. They initiated research and sparked debate on public experiences of, and demands for, policing and their relation to extant police priorities (see, for example, Kinsey 1985). They put in place new forms of monitoring and accountability—such as suspects' rights cards and lay visitors schemes. And they sought to give voice—through 'local public forums' (former chairperson, metropolitan police authority) as well as inquiries into the policing of specific localities (Independent Committee of Inquiry 1989) or events (Independent Inquiry Panel 1985)—to the claims of both 'the community' in general and those fragments of it that felt most alienated from the police in particular (see, further, Jefferson *et al.* 1988). The following account encapsulates well both this range of institutional effort and the reaction it provoked:

When we arrived on the police authority, it met once a month. And there was a finance committee which met I don't think even once a month. And it had been chaired by a bookmaker who was very pally with the chief constable. And it was just a nice gentle sort of arrangement. So we turned up with this strong view that police should be more accountable, and set about setting up whole structures for dealing with things. By the time I was chair, in addition to the finance committee, you had a community relations committee, which actually set up the first lay visiting scheme of any police force in the country. Brixton was not the first. We were actually the first. The chief constable said over my dead body basically. You can't imagine the kind of work it took to achieve it, having to get the Home Office to back you, and all sorts of things going on. Work on the training, the procedures, the rules, forms. That was the first lay visiting scheme ever in any police force in the country. We also set up all these community liaison panels [former chairperson, metropolitan police authority].

As this account suggests, what followed in the early 1980s was a period of high-profile political conflict between several metropolitan police authorities and 'their' chief constables—notably involving chief constable James Anderton and the chairperson of the police authority, Gabrielle Cox, in Greater Manchester (Prince 1988; McLaughlin 1994) and their respective counterparts, Kenneth Oxford and Margaret Simey, in Merseyside (Simey 1988). 'The political atmosphere in the 1980–5 years was'—in the words of one ex-chief constable of a metropolitan force we interviewed—'pretty steamy' and it gave rise to much 'high drama' (former chairperson, metropolitan police authority) as the *dramatis personae* took up and defended publicly some markedly polarized positions. For some—including many among the former chief constables and Home Office officials we spoke to—these 'clashes of personality' were the crux of the matter, serving to unsettle what were viewed as a set of arrangements that 'on the whole worked reasonably well' (retired Home Office civil servant). There is clearly something in this view. The rhythm of politics of course depends in part on the characters involved. It is also the case that in many parts of England the architecture of the 1964 Police Act remained uncontested. Yet this judgement remains unhelpfully reductive, missing what is most significant about this political 'moment'. It ignores the fact that some settled taboos were clearly being prised open: 'for the first time ever they [the police] were asked to explain why there were far more burglaries in Bolton than Rochdale, or whatever. We had a very long serving CID man, who was the assistant chief constable for crime, who just didn't know what to do. They'd never looked at the figures. They didn't analyse the figures. Didn't know how to respond to questions on statistics' (former chairperson, metropolitan police authority). And it fails to register both the ways in which this conflict exposed the limitations of the under-specified—for some, simply 'unworkable' (former chairperson, metropolitan police authority)—arrangements set out in the 1964 Act, and the different ways of imagining the connection between police, government, and citizen that were—for a short while—in the process of emerging:

I think we did a lot of good work, and I think we got a lot of respect from probably the senior officers who saw us at work. And a lot of aggro from the general public, and from serving policing officers, because Jim Anderton was seen as defending his officers against these maniacs. But the HMI, and the Home Office and so on, they didn't like the fact that we were constantly having these rows, but as a police authority couldn't fault us, I don't think. And said that we were a good police authority. We delivered. They were well resourced. We didn't do anything foolish. We were not trying to interfere in things that we shouldn't interfere in. What we were doing was legitimate [former chairperson, metropolitan police authority].

The onus of calling him [the chief constable] to account was ours, but the onus of finding a solution was his, professionally. I think it began to dawn on them [the police] that this was a workable arrangement. And our members, without articulating it, began to grasp 'that's his job'. And they, from all of the records of demarcation strikes, they knew all about demarcation, it was familiar territory. I think we were really on the way to evolving the pattern of the relationship between all public servants and the public. It really breaks my heart that nobody wants to know [former chairperson, metropolitan police authority].

That these questions were indeed central is brought out by the *second* aspect of what one might loosely term a movement for democratic policing, one that made the tripartite structure itself (and the thought styles that underpinned it) an object of critique and site of political struggle. The overarching objective of this 'movement' was to shift responsibility for determining general police policy from chief officers to local police authorities (or some other democratically elected body), thereby bringing police policy-making within the ambit of the political process (Hain 1979; Spencer 1985; cf. Regan 1991). It represented an attempt to render policing *democratically profane* (to treat it, in other words, as one might in a democratic polity treat questions of housing or education)—something that offered a resolute challenge to the hallowed doctrine of police autonomy. As one of the protagonists put it at the time, 'the myth of operational independence has become as emotive, sacred, unchallengeable and zealously defended as the Divine Right of Kings. Neither can be acceptable in a democratic society' (Cox 1984: 2208).

This issue was seldom far from the surface of the dramatic disputes between police authorities and chief officers that littered the early 1980s—indeed one feature of this period was just how 'accountability' appeared to condense many disparate political concerns about such matters as stop and search, deaths in custody, paramilitarism, and the like. But the battle lines were also more expressly drawn in a number of ways. The goal of democratic policing clearly animated the work of the Greater London Council's Police Committee (and funded support group), established in 1981 to monitor the Metropolitan Police and campaign for a directly elected police authority for London (Greater London Council 1983).[6] It was championed by the National Council for Civil Liberties (which in the early 1980s commissioned a research project on the matter—Jefferson and Grimshaw 1984), as well as forming the central plank of two Private Members' Bills introduced—without success—by the back-bench Labour MP Jack Straw in 1979 and

1980. For a period in the early 1980s democratizing police policy-making also became official Labour Party policy—something that contributed greatly to the frosty relationship that existed at the time between the Her Majesty's Opposition and the police.[7]

Yet for all its intensity and the bitterly fought contests it provoked, this movement had by the latter part of the 1980s largely evaporated as a political force, having failed to accomplish its principal aim. It was undone, numerous commentators have argued, by a combination of factors—by the introduction in 1985 of police–community consultation committees that appeared to concede at least some of what was being demanded (Morgan 1989, 1992); by the attempts of the Labour Party from 1985 onwards to mend fences with the police and reorient its policy towards crime prevention and community safety (Kettle 1985b); and by a small, vindictive act of constitutional surgery that saw Margaret Thatcher in 1986 simply abolish the Greater London Council and other Metropolitan Authorities, and with them the police committees that had served as the nerve-centre of the movement for police accountability (Reiner 2000a: 188–91; Walker 2000: 87–8).[8] This at least is the view of one of the main protagonists:

> Maggie destroyed it. And the piece of machinery that made it work, she's demolished. In its place she's got a quango, and they're not accountable to anybody. It's a very dangerous thing. The police, because they're not accountable to anybody, the police ride roughshod over them. That's not democratic policing [former chairperson, metropolitan police authority].

Matters cannot, however, be left to rest here. Other questions were also—culturally and politically—in play during the early 1980s, and some attention to them can enable us to secure a better grasp of the peculiar intensity of police politics at this juncture. Just why did the campaign for democratic policing meet with the reaction that it did? What interests and values were deemed by the movement's opponents to be under siege? The answer to these questions lies, we think, in the fact that this movement was striving to render the police democratically profane at a time of deep social, economic, and political crisis. This prompted various agents and agencies of the English state to imagine policing first and foremost in terms of the task of shoring up an embattled social order and to cleave to the idea that the police were a unique social institution whose independence (and received 'traditions') needed to be defended to the hilt. No matter that, in another part of the woods, this crisis was giving rise to some significant breaches of the very 'traditions' in whose service so much rhetoric was being energetically deployed. The moment was one that appeared to many in official circles to require a concerted effort to see that the role of local authorities in the governance of police was in no significant respects enhanced.

The campaign for democratic policing rubbed up, for instance, against a generation of chief constables determined to safeguard their forces and their independence from what they viewed as 'extreme' 'left-wing' politicians—and to give little or no ground in so doing. 'There was', as one retired chief constable we interviewed put it, 'a tendency for the police to retreat into a kind of mental *laager*, a stockade, and sort of view the world from a very defensive position.' This stance—which accorded police authorities almost no legitimate place in the architecture of police governance—was most forcefully and unbendingly adopted by James Anderton. In the face of efforts by 'his' (and that was very much how he saw the matter) police authority to call him to account for the conduct of his force, Anderton very publicly portrayed its motives as 'the political control of the police service without which the dream of a Marxist totalitarian state in this country cannot ultimately be realised' (Anderton 1982: 584). He put on record his view that the campaign for greater accountability represented 'one of the most shameful, disgraceful and harmful episodes in the whole history of the British Police Service' (Anderton 1985a: 2312), an episode he interpreted as a battle to preserve 'our traditional democracy' against 'an enemy more dangerous, insidious and ruthless than any faced since the Second World War' (Anderton 1982: 585). And he sought to defend a conception of 'accountability' that meant little more than the police being controlled by the 'good management', 'applied common sense', and 'professional understanding' of chief constables (Anderton 1981: 269): 'At the end of the day, real "accountability" has little to do with Police Committees, County Councils, or even Parliament. It is a matter which lies directly between the police and the people they serve' (Anderton 1982: 584).[9]

This is clearly extravagant, over-heated stuff, and Anderton was, as we indicated in Chapter 7, in many respects an idiosyncratic figure—a maverick among mavericks. But his views on these issues were far from unrepresentative of elite police opinion of the time.

The view that the police can and should be in some direct fashion accountable to 'the public'—what one might call 'accountability without institutions'—has long been central to senior police ideology. So too has the attendant distaste for politics and politicians and, in particular, the then prevalent view 'that local politics had got nothing to do with policing' (male inspector, Greater Manchester Police (GMP)). And Anderton's opinions on the proper relationship between the police and police authorities closely echoed those of many of his colleagues—a cohort of chief officers who remained generally reluctant to 'take police authorities into their confidence', let alone discuss operational matters with them: 'there was this vogue among a lot of chiefs at the time that you should stand four-square as chief on the operational plans of the police. You should not entertain any discussion at all with the police authority on operational matters' (retired chief constable, metropolitan force). The prevailing elite police temper in this regard is nicely summed up in the reflections of this chief constable—who headed a provincial force in the 1990s—on the disposition of his immediate predecessor:

I inherited appalling relationships with the police authority and the county council. My predecessor only marginally accepted the right of the police authority to be there, and didn't accept that the county council had any role at all. I asked who he felt he worked for, and he said that he worked primarily for the Queen, because his oath of office was to the sovereign when he joined. And secondly for the Home Secretary. And very begrudgingly he accepted that the police authority had a role because they appointed him. But he didn't tell them anything, and he wouldn't work with them. They were at constant loggerheads.

A further—related—reaction to the movement for democratic policing came from within the governing Conservative class. In part it too was driven by a concern to defend the notion of constabulary independence and the role it was considered to play in guaranteeing 'those high standards of impartiality, fairness and effective policing [that] have been the fame of our country and our police force'.[10] Their reaction flowed too from an evident discomfort at hearing the words 'police' and 'politics' so frequently uttered in the same breath and, in particular, from the sight of the political Left calling into question (and seeking to remedy) the actions of an institution sentimentally viewed by many conservative-minded individuals as 'our police'. As Edward Gardner MP somewhat hysterically put it in the aforementioned debate, 'it is legitimate to ask in all seriousness how one can compel the police to consult local politicians who are fanatical Marxists, pro-IRA and anti-police'. Their response was conditioned mainly, however, by a par-ticular—heavily police-centred—reading of the social and industrial conflicts that the New Right's attempt to shift Britain to a new mode of rule had unleashed. This prompted, on the one hand, an intensified emotional identification among many govern-ing elites with the institution that 'stood between our society and the collapse of law and order' (that man Gardner again); while making it appear politically imperative, on the other, that the police were properly motivated and resourced to handle the conflicts in which they were so deeply and controversially embroiled. This of course meant in practice that the English 'traditions' of constabul-ary independence and local policing were—behind the scenes—being severely undermined, as efforts were made to co-ordinate centrally an effective police response first to the riots and then to the miners' strike (Cowell *et al.*, 1982; Fine and Millar 1984). These events also delivered—as we saw in Chapter 4—a number of severe blows to a once more settled conception of the benign English police. Yet at the same time they appeared crucially to demand that the symbolic imagery associated with this conception was dusted down and put to use in order to back the police against their critics. This speech by the then Home Secretary, Leon Brittan,—delivered to the Police Federation in the midst of the miners' strike—illustrates this discursive positioning rather well:

Throughout the dispute you displayed the qualities of patience, common-sense and good humour which have come to be regarded as the hallmark of police officers in this country. As a result, in very difficult conditions you upheld the finest traditions of the police service. I am glad to have this opportunity of saying thank you to you all [cited in Kettle 1985c: 1260].

Thus it was that the movement for police accountability came to be represented culturally and responded to politically, not as an exercise in 'practical democracy' (Simey 1988), but as *so many small acts of treachery*. Such were the political imperatives and dominant ideologies of the early 1980s—ones that made policing 'so intimately bound up with patriotic symbols that any critical questioning of its functions and functioning tend[ed] to be perceived as *treason* and sacrilege' (Bourdieu 1998: 62, emphasis in original). As a reading of the cultural politics of the time, this may appear a mite over-stretched, fanciful even. But how else does one explain the response those involved with metropolitan police authorities in the 1980s evoked from some among their co-citizens: 'there was graffiti on the walls in [the] city centre, which had a picture of a gallows and somebody hanging from it, and it said "[X] and co out, law and order in". I used to get hate mail and all sorts of things.'[11] Why else would individuals who sought to ask questions of the police, and place them on the same policy-making footing as other public authorities, come to be depicted as meddling in matters that ought not to concern them: 'the police had become the last bastion of security in what had suddenly become so frightening a world, and not a word of criticism of them was to be uttered... There was widespread acceptance of the assumption that policing was police business and politicians must keep out' (Simey 1988: 49). And by what more adequate means can we make sense of the politically and emotionally charged way in which those who endeavoured to grapple seriously with the vexed problem of accountability were so determinedly represented as 'anti-police':

It was weird. It was a perfectly sound, academic, legal, you know, sort of issue around how do we run particular bits of the police. But it became a kind of circus, and was portrayed in very peculiar ways. So I mean it was a strange, strange time, and there's never been another like it. And then, when the police authorities were abolished, most of the authorities that replaced them took fright in a sense, didn't want to be perceived in the same way, I think. Probably believed most of what was said about people like me in the press. They effectively, I think, gave up the whole notion that you should actually try to make the police more accountable. Interestingly, when people like us raised issues about police corruption, about racism, about violence, we were seen to be anti-police. Since then there's been all this stuff about the West Midlands, you know. All these notorious cases. All the stuff, culminating now with Stephen Lawrence and everything, where it's almost taken for granted that these things have happened and do happen. They were happening far more at the time when we were around. But to attempt to try and deal with them, or talk about them, in a perfectly reasonable way, was regarded as though you were undermining society [former chairperson, metropolitan police authority].[12]

This extract captures something of how the policing scene has altered in the decade and a half since the movement for democratic accountability began to recede in prominence. One also encounters a sense of vindication in respect of what that movement was striving to accomplish, coupled with a certain resignation in the face of what appears as the withering significance of *democratic* account-ability as a live political question: 'the whole of that debate has disappeared, and nobody wants to really take it up again. But it still seems to me that there's... because if you've got a decent and fairly good chief constable, okay, you can actually probably pursue a lot of those issues, and work together, without having to change the legal framework. But if you don't have a good chief constable, then you really just have to put up with whatever he decides.' There is clearly—as we shall shortly see—much in this assessment, and it certainly highlights something important about where—in consti-tutional terms—the balance of power within the tripartite structure presently resides. Yet it is also necessary to take note of the political and cultural space that the movement for democratic accountability helped open up and to recognize some of the traces—and possibilities—it has bequeathed. Let us conclude this section with a few remarks on this question.

Mention ought to be made first here of the various—generally autonomous, non-party-political—campaigning groups and move-ments that have continued to articulate the claims and concerns of ethnic minority, gay and lesbian, and other disadvantaged con-stituencies *vis-à-vis* the police and, in so doing, to advance the case for more accountable, transparent, and human rights-sensitive policing. The work of the Moss Side and Hulme Community Forum—set up in 1991 as a 'mechanism' for 'local people to engage with the police on their terms' (male community worker, inner-city Manchester)—provides one instance of this style of police politics that we encountered during our research (Moss Side and Hulme Community Forum 1994).[13] The continued campaigning—undertaken both within local government and by pressure groups beyond it—around police relations with gay and lesbian communities—offers another (see Chapter 4); and, in both cases, these processes of political engagement have served to keep the issues alive and maintain pressure on the police to respond to them.

We need to note, secondly, that the complex of issues first raised in the early 1980s—to do with the treatment of minority com-munities, miscarriages of justice, police responses to violence against women—have come to occupy a much more central place within English political discourse—to the point that they are now pressed, not merely by 'oppositional' pressure groups, but by established national mechanisms of oversight and accountability such as Her Majesty's Inspectorate of Constabulary (1997, 1999). Moreover, this activity now takes place within, and serves in its turn to reinforce, a wider cultural climate that has become rather more receptive to the idea that the police can and should be brought to account for their shortcomings—a social transformation to which the struggles of the early 1980s made its own small but significant contribution. One of the key players in those struggles reflected on the nature and extent of this change thus: 'in no way was it permissible to utter any word that seemed to imply criticism of the British bobby. The power of that intangible taboo, supported as it was with emotion and vehemence by police and public alike, is hard to convey, all the more so because it is now so freely challenged' (Simey 1988: 33).

One needs to register, thirdly, the altogether different reception these movements and issues are now accorded within professional police circles. Our work suggests—as we began to indicate in Chapter 7—the emergence over the last decade or so of a strand of (often, but by no means only, senior) police opinion that has become both cognizant of these altered cultural conditions and more open to the overtures of the outside world. As one serving chief constable put it, 'you can't just sit like a God and give orders from your office. Anyone who tried to do that would not last very long. You just could not do it' (chief constable, provincial force). It is an outlook that appears less eager to lay claim to exclusive ownership of 'policing' issues; more willing to learn from past experience and concede mistakes, and more open to the idea of connecting policing to local political institutions: 'I think the police service has suffered from not having a sufficient shared responsibility which involves the democratic process...the independence I inherited was anachronistic and counter-productive' (chief constable, metropolitan force). On the question of accountability, this view finds expression in a greater readiness both to appreciate the importance of local democracy ('let's have directly elected police authorities. Let's dump these so-called independents' (ex-chief constable, provincial force)) and to work with police authorities ('we're [now] much more likely to see chief constables and police authorities speaking with one voice against the Home Office' (ex-chief constable, provincial force))—albeit that this newly embraced spirit of 'partnership' retains some clearly discernible limits:

The best analogy I can give for the role I think the police authority ought to play is that they are the commissioners of a painting. They have the finance, theirs is the money, although it's largely devolved now to the chief constables. They ultimately have the money to spend on a painting. They have a picture in their mind of how they want police to be seen in [force area] for the following year. So they commission me to paint that, if you like. They describe to me how they want it to be. Periodically they come along and have a look and see how it's going, and they can criticize me and say 'that's not how we want it, and we didn't want you to do it this way, and we wanted more emphasis on this'. And they're also quite entitled at some point to say 'you've got it completely wrong, that is not what we wanted at all, and we're going to take the commission away from you and you won't get any money' and so on. The cross-over point for me is where they come along to one of these sittings, if you like, and they're looking at the progress that I'm making on this painting, and actually get hold of the brush and tell me to put a bit of red in there because that's what they want. As soon as they put their hand on the brush, then what I will say to them is 'well this is beginning to look like your painting now, not mine' [chief constable, shire force].

It finds expression also in an evident willingness to engage in dialogue with a diverse range of populations about crime and policing issues—and to include in that process those 'critical' individuals and groups who would not so long ago been dismissed as 'anti-police' and kept firmly at bay (Jones and Newburn 2001). One police manager we interviewed spoke in this regard of the police's tendency in the 1980s to use consultation as a device for forging 'consensus' with 'the respected and the respectful', an outcome he appeared keen to avoid: 'as a superintendent sitting here, I can pick up the phone book and give all the old colonels around here a ring. We can have a lovely cup of tea and they will tell me what a wonderful job I'm doing. But is that really a scientific way of measuring the clinching indicators in my community? No, it isn't. The real way is you actually go out there and be a little bit more imaginative and work hard to get people in here who are going to give you an ear-bashing. But, if you hang your ego at the entrance to your office, maybe that ear-bashing will actually help you move forward' (spokesperson, Black Police Association). One member of the Moss Side and Hulme Community Forum also noted a change in police outlook towards the concerns and demands being articulated by that organization (Moss Side and Hulme Community Forum 1994):

> The views in that [report] are obviously not particularly good about the police. They took it all on board. In James Anderton's day there would just have been a screaming match—'this is just political propaganda'. The police took it very seriously, and sensibly. They've stopped being defensive all the time basically. A real recognition that you have got to work with others. And even you see, in the old days, even when the police said inter-agency work, it was always they were the leaders, they set the agenda, it was on their terms. Whereas there's much more sense now that this is a joint thing...Unthinkable in the old days. Absolutely unthinkable.

These various shifts—which must form part of any rounded judgement on the movement for democratic policing that briefly held centre-stage in the early 1980s—seem to us to call into doubt any simple-minded assessment of that movement as a political failure. Sure, the struggle for democratic accountability was—for the reasons we have suggested—seen off without having accomplished its principal legislative goals. But we can see now that the questions and concerns about policing that it sought to pursue (claims that were at the time dismissed as hailing from the unrepresentative margins of English political life) have come to assume a place within mainstream policing debate—albeit that they occupy the edges of that mainstream and are at best unevenly couched in the language or spirit of democracy. More often today they stand alongside—and exist sometimes in alliance, for the most part in competition, with—another mode of thinking about how policing ought properly to be governed, one that has over the last two decades become increasingly pre-eminent.

Making Policing Profane?: The Triumph of a Limited Kind of Scrutiny

Reflecting on the changing relationship between police and government in the last two decades of the twentieth century, one serving inspector from Greater Manchester Police settled on the following conclusions:

> In the Thatcher era the police service were the golden service. There was a political reason for that. They knew the trouble that there was going to be

in the country didn't they, from the Scargill strikes and things like that. So the police had to be looked after. We were the golden...I think we were, we were looked after then. We were built up by politicians and talked favourably about, and nurtured a bit, and things like that. So I think we felt wanted, for want of a better word, then. For the wrong reasons maybe. But we felt that. The agenda has moved away from that now. It's not a sexy thing now the police service, to get into, for politicians. It's health, education, things like that. They're the issues.

This officer's account helps to indicate the short-lived nature of the relationship between police and central government that emerged in the early 1980s. This relationship was the product of a mutually corroborating combination of some urgently felt political imperatives and some deeply felt political sentiments. Yet it was destined not to last. As the social conflicts that marked the early 1980s began to abate, and as English society entered what Reiner et al. (1998) have termed a 'post-critical' period, so a different kind of policing agenda began to unfold. By the mid to late 1980s criminal-justice politics had entered what one Home Office official recalled as a 'curiously tranquil period' in which 'fundamental questions were not being posed by events'. These conditions, in turn, made it possible for the (at the time electorally secure) Conservative government to begin posing some fundamental questions of the police; questions—pertaining both to how adequately the police carried out their role *and* to the precise nature of that role— that would a few years earlier have appeared at best indecent, at worst foolish and politically irresponsible. It heralded the onset of a reform agenda that has come—in Raymond Williams' terms— to assume a dominant place in the formation of English policing culture.

This revised governmental approach to the policing question had in fact been signalled in the midst of that earlier—more tumultuous— moment, when, in 1983, Home Office Circular 114 made additional police resources conditional upon forces being able to demonstrate improved 'economy, efficiency, and effectiveness'. This was, however, an initiative driven more by government officials than by politicians—officials concerned for mainly fiscal reasons to rein in the enthusiasms of ministers who at that time seemed far from committed to any considered programme for over-hauling the police. It formed part, in particular, of an emergent Home Office position that came to question quite radically policies

that placed the police at the forefront of the 'fight against crime'
(e.g., Morris and Heal 1981). As one retired Home Office civil
servant recalled, 'they [the police] were, in the Thatcher view, to
be given more or less whatever they asked for. But, and this is the
important thing, it didn't stop the increase in crime. Indeed in
the Home Office, we used to plot the graphs and so on, and the
increase in crime was still going up like that and the increase in
the number of policemen was going up almost exactly the same. So
more policemen didn't mean less crime'. That this initial shift
of policy direction was not the brainchild of ministers is well
illustrated by this account:

I think if you put it to [then Home Secretary] Willie Whitelaw, he would
not disagree with that [the view that more police didn't mean less crime],
but I think his sympathies were for giving the police what they want
because they have a difficult job on—they were having missiles thrown at
them, and they really ought to be given every support. And I think emotionally, he was pro-police, as indeed Margaret Thatcher was pro-police,
and that's where their sympathies lie. I think officials were perhaps a bit
more hard-headed about this, I think because they had to answer to the
Treasury. They were very hard-headed about these things. And so I think
there was perhaps a greater recognition among officials that you had to be
looking for better value-for-money and more cost-effective solutions. I
think there was perhaps a bit of a distinction here between politicians and
officials [retired Home Office civil servant].

As the 1980s unfolded, however, and the imperatives and conflicts
that had made such sense of the Conservative administration's
robust pro-police disposition receded in importance, the governing
classes began to call into question the performance of the institution they had hitherto so steadfastly defended. Fuelled by what
they saw as the failure of a well-resourced police force to stem what
for the party of 'law and order' were some steep, politically embar-
rassing climbs in levels of recorded crime, government ministers
began to speak in much less glowing terms about the police as an
'inflexible organization' (former Conservative Home Secretary)
whose performance was 'patchy' (former Conservative Home
Secretary); terms that appeared to signal that an old, once-trusted
friend was somehow letting them down. One former Conservative
Home Secretary records this change of mood in his memoirs thus:
'while several of my ministerial colleagues and Tory MPs
supported the police in public, they were highly critical of them in

private. There was impatience, if not anger, that although we had spent 87 per cent more in real terms since 1979, and had increased police numbers by 27,000, there had been a substantial rise in crime. "Where is the value for money?", asked my colleagues. I had even heard Margaret Thatcher criticize the management and leadership of the police' (Baker 1993: 450).[14]

Thus it was that the police came to be brought within the ambit of the neo-liberal reform programme that the Conservatives had since 1979 been unleashing elsewhere across the public sector—a programme the police had during the early to mid 1980s largely been exempted from (Loader 1996: 14–22; McLaughlin and Murji 1997). This reform agenda—a series of initiatives commonly corralled together under the rubric 'managerialism' (Pollitt 1990; Clarke and Newman 1997)—saw the police increasingly spoken of in the lexicon of efficiency and value for money, performance targets and auditing, quality of service and responsiveness to customers (McLaughlin and Murji 2000). It represented a novel means of configuring the connection between police and government, one that saw the police subjected to new political rationalities and regimes of rule. It amounted to an assault on the police not from the political Left, but from the New Right; one that strove—in the name of *financial* accountability and *consumer* interests—to make the police *profane*; no different from any other public bureaucracy, and able, like them, to learn from organizations that have to compete and survive in the marketplace. Coming from this particular quarter, from those the police had come to think of as 'on our side', this sustained programme of reform came to many as a nasty shock:

Willie Whitelaw had come into office and the impression was that there was loads of money. You know, 'No problem—how much do you want lads? And is that enough? Are you sure?' You know, and all this was lavished on the police at the time … The police were really on a high and they really thought that all the years of denial and shortage of resources were gone. And then suddenly—bang—along comes the circular 114 of '83, the value-for-money thing, you know. The party's over [spokesperson, Police Federation].

What then are the key moments and motifs that mark this shift? How have they been registered and assessed by different audiences? What visions of policing—and of the police's proper relation to

government—are inscribed within the 'managerialist' reform programme and the array of responses to it? What broader cultural
formation does this particular—in many ways limited—form of
police scrutiny reflect and contribute to? Let us, in concluding this
chapter, address these questions.

Two organizing thematics of this 'new managerialist' agenda can
usefully be discerned here. The first—a move to render the police
more business-like, cost-effective, and performance-oriented—itself
comprises a number of strands. The early attention—originally heralded by circular 114/83—was on improving 'economy, efficiency,
and effectiveness' and the strictures of that watershed Home Office
edict were buttressed in like terms by a subsequent, more robust
circular issued in 1988 (Reiner 2000a: 191). This in turn helped
condition the emergence among senior officers themselves of an
initially cost-conscious focus on 'policing-by-objectives' (Butler
1984); followed from the late 1980s onwards by a concern to
reconfigure the organization around an agenda of service 'quality'
and meeting 'consumer' demand (Hirst 1991; Waters 2000). The
Metropolitan Police's 'Plus Programme'—launched in 1987 by
Commissioner Peter Imbert—was clearly the 'brand leader' here,
though it was followed—in spirit with the government's 1991
Citizens' Charter initiative—by a proliferation of customer-satisfaction
surveys, force 'mission statements', and other associated trappings
of 'responsive' policing (Joint Consultative Committee 1990;
Butler 1992). It amounted to the application of private sector tech-
niques and ethos to many of the 'time-honoured' orientations and
practices of the police, something its proponents saw as long
overdue: '[the police] should be part of real life. As an institution it
should be part of real life. It should be constantly asking itself
questions, evaluating itself. Looking to do things differently' (former
senior Conservative MP).

The emergence of these ways of thinking and acting *vis-à-vis*
policing was novel enough, representing at it did an attempt to
re-make the police—in Walter Baghot's terms—as a more routinely
'working' component of the British state. But the application of
a regime of economy and performance signified much else besides.
It signalled the start of a process that has chipped away at the cultural boundaries that once set the police apart from other public
sector institutions—boundaries that Home Office ministers and
officials had for much of the post-war period been eager to patrol

and protect. It indicated that (New Right) politicians were no longer prepared to trust the police (or any other set of public sector professionals) to deliver an adequate 'product' to a public suddenly re-imagined as its 'customers'. And it spelt the end of the police's time as the Conservatives' 'golden service' and, with it, the emergence of a period in which government acted not so much *for* or even *with* the police, but *upon* them.

No single better indicator of this altered relationship can be found than the Sheehy Report, published in 1993 (Sheehy 1993*a*). The Sheehy enquiry—chaired by 'a tobacco baron' (male chief superintendent, GMP) and made up of members consciously selected for their *lack* of a police background or expertise[15]—was established by Home Secretary Kenneth Clarke (a man who came to the job with a reputation for having 'roughed up' two other bodies of public sector professionals—teachers and doctors) to examine 'police responsibilities and rewards'. Its subsequent report recommended, *inter alia*, short-term contracts and a reduced starting salary for new recruits, performance-related pay, and the abolition of three police ranks; a panoply of measures that amounted to a thorough-going application of private sector thinking to the question of how police organizations might efficiently and effectively be run. The police, needless to say, were outraged, both by the manner in which this report was foisted upon them without proper consultation (one Police Federation spokesman recalled the atmosphere in the room during the 'one hour' the Federation was granted to meet the enquiry team as 'appalling'), and by what they considered to be a sustained assault by an 'alien culture' on the 'proud vocation' of British policing (Coyles 1993; cf. Sheehy 1993*b*).[16] As it turned out, many of Sheehy's recommendations were either shelved or watered down, and the Report implemented only in part. The reasons for this are numerous. They have in part to do with the campaign the Police Federation waged against Sheehy, one that included a series of full-page newspaper advertisements (see, for example, *Guardian*, 14 July 1993, *Guardian*, 6 October 1993, *The Times*, 6 October 1993) and a protest rally of 23,000 police officers at Wembley Arena addressed by leading opposition politicians, including Tony Blair (*Police Review*, 23 July 1993; cf. McLaughlin and Murji 1998). The Federation's stance was publicly supported by chief officers, at least five of whom—including Metropolitan Police Commissioner Paul Condon and the chief constable of the

RUC—vowed that they 'would consider their position' if the Sheehy Report was fully implemented (*Police Review*, 30 July 1993). The success of this campaign was much assisted, however, by the advent in June 1993 of a new Home Secretary, Michael Howard, whose sympathies and 'tough', 'crime-fighting' agenda were rather more attuned to those of many rank-and-file police officers; and by the Conservative Government's thin Parliamentary majority and deep unpopularity, a situation that made a high-profile dispute with the police over Sheehy a politically imprudent course of action to pursue. Yet Sheehy still stands as a watershed, a powerful symbol of the fact that English policing was no longer considered 'unique' or 'sacrosanct' by government, that its received wisdoms were simply no longer cutting a great deal of ice:[17]

All the concepts which are now part and parcel of the way the police is run and organized were totally foreign to the police tradition. The idea that you could bring management sciences into the running of police forces was regarded as laughable. And we comfortably assumed that the police were different and the police could not be measured. How did you measure the preventive effect of a constable? We were shattered to discover that such scientific measurement as there was suggested that it was very ineffective and wasn't much of a prevention. We think that the science is very badly flawed and doesn't take account at all the human nature factors that are involved. But, the fact was that, when challenged to prove the effectiveness of the patrolling officer, we've never been able to do that. But it's a difficulty that we've got, because there is this clash between value for money, cost effectiveness and the British policing ethos that we've inherited from the days of Robert Peel [spokesperson, Police Federation].

The second key thematic of the 'new managerialist' agenda—what we might call *a regime of audit and inspection*—also received an important outing in 1993, with the publication of the White Paper on *Police Reform* (Home Office 1993*b*).[18] This was to form the basis of the Police and Magistrates' Courts Act 1994 (since consolidated in the Police Act 1996), a piece of legislation that significantly reconfigured the tripartite arrangements for police governance established over three decades earlier. Dubbed by Kenneth Clarke 'the most important reform of the police for thirty years' (Clarke 1993: 15), this measure—which, like Sheehy, was subject to little or no consultation with police interest groups (Jones and Newburn 1997: 21–2)—was intended by government to streamline these arrangements in order that the revised structure was better able to ensure the provision of effective and efficient policing. To this end, it sought to clarify and render transparent the under-specified set of roles and relations laid down in the Police Act 1964—albeit in ways that generated much acrimony and dispute. The principal changes (and bones of contention) were as follows (see further, Walker 2000: ch. 4). Two substantial revisions were made to the role of the Home Secretary, giving him/her the power to cash-limit police budgets (the Home Office had previously contributed 51 per cent of whatever budget a police authority set) and a power to set national police objectives and related performance targets for local police authorities. Significant changes were, in turn, made to the composition and remit of these authorities. Police authorities were, firstly, reduced in size to seventeen, with (nine) elected councillors and (three) magistrates being joined by five 'independent members' (to be appointed by a procedure of labyrinthine complexity (Walker 2000: 159)). Under a revised remit to guarantee an 'efficient and effective force', police authorities are (jointly with their chief constable) now tasked with the job of producing—following public consultation—annual 'policing plans' and force objectives, though such local priorities have to be consistent with those laid down by the Home Secretary. Chief officers, finally, were granted greater freedom to allocate their resources and acquired, in particular, 'detailed powers of financial management in respect of manpower, buildings and other equipment' (Walker 2000: 127). While chief officers retain responsibility for the direction and control of their forces, this is now explicitly qualified by a requirement 'to have regard to' the local policing plan.

The Police and Magistrates' Courts Act was at the time of its passage the subject of much heated political dispute and—in what might well prove the death-rattle of that once axiomatic doctrine of constabulary independence—a powerful lobby in the House of Lords (led by at least three erstwhile Home Secretaries) forced some significant amendments to the government's original plans. Proponents of these plans justified them in terms of enhancing the status and autonomy of authorities they rightly identified as having been a for the most part ineffectual backwater of local government. The aim, Home Secretary Clarke informed the House of Commons, was to create 'more powerful and businesslike police authorities which will give more leadership to the local police service and ensure that money is spent more effectively' (*Hansard*, vol. 221, col. 765, 23 March 1993; see also Clarke 1993). Yet this—as critics pointed out—seems hard to square with the weight of legislative provision whose purpose appeared so plainly centralizing. One such provision—a proposal to enable the Home Secretary to appoint the chairperson of each and every police authority in England and Wales—was thrown out by the House of Lords. A second—the unprecedented introduction of *centrally* determined performance indicators—made it to the statute book, and clearly signalled that the Home Office was intent on becoming the primary strategic player in police policy-formation and performance-monitoring. In a further sign of the altered political context of policing, an alliance of chief constables, the Police Federation, and Labour-run local authorities joined forces to take issue with these measures on the ground that they 'break with the tradition of local democratic control' (Pead and Hilliard 1993: 16).

Yet these revised arrangements form but part of what we have called a regime of audit and inspection. The tripartite structure came increasingly in the 1980s and 1990s to be supplemented (and to some extent decentred) by a complex of national institutions that presently play a much enhanced role in the governance of police. Foremost among these were the Audit Commission and Her Majesty's Inspectorate of Constabulary (HMIC). The former—a body established by the Conservative Government in the early 1980s to monitor local authority spending—published a host of often influential reports on various dimensions of police work during this period (Audit Commission 1993; 1996) and has recently—under the New Labour government's 'Best Value' arrangements—assumed an even more prominent place in the regulation of policing.[19] The latter has also, since 1990, adopted a higher profile. Gone are the days when the Inspectorate provided a cosy retirement home for ex-chief constables and inspections were ritualized, hit-and-miss affairs. In their place has come a system of more rigorous annual inspections (Derbyshire Police was on three occasions in the early 1990s refused its 'efficiency certificate' by HMIC) and published reports. The advent of transforce 'thematic' inspections has also enabled the Inspectorate to gaze into 'the crystal ball' and 'lay some sort of metaphorical stepping stones out for forces to follow' (ex-chief inspector of constabulary). To supporters, this has enabled HMIC to act as 'the architect of the spreading of best practice' (ex-Chief Inspector of Constabulary), a view the Home Office quietly endorses.

To critics, such as one recently retired provincial chief constable we interviewed, they have become 'a tool for centralization': 'They're less and less willing to recognize, or to support, local diversity. In a sense one shouldn't really expect anything else. They are employees of the Home Office.'

What though have been the meanings and effects of these newly pre-eminent governmental arrangements? What cultural sensibilities towards policing and police governance have they brought to the fore? Which in the process have been rendered residual, perhaps even oppositional?

The *first* point to note is the dominant part that cost-effectiveness, value for money, economy, efficiency, performance measurement, and the like have come to play in structuring how policing is thought about and routinely enacted—an effect that can be discerned in the occupational consciousness of even relatively junior officers: 'I am not a business person. Other than a household budget I've got no experience of that. But I'm thinking about cost all the time, how can I save money?...I've become very aware [of that] even at my level, and I'm not a budget holder' (male sergeant, GMP). This ascendancy has clearly upset an array of professional—and, as we have seen, lay—sensibilities that take it as given that the police are different from other social institutions, both public and (especially) private, and see only deleterious consequences flowing from governmental efforts to make it otherwise. One superintendent from Greater Manchester Police bemoaned the eclipse of this once more settled cultural axiom and its effects thus:

I worry about unit costs, cost benefit analysis but I still, I mean, you know, it's appalling that my time is being wasted and that of a lot of other senior management officers, on plans, strategies, performance measuring. The amount of stuff that's piling in internally and externally in the modern police service is debilitating to management and debilitating to the service itself, because you're not concentrating on the basics...It doesn't matter what government persuasion it is, you cannot run a public service like a business.

There are a number of complex, contradictory, and sometimes competing vocabularies of motive helping to make up assessments of this kind. Some—though articulated around the impact this one particular set of 'alien' values and interests has had on the police— are plainly tied up with an idea of policing as 'special', *necessarily* opaque to outsiders, and as such immune to *any* external influence or determination. They are, without doubt, anti-democratic 'rhetorics of reaction' (Hirschman 1991). Others, however, stand in opposition not to accountability *per se*, but to a version of it that is viewed as placing in jeopardy a valued, public service conception of what English policing ought properly to represent. These project a series of somewhat different possibilities.

Such meanings are not easily disentangled. Yet the former appears most evident in police reactions to the emergence of budgetary constraints and financial accountability as structuring levers of police work; something that plainly jarred among many with memories of an age when 'you always knew that the money was going to be there to pay' (retired chief constable, shire force). For some officers, the principal objection here is to the *civilian* agents whose presence in the organization (often in quite senior positions) has appeared to accompany this altered climate of governance. Such agents, in their view, could simply never hope to grasp the 'essences' of policing: 'we've got a civilian now in charge of the budget. And he's dictating to our bosses now what they use on various things. How does he know what policing needs are on the streets? . . . Civilian staff, they haven't got a clue how the job works, yet they want to impose their ideas' (constables' group, GMP). Others seem offended that the profane matter of money has touched policing at all, as if the institution possessed a symbolic value that ought properly to place it beyond the reach of a financial economy. The regime of economy and performance has clearly effected a 'destructive alteration' (Bourdieu 1998: 113) to this unstated article of police faith, and it is telling how often officers reached for that most affectively-charged police form—the murder enquiry—to register the point (cf. Innes 2002):

I had an HMI who, during an inspection, actually counselled me to put down a murder enquiry because it was costing too much, had been running too long, and it's only one crime at the end of the day. I chose not to do that. And at the end of two and a half years we had a full team running, who detected that murder. A person was convicted. The sense of relief in that community, it was a particularly horrific murder of an old lady who was a pensioner. It was a little village up the rural [area]. But the string of villages around there were terrified by it. It was apparently motiveless. It affected people's lives. We didn't have a serial killer—eventually, as always, it was a distant relative, there was a link. The sense of gratitude of those local communities, that we'd never forgotten them, so they were always important, one person was important, and we were going to continue doing something as long as we could. The people said that they started unlocking their doors again when first of all the arrest was made. And subsequently when the sentence of life imprisonment was given, they felt safe. It had affected their life. That was two and half years. It cost us a small fortune. That's about being value driven rather than being cost driven. The value of us doing that is incredible. We'll be reaping the benefit of that for the next ten years [retired chief constable, provincial force].

This account also points to another set of police—and, again, lay—dispositions that the ascendent rituals of audit (Power 1997) have served (further) to residualize; ones concerned to register a set of practices and values that, it is felt, are being *eroded* or even *lost* by an energetic concentration on those police activities government believes can reliably be measured (cf. Walker 2000: 139–45). The array of motives in evidence here centres largely upon the quality and styles of policing and issues of public service and trust. Forceful reference is made by some, for example, to the crucial, if intangible, promise 'of peace and tranquillity' (retired chief constable, provincial force) offered by visible police patrols: 'how could you measure the usefulness of a policeman walking round on foot? "So he doesn't make an arrest, so he doesn't detect a crime, therefore, he's unproductive, therefore he's a waste of space." Rubbish. The public like to see in some sorts of surroundings a policeman on foot, or two policemen on foot. It's a very, very hard thing, public reassurance, but it's liked' (male superintendent, GMP). Others spoke warmly of the 'street craft' that such officers possess—the 'knowing problems on your beat, knowing your people, knowing the offenders on your division' (male black officer, GMP); skills in managing the unexpected that current regimes of performance appear radically to underestimate. And a number of chief officers spoke, not of their objection to accountability and performance, but of a dispute about 'what I'm being held accountable for and what performance is important' (retired chief constable, provincial force); and often sought in these terms to defend the kind of omnibus 'public service' mandate the new performance regimes had, in their view, imperilled: 'should the police service have to go to Mrs Jones' house at three o'clock in the morning to put 70 year old Mr Jones back in bed?...The answer, clearly, is no if you can avoid it, yes if that's Mrs Jones' only hope' (chief constable, metropolitan force). Taken together, it amounts to a view of a performance measurement as a regime of governance that risks—in the name of economy, efficiency, and effectiveness—atrophying the 'bonds of trust' upon which public consent and legitimacy depends:

> I'm a bit concerned that our response to limited resources is leading us to, or potentially could lead us, to neglect some complaints and that the focus on targeting resources could really cause problems in the long term because we'll be leaving people behind who have legitimate complaints which may be perceived by the police to be trivial. I think that we'll lose a lot of support [male inspector, GMP].

A *second* noteworthy effect concerns the impact of these new 'managerialist' regimes on the status of that ideological cornerstone of post-war English police governance—constabulary independence. It is difficult here to register any other conclusion beyond one that points to its perhaps terminal decline (Loveday 2000). Sure, ritualized defences of the unimpeachable importance and cultural significance of police autonomy continue to fall from the lips or pens of chief officers and politicians alike, sometimes still in puffed-up, patriotic tones: 'there's obviously a doctrine in this country, as you will know, called constabulary independence of which I'm very strongly in favour. In my view, that is the correct way to do things. In Germany, ministers do in fact involve themselves in operational policing decisions, with very disastrous consequences I may say' (former Labour Minister of State, Home Office). Some version of what in the context of Northern Ireland the Patten Commission recently reformulated as the 'operational *responsibility*' of chief officers is also—quite properly—likely to remain a significant structuring force (Patten 1999: 32–3). Yet the broad mid-twentieth-century version of the doctrine—that which gave chief constables such capacious freedom for manœuvre in the determination of police policy (Jefferson and Grimshaw 1984: ch. 5)—appears to have lost its once hegemonic grip over the field. It is simply no longer axiomatic, no longer a trump card, no more the article of faith to which any proposal for reform of the English police must defer.

In part—as we saw at the end of the previous section—this has to do with the small victories and advances of local democratic politics, and the engagement of members of minority groups with a generation of senior officers more willing to enter a dialogue with critics. It is true also that greater efforts are now made to generate more inclusive forms of local consultation; that much internal police decision-making has been devolved to local (basic command unit) level; and that sector, geographic, problem-solving, and other variants of 'community policing' have since the early 1980s been more or less in vogue. Recent legislative developments have, in addition, served to blur the once heavily defended border between police and local government. The aforementioned provisions of the Police and Magistrates' Courts Act 1994 (pertaining to local policing plans) and the statutory requirement under the Crime and Disorder Act 1998 for police and local authorities to form 'local crime reduction partnerships' have both served to close down the expansive decision-making space that chief officers once occupied in ways that renew and multiply the potential for local conflict about 'who' in the final instance 'is the boss' (chief constable, metropolitan force). The recent 'Best Value' initiative seems likely to erode still further both that distinction and that space. Yet for all that—note that many of the above developments are also about the exercise of central control and that local (police) authorities remain in practice often compliant, junior partners (Jones and Newburn 1997: 208)—locally governed policing is not the principal cause of constabulary independence's secular decline.

That impetus has come rather from the centre, whence has emerged, not so much any explicit, deliberated-upon move to shift the locus of police governance to a regional or national level as the further, steady accretion of agenda-setting and performance-monitoring powers at the centre. Many individual chiefs of course remain important figures in shaping—or responding to—these agendas. They also retain some capacity—and, among many, a strong professional inclination—to dissent from the national mood in order to accommodate (their sense of) local feeling and priorities: 'If we don't listen to that, don't do something about it, then you might just as well say let's not bother to have local constabularies and local police authorities, let's have a national police force directed by the Home Office and have area managers' (chief constable, shire force). Yet none of this can disguise the emergence—in respect of key strategic directions—of a complex of agencies that have come in recent decades to form a relatively closed national 'policy community' (Wall 1988: 306); at the hub of which lies the Home Office, an agency that increasingly 'rules at a distance' in *concert* with and *through* the offices of organizations such as the

Audit Commission, HMIC, ACPO, and the Association of Police Authorities. In the early years of the twenty-first century, the focal point of English police governance is to be found, no longer in a tripartite relationship between police, local authorities, and central government (with all its attendant habits of thought and feeling), but in this more extended network of governing institutions.

If the doctrine of constabulary independence has—in the manner we have tried to indicate—lost ground as a political and cultural force, it has done so not in the name of *local* democracy, not to some set of robust political institutions capable of supervising policing in the name of equity, representation, and public participation. Such acts of democratic politics have in recent decades been largely sporadic and incident-focused. Rather, this once hegemonic doctrine has fallen to the political centre, to a set of opaque, self-corroborating, and at best thinly 'democratic' institutions whose purpose is to deliver to individual consumers of policing an efficient and effective service. In being rendered profane, policing has, it appears, succumbed to *this* limited but currently dominant regime of scrutiny.

PART IV

Past and Present in Contemporary Policing

9

English Policing and Contemporary Culture

Whose culture shall be the official one and whose shall be subordinated? What culture shall be regarded as worthy of display and which shall be hidden? Whose history shall be remembered and whose forgotten? What images of social life shall be projected and which shall be marginalized? What voices shall be heard and which silenced? Who is representing whom and on what basis? This is the realm of cultural politics [Jordan and Weedon 1995: 4].

We have in this book endeavoured to outline the contours of what we have called *English policing culture*, by which we mean the amalgam of institutions, practices and policies, myths, memories, meanings, and values that, at any given time, constitute the idea of policing within English society. Drawing upon a range of police representations and oral testimony generated in interviews with politicians and civil servants, police officers, and different strata of the English populace, we have sought over the six chapters that comprised Parts II and III to document, and make sense of, the lay and official mentalities and sensibilities that struggle to determine the form this culture shall take. We have, in so doing, endeavoured to flesh out substantively our claim that English policing has not in the latter half of the twentieth century travelled speedily along a one-way path towards desacralization (cf. Reiner 1995*a*), but has, rather, come to be encircled by an uneasy, conflicting mix of profane *and* sacred dispositions. Contemporary English policing *is* made up of a range of utilitarian dispositions, technologies, and practices. But it *also* remains animated by memory, emotion, and myth.

Policing—we have suggested and hope to have demonstrated—can fruitfully be understood as an aspect of mundane and political culture. It is a cultural institution and performance, a condensing symbol through which people evoke and interpret the past, form judgements on the present, and channel fears and longings for the future. Police work and policy, whether oriented to maintaining order, controlling crime, or any other stated objective of policing, are always at the same time cultural work and policy, an authoritative means of allocating risk and blame, of affirming lines of affiliation and exclusion, of constituting the boundaries and identity of cultural and political community (cf. Christie 2000: ch. 13). It is from this standpoint, using this theoretical lens, that we have tried in the preceding pages to assess the intersections that obtain between police practice and legitimacy and the social, political, and cultural transformations that English society has undergone since 1945—between, in the words of our title, policing and the condition of England. And it is with this in mind that we have sought to understand the forms that public sensibilities towards policing take and the experiences, associations, vocabularies, and imagery that compose them. The durable, pre-conscious, emotionally-charged character of many such dispositions makes it, in our view, unlikely that public trust in the police can be 'restored' merely by improving institutional performance or enhancing the amount or quality of information that people possess about it. Political struggles over the futures of English policing are always also cultural struggles— contests deeply entangled with questions of subjectivity, recognition, belonging, and collective identity.

We want, in this concluding chapter, to offer an assessment of the current condition of English policing culture. This entails us revisiting Raymond's Williams' threefold typology of cultural forms— the *dominant*, the *residual*, and the *emergent*—that we sketched towards the end of Chapter 2 and which has quietly guided our subsequent efforts at interpretation (Williams 1977: 121–7; 1981: 204–5). In recapitulating the principal themes that featured in Parts II and III, we aim to further a sociological and political analysis of the mix of lay, professional, and governmental sensibilities that struggle with one another to constitute (and re-constitute) English policing culture. What are the historical trajectories and contemporary force of the diverse cross-currents of this culture? Which elements among them stand dominant today? Which are mere vestiges, survivors from the past? What alternative meanings and political possibilities stand immanent within the present? If, as we have argued, policing is a vehicle for mediating belonging, what forms of social order and political authority do different English 'structures of feeling' reinforce, recover, or anticipate? More on this in due course. Let us begin with the cultural formation that we believe has today become—in Williams' terms—dominant.

Dominant: A Culture of Scrutiny and Complaint

Raymond Williams, we noted in Chapter 2, characterizes as 'dominant' those meanings and values that govern the way in which—in the present case—policing is rendered intelligible; practices that seek to forestall political conflict by 'naturalizing' particular preferred readings, making them appear 'common sense', the only way in which policing can plausibly be understood, organized, or brought to account.

English policing, we suggest, is currently dominated in something approaching these terms by what may be characterized as *a culture of scrutiny and complaint*. Among the cluster of official, professional, and lay dispositions that comprise this culture, three are particularly salient. First, *managerialism*, the view that policing ought to be organized—in a manner akin to commercial enterprise—to deliver its stated purposes with the maximum 'economy, efficiency, and effectiveness'; that it must be disciplined by national performance measures and targets, and that it should, accordingly, be subject to the routine scrutiny of external inspection and audit. Secondly, *consumerism*, the belief that 'the public' are to be treated—the analogy, once more, is with private business—as 'customers' of policing services, and that their demands need to be elicited and satisfied as such. Thirdly, *multiculturalism*, the notion that police policy and practice must recognize the experiences and claims of the diversity of social groups that today compose English society and respond in ways that are anti-discriminatory, sensitive to the situational definitions and emotional needs of victims (especially of 'hate crime'), and protective of human rights. (Given that minority groups are, on this basis, to be included as consumers, and that police performance in meeting their demands is measured in managerialist terms, multiculturalism might best be described—borrowing a formulation from Bourdieu—as the dominated fragment of the dominant culture.)

We have, in the course of our enquiry, encountered several instances that point to the current ascendancy of these outlooks and practices. The prominent place that managerialist imperatives and rhetorics have come to assume among political elites offers one significant case in point here; their emergence under successive Conservative administrations in the 1980 and 1990s having been reinforced by New Labour since it took office in 1997. The determined readiness of the governing classes to treat the police as a mundane public sector organization (rather than as a 'special case'), and the *de facto*—perhaps even terminal—demise of the once untouchable doctrine of constabulary independence, both stand as indicators of this new political landscape, as does the assemblage of *new* measures recently proposed by the Labour Government in its White Paper, *Policing for a New Century: A Blueprint for Reform* (Home Office 2001), and the ensuing Police Reform Act 2002. These include: the Police Standards Unit ('to identify good practice and work out how best to spread it' (Home Office 2001: 128)); the National Policing Plan (and associated National Policing Forum); the National Centre for Policing Excellence; the National Intelligence Model; the Police Skills and Standards Organization, and a series of measures designed to replace outmoded, 'inflexible' police working practices with 'modern management and reward systems' (Home Office 2001: 108).

We might point further to the entry into the political and professional 'mainstream' of what has come—in management-speak—to be called 'policing diversity', to the fact that a set of concerns that in the 1970s and early 1980s was the province of the political Left in Britain is now energetically—if selectively—pursued by the likes of the Home Office, Her Majesty's Inspectorate of Constabulary, even the Police Federation. We might also recall the onset, described in Chapter 7, of a less authoritarian and strident, somewhat more humble and pragmatically liberal, elite police voice—of senior officers taking more seriously both the performance of their organizations and racism, sexism, and homophobia among their officers. This, in turn, needs to be considered alongside the fracturing of a once more politically and socially uniform 'police culture'—as evidenced by the advent of staff associations representing black and ethnic minority, and gay and lesbian, constituencies.

Finally, we need to note the emergence of that which these shifts in part reflect and contribute to—the coming to the fore in the latter decades of the twentieth century of what we might term *post-traditional* public sensibilities towards policing; structures of feeling that are less quiescent, deferential, and habituated to accepting the word of authority *qua* authority and characterized, instead, by raised expectations of public and private institutions; by reduced levels of trust and a propensity to scrutinize, and by a greater readiness to voice grievances and demand redress. Testament to the dominance of such dispositions is to be found not merely in the outlooks of those we described in Chapter 4 as the 'disenchanted' middle-class and working-class 'atheists', but, tellingly, in the fact that those who yearn for the 'return' of a more orderly, 'disciplined' English past themselves condemn the present in a manner deeply permeated by the prevailing culture of complaint.

This dominant cluster of meanings and values appears—and in certain official quarters prides itself on being—instrumentally rational in its impulses and pursuits—an outlook that is hard-headed, 'cold', and actuarial, one stripped of cultural resonance and concerned purely with 'what works', with the careful weighing of evidence, with value for money, with the delivery of high-quality policing services to quite properly demanding customers. In each of these respects, this formation appears to signal a sharp rupture with the past, not only in its impatience with traditional symbols as devices for legitimating police practice, but, also, in its abandonment of the 'myths' of omnipresence and omnipotence that loom large in social memories of the post-war English police, and its conscious striving to deploy the 'facts of the matter' in a bid to circumvent, or neutralize, the febrile passions that so often attend popular demands for policing. This seems, in short, a steadfastly rationalist outlook, one frequently condensed in the idea that the key to managing the demand for order and to 'restoring' public confidence in the police lies in providing customers with reliable statistical indicators of how 'their' police are performing, and disseminating better information on what policing can, and cannot, contribute to social order (Audit Commission 1996).[1]

Such assumptions and self-understandings paint an incomplete picture, however. They forget, first of all, that this evidenced-based rationalism continues to harbour, and thereby reproduce, a series of doxic/paleo-symbolic beliefs about English policing—something one can encounter in even the most self-consciously hard-headed official prose. Take, for example, the Labour Government's aforementioned *Blueprint* for policing in the twenty-first century, one whose avowed purpose is to 'modernize and reform the police service' in order that it can 'meet modern needs' (Home Office 2001: 10).

While this document acknowledges that 'the police alone cannot win the fight against crime and disorder' (Home Office 2001: 84) nor 'build better communities' (Home Office 2001: 13), it nonetheless proceeds in ways that implicitly and expressly reinforce the symbolic power of the English police. Let us note three. First, the faithful homage (and promises of wholehearted support) that government persists in feeling compelled to accord the police— 'we owe an immense debt to the police . . . The Government pays tribute to the police service—officers and support staff—and values their dedication; *they have our full backing*' (Home Office 2001: 12, emphasis added). Secondly, the fact that the White Paper does little to unsettle the 'obviousness' of the crime–policing couplet, quite the reverse in fact: 'progress has been made in tackling crime, and overall *levels of crime have fallen*. The Government has provided substantial *additional funding for the police*; the decline in police numbers has been reversed and the Government has set a new target of 130,000 officers by March 2003' (Home Office 2001: 1, emphasis added). Thirdly, the active celebration and championing of what criminological research has long since demonstrated to be simplistic, even illusory, 'solutions' to the problem of order—notably, as the above extract intimates, the idea that greater police numbers correlate with safer societies (cf. Bayley 1994: ch. 1).[2]

But they also forget that managerialism is itself a cultural formation, a communicator of meaning (cf. Hood 1998)—a practice that remains ineluctably entangled with the processes of detraditionalization that both shape it and are, in part, shaped by it. There exists, in other words, a deep—mutually, if asymmetrically, conditioning—affinity between the dominant elements of English policing culture and what has in the last several decades of the twentieth century become a pluralistic, individualized, consumerist society.

The culture of scrutiny and complaint that today marks English policing can, in this respect, be viewed as 'part and parcel' of what Jock Young (1999: 76) describes as 'essentially progressive and democratic processes occurring throughout the world in the late twentieth century'. It is, as such, a culture that intersects closely with the shifts in late modern social relations outlined in Chapter 1; notably, a democratization of everyday life that has called once-settled hierarchies (between men and women, parents and children, employers and employees, police and citizens) into dispute and exacerbated both the demands made of social institutions and the levels of public scepticism exhibited towards their claims to 'expertise'. But it is a culture conditioned too by over three decades of identity politics in which feminist, black and ethnic minority, and gay and lesbian social movements have mobilized to have their experiences and demands taken seriously by governmental institutions. The result is a public no longer so enthralled by the English police and less willing to let officers simply 'get on with the job' as they see fit; a police force no longer controlled by 'producers' who doggedly defend their independence from 'outsiders'; a more visible (and watched) police force that operates under the glare of—selective—media spotlights and the routine gaze of sceptical consumers. The result, also, is a police force that has slowly, and unevenly, given ground in the face of claims for recognition by social movements, one that has been forced to refigure—in the face of political pressure and periodic scandal—how it deals with matters such as rape, domestic assaults, homophobic and racist violence, how it polices minority communities, and how it treats its own—now more diverse, less habitually 'disciplined'—workforce. Perhaps, in the light of this, it is sage to avoid characterizing contemporary culture solely or even mainly in terms of 'control' (cf. Garland 2001) in favour of an approach that gives fuller acknowledgement both to the 'democratic' scepticism that marks relations between citizen and state, and to the social and political effects—in the field of policing as elsewhere—of three decades of identity politics. In both instances, as Jock Young (1999: 76) puts it, it is possible to detect signs of a 'general desire that citizenship should encompass a degree of control of the world that surrounds us, from the quality of life in the streets of our cities, to the accountability of public bodies'.

We shall return to this 'desire', and the political possibilities it may portend, below. But we must first take care to apprehend both the limits and lacunae of these more 'sceptical' public sensibilities, and the ways in which the concerns of oppositional politics have—in Williams' terms—been 'selectively appropriated' within a policing culture marked by managerialism and consumerism and a wider public culture attuned more to difference and self-realization than to equality and social justice (Young 1999; Barry 2001). In our judgement, the culture of scrutiny and complaint we have highlighted in this book embodies and reinforces a society of atomized consumers voicing demands for resources, rights, and redress *as* atomized—and, moreover, often disgruntled—consumers. It is a society of thin social bonds, with little sense of common identification with the polity, and a poorly developed notion of the public good; one in which the claims of a multiplicity of victims (of racist violence, of paedophiles, of rampaging teenagers, of police misconduct) vie for public attention, and where 'victimhood' (and, by extension, resentment) has become, arguably, *the* category through which belonging to a political community is enacted, solidarity between individuals fleetingly established, and claims for recognition and resources pressed (see, on this, Taylor 1994; Brown 1995; Garland 2001: 200–1).[3] It is a highly mediated, scandal-centred society in which the print and broadcast media have assumed a culturally significant power to bring the police to book—a mode of scarcely accountable accountability preoccupied with 'scandal' and *causes célèbres* in ways that contribute more to a climate of suspicion and complaint that to informed public deliberation.[4] It is, in short, a society of multiple claims made against numerous authorities, but one in which those claims have a limited connection to the kind of democratic processes that might transform the grievances of individual consumers into an effective citizenship-based politics. As Zygmunt Bauman (2000: 23) remarks:

We are perhaps more 'critically predisposed', much bolder and intransient in our criticisms, than our ancestors managed to be in their daily lives, but our critique, so to speak, is 'toothless', unable to affect the agenda set for our 'life-political' choices. The unprecedented freedom which our society offers its members has arrived, together with unprecedented impotence.

This, furthermore, is a society in which the English police have lost much of their symbolic aura, their capacity to command widespread implicit trust, their ability to signify a common moral and political community—something that has flowed from both some police-specific shortcomings and misconduct and a more pervasive erosion of public 'faith' in the capacity and legitimacy of state (as opposed to market) solutions to social problems. The police have, in the process, been stripped of the cultural resources they might once have effectively deployed to set them apart from the array of actors who today compete for business in what is a burgeoning security market (Jones and Newburn 1998; Loader 1999; Rigakos 2002).

Under such conditions—'when the authorities are many, and the sole effective authority in the field is the one who must chose between them' (Bauman 2000: 64)—it is perhaps no surprise that the police have become increasingly embroiled in efforts to 'tempt and seduce' (Bauman 2000: 64) no longer so uniformly loyal 'customers' by eliciting their preferences and enacting measures aimed at demonstrating that the police retain the capacity to satisfy them. These, we think, are the structuring cultural dynamics of the present—dynamics that have robbed *the police* of their symbolic aura while leaving the socio-cultural centrality of *policing* undisturbed. As such, they make it difficult to think imaginatively about how, equitably and effectively, to govern apparently insatiable demands for policing; difficult to generate and sustain an intelligent public conversation about the limits of policing as a solution to the problem of order, and difficult to obtain any kind of critical purchase over the exclusionary, xenophobic sentiments that continue to animate certain, in our judgement residual, public dispositions towards English policing. It is to these we must now turn.

Residual: Looking Forward to the Past

Our past, whatever it was, was a past in the process of disintegration; we yearn to grasp it, but it is baseless and elusive; we look back for something solid to lean on, only to find ourselves embracing ghosts [Berman 1983: 333].

When the moral survival of a society is threatened there can be no cost-benefit analysis [Simon 2001: 29].

In an understandable desire to chart the impact of tradition-eroding social change on a once revered national institution, Robert Reiner and other proponents of the desacralization thesis have tended to overlook the persistent presence of public mentalities and sensibilities that cleave to the idea—and promise—of a particular reconstructed vision of English policing. We think these sentiments have, in Raymond Williams' terms, been rendered 'residual'. Forged in the privations of war and its aftermath in the mid-twentieth century, they struggle to find verification in the altered political and cultural settings of the present. They nonetheless, as we have endeavoured to show throughout Parts II and III, retain a contemporary presence and potential political force, often today assuming an oppositional relation to the dominant elements of English policing culture.

The outlook we are referring to is one that hankers after and seeks to recover—the 1950s being the key cultural reference point here—what is taken to be a better, and lost, past. It is a past reconstructed as safer, more stable, more socially cohesive, and disciplined; a past where the authority of authority figures (teachers, doctors, vicars, policemen . . .) was quite properly taken as given, a past where local beat officers not only provided a visible, authoritative, pastoral presence in community life, but, in so doing, stood as an avatar of a proud, settled, uncomplicated, and white 'England'. This worldview—which *looks forward to a past* that it mobilizes to assess and condemn the present—today forms a residual element of English policing culture. It is a cluster of meanings and values located largely in a particular generation, and in specific ('respectable' working- and middle-) class fragments; the reactionary posture of a once supposedly 'silent majority' (it is telling that this utterance has largely disappeared from English political discourse) who now feel themselves to be a displaced, beleaguered minority. It is an outlook—as we have seen—that has pretty much lost the battle in governmental and elite police circles, where it has become a grumbling, subterranean, oppositional presence—the view that dare not speak its name. As such, these sentiments remain capable of being appealed to and mobilized by political and social actors seeking to fashion them into a convincing ideology. They also loom as a potential resource and constant temptation for hard-pressed police managers seeking an instant fix of legitimation. They retain in these respects the power to shape events. But they are, for the most part, voices on the margins, voices with only occasional—if occasionally noisy—echoes in the social and political centres of English public life.

The recent bouts of frenzied activity surrounding 'zero-tolerance' policing exemplify both the *capacity* of these residual forms to make sporadic, media-inspired incursions into the political process and their *incapacity* to secure any kind of foothold from which to effect a more enduring shift in the political and organizational landscape of policing (Dennis 1997; cf. Stenson 2000). Two features of the short history of zero-tolerance policing lend support to this view. First, the fact that it was associated largely with maverick, 'anti-authority' figures (notably, Detective Superintendent

Ray Mallon of Cleveland Police), energetic populists forced to proceed in the face of at best silence, at worst active opposition, from the vast bulk of senior police officers. Secondly, that popular support for zero tolerance was principally, if not exclusively, located among those who yearn to 'turn back the clock' to a set of hierarchical, absolutist authority relations that processes of detraditionalization have rendered 'structurally obsolete' (Boutellier 2000: 156). The zero-tolerance episode nonetheless offers a telling instance of how remote public bureaucracies which are perceived to be failing in their defining objectives are liable to 'takeover' by charismatic personalities pursuing populist agendas (cf. Gamble 2000: 71–2; Thompson 2000: 257).

We can cite several examples from this study that indicate *both* the persistence of this structure of feeling *and* the residual, oppositional place that it occupies within contemporary culture. The clearest such manifestation is to be found in the memories of, and mourning for, the social authority associated with the—now absent—'local bobby'; memories frequently suffused, as we demonstrated in Chapter 3, with wistful narratives of a police force largely unfettered by law and bureaucracy securing order by administering firm but appropriate summary justice to unruly citizens. Public—and far from residual—demands for more 'bobbies-on the-beat' stand today as the component of this structure of feeling with the greatest capacity to influence political debates and policing priorities—albeit amid a recognition in official quarters that this particular demand for order *cannot* be met in the exact terms in which it is expressed. Such demands continue, for instance, to attract much warm political rhetoric: 'the public wants to see more police officers on the beat—so does the Government . . . The increase in police numbers will only result in a more visible police force if we deal with the bureaucracy and blockages which are keeping officers off the beat' (Home Office 2001: 62, 71). They have also animated the decentralization of police service delivery (and performance monitoring) to local—basic command unit—level, as well as spawning two innovations—organized around the idea of the 'extended police family' (Home Office 2001: ch. 5)—aimed at ensuring that the police remain a significant player in, and regulator of, security markets in which they are no longer the only, or indeed obvious, supplier of visible patrolling. First, the introduction in late 2002 of an integrated second tier of 'police community support officers' with dedicated responsibilities—and limited powers—for managing order in specific territories. Secondly, the proposal for the police to train and accredit—and thereby lend their symbolic capital to—alternative suppliers of patrol services (see, further, Blair 2002*a* and *b*).

But this outlook also found expression in other ways. We might recall, first, those who believe that the English police have become hamstrung by paperwork, human rights, and political correctness— 'got at' by lawyers and liberals, 'captured' by minority interests; a view that loomed large—as we saw in Chapter 5—in certain white reactions to the report of the Stephen Lawrence Inquiry (Macpherson 1999). We might point further to those 'defenders of the faith' who manage to combine some often stinging assessments of police priorities and performance with the unflinching belief that the English police remain 'the best in the world'—a socially indispensable institution that needs defending as such against misbegotten criticism. We might recall also those—citizens and police officers alike—who stand 'hotly' opposed to the application of 'cold' economic reasoning (and budgetary constraints) to an institutional practice as deeply significant as policing. And we might, finally, mention the displaced rank-and-file police officers—considered in Chapter 6—who bemoan the demise of their preferred vision of 'the Job' and 'the force'—a demise they see registered in the advent of 'liberal' senior officers, the erosion of organizational 'discipline', the attributes and attitudes of today's constables, and the lost art of that which stands at the ideological core of their memories and understanding of English policing—namely, 'bobbying'.

This, it should be said, amounts to a body of sentiment and belief that is not entirely lacking in progressive political potential. It stands passionately committed not merely to the reassuring figure of the local 'beat bobby' but, by extension, to the more capacious idea of locally delivered and accountable policing. It responds to managerialist strictures and performance tables in tones ranging from bemused apathy to barely concealed disgust. It remains strongly attached to the notion that policing is (and should be) a collectively—and hence state—provided function that ought not to be thrown open to the market. And its wistful nostalgia for the social world of the 1950s harbours the belief that 'good' policing is that which somehow contributes to civic cohesion, even if this nostalgic disposition cannot—in the altered conditions of the present—begin to grasp what social solidarity (and its relationship to police work) might possibly entail in a pluralistic, post-traditional society.

These, however, are not the dominant, explicitly expressed values of what stands in the main as a *police-centred* and *politically reactionary* cultural formation; one whose impulse is to 'spring to the defence of certain kinds of order, certain social hierarchies and moral stabilities' in ways that possess 'dangerous contemporary application' (Williams 1973: 36). In respect of the former, we are concerned with a disposition that evinces a high level of emotional attachment to policing; one possessed of an extravagant sense of what the police can contribute to the production of social order; one prepared to offer almost unconditional support to the police and engage in various forms of denial of police misconduct (cf. Cohen 2001). This viscerally pro-police sentiment appears, paradoxically, to co-exist with some robust, heart-felt criticism of actual police performance. The paradox however is more apparent than real. 'The police' are bemoaned because they fare poorly when measured against a 'police force of the imagination', because they fail to represent adequately the promise inherent in the idea of English policing. It is, it seems, this *idea* that remains compelling and sacred: one of the 'foundations stones of the national identity', an entity 'too important to be compromised' (Gamble 2000: 65).[5]

In terms of the latter, this disposition towards English policing stands intimately enmeshed with a yearning for, and bid to rein-state, the unthinking solidarity of a more ordered, hierarchical community, one that binds policing to the nation around a narrow 'ethnic' articulation of English national identity. It is a defensive, xenophobic conception of imagined community that inscribes—and depends upon—a whole series of exclusions—of those who are strangers to the social memories that constitute it (the young); of those 'outsiders' who threaten the safety that it promises (criminals), and of those whose presence signifies its seemingly terminal decline (blacks, ethnic minorities, asylum-seekers). These processes of essentialism and demonization have, as their corollary, a certain pre-rational commitment to the social institution tasked with the control of such demons—a police force (of the imagination) that protects 'us' from 'them', keeps entropy at bay, and which must therefore be protected from those who would drag its good name into disrepute.[6] Jock Young (2003) has written recently of the feelings of indignation and vindictiveness towards the Other that suffuse social relations under conditions of late modernity. One might add that such sentiments appear to coalesce with an impassioned, uncritical devotion towards police power and authority.

We have described here a worldview that elevates 'nostalgia over reflection, retrenchment over innovation, dominant over minority values, archetypes over deviant types, and citizens over aliens' (Walker 2002: 314–15). It tends, as such, to be the outlook of those displaced by economic dislocation and precariousness, disaffected by processes of detraditionalization and social fragmentation, marginalized from democratic politics. They are those who feel discomforted by a diverse, contentious world in which 'there are no longer authoritative accounts of how to live' (Gamble 2000: 65) and who react to the emergence of a multicultural England with what John Keane—writing about nationalism more generally—has called 'a bovine will to simplify things' (1998: 95). It is under these conditions, and from this vantage point, that the police (or, more accurately, a vision of sectarian policing) are mobilized as a 'primal shelter' for the insecure (Bauman 2000: 214), one imagined as capable of delivering order and security to a world experienced as changing, dynamic, dangerous, and unstable. An institution that ought to assume a marginal place within any mature democratic society is by these means made symbolically central. It is a process of centring that obviates the need for more searching thought about what it is that 'unites and divides society' (Wrong 1994); one that channels reflection about the problem of order down some misguided paths and saddles the English police with unquenchable, ultimately de-legitimating, expectations.

Emergent: Democratic Moments in English Policing Culture

In his writings on culture, Raymond Williams is at pains to emphasize that dominant meanings and values—however hard their adherents might seek to naturalize them—do not exhaust, and cannot hope to colonize, all human experience, practice, and intention (Williams 1977: 125). We have—in the case of policing—demonstrated this by reference to those backward-glancing sensibilities that today exist in oppositional relation to ascendent managerialist and consumerist logics. But Williams also speaks in this context of 'emergent' structures of feeling, a term he uses to describe meanings and values that connect with, and articulate, experiences the dominant mode of ordering excludes, represses, or neglects, and which harbour, prefigure, or project—often in pre-political forms—alternative social arrangements and political futures.

We have in this study discerned several *democratic moments* in English policing culture that might be characterized as emergent in something approaching these ways. They take the form of movements and outlooks that attempt either to demystify the symbolic power of the police, or else construct meanings and narratives that connect policing in revised, potentially more inclusive and democratic, ways to questions of recognition, citizenship, and political community. Three such moments seem especially worthy of elaboration.

This democratic impulse is most readily apparent in those campaigns and movements that continue to struggle for forms of anti-discriminatory and politically accountable policing in ways that reach beyond the selective appropriation of black, gay and lesbian, and community politics into the dominant culture—something we documented in our account of 'the hopeful' in Chapter 4 and in respect of the policing politics of inner-city Manchester in Chapters 5 and 8. These movements, we noted, are organized around different social memories, and a different sense of English policing's post-war historical trajectory, from the tales of love and loss encountered in—especially residual—white narratives. The story they recount is of police–minority relations that reached a nadir in the 1970s and early 1980s before undergoing a slow, uneven, but nonetheless significant alteration. Against this backdrop, these often local, incident-oriented campaigns and movements engage with, and press the limits of, an altered police disposition towards questions of 'diversity'. They refuse to allow a more liberal police voice to pass unchallenged; resist the complacent presumption that 'the hard work is in the past', that 'there is nothing else to be done' (Gilroy 2002: 151), and continue to provoke questions about what democratic, equitable policing means and how it may best be institutionalized. This adds up to what one might call a radical profaning of the English police, one that aims to disturb the doxic symbolic power of the police and enact policing forms that operate in ways that affirm black, ethnic minority, gay and lesbian, and other dispossessed social groups as full members of the English cultural and political community.[7]

We might, secondly, revisit aspects of those public sensibilities towards policing that we earlier coded as either 'dominant' or 'residual'. Consider, in respect of the latter, the aforementioned white reactions to the Stephen Lawrence case. Here, amid all the expressed disquiet about the effects of this tragedy on 'our' police, and the mental gymnastics aimed at neutralizing the consequences of scandal, one finds some public acknowledgement that injury had been done by the police's failure to investigate the murder of Stephen Lawrence with due competence—an acknowledgment that contains at least an implicit, doxic recognition that questions of fair and equal treatment are, and should be, integral to English policing. We might also, more promisingly, recall the various post-traditional sensibilities towards police authority set out in Chapter 4. These, we think, can be re-read in ways that reach beyond their dominant consumerist articulation and render them, instead, resources for an alternative politics of citizenship. We have in mind here the advent of a disenchanted and no longer so silent majority that is today more attuned to shortcomings in police performance, more minded to accept the existence of police wrongdoing, and more willing to recognize the significance—for 'us' *and* for 'Others'—of accountability and human rights. Such dispositions, though by no means always finding conscious political expression, nonetheless offer a reservoir of thought and feeling upon which a democratic politics of policing can today draw. They bespeak concerns that are no longer confined to the—civil libertarian— margins of English public life.

Finally, we might make reference to the emergence *inside* the police of constituencies and outlooks that appear more amenable to a vision of policing in which considerations of equity, the search for inclusive public consultation, and a culture of human rights figure centrally. The advent—and subsequent political and cultural work—of bodies such as the Black Police Association and the Gay and Lesbian Police Association can readily be understood in this light. So too can the presence of senior police managers who are troubled—on grounds that anticipate more democratic policing forms rather than hark back to an age when the mysteries of police work remained opaque to outsiders—by the narrow, myopic predilections of a dominant audit culture; officers more willing to acknowledge and address police wrongdoing, and who appear at ease with, and in some cases actively champion, a language of ethical, equitable, responsive, rights-sensitive policing (e.g., Neyroud and Beckley 2001; Neyroud 2002). There is, it seems reasonable to suppose, a diverse and entangled vocabulary of motives in play here, ranging from genuine political commitment, to a pragmatic professional recognition of the altered conditions of police legitimacy and effectiveness, to an instrumental, career-minded adaptation to revised political imperatives.[8] They amount nonetheless to a small but hardly insignificant democratic moment within contemporary English policing culture, one that offers some potentially fertile ground upon which to forge—in local settings and through national interventions—a more deliberative vision of what that culture could become.

These shifts and partial incorporations pose a number of distinct challenges, not only to the movements whose struggles helped to effect them, but also to the claims made, and stances adopted, by the radical criminologists who for much of the 1970s and 1980s were instrumental in campaigning for politically accountable policing (e.g., Hain 1979; Baldwin and Kinsey 1982; Cowell *et al.* 1982; Jefferson and Grimshaw 1984; Scraton 1985). Often—in policing as elsewhere—critical criminologists seem reluctant to acknowledge such practical effects, but they raise for us some intriguing questions: what does critical criminology (or, in the present case, a radical politics of policing) do when it finds its concerns selectively echoed in official discourse and practice? What kinds of re-appraisal are called for? What positions and strategies should it adopt? For us, such re-appraisal seems to demand minimally that we seek to navigate a course between two unhelpful positions that recur within debates about police reform. On the one hand, a sociologically naïve view (often found in professional talk about 'drivers of change', 'change agents', and 'change management') that underestimates the durability of institutional practices and cultures, whether due to active/passive resistance or the dead weight of habit and routine. On the other hand, those postures (which remain prevalent within some strands of critical criminology) prone to dismiss internal police reform efforts, or apparent shifts in the occupational habitus, as so much window-dressing—devices aimed at co-opting critics, keeping more radical reform at bay, disguising the fact that *plus ça change, plus c'est la même chose.*

These various sightings provide, in our judgement, reasons for thinking that a more democratic understanding of English policing and its relationship to mundane and political culture lies immanent within the present configuration of public sensibilities—a prospect that remains, politically and culturally, open to us. Some elements of this configuration are consciously voiced as demands for democratization, as we have seen. Others take more diffuse, pre-political forms. Yet these remain capable of being re-articulated and radicalized in ways that project alternatives to the politics of atomized consumerism on the one hand, and that of unthinking community on the other. With this prospect in mind, let us conclude by considering how the cultural connection between policing, state, and nation might be reconstituted in more inclusive, cosmopolitan forms, and how policing might, on this basis, offer a site for the articulation of new styles of deliberative political authority and democratic citizenship.

Towards a Cosmopolitan Policing Culture

A public sphere has the effect of desacralizing power relationships. It is the vital medium of naming the unnameable, pointing at frauds, starting arguments, shaking the world, stopping it from falling asleep [Keane 1998: 169–70].

English policing culture appears today to be structured around a conflict between the 'modernizing' zeal of consumerism and managerialism and a nostalgic yearning for the solidarity of community. Yet for all that they differ in outlook and emotional tone, these 'dominant' and 'residual' forms contribute to a broadly similar outcome: namely, a cultural complex of impatient, other-disregarding, and seemingly insatiable demands. This situation can be interpreted, or so we have argued, as a consequence of processes of individualization and detraditionalization. But it is also the product of a failure of democratization—an outcome, in the specific field of policing, of the absence of any viable democratic narrative of Englishness (cf. Nairn 2000: 88–9). Public sentiments marked by anger, frustration, and disenchantment arise, in other words, from a polity that lacks institutional spaces through which competing demands can engage in mutual dialogue, and by these means be subject to democratic governance.

What though is entailed, culturally and politically, in seeking to address this impasse by extending and deepening the democratic moments that also, however peripherally, compose English policing culture? We cannot hope to offer here anything approaching an adequate account of what this might involve, not least because such an account requires the cultural sociology we have undertaken in this book to be supplemented by a fuller engagement with normative political theory.[9] We do, however, want to outline certain key elements of what one might call a *cosmopolitan policing culture* and, in so doing, indicate what might be required in order to generate and sustain a more inclusive and deliberative conception of English policing.

This prospect requires first that we transcend the kind of naïve rationalism that either expressly desires, or implicitly presumes, that policing can be stripped entirely of its *symbolizing force*—its capacity to condense and signify a series of considerations pertaining to such matters as morality, community, identity, power, and authority. Given the intimate connection of policing to questions of life and death, order and entropy, protection and vulnerability, and its constitutive association with the coercive authority of the state, any such severing seems a remote, sociologically implausible, prospect. The question, therefore, is not whether, but how and in what form, policing comes to be encoded within mundane and political culture. It is a matter, not of denuding policing of myth and meaning, but of the kinds of collective myths and meanings that are attached to it, of the character of the social and cultural relations that policing is conditioned by and a contributor towards. The communicative power of policing may be an enduring, deeply-rooted dimension of late modern societies, one whose broad parameters are delimited by the coercive foundations of the policing function. Yet the precise form such signification takes remains a variable, contested, and politically contingent matter, as we have shown. There are no *a priori* reasons why policing cannot affirm and symbolize more egalitarian forms of civic solidarity, or a more deliberative, thinking polity.

The vexed nature of the policing question within the Northern Ireland peace process illustrates well both the structural and contingent aspects of this issue. In a deeply contested polity where the police either represent (for nationalists) the coercive power of an illegitimate, sectarian state, or stand (among unionists) as brave defenders of the union from terrorist outrage, it is no surprise that policing has been among the most bitterly disputed issues within the peace process (at times threatening to derail it), nor that the iconography of policing (the force's name, badge, uniform, oath of allegiance, etc.) have assumed great salience as a dimension of police reform (Patten 1999: ch. 17; Ellison and Smyth 2000: ch. 9; Smyth 2002). Yet the fact that small steps forward have been taken in even this most unpromising terrain demonstrates that it *is* possible for policing to assume new social meanings and contribute in modest but pivotal ways to the remaking of cultural and political community (see, generally, Ellison and Mulcahy 2001).

Much the same can be said, secondly, about the place of *emotions* in contemporary policing culture. Given its aforementioned entanglement with questions of order and security, with morality and authority, with the lines of affiliation within, and boundaries of, community, it is readily understandable that policing—together with criminal justice and punishment—is a social institution liable to be suffused by the passions. It is difficult, once again, to envisage that this linkage can be entirely uncoupled, to imagine that human emotions will not continue to play some part in animating demands for policing and in structuring institutional practice. Yet while policing seems likely to retain some form of connection to public sentiment, one can also identify grounds for supposing that there is little fixed or predetermined about the form or intensity of this bond. As David Garland (2000: 352) remarks of the closely analogous case of 'popular-punitive' sensibilities towards punishment:

> Outrage and anger are the culture's antidotes to fear and anxiety, and the open expression of these emotions is part of the consolation and therapy it offers. But these sentiments are quite specific ones, grounded in definite features of our social organization rather than in some timeless punitive instinct. They are conditioned, evoked and channelled by the social routines and cultural practices of contemporary society.

Policing—like punishment—is encircled by a complex, contradictory, and differentially felt range of emotions ranging from anger, fear, and resentment, to guilt, empathy, even pleasure. It is also—given the paradox of housing coercive power in an institutional container that is thereby able to undermine the very security it exists to uphold (Berki 1986: ch. 2; Walker 2000: ch. 1)—perfectly possible for citizens simultaneously to feel anxious of both crime *and* policing. There is, furthermore, no reason why policing has to attract the depth of emotional investment that it has come to assume within contemporary culture. The 'heightened emotional tone' that Garland (2001: 10) identifies as part of a 'culture of control' is both a relatively recent and unevenly patterned phenomenon (cf. Karstedt 2002). For much of the post-war period (at least until the 1970s) the punitive passions appear to have had nowhere near the cultural prominence or political take-up that they possess today (Garland 2001: ch. 1; see also Windlesham 1987, 1993; cf. 1996). As our discussion of the 'agnostics' in Chapter 4 demonstrates, there also remain those for whom policing has little emotional resonance, citizens who form subjectivities in which the idea of policing plays but a marginal, background part. The emotionality of policing has, it seems, specific conditions of possibility. It depends on the 'thickness' or otherwise of the social relations the police are tasked with regulating—on prevailing patterns of economic inequality and social marginalization (Young 1999). It depends too on the ways in which the affects manifest in policing are 'handled' institutionally—with whether they are given space for legitimate expression, and with how they are (or are not) channelled through processes of public dialogue and deliberation. Ignoring, or seeking to bracket off, or keep at a 'safe' distance the passions that attend policing is no recipe at all for the construction of a cosmopolitan policing culture.

There is, thirdly, little to be gained in these terms from aiming to suppress (rather than debate and render reflexive) *the cultural connection between police, state, and nation*. Given the exclusionary, defensive, xenophobic form this link appears currently to assume, one liable to invest extravagantly in the police as a source of security, and prone to overlook abuses of police power, this is, at first glance, an understandable, even appealing, political objective (Loader and Walker 2001: 20–5; Walker 2002: 314). Yet it remains, in our judgement, a wrong-headed one. In part, this is simply to acknowledge that the police's place as a constitutive element, and icon, of sovereign statehood and its promise of security secretes this cultural connection in ways that are deep, often pre-rational, and difficult to erase. Yet it is also, in a more constructive spirit, to suggest that this relation can be remade in a more affirmative form, such that policing comes to contribute, materially and symbolically, to a more open, reflexive, non-racialized notion of 'civic nationality' and its attendant institutions of democratic citizenship (Barry 2001: 80; see also Miller 1995; Beetham 1999: 16–17). In his account of the 'cosmopolitan nation', Giddens (1998: 134) puts the matter thus:

Today, national identities must be sustained in a collaborative milieu, where they won't have the level of inclusiveness they one did, and where other loyalties exist alongside them. What is implied, as elsewhere in society, is a more open and reflexive construction of national identity—which marks out what is distinctive about the nation and its aspirations, but in a less taken-for-granted way than before.

The English police might, in other words, help to foster the nation as a 'community of attachment', one that 'promotes the trust and concern for "anonymous others" necessary to sustain the redistributive politics which centre any system of public provision of services, including policing services' (Walker 2002: 315).[10] In so doing, the police might, in turn, derive benefit from being apprehended as a part of a 'common public culture' (Miller 1995: 21–2), whether in respect of an enhanced capacity to draw currently atomized or antagonistic demands into forms of deliberation that encourage reflection on both the claims of others and the limits of policing, or from fashioning the forms of inclusive public consent that stand as the precondition of effective policing.

How though, from such starting points, might we begin to remake and re-imagine English policing and its relation to mundane and political culture? Given the analytic purposes of the present study, it is not our intention to detail the institutional architecture upon which any such reconfiguration ultimately rests.[11] Let us, instead, offer some brief concluding, but at the same time *opening*, remarks on what we take to be the core elements of a cosmopolitan policing culture. Such a culture requires, minimally, the creation of institutional forms and practices that expressly recognize the social and ethnocultural diversity of contemporary English society (cf. Kymlicka 1995). This means not only embedding in the police a legal regime and occupational ethos that is attuned to the lived experience and entitlements of *all* social groups—what the Patten Commission on policing in Northern Ireland called a 'human rights culture' (Patten 1999: ch. 4). It also requires a public sphere—one composed of a range of deliberative institutions and a willingness to practise what Unger (1998: 5–29) calls 'democratic experimentalism'—through which the sometimes impassioned demands of different constituencies can be voiced, the question of how, indeed whether, they can practically and equitably be met and addressed, and competing priorities and practices discussed and determined.

But it must, in addition, be recognized that 'recognition of cultural variety is the beginning, not the end of the matter; it is but a starting point for a long and perhaps tortuous, but in the end beneficial, *political process*' (Bauman 2001: 136, emphasis in original). Such a process would—in attending to the thorny question of how to allocate scarce policing resources on an inclusive, equitable, rights-protecting, basis—seek to involve all interested parties in ways that subject the conflict of identities and convictions to what Paul Ricoeur (1998) calls an 'ethics of argumentation'. This means bringing out from the shadows the emotions, desires, and fantasies that animate demands for policing and exposing them to the light of democratic dialogue. It means seeking—in a radical Durkheimian spirit—to bring to social consciousness and public reflection those doxic/paleo-symbolic beliefs that currently burden the police with unhappy, de-legitimating expectation (Durkheim 1992/1957; see also Stedman Jones 2001: ch. 9). And it means creating spaces of deliberation that seek to disrupt and unfix the habits and outlooks of those who present their cultural identities and policing preferences '*non-negotiably* to others' (Waldron 2000: 231, emphasis in original) in ways that open up the possibility—in the field of policing and security—of a solidarity-building 'politics of compromise' (Bellamy 1999).

These, it seems to us, are the minimum necessary ingredients of a cosmopolitan policing culture, one in which the institutional resources of policing make a modest material and symbolic contribution to the recognition of cultural diversity and to forging the social bonds of a common political community. Such a culture will not of course be easily or quickly constructed. Nor will its creation be free of obstacle or opposition. It will require patient cultural and political work aimed at deepening and extending those democratic moments within the present that are conducive towards it; work that seeks to animate English policing with a new, non-ideological, social imaginary. Such work will involve a struggle to de-centre the police from their iconic status as symbols of order and security, and conduits for the formation of individual and collective identity. It will mean coming to terms with the essentially 'tragic' quality of policing (cf. Garland 1990: 288–9), with the fact that the levers inducing order and conformity lie beyond the police in a manner that radically limits the role they can play in the production of safer societies. And it will demand greater attention not only to the ways in which the broader pattern of economic and social relations structure police practices, but also, in a more reconstructive spirit, to how policing might contribute to, and be mutually and virtuously conditioned by, more egalitarian social relations and more democratic institutions of governance (see Bayley 2002). This is, to be sure, a tall order. But it offers the only viable basis, in a post-traditional society, for making democratically legitimate a social institution in which citizens have come to possess little, or retain too much, faith.

Notes

Chapter 1

[1] This conclusion came in for a certain amount of criticism at the time from commentators accusing the Commission of having misinterpreted its own data. Whittaker, for example, points to the fact that 42 per cent of the public thought policemen took bribes, and 35 per cent that the police used unfair methods to obtain information, before charging the Royal Commission with 'complacency' (1964: 14–17; see also *Times Literary Supplement*, September 1962; Hart 1963: 294–8).

[2] The phrase was used by incumbent Conservative Prime Minister Harold Macmillan during the 1959 general election.

[3] The then Prime Minister, Edward Heath, called an early election in February 1974 in part around the issue of 'who governs Britain?' He suffered a narrow defeat.

[4] The 1997 figure takes account of the *fall* in recorded crime levels that began in 1993 and persisted throughout the 1990s; a fall that was subsequently corroborated by evidence from the British Crime Survey (Kershaw *et al.* 2000).

[5] More detailed elaboration of these figures can be found in Hough and Mayhew (1983); Mirrlees-Black *et al.* (1996); Smith (1996); Morgan and Newburn (1997: 30–8); Barclay and Tavares (1999: ch. 1); Maguire (2002). On the interpretation of post-war crime trends see, variously, Field (1990); Bottoms and Wiles (1995); Felson (1998); Wouters (1999); Garland (2001: 90–2).

[6] Mark publicly coined this phrase in an interview he gave to Desmond Wilcox shortly after his retirement in 1977 ('Robert Mark on Villainy, Virtue and "Vanessa's Loonies"', *The Listener*, 4 August 1977).

[7] We may also add in this regard the de-legitimating effects of Roger Graef's 1982 'fly-on-the-wall' documentary series on Thames Valley Police that depicted detectives engaged in what was widely viewed as the insensitive, bullying interrogation of a woman who alleged that she had been raped.

[8] This latter charge has been pressed most forcefully in an intervention by Pat O'Malley (1997). O'Malley argues that there is an 'enormous interpretive gap' in Reiner's (1992) account between 'the hypothesized operation' of the global processes that Reiner labels 'postmodernity' and particular 'processes of public police reform' (1997: 376). This analytic strategy, O'Malley contends, underplays the specific role of neo-liberal political rationalities in driving contemporary transformations in policing and, in

so doing, risks depoliticizing police reform by 'casting analysis into the kind of pessimism that has become the hallmark of certain brands of postmodern theorizing' (O'Malley 1997: 376). From different theoretical starting points, McLaughlin and Murji (1999*a*: 226) cognately claim that Reiner's account portrays the police 'as the victim of long-term structural shifts over which it has little control, direction or agency'; something that treats 'the police' as somehow distinct from an entity called 'society', of which it is a mere 'reflection' (cf. Latour 2000: 113–14), and under-emphasizes the ways in which policing *contributes* to the formation of social categories, divisions, and imaginings.

[9] Reiner has, it should be noted, demonstrated some awareness of these complexities. In the third edition of *The Politics of the Police*, he writes: 'the police are, in some senses, a Teflon service: they have survived all manner of scandal and controversy and remain a powerful political and cultural force, more so than any other state institution in an increasingly neo-liberal, privatized world in which the state has "hollowed out"' (Reiner 2000*a*: 47).

Chapter 2

[1] A body of recent work—including contributions from one of the present authors—has also demonstrated that *the police* today stand as but one among a plurality of *policing* agencies—one node with loosely-coupled networks of civil, municipal, and commercial policing forms operating at subnational, national, and transnational levels (e.g., Sheptycki 1995; Bayley and Shearing 1996; Shearing 1996; Jones and Newburn 1998; Johnston 1999; Loader 2000). Against this backdrop, studies that focus analytic attention solely on bounded state institutions composed of sworn, uniformed officers ('*the* police') tend nowadays to be increasingly regarded as anachronistic—something aptly demonstrated by the gently critical reception accorded to the latest edition of Reiner's *The Politics of the Police* (Reiner 2000*a*; cf. Jones 2001; Sheptycki 2001). We nonetheless persist in *this* study in taking state policing as our point of departure. We do this, in part, because state police forms continue to assume a significant place among the patchwork of providers that comprise contemporary security networks (Loader and Walker 2001). But we do so, more pertinently, because our object of enquiry is the *social meanings* of policing—meanings that continue, it seems to us, to be largely constituted around the idea of state policing. In striving to make sense of these processes of constitution (and the cultural linkages that exist between police, state, and nation), we will in the analyses that follow nonetheless remain alive to the possibility that the cultural category 'policing' is coming to have as its referent a more diverse range of institutions and processes.

[2] The use of the word 'idea' here is intended to signify the desires and longings, or, conversely, the fear and loathing, that police powers and interventions arouse in people. One might also speak in this regard of a *police force of the imagination*, one against which 'real' policing institutions are (frequently) measured and (all too often) found wanting. On the importance of analysing the category of the state as an idea, a 'collective misrepresentation' see Abrams (1988).

[3] As Giddens (1979: 39) notes, 'there are no signifying practices; signification should be seen as an integral element of social practices in general'.

[4] A cognate point can be made about the mobilization and display of police symbols. Bourdieu (1991: 75) emphasizes that there can be 'no symbolic power without the symbolism of power'. This does not mean, however, that the ceremonies, rituals, and imagery associated with police-work themselves generate the symbolic power of the police. They do not. Rather, the iconography of policing—the handcuffs, fingerprints, cop shows, uniforms, photofits, picture postcards, memoirs, cars, sirens, helicopters, riot shields, and so forth—connect with and re-articulate dispositions towards, and fantasies of, policing that already pertain within the wider culture (Sparks 1992*a*). As Bourdieu (1991: 126) again says, perhaps overstating the case, 'the belief of everyone, which pre-exists ritual, is the condition for the effectiveness of ritual. One only preaches to the converted'.

[5] By 'penal culture' Garland (1990: 210) means 'the loose amalgam of penological theory, stored-up experience, institutional wisdom, and professional common sense which frames the actions of penal agents and which lends meaning to what they do'.

[6] The relative contrasts in scope between recent social analyses of policing and punishment are brought into sharper focus when one considers the sheer impossibility of writing—on the subject of policing—a book equivalent in ambition to Garland's synthetic social theory of punishment. In part, of course, this derives from the fact that policing was never visited by sociology's 'founders' in the way that punishment was—not least by Durkheim. This lack of 'giant's shoulders' upon which to stand at least partially explains why policing has attracted so little of the kind of bold theorizing that has marked the sociology of punishment and social control in recent years (though see Ericson and Haggerty 1997). In this respect, Reiner (1992: 762) is undoubtedly right: police studies is crying out for some more 'fundamental social analysis' of the place that policing occupies within contemporary social relations.

[7] In similar terms, Garland (1990: 180) observes, 'there are two contrasting visions at work in contemporary criminal justice—the passionate, morally-toned desire to punish and the administrative, rationalistic, normalizing concern to manage. These visions clash in many

important respects, but both are deeply embedded within the social process of punishing' (cf. Sparks 2003).

[8] It should, however, be noted that the official data we draw upon in the study cover the legal jurisdiction of England and Wales.

[9] There are in fact two—not wholly unconnected—strands to these disputes. In part they have been sparked by the establishment of devolved government in Scotland and Wales in 1999 and been concerned with the post-devolution 'emergence' of a specifically English national identity—its meanings, desirability, likely effects etc. (Paxman 1998; Heffer 1999; Marr 2000; Nairn 2000). But they also represent the latest bout of a more longstanding contest about the nature of 'membership', 'community', and 'citizenship' in a multicultural Britain (Parekh 2000; Alibhai Brown 2001). We will have cause to touch on aspects of these disputes at various points throughout the book.

[10] The political, cultural, and legal context of policing in Northern Ireland is of course—for reasons too complex for us to do justice to here—in significant respects different (see McGarry and O'Leary 1999; Ellison and Smyth 2000; Walker and Telford 2000; Ellison and Mulcahy 2001).

[11] The point of departure for much of this now extensive literature is Maurice Halbwachs' *On Collective Memory* (1992/1941). It encompasses important contributions from, among others, historians (Fentress and Wickham 1992), sociologists (Connerton 1989), social psychologists (Middleton and Edwards 1990), and anthropologists (Tonkin 1990).

[12] By 'structural' we refer here to those features of policing (such as the capacity to exercise legitimate coercion) that constitute relatively durable—and universal—elements of state policing in complex, modern societies. By 'conjunctural' we mean those aspects of police operation (forms of involvement in the mediation of social conflicts, policing styles and technologies, specific professional ideologies, and legitimation claims) that emerge in particular times and places as variations within these basic structural configurations (cf. Melucci 1996: ch. 4).

[13] These issues have—somewhat surprisingly—received relatively little attention in historical and sociological accounts of the English police (though see Emsley 1992, Taylor 1999: 20–7; and compare, for Canada, Walden 1982). They are even less apparent in the contemporary literature on national identity and constructions of the English/British national past, much of which we have nonetheless found useful in extending and refining our analyses (see, e.g., Wright 1985; Schlesinger 1991; Billig 1995; Miller 1995; Weight 2002).

[14] Readers will have noticed that we have had relatively little to say in the preceding few pages about the role played by the media in constituting patterns of opinion and belief *vis-à-vis* policing. This is not because of a failure on our part to recognize the mass media as significant producers

and carriers of the social meanings of English policing, as the attention we have paid in the opening two chapters to relevant work on media representations of policing and their effects should attest. It is nonetheless the case that analysis of media discourse *per se* does not form a significant component of the account that follows. This is partly a question of human resources and capacity—there is only so much a research team of two can adequately accomplish in the time available and, even in the absence of a dedicated media element, our proposed enquiry already seemed ambitious enough. And it is partly because we saw little to be gained from pursuing an investigation that would in important respects have covered the same terrain as that mapped by Jessica Allen, Sonia Livingstone, and Robert Reiner in their recently completed research on post-war media representations of crime and criminal justice (Allen *et al.* 1998; Reiner *et al.* 2000*a*; 2000*b*). Having said this, our concerns in the present study do very much extend to analysing the traces of mass mediated discourse as they appear in various official representations of, and ordinary conversations about, policing.

[15] This does not, we ought to re-emphasize, imply any lack of interest on our part in processes of historical change. Nor does it entail the abandonment of 'controls' on interpretation and their replacement with the predilections of the researcher(s). It merely means orientating oneself to 'the study of the cultural forms and processes through which individuals express their sense of themselves in history' (Portelli 1991: p. ix).

[16] These forces represent, respectively, England's most influential (and nationally prominent) police organization, a significant metropolitan force, and a shire county constabulary, and were chosen to represent a range of outlook and experience. Cognate reasoning informed our decision to interview police officers and citizens from different locations across Cheshire and Greater Manchester.

[17] Given the oral historical orientations of our study (and the ensuing methodological requirement for respondents to reflect upon processes of biographical and social change) it did not make much sense for our interviewees to be much below the age of about 35.

[18] Transcripts of the interviews conducted for this study have—with the exception of the few interviewees who wished their transcript for various reasons to be withheld—been deposited in the Economic and Social Research Council's *Qualidata* archive based at the University of Essex (www.qualidata.essex.ac.uk). Copies of the material have been lodged by *Qualidata* in the British Library of Political and Economic Science, London School of Economics, and the Radzinowicz Library, University of Cambridge, as well as with the UK Data Archive (www.data-archive.ac.uk). They can be accessed—for legitimate research and journalistic purposes—with the permission of the authors.

Chapter 3

[1] The names of all our interviewees and discussants, and of any persons referred to by them during our conversations, have been replaced with pseudonyms.

[2] Such 'violence' was, in fact, rather more contested during the 1950s than these recollections suggest, as the setting up of an official tribunal into the alleged assault by two Scottish police officers on the 'Thurso boy' in 1957 indicates (Home Office 1959). But it is also evident that public sentiments such as these offer an emotive reservoir of support for those officers—such as the Avon and Somerset police constable Steve Guscott who in May 1994 was convicted of common assault against a 15-year-old boy (McKenzie 1995)—who find themselves sanctioned for such behaviour. In the public/media frenzy that followed PC Guscott's conviction not too many voices could be heard demanding that he be sacked.

[3] This 'community' is, it should be said, also implicitly white, an implication we explore at greater length in Chapter 5.

[4] The cover photo of the inaugural issue of *Police*, for instance, has two policemen standing beside a Mini car, the legend underneath them reading '...world's finest police!' (*Police*, September 1968).

[5] The view that 'unit beat policing' represented a scientific remedying of old inefficiencies—the application to policing of Harold Wilson's 'white heat of technology'—was widely echoed in official circles at the time of its inception (see Weatheritt 1986). As one former Minister of State at the Home Office recalled, 'it was hailed as a great advance without any controversy at all. [Defending fixed-point patrol] was like saying you defend the existence of stage-coaches. It just wasn't appropriate'. In this spirit, an editorial in *Police* magazine in 1971 complained that the public does not seem to realize that, 'were it not for the car, whole areas of urban Britain might not see a policeman' (*Police*, October 1971: 4).

[6] This emerging disposition towards authority is characteristically represented in a *Police* magazine cartoon in 1991. The cartoon depicts a 'Toytown' setting in which the avuncular and rotund PC Plod is attempting to deliver some wise words of authoritative guidance to Noddy and Big Ears. Noddy is contemptuous of his efforts: 'leave it out copper, I know my rights' (*Police*, March 1991).

[7] Though it should be noted, as well, that the sentiments outlined here might be fashioned in support of 'community' or 'problem-oriented' policing. In this spirit, perhaps, one retired chief officer we interviewed ventured to suggest the following: 'when you walked the beat in your uniform, you were a symbol of peace and tranquillity. It worked, it would still work today. Whatever anti-police feeling there might be in some parts of society they still want to see the bobby-on-the-beat. I can't help

thinking that if some forces said "let's stop all this specialism. Let's sort of flood the place with bobbies-on-the-beat". I think it's effect would be absolutely magical' (retired chief constable, provincial force).

Chapter 4

[1] These categories are analytic constructions designed to help clarify the various *clusters of doxic/paleo-symbolic sentiment* that can be discerned from our conversations—clusters, as we shall see, that overlap in certain respects while remaining mutually incompatible in others. They are *not*, it should be stressed, typologies of individuals or groups. While we necessarily utilize the utterances of specific individuals to illustrate our selected categories, and indicate the social positions that seem to us to generate them, the habitus of any single person is rarely, if ever, confined entirely within any single cluster. It should be also noted that these categories are by no means intended to exhaust the possible range of doxic opinion towards the police.

[2] In summer 2002 the *Daily Mail* sought to mobilize such sentiments in a campaign against what it chose to call 'part-time policing'. The police station mentioned in the above account was featured in the lead story that launched the campaign under the caption: 'Hello, hello: Nobody opens the doors to Altrincham police station on Sundays and Bank Holidays' ('ROBBED OF OUR POLICE', *Daily Mail*, 10 June 2002). A sympathetic 'insider' account of the emergence of this kind of 'right-wing rancour' towards the police can be found in Montgomery (1999).

[3] A common—middle-class—response to these matters centred on how the police are today being diverted away from ('real') crime by petty traffic infringements. The following is fairly typical: 'there's resentment of so many people... "why should they stop me for doing 32 miles an hour in a 30 limit when they could be fighting crime", that sort of thing. The things which we think are important, which are fighting crime, are being overtaken by all this' (women's organization, south Manchester). See further Girling *et al.* (2000: 133–7).

[4] Joan was both a participant in our group discussion with members of a tenants' association in inner-city Manchester and the subject of an extended biographical interview. Joan Cromwell is, of course, a pseudonym.

[5] This had in fact been preceded, in the early 1960s, by someone her mother had attended school with, and who went on to become a police inspector, being charged with corruption. This was, Joan recalls, 'the first inkling that I ever had that perhaps they weren't quite, you know, these pillars of society.'

Chapter 5

[1] The concept of 'racialization' refers, according to Miles, 'to those instances where social relations between people have been structured by the signification of human biological characteristics in such a way as to define and construct differentiated social collectivities' (1989: 75). 'Race' on this view is an ideological construct of racialized relations and has no meaning beyond them; biologically speaking, there are no such entities as 'races'. In a policing context, racialization describes the ways in which wider relations of domination and subordination organized around 'race' impact upon and shape the social patterning and effects of police activity, as well as the means by which the distribution and deployment of police resources contribute to the production and reproduction of such relations. On racialized relations generally see Miles (1989); Solomos and Back (1996); on racialization and policing see Keith (1993); Holdaway (1996).

[2] We did not originally set out to ask our respondents about the Lawrence case and the police mishandling of it. The Macpherson Report was, however, published in the midst of our period of interviewing and the case was subsequently either raised without prompting by many of our discussants or explicitly introduced by us as a way of initiating or wrapping up discussions of the post-war intersection of race and policing. As such, we are—to some extent serendipitously—in the position of being able to present in this chapter an analysis of how the issues raised by Lawrence/Macpherson were *received and appropriated by different audiences*, something that has not thus far figured highly in sociological commentary on the case (cf. Bridges 1999; McLaughlin and Murji 1999*b*; *Sociological Research Online* 1999). The development of such an analysis also enables us to advance one of our broader explanatory purposes—namely, to elicit understanding of the ways in which public sensibilities towards policing and particular police scandals condition one another.

[3] A telling instance of this can be found in the *Sun*'s initial reaction to the Stephen Lawrence Inquiry report. On a day when all other national dailies devoted extensive front-page coverage to the Macpherson report's publication, the *Sun* relegated the story to the inside pages, choosing instead to give front-page prominence to the latest instalment of its pro-Sterling campaign ('121,764 VOTE TO SAVE £', *Sun*, 25 February 1999). One week on, the paper then opted to deploy its front page *in defence* of the beleaguered police, reporting the 'findings' of another readers' poll under the headline: 'BRITAIN BACKS OUR BOBBIES: SUN POLL BOOSTS UNDER-FIRE COPS? (*Sun*, 1 March 1999).

[4] This response to the Lawrence case was almost exclusively confined to some of the white citizens and police officers we spoke to. On the rare occasions such sentiments were voiced among senior police officers or politicians they emerged in heavily muted form. This suggests to us both a

degree of barely articulated, 'backstage' disgruntlement among certain police and political elites about the criticism piled onto the police by Macpherson and—tellingly, from this perspective—his aides; and the inability of this sentiment to cohere into an effective political form at the present time. This much seems clear at least from the observations of this retired chief constable: 'we can talk forever about the Lawrence case. It's almost a total miscarriage of justice, but that's by the way. If you acknowledge that a judge sitting by [left-wing barrister] Michael Mansfield might be going to sort of clobber the service, you've got to get out of bed and do something about it. It is fair to say that the investigation of the crime has clearly not been all it should be. It's certainly not been racial . . . But if I say that, it's "You're racist, that's what your problem is".' It is also present, albeit rather more obliquely, in the grudging comments made by this former Conservative Home Office Minister about Macpherson: 'unfortunately it is written in a way, and it makes findings which have created quite new controversy. I mean I'm bound to say that I thought it was disappointing. I know the judge, and I was disappointed because it has created criticism, which I think in some respects isn't very well grounded . . . I don't really want to discuss that report.'

⁵ The term 'institutional racism' has, since it was first suggested to—and rejected by—Lord Scarman in his report on the Brixton disorders some two decades ago (Scarman 1982: 105–6), become a key symbolic marker in the cultural politics of race and policing. A categorization strenuously resisted by chief officers throughout the bulk of this period, it was only in the aftermath of the Lawrence Inquiry (and only then following a final, anguished bout of semantic jockeying) that some senior officers began to concede that racism could be embedded in their forces in ways that went beyond the discriminatory actions of—a few—prejudiced officers. The definition proposed by Sir William Macpherson and accepted by the Metropolitan Police reads as follows: ' "Institutional racism" consists of the collective failure of an organisation to provide an appropriate and professional service to people because of their colour, culture or ethnic origin. It can be seen or detected in processes, attitudes and behaviour which amount to discrimination through unwitting prejudice, ignorance, thoughtlessness, and racist stereotyping which disadvantage ethnic minority people' (Macpherson 1999: 321).

⁶ For one such attempt to mobilize these sentiments in the aftermath of, and in reaction to, the Stephen Lawrence Inquiry Report see Dennis *et al.* (2000).

⁷ This shift in police outlook was also acknowledged by others among our ethnic minority discussants, including this female member of our Pakistani discussion group who had long been involved in working with Asian victims of domestic violence: 'they [the police] are more willing to

listen to the community, like now they will phone us up. Say if there is a woman missing from home or something like that, they would phone us up. We know their procedures of confidentiality are the same as ours. We know if we tell them we know where this woman is, there is no danger they are going to go to the husband and say 'your wife is there go and collect her', which you could not have been sure of twenty, well fifteen years ago...So we have built a kind of rapport with them.'

Chapter 6

[1] According to the information accompanying the survey, *Protect the Protectors* was 'Est. 1993 in order to campaign for the rights, interests and protection of British Police Officers'. Its logo reads: 'Protecting those who protect society'.

[2] The joining dates of the thirty-three retired and long-serving police officers we interviewed can be subdivided as follows: two enlisted between 1930 and 1939; two between 1940-9; four between 1950-9; thirteen between 1960-9; ten between 1970-9, and two post-1980.

[3] The 1993 Sheehy Report was also—less happily for police officers—concerned with police conditions and remuneration. We examine this report—and police reactions to it—in Chapter 8.

[4] He continued, tellingly, 'then it waned in the 1960s, and it's all gone now of course'.

[5] One of our interviewees noted in this regard that 'well into the 1950s', constables' reports 'started off "Sir, I respectfully beg to inform you" and finished off "I am, Sir, your obedient servant"' (retired chief constable, metropolitan force). See further on this, Young (1991: 356).

[6] The interpretative sketches that follow are intended as a provocation to a renewal of work in this field. They represent a challenge, in particular, to those strands of the literature on 'police culture' that tend to situate the dispositions of police officers principally in the structural features of the job at the expense of their wider connections to the social, thereby depicting this culture as a rather too spatially invariant and temporally static phenomenon (Waddington 1999; cf. Reiner 2000a: 105-6). It is often forgotten in this regard that the preponderance of work on British police culture was undertaken during a moment of political turmoil in the 1970s and 1980s with the attendant risk that a bundle of sentiments forged in the specific milieu of that time has come—in a de-historicized fashion—to be seen *as* police culture (see, e.g., Cain 1973; Holdaway 1979, 1983; Reiner 1978; Baldwin and Kinsey 1982; Smith and Gray 1985). Revisiting and revising this work in the context of the political climate that now surrounds policing (managerialism, partnership working, competition with alternative providers etc.) and the socio-cultural shifts of

the last two decades (individualization, democratization, multiculturalism etc.) seems to us to be a significant sociological and political task (cf. Chan 1997; Fitzgerald *et al.* 2002).

[7] According to one chief constable we interviewed, it is possible today to detect signs that such generational differences are emerging in a new form. He cited in this regard the following incident: 'I went out on patrol a few months ago in the city centre here with some officers, and was actually told by one of the younger officers "chill out boss, you're making it worse". I wanted to intervene in a situation which I thought was intolerable. And they said "no, that was the norm". They were quite happy with that, they could manage that. It was an affront to me. In effect they were telling me that the generation gap was clearly there, and they had more in common with the young people who are not police officers of their own age, than they had with me who was also a police officer but was past it' (chief constable, provincial force).

[8] Mention should also be made here of the—chronically under-investigated—cultural effects of the advent within the police of a greater number of 'civilians', some in senior, policy-making positions. (The term 'civilian' of course is itself a vestige of the police's military traditions and has now been superseded in many forces by the more neutral sounding, if scarcely accurate or illuminating, 'support staff'.) Those among our interviewees who deemed that policing could be done effectively only by those with what one Greater Manchester Police superintendent called a 'police instinct' often stood aghast at this development: 'It's now turning. We're working for them in some respect. Civilian staff, they haven't got a clue how the job works, yet they want to impose their ideas' (constables' group, GMP).

[9] Some interpretative caution needs to be exercised here. It may well be that these 'changes' reflect more the career trajectories (and associated dispositions) of the officers making the claims than they do any genuine shift in the habitus of today's police officers—our respondents, in other words, recall their days as novice constables as being marked by steely discipline, in contrast to now, where, as supervisory officers, they see themselves surrounded by the argumentative, 'ill-disciplined' young. It is worth recording in this regard that on each of the three occasions we arranged discussion groups with serving officers, they duly turned up at the appointed place and time with *little or no* idea of why they had been asked (told?) to come along. They had simply done as instructed. This—like the other matters discussed in this section—plainly stands in need of dedicated empirical enquiry.

[10] Aspects of this diversification have been widely investigated and analysed over recent years, most heavily in respect of gender (Heidensohn 1992; Martin and Jurik 1996; Brown and Heidensohn 2000; Westmarland 2001) and ethnicity (Holdaway 1991, 1996; Holdaway and Barron 1997), but also in relation to sexuality (Burke 1993).

[11] One indicator of the active reluctance on the part of the police in the 1960s and 1970s to take seriously these issues was their successful lobbying for an exemption from the anti-discrimination provisions of the Race Relations Act 1976. One former Home Office Minister recalled in this regard the reception given to the then Home Secretary, Roy Jenkins, when he raised the possibility at a conference of the Metropolitan Police Federation. 'It was clear', the minister recalled, 'that there was entrenched attitudes amongst some of them that were frankly disturbing, howling at the mention of the Race Relations Board. I suppose you could argue, looking back, that some of it was inevitable, newly arrived immigrant community and so on, but it was very worrying in terms of people who had a responsibility for enforcing the law and maintaining the Queen's peace. There were some of them who walked out.' The police exemption was removed—in the aftermath of the Stephen Lawrence case—by the Race Relations (Amendment) Act 2000.

[12] Given their—still—small numbers within Greater Manchester Police, the ranks of the black and Asian officers we interviewed have been concealed in order to protect the anonymity they were promised.

[13] Robert Reiner has pointed out to us (personal communication, 22 October 2002) that many of these motifs—'declining discipline, managerial change, etc.'—arose in 'similar' or 'identical' forms in the interviews he conducted for *The Blue-Coated Worker* in the early 1970s (Reiner 1978). It may be, as he suggests, that these represent 'almost constant themes of police talk' and that officers are inclined to project into the past a 'Golden Age' located some twenty to thirty years earlier. At the very least they suggest that a reactionary reflex to change (one predisposed to feel that change is making the world worse and the job more difficult) stands as one relatively enduring element of the police occupational habitus.

Chapter 7

[1] Like all periodizations, this one does some violence to actual historical events and processes, and the precise dating plainly obscures certain continuities and overlaps, the most important of which we will endeavour to draw out in discussion. We nonetheless hold that this categorization captures what *are* in important respects distinct moments in the contemporary history of elite police mobilization; and note in this regard that our typology roughly parallels that adopted by Reiner and his colleagues in their recent analysis of post-war media representations of crime and criminal justice (Reiner 2000b; Reiner et al. 1998). We are grateful to Robert Reiner for bringing these convergences to our attention (personal communication, 3 August 1999).

[2] This relative silence is echoed in the disposition of the Police Federation. Though it had appointed its first parliamentary spokesperson,

James Callaghan, in 1955, and lobbied successively for more pay around the time of the 1960–2 Royal Commission, the Federation remained during this period a rather modest outfit ('two rooms above a grocer's shop in Camden', as one of its ex-presidents put it to us) that evinced little inclination to proselytize about social issues. 'We didn't talk to the press', our informant continued, 'the press wasn't admitted to our conferences, or anything of that nature.'

[3] Despite this, senior officers continued during this period to encourage the public to report crime. Consider, for instance, the Commissioner's evident pleasure at the rise in '999' calls: 'it is an encouraging sign that, year by year, more and more calls are being received from members of the public who see or hear something suspicious and are public-spirited enough to do something about it. We cannot get too much help from this source and I hope to see an ever-increasing flood of calls from people who are in a position to direct police attention to suspicious incidents or noises. We never resent it if suspicions prove to be wholly unfounded' (MPAR 1954: 7). This encouragement stands in obvious contrast to recent police campaigns seeking to restrict use of the '999' system to genuine emergencies.

[4] Throughout the post-war period Cheshire Police has represented a resolute exception to this. The forewords of successive chief constables have for the most part remained local in orientation and evinced little interest in questions of social change—indeed in the (increasingly conflict-ridden) 1970s the issue that seemed paramount in these reports was the force's response to burglar alarms. This is not to say, of course, that the outside world never impressed itself upon policing in Cheshire: 'In the changing society in which we live it is not sufficient merely to deal with the problems on our own doorstep. National or international events also influence our actions. During 1970 numerous demonstrations were staged for a variety of reasons and international hijackings led to special attention at Ringway [Manchester] Airport' (Cheshire Police annual report (CAR) 1970: 5).

[5] This public campaigning was to intensify from the mid-1970s onwards and cause no little consternation among—usurped—chief officers (Reiner 1978, 1980; Murji and McLaughlin 1998; for an 'official' Federation view see Judge 1994, for that of chief officers, Mark 1978: 159).

[6] Mark's campaign was to have an almost immediate impact in that the first two of the measures he promoted (majority verdicts and pre-trial disclosure of defence alibis) were implemented by the Labour government's Criminal Justice Act 1966—Roy Jenkins (1991: 205) later put on record Mark's 'considerable influence on me on this issue'. The other two of his demands (both concerning the effective abolition of the 'right to silence') remained high on the political agenda of chief constables for the next three

decades, until in 1994 they too were given legislative effect by the Criminal Justice and Public Order Act (Savage *et al.* 2000: 178–81).

[7] This stands in marked contrast to the position adopted by the Police Federation during two high-profile 'law and order' campaigns launched in the 1970s—one in November 1975, a second in the run-up to the 1979 general election (Reiner 1980; McLaughlin and Murji 1998). These campaigns—which explicitly strove to mobilize the so-called 'silent majority' against 'liberal' criminal justice policies—saw the Federation align itself closely with the policies being promulgated at that time by Margaret Thatcher's Conservative Party: 'I think the service did politically move quickly to the right [in the 1970s]... The great majority of the police service were Conservative voters and saw the Conservative Party as the savior of the police service' (spokesperson, Police Federation). The Police Federation's single voice also arguably enabled it to position itself more effectively than senior officers as an authoritative police presence within English public life. As one former Home Office official we interviewed put it, 'they were capable of putting up a spokesman, a convincing articulate spokesman, on pretty well any issue at no notice, and did... They were much better briefed, better educated, willing to argue, and increasingly sophisticated; though not always beautiful to hear'.

[8] This was also one issue on which chief constables and the Police Federation were able to make common public cause. According to Paul Gilroy (1987: 95), the emergent police mobilization around questions of 'black crime' also served during the early 1970s as 'common ground' between senior and rank-and-file officers.

[9] Following falls in levels of recorded crime in the early 1990s it is also possible to detect (following a number of years during which senior officers had generally played down the police's crime-fighting capacity) a gradual increase in elite police confidence about the police's ability to deal with crime. In London, Paul Condon expressed a certain pride in the force's apparent success in targeting and reducing levels of burglary and 'mugging': 'through intelligence-led policing and partnership initiatives, we are making our great city a safer place to work, live and visit' (MPAR 1997: 2). Similar sentiments were expressed in Cheshire: 'Over recent years... there is no doubt that Cheshire has become a much safer place to live, work and visit. A very clear message can be drawn from the crime statistics and performance indicators in this report. That message is that it *is* possible to catch those who thieve, defraud, threaten or inflict violence, or peddle drugs' (CAR 1996: 4–5; emphasis in original).

[10] Mark himself noted, in an interview with Desmond Wilcox published in *The Listener* in 1977 ('Robert Mark on Villainy, Virtue and "Vanessa's Loonies"', 4 August 1997), that his forays into the realm of media and politics had tended to 'isolate' him from his peers in the senior police world.

'I think my colleagues generally disapproved of this very strongly', he opined, 'irrespective of any public good that might arise from it.' Interviewed for this study, one of the 'silent' chief constables who was the implicit target of Mark's attention (a man who says he felt 'no desire to thump the table') made oblique reference to this while discussing how ACPO presidents were appointed during this period: 'There were one or two who were quite rogue chief constables and they did just not get considered for the presidency at all'. One former chairperson of a metropolitan police authority echoes this view: 'there was an enormous amount of embarrassment, even anger, on the part of the police establishment about these mavericks who made life so difficult'.

[11] This outlook is, it appears, one shared by the Police Federation. 'It seems to me a trap', one of its spokespeople opined to us, 'to get too involved in social issues.'

[12] It was a common refrain among both the Home Office ministers and (especially) civil servants we spoke to that the 'police heroes' of the 1970s and 1980s had exercised little influence over government policy. As one senior civil servant reflected, 'they of course were mavericks. They didn't speak for anybody but themselves, and their forces as long as they were in charge. I maintain my position, that there may have been some louder noises being made, but they were not made by the leading members of the cast.'

[13] In 1981 not one of the forty-three serving chief constables had attended this course. Some ten years later 60 per cent had done so (Wall 1998: 227). In 1991, the Home Office made completion of the Senior Command Course (or what has now been redesignated the 'Strategic Leadership Development Programme') a condition of appointment to ACPO rank (assistant chief constable and above).

[14] Further details of this 'professionalization' of ACPO can be found in Barton (1996); Charman and Savage (1998); and Savage et al. (2000: ch. 3).

[15] The conditions of production of such 'rogue' figures have been further undermined by the Police and Magistrates' Courts Act 1994 (now s. 50(6) of the Police Act 1996), which placed all assistant and chief constables on renewable four- to seven-year contracts.

[16] The capacity of the police during this period to tap into and articulate the fears and longings of a significant section of the English populace (and the realization on the part of police leaders that such was the case) is interestingly revealed by the mute acceptance of (even perhaps welcome for) the police's confession in the late 1970s—during McNee's campaign for more police powers—to what Paul Condon was later to call 'noble cause corruption'. As Baxter and Koffman (1985: 1) comment, '[It is an] indication of the power and prestige of the police that an admission of

such unconditional and lawless behaviour should be accepted with such equanimity in a liberal democratic society'.

[17] There has throughout police discourse of recent decades appeared an unresolved contradiction between, on the one hand, this view of the police as an 'anvil' or 'bastion' holding steadfastly firm against the choppy waters that surround it, and, on the other, a conception of the police—much in evidence whenever police racism is under discussion—as merely 'a reflection of society', prone to being swept along by the prevailing cultural currents. Mark, at various times, sought to advance both these propositions.

[18] Consider in this regard the enthusiastic cultural reception given to probably the most prominent 'police hero' of the 1990s—Detective Superintendent Ray Mallon of Cleveland Police (Stenson 2000). While Mallon's get-tough, zero-tolerance, exclusively police-centred approach to the crime question, and his much publicized promise to resign if he did not reduce the local crime rate, generated great excitement in the tabloid press, it was notable that not one of the forty-three serving chief constables publicly supported his stance. Mallon was subsequently charged with a number of disciplinary offences relating to his time as superintendent in Cleveland, allegations that remained unproven and the subject of bitter dispute when he eventually resigned from the police in order to pursue a political career. In 2002 Mallon was elected Mayor of Middlesborough.

[19] Those (senior) police officers who continue to subscribe to this outlook (of whom there are still surely some) have thus come to think twice before emitting their opinions in public. One can see evidence of this, we think, in some of the unofficial police mutterings that followed the publication of the Macpherson Report (1999) into Steven Lawrence's murder, mutterings whose substance ('we can't arrest blacks these days') stood in stark contrast to Paul Condon's resolutely liberal—'we will tackle racism'—response; as well as in the 'off-the-record' remarks one sometimes hears in (senior) police circles about the 'guilt' of the Birmingham six and Guildford four.

Chapter 8

[1] In a recent critique, Walker (2000: 54–67) concedes that the doctrine offers a plausible—if ultimately misplaced—resolution of what he calls 'the paradox of police governance'—the paradox being that the national and local state is both the source of regulatory control over the police and, as a main beneficiary of the police's ordering capacity, part of the problem that regulation seeks to address. The solution constabulary independence purports to offer is one that restricts the state's ability to intervene in policing matters either on its own behalf, or in order to secure the interests of particular social groups, by placing a protective legal capsule around

police institutions. Such a view is flawed, Walker believes, by its failure to recognize the possibility and necessity in a democratic polity of distinguishing between legitimate and illegitimate forms of political 'interference' into policing, and by its inability to grasp the chronic limitations of law as a device for controlling police discretion (see also Jefferson and Grimshaw 1984: ch. 5; Loader 1996: ch. 1).

[2] It is noteworthy in this regard that police officers continue to swear the following oath of allegiance *to the Crown*: 'I solemnly and sincerely declare and affirm that I will well and truly serve our Sovereign Lady the Queen in the Office of Constable without favour or affection, malice or ill will, and that I will, to the best of my power, cause the peace to be kept and preserved, and prevent all offences against the persons and properties of Her Majesty's subjects, and that while I will continue to hold the said office I will, to the best of my skill and knowledge, discharge all duties of thereof faithfully according to law.'

[3] Further amalgamations in the wake of local government reorganization in 1974 reduced the total number of forces to the present forty-three.

[4] Governmental concerns about the quality of police leaders have been a recurrent feature of post-war policing—something that was illustrated during our conversations with former government ministers and civil servants by the use of phrases such as 'pedestrian sort of types', 'the occasional star in an otherwise evenly lit background' and 'less than fruitful' or 'dead wood' to characterize senior police management. This concern at least in part appeared to underpin the amalgamation programme in the 1960s—there being a feeling that whereas 'you might be able to find thirty or forty really top commanders', 'you wouldn't find 120' (retired Home Office official). It has also given rise to periodic bouts of interest in the idea of a direct-entry, 'officer class', something Margaret Thatcher is known to have 'been rather keen on' (former Conservative Home Secretary) in the late 1980s and early 1990s (see also, Baker 1993: 450). As Reiner (1980: 406) has noted, the possibility that the treatment of chief constables as cuckoos in the governmental nest represents a form of class prejudice against a body of people that are not—by origin—'one of us' (and who have as police officers been exposed to 'unsavoury' aspects of English society) cannot entirely be ruled out.

[5] One notable example of this concerns what one retired chief constable we interviewed described as the 'comical' force inspections of the 1950s and 1960s, a system that was recalled by many officers as combining symbolic ritual with random acts of thoroughness: 'There was actually a parade. They cleared the car park at divisional headquarters and the whole division paraded, in military terms, and the HMI inspected you. What you feared was of course that he'd stop in front of you—"what's your name", "get your pocket book out". And he would say, "tell me

about a case you've dealt with", and his staff officer would then take your pocket book from you and go into the building and he would follow it through the files' (retired chief constable, provincial force). 'Terrifying' though this must have been for the officers concerned, this mode of regulation—what one serving superintendent recalled as 'the white glove, dust on the top of the cupboard' approach—did not appear to result in an overly systematic enquiry into the organization: 'the inspection system was not there very much... There was one particular man called Colonel Inglis, he used to say, "the men were very well turned out on parade and the force is efficient" ' (retired Home Office official). It is worth recalling in this regard that those forces involved in fraud and corruption scandals during the 1950s were routinely issued with their efficiency certificates throughout this period (Hart 1963: 283–5).

[6] The Metropolitan Police had since its formation in 1829 been answerable to the Home Secretary rather than a police authority and was exempt from the arrangements set up by the 1964 Police Act. This remained the case until 1999, when the new Labour Government established the Greater London Police Authority.

[7] These relations, which had been declining since the mid-1970s, went into apparent free fall in the early part of the 1980s, as many Labour politicians locally and nationally became fierce critics of the police's handling of the riots, their increasing resort to paramilitary equipment and styles, and their role in a number of industrial conflicts—notably the 1984–5 miners' strike. They reached their nadir in the aftermath of the 1984 Labour Party Conference, at which the party passed resolutions calling for democratic control of the police, abolition of the Special Patrol Group, and the introduction of an independent complaints system. This prompted the president of the Police Federation, Leslie Curtis, to issue a coded—though barely coded—warning to the effect that the police might not be able to work with a future Labour government (Curtis 1984)—a 'warning' that was repeated in more polite terms by Metropolitan Police Commissioner, Kenneth Newman, in an address to the Howard League the following year (Newman 1985). One of those who drafted Curtis' speech conceded—during an interview with us—that 'it was deliberately intended to fire a shot across the bows of the Labour Party'.

[8] The police authorities were replaced by 'joint boards' comprised of councillors and magistrates from the district council areas covering the territory of the former metropolitan authorities. These proved to be generally more quiescent bodies than those they had replaced (Loveday 1991).

[9] Anderton's view of the proper role of politicians *vis-à-vis* the police is well illustrated by the eight-point 'prescription for effective crime prevention' he issued in 1985, the fifth of which reads as follows: 'that all political parties in this country give police the unequivocal and unqualified

support they deserve' (Anderton 1985*b*: 1208). One Home Office official we interviewed indicated his dismay at the tendency of chief officers to think about the wider world in this manner in the following terms: 'they used this phrase which I tried to change. They talked about civil servants, local politicians, newspaper editors and they used the phrase "he is very supportive of the police". I said I hate that expression. It carries with it the notion that they will support you whether you are right or wrong. Understanding, helpful, cooperative, yes, by all means. But this notion that they are supportive is a dangerous concept. You still hear it occasionally.'

[10] Conservative MP Edward Gardner speaking in a House of Commons debate on the Scarman Report (*Hansard*, vol. 16 col. 1016, 10 December 1981).

[11] The former chairperson of another metropolitan police authority similarly remarked to us that 'my hate mail was so enormous I stopped reading it. I couldn't cope'.

[12] The uses and effects of the little phrase 'anti-police' within recent English political discourse would repay some careful attention. Suffice it to note here that this phrase was an important structuring trope of police politics in the early 1980s; one that served—like an act of paint-throwing—to taint 'critics' of the police and leave them needing to 'clean themselves up' before they could continue—with any realistic hope of success—to advance their case. One also suspects that the repeated, ritual-istic, and, in all important respects, compulsory denials issued by such 'critics' ('we are not anti-police') rarely stood much chance of recovering the lost ground. In the political atmosphere of the time, the accusation 'anti-police' served to condense very effectively what many anxious, 'law-abiding' citizens (and a good proportion of newspaper editors) were already inclined to think and feel. The damage was done. There was no way back.

Two wider theoretical points arise from this. It illustrates, first, how the police's symbolic power can operate to shape the contours and limits of political discussion about the problem of order—determining, at the very least, the space within which politicians in search of elected office must position themselves. Even today, when this particular police power is less in evidence and arguably less secure, such politicians (especially those pursuing a liberal-left agenda) still have to tread relatively carefully over policing—and police-related—terrain, lest that telling attribution is once more ushered forth and put to practical use (though it is noteworthy that the ascription was rarely, if ever, applied to later Conservative assaults on the police). It reminds us, secondly, how the police are capable of evoking emotions that can be mobilized politically to forestall or disrupt the possibility of considered democratic deliberation over questions of crime, authority, and order—a situation that has no easily discernible parallel in other fields of public policy. A community worker we interviewed from inner-city Manchester neatly pinpointed the paradox this entails:

> When you give a group of people, in this instance the police force, power, real power, and they are the only people in the land that I know that have the power to take away your liberty... then unless you actually have some kind of accountable control on those people, being human beings, there's a real danger of abusing that power. I find it interesting that we put, or we try to put, blocks and limits on doctors, social workers, teachers—we have a range of systems in place. And it's quite interesting that the most powerful set of people, which is the police, when anybody talks about them, and talks about challenging them, people say 'you're anti-police'. But they never say you're 'anti-doctor', 'anti-teacher', 'anti-social worker'.

[13] The Forum was established—at a time of reportedly poor relations between the police and especially black youths in the Moss Side area of inner-city Manchester—following a public meeting attended by 'over 400 people'. One community worker recalled the moment thus: 'people wanted something that they could control, that they directed, that they influenced, because most PCC's [police consultative committees] are actually run by police authority officers'. The Forum has subsequently had to tread a difficult path between, on the one hand, pressing the police on issues that trouble local people (stop and search, allegations of violence towards suspects, and so forth) and thereby maintaining confidence locally; and, on the other hand, avoiding the allegation that they are 'anti-police'. The arrival of a senior management team in Greater Manchester Police 'with a preparedness to admit there were problems' and a willingness to 'address them' (male community worker, inner city Manchester) was no small help in this regard.

[14] In the midst of this shifting climate, the police's 'vested interests' and capacity to generate warmly supportive passions among elements of the English populace came to be seen by some Conservatives as an irritant and obstacle to reform. Having recalled how he had failed to persuade Margaret Thatcher to reform radically the structure of the police in the late 1980s (she had apparently retorted, 'I'm too busy dealing with the economic issues, I can't fight everybody'), one former senior Conservative backbencher opined to us: 'hells bells, dealing with doctors and people like that, very difficult. To take on the Police Federation, ACPO, this great army of Middle England "losing our boys in blue" and all the rest of it. You just couldn't do it, so you had to proceed by stealth'.

[15] Sir Patrick Sheehy is head of the multinational conglomerate British American Tobacco. The enquiry team comprised two academics and two other members from a commercial background.

[16] This clash over the social meanings of policing is nicely illustrated by the following account, reported to us by one of the civil servants we

interviewed: 'I'd love to tell your recorder a short story about Sheehy. It was about the performance-related pay of chief officers. Sheehy was of course very keen on it. He came to see Sir Patrick Mayhew [Secretary of State for Northern Ireland], who in very short order informed Sir Patrick Sheehy, "that if he, the Secretary of State for Northern Ireland, responsible for the RUC, felt that he could get more out of a chief constable in the RUC than he was already getting by paying a bit more money, he wouldn't want the man anywhere near him, thank you very much." Sheehy had just never seen this worldview before. It was a total non-meeting.' It is noteworthy in this regard that the Police Federation's campaign against Sheehy made much of the Report's apparent insult to the bravery and sacrifice of RUC officers (*Police Review*, 23 July 1993).

[17] It is noteworthy that a strong—if not always obviously confident— Labour government began in 2001 to re-engage the police on these issues (Home Office 2001: ch. 6).

[18] The pervasive mood of fundamental upheaval that obtained at this juncture was exacerbated in December 1993 when Michael Howard set up an *internal* Home Office review into police 'core and ancillary tasks' under Ingrid Posen. It was widely feared in police circles that this was to be a vehicle for a radical cost-cutting exercise which would see many supposedly 'ancillary' police functions transferred to other (commercial) agencies (see *Police Review*, 15 July 1994; Smith 1994). The final report turned out, however, to be something of a damp squib, recommending only that a number of mainly uncontentious police responsibilities could more effectively be assumed by others (Home Office 1995; for some further context and a critique, see Loader 1997: 145–9).

[19] Introduced by the Local Government Act 1999, 'Best Value' places a legal requirement on local authorities, police, and fire services to 'make arrangements to secure continuous improvements in the way [their] functions are exercised, having regard to a combination of economy, efficiency and effectiveness' (cited in Geddes and Martin 2000: 380). The Audit Commission is afforded a key strategic role in the audit and inspection regime that accompanies these arrangements (see generally, Geddes and Martin 2000; and, in respect of policing, Alexander 2000).

Chapter 9

[1] For a cognate approach to—changing—public attitudes towards criminal justice and sentencing policy see Chapman *et al.* (2002); Roberts *et al.* (2003).

[2] All this could of course be said to be a matter of electoral necessity, the felt imperative to secure and retain a stock of political capital (what politician, for instance, would dare to suggest that we should cut police

numbers and spend the money elsewhere—on adult literacy, say, or children in care?). This may be so. But such a retort requires one to concede that the affective allure of policing continues to suffuse the outlooks and demands of what today is an apparently more informed and sceptical English populace.

[3] It is no part of our purpose here to deny that such victim mobilization often stems from legitimate grievances or injustice. We merely wish to highlight the tendency of such grievances today to be articulated, and responded to, through an individuated discourse of rights, legal redress, and compensation in preference to the political language of democracy and social justice—a process, one might say, that turns *victims* into *Victims*. The relative absence of questions of *democratic* accountability from the gamut of official reactions to the racist murder of Stephen Lawrence (Macpherson 1999; Home Office 1999*a*) can in part be interpreted in these terms.

[4] The contribution a now bewildering array of media forms makes to the production of English policing culture has not—for reasons we set out in Chapter 2—figured prominently in the present study. This is not, however, to disregard the significance of this role, nor to dispute the need for further dedicated social enquiry in this field. Among the topics such investigation might fruitfully consider is the way in which the media today operate as an *institution of police governance*—shaping (even, on occasions, driving) police policy and practice and forming a significant part of the cultural and political environment that forces are routinely required to attend to and try, as best they can, to 'manage' (Mawby 2002). This daily scrutiny has undoubtedly increased the public visibility and transparency of policing, and in this sense its accountability. But it has done so in a manner that is selective and unsystematic in how it takes up (and, just as rapidly, drops) police stories and 'scandals', one that plays a key role in fuelling the volatile and contradictory emotional ferment so often surrounds policing controversies today (cf. O'Malley 1999). The part played by the *Daily Mail* in the Stephen Lawrence case offers a telling case in point here—the *Mail*, you may recall, campaigned vigorously to highlight police failings in pursuing those it named on its front page as 'racist murderers', only to perform a *volte-face* in the wake of the Macpherson Report when it decided that 'our' police stood in need of stout defence from Macpherson's critique. So too does the recent high-profile media coverage of paedophiles and child murders, coverage that now routinely appears to combine celebration of the heroic idea of policing with populist dissection and—sometimes obstructive—vilification of the ways in which it is actually being performed (see Silverman and Wilson 2002: ch. 8).

[5] An analogy might be drawn in these respects with those Catholic believers who—faced with authoritative public knowledge of criminal

sexual assaults committed against boys by a number of Catholic priests—nonetheless find ways of rescuing the infallible doctrine (Catholicism) from its embodiment in a fallible institution (the Catholic church). We are indebted to Laurence Lustgarten for this point.

[6] Hence the almost intuitive resort to various forms of denial and neutralization when faced with such officially acknowledged matters as miscarriages of justice (the Guildford four, Birmingham six...) and police failures to respond seriously and professionally to violence towards members of black and ethnic minority communities (notably in the case of Stephen Lawrence). Such denials generally start from one of two unstated premises: either '*they* were guilty anyway' or '*our* police could not possibly do such a thing'.

[7] It is notable that these movements and campaigns—though they in many cases involve *economically* marginalized groups and make demands entailing both recognition *and* redistribution (Fraser 1997)—tend not to be organized explicitly around class. The question of class does, by contrast, continue to condition the outlook of those we termed 'atheists', their demands for policing encompassing not only a claim for a 'fairer' share of policing resources, but also a concern with the lack of recognition shown by the police to 'the local community' (and especially its young).

[8] We should not entirely underestimate the potentially positive outcomes of such careerist motivations. Hypocrisy, as Jon Elster reminds us, can have civilizing effects (Elster 1997: 12).

[9] One of the present authors has begun elsewhere to advance this more conceptually expansive project: see Loader and Walker (2001).

[10] Brian Barry (2001: 79) expresses much the same point in the following more general terms: 'we cannot expect the outcomes of democratic politics to be just in a society that contains large numbers of people who feel no sense of empathy with their fellow citizens and do not have any identification with their lot. This sense of solidarity is fostered by common institutions.'

[11] For a fuller specification of such possible institutional arrangements, and the normative democratic principles that underpin them, see Loader (1996: ch. 7; 2000).

References

Abrams, P. (1988). 'Notes on the Difficulty of Studying the State'. *Journal of Historical Sociology*, 1/1: 58–89.

Alderson, J. (1979). *Policing Freedom*. Plymouth: Macdonald and Evans.

——(1984). *Law and Disorder*. London: Hamish Hamilton.

——and Stead, J. (eds.) (1973). *The Police We Deserve*. London: Wolfe Publishing.

Alexander, A. (2000). 'The Police and *Best Value*: Applicability and Adaptation'. *Policing and Society*, 10/3: 263–76.

Alexander, J. (1989). *Structure and Meaning: Relinking Classical Sociology*. New York: Columbia University Press.

Alibhai Brown, Y. (2001). *Who Do We Think We Are?* Harmondsworth: Penguin.

Allen, J., Livingstone, S., and Reiner, R. (1998). 'True Lies: Changing Images of Crime in British Postwar Cinema'. *European Journal of Communication*, 13/1: 53–75.

Almond, G., and Verba, S. (1963). *The Civic Culture: Political Attitudes and Democracy in Five Nations*. Princeton, NJ: Princeton University Press.

Anderson, B. (1991). *Imagined Communities: Reflections on the Origin and Spread of Nationalism* (rev. edn.). London: Verso.

Anderton, J. (1982). 'Accountability'. *Police Review*, 6 February, 268–9.

——(1982). 'The Reality of Community Policing'. *Police Review*, 26 March, 582–6.

——(1985a). 'How an Earth do they Expect us to Cope?'. *Police Review*, 15 November, 2312–13.

——(1985b). 'What Price Law and Order?'. *Police Review*, 14 June, 1206–8.

Arendt, H. (1970). *On Violence*. Harmondsworth: Penguin.

Audit Commission (1993). *Helping with Enquiries: Tackling Crime Effectively*. London: HMSO.

——(1996). *Streetwise: Effective Police Patrol*. London: HMSO.

Baker, K. (1993). *The Turbulent Years: My Life in Politics*. London: Faber & Faber.

Baldwin, R., and Kinsey, R. (1982). *Police Powers and Politics*. London: Quartet Books.

Banton, M. (1964). *The Policeman in the Community*. London: Tavistock.

Barclay, G., and Tavares, C. (eds.) (1999). *Digest 4: Information on the Criminal Justice System in England and Wales*. London: Home Office.

Barry, B. (2001). *Culture and Equality: An Egalitarian Critique of Multiculturalism.* Cambridge: Polity.

Barton, M. (1996). 'Double Vision'. *Policing Today*, April: 8–9.

Bauman, Z. (1987). *Legislators and Interpreters: Modernity, Post-modernity and Intellectuals.* Oxford: Basil Blackwell.

—— (1990). *Thinking Sociologically.* Oxford: Basil Blackwell.

—— (1992). *Intimations of Postmodernity.* London: Routledge.

—— (1998). *Globalization: The Human Consequences.* Cambridge: Polity.

—— (1999). *In Search of Politics.* Cambridge: Polity.

—— (2000). *Liquid Modernity.* Cambridge: Polity.

—— (2001). *Community: Seeking Safety in an Insecure World.* Cambridge: Polity.

Baxter, J., and Koffman, L. (1985). 'Introduction', in J. Baxter and L. Koffman (eds.), *Police: The Constitution and the Community.* Abingdon: Professional Books.

Bayley, D. (1985). *Patterns of Policing.* New Brunswick, NJ: Rutgers University Press.

—— (1994). *Police for the Future.* Oxford: Oxford University Press.

—— (2002). 'Policing Hate: What Can be Done?'. *Policing and Society*, 12/2: 83–91.

—— and Shearing, C. (1996). 'The Future of Policing'. *Law and Society Review*, 30/3: 585–606.

Beck, U. (2002). 'Zombie Categories: Interview with Ulrich Beck', in U. Beck and E. Beck-Gernsheim, *Individualization.* London: Sage.

Beckett, K. (1997). *Making Crime Pay: Law and Order in Contemporary American Politics.* Oxford: Oxford University Press.

Beetham, D. (1999). *Democracy and Human Rights.* Cambridge: Polity.

Bellamy, R. (1999). *Liberalism and Pluralism: Towards a Politics of Compromise.* London: Routledge.

Belson, W. (1975). *The Public and the Police.* London: Harper & Row.

Berki, R. (1986). *Security and Society: Reflections on Law, Order and Politics.* London: Dent.

Berman, M. (1983). *All That is Solid Melts into Air: The Experience of Modernity.* London: Verso.

Billig, M. (1995). *Banal Nationalism.* London: Sage.

Bittner, E. (1990). *Aspects of Policework.* Boston, Mass.: NorthEastern.

Blair, I. (1998). 'Where do the Police Fit into Policing?', speech to Association of Chief Police Officers' Conference, July.

—— (2002a). 'Surprise News: Policing Works', paper presented to the British Criminology Conference, Keele University, 17–20 July.

—— (2002b). 'The Policing Revolution: Back to the Beat'. *New Statesman*, 23 September, 21–3.

Bottoms, A., and Stevenson, S. (1992). 'What Went Wrong?: Criminal Justice Policy in England and Wales, 1945–70', in D. Downes (ed.), *Unravelling Criminal Justice*. Basingstoke: Macmillan.

—— and Wiles, P. (1995). 'Crime and Insecurity in the City', in C. Fijnaut, J. Goethals, T. Peters, and L. Walgrave (eds.). *Changes in Crime, Society and Criminal Justice in Europe, Vol. 1*. The Hague: Kluwer.

Bourdieu, P. (1987). 'The Force of Law: Toward a Sociology of the Juridical Field'. *Hastings Law Journal*, 38: 805–57.

—— (1990). *The Logic of Practice*. Cambridge: Polity.

—— (1991). *Language and Symbolic Power*. Cambridge: Polity.

—— (1998). *Practical Reason: On the Theory of Action*. Cambridge: Polity.

Boutellier, H. (2000). *Crime and Morality: The Significance of Criminal Justice in Postmodern Culture*. Dordrecht: Kluwer.

Bowling, B. (1999). *Violent Racism: Victimisation, Policing and Social Context*. Oxford: Oxford University Press.

Bradley, D., Walker, N., and Wilkie, R. (1986). *Managing the Police*. Hemel Hempstead: Harvester.

Brake, M., and Hale, C. (1992). *Public Order and Private Lives*. London: Routledge.

Bridges, L. (1999). 'The Lawrence Inquiry: Incompetence, Corruption and Institutional Racism'. *Journal of Law and Society*, 26/3: 298–322.

Brodeur, J.-P. (1983). 'High Policing and Low Policing: Remarks About the Policing of Political Activities'. *Social Problems*, 30/5: 507–20.

Brogden, M. (1977). 'A Police Authority: The Denial of Conflict'. *Sociological Review*, 25/2: 325–49.

—— (1982). *The Police: Autonomy and Consent*. London: Academic Press.

—— (1991). *On the Mersey Beat: An Oral History of Policing Liverpool Between the Wars*. Oxford: Oxford University Press.

Brown, J. (1997). 'Equal Opportunities and the Police in England and Wales: Past, Present and Future Possibilities', in P. Francis, P. Davies, and V. Jupp (eds.), *Policing Futures: The Police, Law Enforcement and the Twenty-First Century*. Basingstoke: Macmillan.

—— and Heidensohn, F. (2000). *Gender and Policing*. Basingstoke: Palgrave.

Brown, W. (1995). *States of Injury: Power and Freedom in Late Modernity*. Princeton, NJ: Princeton University Press.

Burke, M. (1993). *Coming out of the Blue*. London: Cassell.

Butler, A. J. (1984). *Police Management*. London: Gower.

—— (1992). 'Police and the Citizen's Charter'. *Policing*, 8/1: 40–50.

Cain, M. (1973). *Society and the Policeman's Role*. London: Routledge and Kegan Paul.

Callaghan, J. (1987). *Time and Chance*. London: Collins.

Campbell, B. (1993). *Goliath: Britain's Dangerous Places*. London: Methuen.

Carson, K. (1984). 'Policing the Periphery: The Development of Scottish Policing 1795–1900: Part I'. *Australian and New Zealand Journal of Criminology* 17: 207–32.

——(1985). 'Policing the Periphery: The Development of Scottish Policing 1795–1900: Part II'. *Australian and New Zealand Journal of Criminology* 18: 3–16.

Castells, M. (1993). 'European Cities: The Information Society and the Global Economy'. *Tijdschrift voor Economische en Sociale Geografie*, 84: 247–57.

——(1996). *The Information Age: Economy, Society and Culture—Vol. I, The Rise of the Network Society*. Oxford: Basil Blackwell.

——(1997). *The Information Age: Economy, Society and Culture—Vol. II, The Power of Identity*. Oxford: Basil Blackwell.

Cathcart, B. (1999). *The Case of Stephen Lawrence*. London: Viking.

Chadwick, W. (1974). *Reminiscences of a Chief Constable*. Ilkley: Scolar Press.

Chan, J. (1997). *Changing Police Culture: Policing in a Multi-Cultural Society*. Cambridge: Cambridge University Press.

Chapman, B., Mirrlees-Black, C., and Brown, C. (2002). *Improving Public Attitudes to the Criminal Justice System: The Impact of Information* (Home Office Research Study 245). London: Home Office.

Charman, S., and Savage, S. (1998). 'Singing From the Same Hymn Sheet: The Professionalisation of the Association of Chief Police Officers'. *International Journal of Police Science and Management*, 1: 6–16.

Chibnall, S. (1979). 'The Metropolitan Police and the News Media', in S. Holdaway (ed.), *The British Police*. London: Edward Arnold.

Christie, N. (2000). *Crime Control as Industry: Towards Gulags Western Style* (rev. edn). London: Routledge.

Clarke, A. (1983). 'Holding the Blue Lamp: Television and the Police in Britain'. *Crime and Social Justice*, 19: 44–51.

——(1986). ' "This is not the Boy Scouts": Television Police Series and Definitions of Law and Order', in T. Bennett, C. Mercer, and J. Woollacott (eds.), *Popular Culture and Social Relations*. Milton Keynes: Open University Press.

Clarke, J., and Newman, J. (1997). *The Managerial State: Power, Politics and Ideology in the Remaking of Social Welfare*. London: Sage.

Clarke, K. (1993). 'My Plans to Improve the Police'. *Police Review*, 26 March, 14–15.

Cohen, P. (1979). 'Policing the Working Class City', in B. Fine, R. Kinsey, J. Lea, S. Picciotto, and J. Young (eds.), *Capitalism and the Rule of Law*. London: Hutchinson.

——(1988). 'The Perversions of Inheritance: Studies in the Making of Multi-Racist Britain', in P. Cohen and H. S. Bains (eds.), *Multi-Racist Britain*. Basingstoke: Macmillan.

Cohen, S. (2001). *States of Denial: Knowing about Atrocities and Suffering*. Cambridge: Polity.

Collini, S. (1999). *English Pasts: Essays in History and Culture*. Oxford: Oxford University Press.

Connerton, P. (1989). *How Societies Remember*. Cambridge: Cambridge University Press.

Corrigan, P., and Sayer, A. (1985). *The Great Arch: English State Formation as Cultural Revolution*. Oxford: Basil Blackwell.

Cowell, D., Jones, T., and Young, J. (eds.) (1982). *Policing the Riots*. London: Junction Books.

Cox, B., Shirley, J., and Short, M. (1977). *The Fall of Scotland Yard*. Harmondsworth: Penguin.

Cox, G. (1984). 'Community Priorities'. *Police Review*, 16 November, 2208–9.

Coyles, D. (1993). 'These Are No Myths'. *Police Review*, 1 October, 22–3.

Crank, J. P. (1994). 'Watchman and Community: Myth and Institutionalization in Policing'. *Law and Society Review*, 28/2: 325–51.

Critchley, T. (1978). *A History of Police in England and Wales*. London: Constable.

Curtis, L. (1984). 'What Leslie Curtis Really Said'. *Police Review*, 12 October, 1966–7.

Dahrendorf, R. (1985). *Law and Order*. London: Sweet & Maxwell.

de Lint, W. (1997). 'The Constable Generalist as Exemplary Citizen, Networker, and Problem-Solver: Some Implications'. *Policing and Society* 6/4: 247–64.

——(1999). 'A Post-modern Turn in Policing: Policing as Pastiche?' *International Journal of the Sociology of Law*, 27: 127–52.

den Boer, M. (1999). 'Internationalization: A Challenge to Police Organizations in Europe', in R. I. Mawby (ed.), *Policing Across the World: Issues for the Twenty-first Century*. London: University College London Press.

Dennis, N. (ed.) (1997). *Zero Tolerance: Policing a Free Society*. London: Institute of Economic Affairs.

——Erdos, G., and Al-Shahi, A. (2000). *Racist Murder and Pressure Group Politics: The Macpherson Report and the Police*. London: Civitas.

Dixon, D. (1997). *Law in Policing: Legal Regulation and Police Practices*. Oxford: Clarendon.

Douglas, M. (1987). *How Institutions Think*. London: Routledge and Kegan Paul.

Douglas, M., and Isherwood. B. (1979). *The World of Goods: Towards an Anthropology of Consumption*. Harmondsworth: Penguin.

Downes, D., and Morgan, R. (1997). 'Dumping the "Hostages to Fortune": The Politics of Law and Order in Post-war Britain', in M. Maguire, R. Morgan, and R. Reiner (eds.), *The Oxford Handbook of Criminology* (2nd edn). Oxford: Oxford University Press.

Durkheim, E. (1915). *The Elementary Forms of Religious Life*. London: Allen and Unwin.

——(1992/1957). *Professional Ethics and Civic Morals*. (Trans. C. Bookfield). London: Routledge.

Eaton, M. (1995). 'A Fair Cop: Viewing the Effects of Canteen Culture in *Prime Suspect* and *Between the Lines*', in D. Kidd-Hewitt and R. Osborne (eds.), *Crime and the Media: The Postmodern Spectacle*. London: Pluto.

Elias, N. (1985). *Involvement and Detachment*. Oxford: Oxford University Press.

Ellison, G., and Mulcahy, A. (eds.) (2001). *Special Issue of Policing and Society on 'Policing in Northern Ireland'*. 11/3–4.

——and Smyth, J. (2000). *The Crowned Harp: Policing Northern Ireland*. London: Pluto.

Elster, J. (1997). 'Introduction', in J. Elster (ed.), *Deliberative Democracy*. Cambridge: Cambridge University Press.

Emsley, C. (1992). 'The English Bobby: An Indulgent Tradition' in R. Porter (ed.), *Myths of the English*. Cambridge: Polity.

——(1993). 'Peasants, Gendarmes and State Formation', in M. Fulbrook (ed.), *National Histories and European History*. London: University College Press.

——(1996). *The English Police: A Political and Social History* (2nd edn). Harlow: Longman.

——(2000). *Gendarmes and the State in Nineteenth-Century Europe*. Oxford: Oxford University Press.

Ericson, R. (1994). 'The Division of Expert Knowledge in Policing and Security'. *British Journal of Sociology*, 45/2: 149–75.

——Baranek, P., and Chan, J. (1991). *Representing Order*. Milton Keynes: Open University Press.

——and Haggerty, K. (1997). *Policing the Risk Society*. Oxford: Clarendon.

Felson, M. (1998). *Crime and Everyday Life* (2nd edn). Thousand Oaks, Cal.: Pine Forge Press.

Fentress, J., and Wickham, C. (1992). *Social Memory*. Oxford: Basil Blackwell.

Field, S. (1990). *Trends in Crime and Their Interpretation: A Study of Recorded Crime in Postwar England and Wales* (Home Office Research Study No. 119). London: Home Office.

Fine, B., and Millar, D. (eds.) (1984). *Policing the Miners' Strike*. London: Lawrence and Wishart.

Fishman, M., and Cavender, G. (1998). *Entertaining Crime: Television Reality Programmes*. New York: Aldine de Gruyter.

Fitzgerald, M. (2000). *Stop and Search in London*. <www.met.police.uk/police/mp>.

——Hough, M., Joseph, I., and Qureshi, T. (2002). *Policing for London*. Cullompton: Willan.

Fraser, N. (1997). *Justice Interruptus: Critical Reflections on the 'Postsocialist' Condition*. London: Routledge.

Gamble, A. (1988). *The Free Economy and the Strong State: The Politics of Thatcherism*. Basingstoke: Macmillan.

——(1994). *Britain in Decline: Economic Policy, Political Strategy and the British State* (4th edn). Basingstoke: Macmillan.

——(2000). *Politics and Fate*. Cambridge: Polity.

Garland, D. (1990). *Punishment and Modern Society: A Study in Social Theory*. Oxford: Clarendon.

——(2000). 'The Culture of High Crime Societies: Some Preconditions of Recent "Law and Order" Policies'. *British Journal of Criminology*, 40/3: 347–75.

——(2001). *The Culture of Control: Crime and Social Order in Contemporary Society*. Oxford: Oxford University Press.

Geddes, M., and Martin, S. (2000). 'The Policy and Politics of Best Value: Currents, Crosscurrents and Undercurrents in the New Regime'. *Policy and Politics*, 28/3: 379–95.

Geertz, C. (1973). *The Interpretation of Cultures*. New York: Basic Books.

——(1983). *Local Knowledge: Further Essays in Interpretive Anthropology*. New York: Basic Books.

Giddens, A. (1979). *Central Problems in Social Theory*. London: Macmillan.

——(1990). *The Consequences of Modernity*. Cambridge: Polity.

——(1991). *Modernity and Self-Identity*. Cambridge: Polity.

——(1994). 'Living in a Post-Traditional Society', in U. Beck, A. Giddens, and S. Lash, *Reflexive Modernization: Politics, Tradition and Aesthetics in the Modern Social Order*. Cambridge: Polity.

——(1998). *The Third Way: The Renewal of Social Democracy*. Cambridge: Polity.

Gilroy, P. (1987). *There Ain't No Black in the Union Jack: The Cultural Politics of Race and Nation*. London: Routledge.

——(2002). 'Joined-up Politics and Postcolonial Melancholia', in S. Lash and M. Featherstone (eds.), *Recognition and Difference: Politics, Identity, Multiculture*. London: Sage.

Girling, E., Loader, I., and Sparks, R. (2000). *Crime and Social Change in Middle England: Questions of Order in an English Town*. London: Routledge.

Goldsmith, A. (2003). 'Policing Weak States: Citizen Safety and State Responsibility'. *Policing and Society*, 13/1: 3–21.

——and Lewis, C. (eds.) (2000). *Civilian Oversight of Policing: Governance, Democracy and Human Rights*. Oxford: Hart.

Goldstein, H. (1990). *Problem-oriented Policing*. New York: MacGraw-Hill.

Goldthorpe, J., Lockwood, D., Bechhofer, F., and Platt, J. (1969). *The Affluent Worker in the Class Structure*. Cambridge: Cambridge University Press.

Gorer, G. (1955). *Exploring English Character*. London: Cresset.

Gouldner, A. (1976). *The Dialectic of Ideology and Technology*. London: Macmillan.

Gray, J. (1995). *Beyond the New Right*. London: Routledge.

Greater London Council (1983). *A New Police Authority for London (Discussion Paper No. 1)*. London: Greater London Council.

Gusfield, J. R. (1981). *The Culture of Public Problems: Drinking–Driving and the Symbolic Order*. Chicago: University of Chicago Press.

Hain, P. (ed.) (1979). *Policing the Police*. London: Calder.

Halbwachs, M. (1992/1941). *On Collective Memory*. (Ed. and trans. L. A. Cover) Chicago, Ill: University of Chicago Press.

Hale, C. (1996). 'Fear of Crime: A Review of the Literature'. *International Review of Victimology*, 4/1: 79–150.

Hall, S. (1980a). 'Reformism and the Legislation of Consent', in National Deviancy Conference (ed.), *Permissiveness and Control: The Fate of the Sixties Legislation*. Basingstoke: Macmillan.

——(1980b). *Drifting into a Law and Order Society*. London: Cobden Trust.

——(1980c). 'Encoding/Decoding', in S. Hall, D. Hobson, A. Lowe, and P. Willis (eds.), *Culture, Media, Language*. London: Routledge.

——(1988). *The Hard Road to Renewal*. London: Verso.

——(1991). 'Old and New Identities, Old and New Ethnicities', in A. King (ed.), *Culture, Globalization and the World-System*. Basingstoke: Macmillan.

——Clarke, J., Critcher, C., Jefferson, T., and Roberts, B. (1978). *Policing the Crisis: Mugging, Law and Order and the State*. London: Macmillan.

Hart, J. (1951). *The British Police*. London: Allen & Unwin.

——(1963). 'Some Reflections on the Report of the Royal Commission on the Police'. *Public Law*. Autumn: 283–304.

Harvey, D. (1989). *The Condition of Post-Modernity*. Oxford: Basil Blackwell.

Hay, C. (1996). *Re-stating Social and Political Change*. Buckingham: Open University Press.

Heelas, P., Lash, S., and Morris, P. (eds.) (1996). *Detraditionalization: Critical Reflections on Authority and Identity*. Oxford: Basil Blackwell.

Heffer, S. (1999). *Nor Shall My Sword: The Reinvention of England*. London: Phoenix.

Heidensohn, F. (1992). *Women in Control? The Role of Women in Law Enforcement*. Oxford: Oxford University Press.

Her Majesty's Inspectorate of Constabulary (1997). *Winning the Race: Policing Plural Communities*. London: The Stationery Office.

——(1999). *Winning the Race Revisited*. London: The Stationery Office.

Hermon, J. (1997). *Holding the Line*. Dublin: Gill and Macmillan.

Hirschman, A. O. (1991). *The Rhetoric of Reaction: Perversity, Futility, Jeopardy*. Cambridge, Mass.: Harvard University Press.

Hirst, M. (1991). 'What do We Mean by Quality?'. *Policing*, 7/3: 183–93.

Hitchens, P. (1999). *The Abolition of Britain: The British Cultural Revolution from Lady Chatterley to Tony Blair*. London: Quartet Books.

Hobsbawm, E. (1994). *The Age of Extremes: The Short Twentieth Century, 1914–1991*. London: Michael Joseph.

Hoggart, R. (1988). *A Local Habitation: Life and Times, Vol. 1, 1918–40*. London: Chatto and Windus.

Holdaway, S. (ed.) (1979). *The British Police*. London: Edward Arnold.

——(1983). *Inside the British Police*. Oxford: Basil Blackwell.

——(1991). *Recruiting a Multi-Racial Police Force*. London: HMSO.

——(1996). *The Racialisation of British Policing*. Basingstoke: Macmillan.

——and Barron, A. (1997). *Resigners: The Experience of Black and Asian Police Officers*. Basingstoke: Macmillan.

Hollway, W., and Jefferson, T. (2000). 'The Role of Anxiety in Fear of Crime', in T. Hope and R. Sparks (eds.), *Crime, Risk and Insecurity: Law and Order in Everyday Life and Political Discourse*. London: Routledge.

Home Office (1947). *Police Post-war Committee, Higher Training for the Police Service in England and Wales*. London: HMSO. Cmd. 707.

——(1949). *Report of the Committee on Police Conditions of Service: Parts I and II (Chairman: Lord Oaksey)*. London: HMSO. Cmd. 7674 and 7831.

——(1959). *Report of the Tribunal Appointed to Inquire into the Allegation of Assault on John Waters*. London: HMSO.

——(1961a). *Royal Commission on the Police: Interim Report*. London: HMSO. Cmd. 1222.

——(1961b). *Police Training In England and Wales*. London: HMSO. Cmd. 1450.

——(1962). *Royal Commission on the Police: Final Report*. London: HMSO. Cmd. 1728.

——(1967). *Police Manpower, Equipment and Efficiency: Reports of Three Working Parties*. London: HMSO.

Home Office (1978). *Committee of Inquiry on the Police: Reports on Negotiating Machinery and Pay*. London: HMSO. Cmd. 7283.

——(1981). *Royal Commission on Criminal Procedure: Report and Law and Procedure*. London: Home Office. Cmd. 8092.

——(1993a). *Royal Commission of Criminal Justice: Report*. London: Home Office. Cm 2263.

——(1993b). *Police Reform: A Police Service for the Twenty-First Century*. London: HMSO. Cm 2281.

——(1995). *Review of Core and Ancillary Tasks: Final Report*. London: HMSO.

——(1999a). *The Stephen Lawrence Inquiry: Home Secretary's Action Plan*. London: The Stationery Office.

——(1999b). *Statistics on Race and the Criminal Justice System*. London: The Stationery Office.

——(2001). *Policing a New Century: A Blueprint for Reform*. London: Home Office. Cm 5326.

Hood, C. (1998). *The Art of the State: Culture, Rhetoric and Public Management*. Oxford: Oxford University Press.

Hope, T. (1997). 'Inequality and the Future of Community Crime Prevention', in S. P. Lab (ed.), *Crime Prevention at a Crossroads*. Cincinnati, Ohio: Anderson Publishing.

——and Sparks, R. (eds.) (2000). *Crime, Risk and Insecurity: Law and Order in Everyday Life and Political Discourse*. London: Routledge.

Hough, M. (1995). *Anxiety About Crime: Findings from the 1994 British Crime Survey*. London: Home Office.

——and Mayhew, P. (1983). *The First British Crime Survey*. London: Home Office.

Humphry, D. (1972). *Police Power and Black People*. London: Panther.

Hurd, G. (1979). 'The Television Presentation of the Police', in S. Holdaway (ed.), *The British Police*. London: Edward Arnold.

Hutton, W. (1995). *The State We're In*. London: Jonathon Cape.

I'Anson, J., and Wiles, P. (1995). *The Sedgefield Community Force*. Sheffield: Centre for Criminological and Legal Research, University of Sheffield.

Independent Committee of Inquiry (1989). *Policing in Hackney 1945–1984*. London: Karia Press/Roach Family Support Committee.

Independent Inquiry Panel (1985). *Leon Brittan's Visit to Manchester University Students' Union, 1st March 1985*. Manchester: Manchester City Council.

Inglis, F. (1988). *Popular Culture and Political Power*. Brighton: Harvester.

Innes, M. (2002). 'Organizational Communication and the Symbolic Construction of Police Murder Investigations'. *British Journal of Sociology*, 53/1: 67–87.

Institute of Race Relations (1978). *Police Against Black People*. London: Institute of Race Relations.

Jefferson, T. (1990). *The Case Against Paramilitary Policing*. Buckingham: Open University Press.

——and Grimshaw, R. (1984). *Controlling the Constable: Police Accountability in England and Wales*. London: Muller.

——McLaughlin, E., and Robertson, L. (1988). 'Monitoring the Monitors: Accountability, Democracy and Police Watching in Britain'. *Contemporary Crises*, 12/2: 91–106.

Jenkins, R. (1991). *A Life at the Centre*. Basingstoke: Macmillan.

Jessop, B., Bonnet, K., Bromley, S., and Ling, T. (1988). *Thatcherism: A Tale of Two Nations*. Cambridge: Polity.

Johnston, L. (1999). *Policing Britain: Risk, Security and Governance*. Harlow: Longman.

Joint Consultative Committee (1990). *Operational Policing Review*. London: Surbiton.

Jones, M. (1980). *Organisational Aspects of Police Behaviour*. Farnborough: Gower.

Jones, T. (2001). 'Review of Robert Reiner's, *The Politics of the Police (3rd edn)*'. *Criminal Justice* 1/4: 480–81.

——and Newburn, T. (1997). *Policing After the Act*. London: Policy Studies Institute.

——and——(1998). *Private Security and Public Policing*. Oxford: Clarendon.

——and——(2001). *Widening Access: Improving Police Relations with Hard to Reach Groups*. London: Home Office.

——MacLean, B., and Young, J. (1986). *The Islington Crime Survey: Crime, Victimization and Policing in Inner City London*. Aldershot: Gower.

Jordan, G., and Weeden, C. (1995). *Cultural Politics: Class, Gender, Race and the Postmodern World*. Oxford: Basil Blackwell.

Judge, T. (1994). *The Force of Persuasion*. Surbiton: Police Federation.

Karstedt, S. (2002). 'Emotions and Criminal Justice'. *Theoretical Criminology*, 6/3: 299–317.

Kavanagh, D. (1987). *Thatcherism and British Politics: The End of Consensus?* Oxford: Oxford University Press.

Keane, J. (1998). *Civil Society: Old Images, New Visions*. Cambridge: Polity.

Keith, M. (1993). *Race, Riots and Policing: Lore and Disorder in a Multi-Racist Society*. London: University College London Press.

Kershaw, C., Budd, T., Kinshott, G., Mattinson, J., Mayhew, P., and Myhill, A. (2000). *The 2000 British Crime Survey*. London: Home Office.

Kettle, M. (1979). 'Anderton's Way'. *New Society*, 8 March: 550–52.

——(1985*a*). 'The National Reporting Centre and the 1984 Miners' Strike', in B. Fine and R. Millar (eds.), *Policing the Miners' Strike*. London: Lawrence and Wishart.

——(1985*b*). 'Realism Softens Labour Rhetoric on Police'. *Police Review*, 11 October, 2052.

——(1985*c*). 'The Danger of Complacency'. *Police Review*, 21 June, 1260.

Kinsey, R. (1984). *The Merseyside Crime Survey*. Liverpool: Merseyside Metropolitan Council.

——(1985). *Crime and Policing on Merseyside, Final Report*. Liverpool: Merseyside Metropolitan Council.

Knight, S. (1980). *Form and Ideology in Crime Fiction*. Bloomington, Ind.: Indiana University Press.

Kymlicka, W. (1995). *Multicultural Citizenship: A Liberal Theory of Minority Rights*. Oxford: Oxford University Press.

Lambert, J. (1970). *Crime, Police and Race Relations*. London: Oxford University Press.

Lash, S., and Urry, J. (1994). *Economies of Signs and Space*. London: Sage.

Laster, K., and O'Malley, P. (1996). 'Sensitive New-age Laws: The Reassertion of Emotionality in Law'. *International Journal of the Sociology of Law*, 24/4: 21–40.

Latour, B. (2000). 'When Things Strike Back: A Possible Contribution of "Science Studies" to the Social Sciences'. *British Journal of Sociology*, 51/1: 107–24.

Lea, J., and Young, J. (1984). *What is to be Done About Law and Order?* Harmondsworth: Penguin.

Lee, J. (1981). 'Some Structural Aspects of Police Deviance in Relations with Minority Groups', in C. Shearing (ed.), *Organizational Police Deviance*. Toronto: Butterworth.

Leishman, F., Cope, S., and Starie, P. (1996). 'Reinventing and Restructuring: Towards a "New Policing Order"', in F. Leishman, B. Loveday, and S. Savage (eds.), *Core Issues in Policing*. Harlow: Longman.

Loader, I. (1996). *Youth, Policing and Democracy*. Basingstoke: Macmillan.

——(1997). 'Private Security and the Demand for Protection in Contemporary Britain'. *Policing and Society*, 7/2: 143–62.

——(1999). 'Consumer Culture and the Commodification of Policing and Security'. *Sociology*, 33/2: 373–92.

——(2000). 'Plural Policing and Democratic Governance'. *Social and Legal Studies*, 9/3: 323–45.

——(2002). 'Policing, Securitization and Democratization in Europe'. *Criminal Justice*, 2/2: 125–53.

——and Walker, N. (2001). 'Policing as a Public Good: Reconstituting the Connections Between Policing and the State'. *Theoretical Criminology*, 5/1: 9–35.

Loveday, B. (1991). 'The New Police Authorities', *Policing and Society*, 1/3: 193–212.

—— (2000). 'New Directions in Accountability', in F. Leishman, B. Loveday, and S. Savage (eds.), *Core Issues in Policing* (2nd edn.). Harlow: Longman.

Lukes, S. (1975). 'Political Ritual and Social Integration'. *Sociology*, 9/2: 289–308.

Lustgarten, L. (1986). *The Governance of Police*. London: Sweet & Maxwell.

Macpherson, W. (1999). *The Stephen Lawrence Inquiry Report*. London: The Stationery Office.

Maguire, M. (2002). 'Crime Statistics: The Data Explosion and its Implications', in M. Maguire, R. Morgan, and R. Reiner (eds.), *The Oxford Handbook of Criminology* (3rd edn.). Oxford: Oxford University Press.

Manning, P. (1988). *Symbolic Communication*. Cambridge, Mass.: MIT Press.

—— (1992). 'Technological Dramas and the Police: Statement and Counter-Statement in Organizational Analysis'. *Criminology*, 30/3: 327–46.

—— (1997). *Police Work: The Social Organization of Policing* (2nd edn). Cambridge, Mass.: MIT Press.

—— (2001a). 'Technology's Ways: Information Technology, Crime Analysis and the Rationalizing of Policing'. *Criminal Justice*, 1/1: 83–104.

—— (2001b). 'Theorizing Policing: The Drama and Myth of Crime Control in the NYPD'. *Theoretical Criminology*, 5/3: 315–44.

Marenin, O. (1982). 'Parking Tickets and Class Repression: The Concept of Policing in Critical Theories of Criminal Justice'. *Contemporary Crises*, 6/2: 241–66.

Mark, R. (1965). 'The Rights of Wrongdoers'. *Guardian*, 18 May.

—— (1977). *Policing a Perplexed Society*. London: Allen and Unwin.

—— (1978). *In the Office of Constable*. Harmondsworth: Penguin.

Marlow, A., and Loveday, B. (eds.) (2000). *After Macpherson: Policing After the Stephen Lawrence Inquiry*. Lyme Regis: Russell House Publishing.

Marr, A. (2000). *The Day Britain Died*. London: Profile.

Marshall, G. (1965). *Police and Government*. London: Methuen.

Marshall, T. (1950). *Citizenship and Social Class*. Cambridge: Cambridge University Press.

Martin, S., and Jurik, N. (1996). *Doing Justice, Doing Gender: Women in Law and Criminal Justice Occupations*. London: Sage.

Marx, K., and Engels, F. (1975/1888). *The Manifesto of the Communist Party*. Peking: Foreign Languages Press.

Mawby, R. C. (1999). 'Visibility, Transparency and Police-Media Relations'. *Policing and Society*, 9/3: 263–86.

Mawby, R. C. (2002). *Policing Images: Policing, Communication and Legitimacy*. Cullompton: Willan.

Maxfield, M. (1984). *Fear of Crime in England and Wales* (Home Office Research Study No. 78). London: Home Office.

McCabe, S., Wallington, P., Alderson, J., Gostin, L., and Mason, C. (1988). *The Police, Public Order and Civil Liberties*. London: Routledge.

McGarry, J., and O'Leary, B. (1999). *Policing Northern Ireland: Proposals for a New Start*. Belfast: Blackstaff.

McKenzie, I. (1995). 'A Clip Round the Ear'. *Policing*, 11/3: 194–202.

McLaughlin, E. (1994). *Community, Policing and Accountability: The Politics of Policing in Manchester in the 1980s*. Aldershot: Avebury.

——and Murji, K. (1997). 'The Future Lasts a Long Time: Public Policing and the Managerialist Paradox', in P. Francis, P. Davies, and V. Jupp (eds.), *Policing Futures: The Police, Law Enforcement and the Twenty-First Century*. Basingstoke: Macmillan.

——and——(1998). 'Resistance Through Representation: "Storylines", Advertising and Police Federation Campaigns'. *Policing and Society*, 8/4: 367–400.

——and——(1999a). 'The Postmodern Condition of the Police'. *Liverpool Law Review*, 21: 217–40.

——and——(1999b). 'After the Stephen Lawrence Report'. *Critical Social Policy*, 19/3: 371–85.

——and——(2000). 'Lost Connections and New Directions: Neo-Liberalism, New Public Managerialism and the "Modernization" of the British Police', in K. Stenson and R. Sullivan (eds.), *Crime, Risk and Justice*. Harlow: Willan Publishing.

McNee, D. (1983). *McNee's Law*. London: Collins.

Melossi, D. (1993). 'Gazette of Morality and Social Whip'. *Social and Legal Studies*, 2/2: 259–79.

Melucci, A. (1996). *Challenging Codes: Collective Action in the Information Age*. Cambridge: Cambridge University Press.

Meyrowitz, J. (1985). *No Sense of Place*. Oxford: Oxford University Press.

Middleton, D., and Edwards, D. (eds.) (1990). *Collective Remembering*. London: Sage.

Miles, R. (1984). 'The Riots of 1958: Notes on the Ideological Construction of "Race Relations" as a Political Issue in Britain'. *Immigrants and Minorities*, 3: 252–75.

——(1989). *Racism*. London: Routledge.

Miliband, R. (1977). 'A State of De-subordination'. *British Journal of Sociology*, 29/4: 399–409.

Miller, D. (1995). *On Nationality*. Oxford: Oxford University Press.

Miller, D. A. (1988). *The Novel and the Police*. Berkeley, Cal.: University of California Press.

Mirrlees-Black, C. (2000). *Confidence in the Criminal Justice System: Findings from the 2000 British Crime Survey* (Home Office Research Findings No. 137). London: Home Office.

——Mayhew, P., and Percy, A. (1996). *The 1996 British Crime Survey* (Home Office Statistical Bulletin 19/96). London: Home Office.

Montgomery, C. (1999). 'The Policeman's Lot is Not a Happy One'. *The Spectator*, 11 September, 11–12.

Morgan, R. (1989). 'Policing by Consent: Legitimating the Doctrine', in R. Morgan and D. Smith (eds.), *Coming to Terms with Policing*. London: Routledge.

——(1992). 'Talking About Policing', in D. Downes (ed.), *Unravelling Criminal Justice*. Basingstoke: Macmillan.

——and Newburn, T. (1997). *The Future of Policing*. Oxford: Oxford University Press.

Morris, P., and Heal, K. (1981). *Crime Control and the Police*. London: Home Office.

Moss Side and Hulme Community Forum (1994). *'Not Good Enough': A Survey of Policing, Crime and Community Safety on Moss Side's Alexandra Park Estate*. Manchester: Moss Side and Hulme Community Forum.

Mulcahy, A. (2000). 'Policing History: The Official Discourse and Organizational Memory of the Royal Ulster Constabulary'. *British Journal of Criminology*, 40/1: 68–87.

Nairn, T. (2000). *After Britain: New Labour and the Return of Scotland*. London: Granta.

National Council for Civil Liberties (1980). *Southall, 23 April 1979 (The Report of the Unofficial Committee of Enquiry)*. London: National Council for Civil Liberties.

Newburn, T. (1992). *Permission and Regulation: Law and Morals in Postwar Britain*. London: Routledge.

——and Sparks, R. (eds.) (2002). *Special Issue of Criminal Justice on 'How Does Crime Policy Travel?'*. 2/2.

Newman, K. (1985). ' "Police-Bashers" Risk to Labour Reputation'. *Police Review*, 11 October, 2060–2.

Neyroud, P. (2002). 'Policing an Unsettled Society', public lecture delivered at the Institute of Public Policy Research, London, 8 July.

——and Beckley, A. (2001). *Policing, Ethics and Human Rights*. Cullompton: Willan.

Offe, C. (1999). 'How can We Trust Our Fellow Citizens?' in M. E. Warren (ed.), *Democracy and Trust*. Cambridge: Cambridge University Press.

Oliver, I. (1987). *Police, Government and Accountability*. Basingstoke: Macmillan.

O'Malley, P. (1997). 'Policing, Politics and Postmodernity'. *Social and Legal Studies*, 6/3: 363–81.

O'Malley, P. (1999). 'Volatile and Contradictory Punishment'. *Theoretical Criminology*, 3/2: 175–96.

Parekh, B. (2000). *The Future of Multi-Ethnic Britain (The Parekh Report)*. London: Profile Books.

Parris, M. (1995). 'Viewpoint'. *Policing Today*, August, 1/6: 1.

Patten, C. (1999). *A New Beginning for Policing in Northern Ireland: The Report of the Independent Commission on Policing for Northern Ireland*. Belfast. HMSO.

Paxman, J. (1998). *The English: A Portrait of a People*. London: Michael Joseph.

Pead, D., and Hilliard, B. (1993). 'Are We Heading for a Police State?'. *Police Review*, 14 May 1993, 16–17.

Philips, M., and Philips, T. (1999). *Windrush: The Irresistible Rise of Multi-Racial Britain*. London: Harper Collins.

Pickering, M. (1997). *History, Experience and Cultural Studies*. Basingstoke: Macmillan.

Piliavin, I., and Briar, S. (1964). 'Police Encounters with Juveniles'. *American Journal of Sociology*, 70: 206–14.

Pimlott, B. (1997). *The Queen: A Biography of Elizabeth II*. London: Harper Collins.

Pollitt, C. (1990). *Managerialism and the Public Services: The Anglo-American Experience*. Oxford: Basil Blackwell.

Portelli, A. (1991). *The Death of Luigi Trastulli and Other Stories: Form and Meaning in Oral History*. New York: State University of New York Press.

——(1997). *The Battle of Valle Giulia: Oral History and the Art of Dialogue*. Madison, Wis.: University of Wisconsin Press.

Power, M. (1997). *The Audit Society: Rituals of Verification*. Oxford: Oxford University Press.

Pratt, J. (2000). 'Emotive and Ostentatious Punishment: Its Decline and Resurgence in Modern Society'. *Punishment and Society*, 2/4: 417–40.

Prince, M. (1988). *God's Cop: The Biography of James Anderton*. London: Frederick Muller.

Punch, M. (1979a). 'The Secret Social Service', in S. Holdaway (ed.), *The British Police*. London: Edward Arnold.

——(1979b). *Policing the Inner City*. London: Macmillan.

Regan, D. (1991). *Local Government versus the Police: The Rise and Fall of Police Monitoring in Britain*. London: Hampden Trust.

Reiner, R. (1978). *The Blue-Coated Worker: A Sociological Study of Police Unionism*. Cambridge: Cambridge University Press.

——(1980). 'Fuzzy Thoughts: The Police and Law-and-Order Politics'. *Sociological Review*, 28/2: 377–413.

——(1991). *Chief Constables: Bobbies, Bosses or Bureaucrats?*. Oxford: Oxford University Press.

——(1992). 'Policing a Postmodern Society'. *Modern Law Review*, 55/6: 761–81.

——(1994). 'The Dialectics of Dixon: Changing Images of the TV Cop', in M. Stephens and S. Becker (eds.), *Police Force, Police Service*. Basingstoke: Macmillan.

——(1995*a*). 'From Sacred to Profane: The Thirty Years' War of the British Police'. *Policing and Society*, 5/2: 121–8.

——(1995*b*). 'Myth vs. Modernity: Reality and Unreality in the English Model of Policing', in J.-P. Brodeur (ed.), *Comparisons in Policing: An International Perspective*. Aldershot: Avebury.

——(1997). 'Policing and the Police', in M. Maguire, R. Morgan, and R. Reiner (eds.), *The Oxford Handbook of Criminology* (2nd edn.). Oxford: Oxford University Press.

——(2000*a*). *The Politics of the Police* (3rd edn.). Oxford: Oxford University Press.

——(2000*b*). 'Romantic Realism: Policing and the Media', in F. Leishman, B. Loveday, and S. Savage (eds.), *Core Issues in Policing* (2nd edn.). Harlow: Longman.

——(2002). 'Media Made Criminality: The Representation of Crime in the Mass Media', in M. Maguire, R. Morgan, and R. Reiner (eds.), *The Oxford Handbook of Criminology* (3rd edn.). Oxford: Oxford University Press.

——Livingstone, S., and Allen, J. (1998). 'Discipline or Desubordination?: Changing Images of Crime in the Media Since World War II', paper presented to International Sociological Association World Congress of Sociology, Montreal, Canada, 31 July.

——— and ——(2000*a*). 'No More Happy Endings? The Media and Popular Concern About Crime Since the Second World War', in T. Hope and R. Sparks (eds.), *Crime, Risk and Insecurity: Law and Order in Everyday Life and Political Discourse*. London: Routledge.

——— and ——(2000*b*). 'Casino Culture: Media and Crime in a Winner-Loser Culture', in K. Stenson and R. Sullivan (eds.), *Crime, Risk and Justice*. Harlow: Willan Publishing.

Rex, J. (1979). 'Black Militancy and Class Conflict', in R. Miles and A. Phizacklea (eds.), *Racism and Political Action in Britain*. London: Routledge and Kegan Paul.

Ricoeur, P. (1998). *Critique and Conviction*. Cambridge: Polity.

Rigakos, G. (2002). *The New Parapolice: Risk Markets and Commodified Social Control*. Toronto: University of Toronto Press.

Roberts, J., Stalans, L., Inermaur, D., and Hough, M. (2003). *Penal Populism and Public Opinion: Lessons from Five Countries*. Oxford: Oxford University Press.

Rose, D. (1996). *In the Name of the Law: The Collapse of Criminal Justice*. London: Jonathon Cape.

Samuel, R. (1994). *Theatres of Memory*. London: Verso.

Sarat, A. (1997). 'Victims, Vengeance and the Identities of Law'. *Social and Legal Studies*, 6/2: 63–89.

Savage, S., and Charman, S. (1996). 'In Favour of Compliance'. *Policing Today*, April: 10–17.

——— and Cope, S. (1996). 'Police Governance, the Association of Chief Police Officers and Constitutional Change'. *Public Policy and Administration*, 11/2: 92–106.

——— and ——— (2000). *Policing and the Power of Persuasion: The Changing Role of the Association of Chief Police Officers*. London: Blackstone.

Scarman, L. (1974). *Report of the Inquiry into the Red Lion Square Disorders of 15 June 1974*. London: HMSO. Cmd. 5919.

——— (1982). *The Scarman Report: The Brixton Disorders 10–12 April 1981*. Harmondsworth: Penguin.

Scheff, T. (1994). 'Emotions and Identity: A Theory of Ethnic Nationalism', in C. Calhoun (ed.), *Social Theory and the Politics of Identity*. Oxford: Basic Blackwell.

Schlesinger, P. (1991). *Media, State and Nation*. London: Sage.

——— and Tumber, H. (1994). *Reporting Crime: The Media Politics of Criminal Justice*. Oxford: Clarendon.

Scott, H. (1954). *Scotland Yard*. London: Mayflower.

Scraton, P. (1985). *The State of the Police*. London: Pluto.

Shaw, M., and Williamson, W. (1972). 'Public Attitudes to Police'. *The Criminologist*, 7: 18–33.

Shearing, C. (1996). 'Reinventing Policing: Policing as Governance', in O. Marenin (ed.), *Changing Police: Policing Change*. New York: Garland.

——— and Ericson, R. (1991). 'Culture as Figurative Action'. *British Journal of Sociology*, 42/4: 481–506.

——— and Stenning, P. (1983). 'Private Security: Implications for Social Control'. *Social Problems*, 30/5: 493–506.

Sheehy, P. (1993a). *Report of the Enquiry into Police Responsibilities and Rewards*. London: HMSO. Cm 2280.

——— (1993b). 'Eight Myths and the Reality'. *Police Review*, 17 September, 12–13.

Sheptycki, J. (1995). 'Transnational Policing and the Making of a Postmodern State'. *British Journal of Criminology*, 35/4: 613–35.

——— (1999). 'Political Culture and Structures of Control: Police-Related Scandal in the Low Countries in Comparative Perspective'. *Policing and Society*, 9/1: 1–32.

——— (2001). 'Review of Robert Reiner's, *The Politics of the Police (3rd edn)*'. *Policing and Society*, 11/3–4: 411–14.

Shils, E. (1975). *Center and Periphery: Essays in Macrosociology*. Chicago, Ill.: University of Chicago Press.

Sillitoe, P. J. (1955). *Cloak Without Dagger*. London: Cassell and Co.

Silverman, J., and Wilson, D. (2002). *Innocence Betrayed: Paedophilia, the Media and Society*. Cambridge: Polity.

Silverstone, R. (1994). *Television and Everyday Life*. London: Routledge.

Sim, J. (1982). 'Scarman: The Police Counter-Attack', in M. Eve and D. Musson (eds.), *The Socialist Register 1982*. London: Merlin.

Simey, M. (1988). *Democracy Rediscovered: A Study in Police Accountability*. London: Pluto.

Simon, J. (1995). 'They Died With Their Boots On: The Boot Camp and the Limits of Modern Penality'. *Social Justice*, 22/2: 25–48.

——(2001). 'Fear and Loathing in Late Modernity: Reflections on the Cultural Sources of Mass Imprisonment in the United States'. *Punishment and Society*, 3/1: 21–33.

Sims, L., and Myhill, A. (2000). *Policing and the Public: Findings from the 2000 British Crime Survey* (Home Office Research Findings No. 136). London: Home Office.

Skolnick, J. (1966). *Justice Without Trial: Law Enforcement in a Democratic Society*. New York: Wiley.

—— and Bayley, D. (1988). 'Theme and Variation in Community Policing', in M. Tonry and N. Morris (eds.), *Crime and Justice: An Annual Review of Research—Vol. 10*. Chicago, Ill.: University of Chicago Press.

Smith, C., Rundle, S., and Hosking, R. (2002). *Police Service Strength* (Home Office Statistical Bulletin 10/02). London: Home Office.

Smith, D. (1996). 'Explaining Crime Trends', in W. Saulsbury, J. Mott, and T. Newburn (eds.), *Themes in Contemporary Policing*. London: Police Foundation/Policy Studies Institute.

——(1997). 'Ethnic Origins, Crime and Criminal Justice', in M. Maguire, R. Morgan, and R. Reiner (eds.), *The Oxford Handbook of Criminology* (2nd edn.). Oxford: Oxford University Press.

—— and Gray, J. (1985). *Police and People in London (Volumes I–IV)*. Aldershot: Gower.

Smith, J. (1994). 'Reviewing the Police: Has the Government got it Right?'. *Policing Today*, 1/1: 4–8.

Smith, M., Sparks, R., and Girling, E. (2000). 'Educating Sensibilities: The Image of the "Lesson" in Children's Talk About Punishment'. *Punishment and Society*, 2/4: 395–416.

Smyth, J. (2002). 'Symbolic Power and Police Legitimacy: The Royal Ulster Constabulary'. *Crime, Law, and Social Change*, 38: 295–310.

Sociological Research Online (1999). 'Rapid Response Section on the Stephen Lawrence Inquiry'. *Sociological Research Online* <www.socresonline.org.uk/socresonline/4/1.html>.

Solomos, J., and Back, L. (1996). *Racism and Society*. Basingstoke: Macmillan.

Sparks, R. (1992*a*). *Television and the Drama of Crime: Moral Tales and the Place of Crime in Public Life*. Buckingham: Open University Press.

—— (1992*b*). 'Reason and Unreason in Left Realism: Some Problems in the Constitution of the Fear of Crime', in R. Matthews and J. Young (eds.), *Issues in Realist Criminology*. London: Sage.

—— (1994). 'Inspector Morse: *The Last Enemy*' in G. Brandt (ed.), *British Television Drama in the 1980s*. Cambridge: Cambridge University Press.

—— (2000). 'Risk and Blame in Criminal Justice Controversies: British Press Coverage and Official Discourse on Prison Security (1993–6)', in M. Brown and J. Pratt (eds.), *Dangerous Offenders: Punishment and Social Order*. London: Routledge.

—— (2003). 'Punishment in Advanced Capitalist Societies', in T. Blomberg and S. Cohen (eds.), *Punishment and Social Control* (2nd edn.). New York: Aldine de Gruyter.

—— Girling, E., and Smith, M. (2000). 'Children Talking About Justice and Punishment'. *The International Journal of Children's Rights*, 8: 191–209.

Spencer, S. (1985). *Called to Account: The Case for Police Accountability in England and Wales*. London: National Council for Civil Liberties.

St. Johnston, E. (1978). *One Policeman's Story*. Chichester: Barry Rose.

Stanko, E. (2000). 'Victims R Us: The Life History of "Fear of Crime" and the Politicisation of Violence', in T. Hope and R. Sparks (eds.), *Crime, Risk and Insecurity: Law and Order in Everyday Life and Political Discourse*. London: Routledge.

Stedman Jones, S. (2001). *Durkheim Reconsidered*. Cambridge: Polity.

Stenson, K. (2000). 'Some Day my Prince Will Come: Zero-Tolerance and Liberal Government', in T. Hope and R. Sparks (eds.), *Crime, Risk and Insecurity: Law and Order in Political Discourse and Everyday Life*. London: Routledge.

Stevenson, S., and Bottoms, A. (1990). 'The Politics of the Police 1955–1964: A Royal Commission in a Decade of Transition', in R. Morgan (ed.), *Policing Organised Crime and Crime Prevention*. Bristol: Bristol and Bath Centre for Criminal Justice.

Stinchcombe, A. (1963). 'Institutions of Privacy in the Determination of Police Administrative Practice'. *American Journal of Sociology*, 69/2: 150–60.

Storch, R. (1975). 'The Plague of Blue Locusts: Police Reform and Popular Resistance in Northern England 1840–57'. *International Review of Social History*, 20: 61–90.

Sumner, C. (1981). 'Race, Crime and Hegemony: A Review Essay'. *Contemporary Crises*, 5: 277–91.

—— (1994). *The Sociology of Deviance: An Obituary*. Buckingham: Open University Press.

Taussig, M. (1992). *The Nervous System*. London: Routledge.

—— (1997). *The Magic of the State*. London: Routledge.

Taylor, C. (1994). 'The Politics of Recognition', in A. Gutmann (ed.), *Multiculturalism: Examining the Politics of Recognition*. Princeton, NJ: Princeton University Press.

Taylor, I. (1995). 'Private Homes and Public Others: An Analysis of Talk About Crime in Suburban South Manchester in the mid-1990s'. *British Journal of Criminology*, 35/2: 263–85.

—— (1999). *Crime in Context: A Critical Criminology of Market Societies*. Cambridge: Polity.

Thompson, E. P. (1980). *Writing by Candlelight*. London: Merlin.

Thompson, J. B. (1990). *Ideology and Modern Culture*. Cambridge: Polity.

—— (1996). *The Media and Modernity: A Social Theory of the Media*. Cambridge: Polity.

—— (2000). *Political Scandal: Power and Visibility in the Media Age*. Cambridge: Polity.

Thompson, P. (1988). *The Voice of the Past: Oral History*. Oxford: Oxford University Press.

Times Literary Supplement (1962). 'Finest in the World?', *Times Literary Supplement*, 14 September.

Tonkin, E. (1990). *Narrating Our Pasts*. Cambridge: Cambridge University Press.

Turner, V. (1974). *Dramas, Fields and Metaphors: Symbolic Action in Human Society*. Ithaca, NY: Cornell University Press.

Unger, R. M. (1987). *Social Theory: Its Situation and Tasks*. Cambridge: Cambridge University Press.

—— (1996). *What Should Legal Analysis Become?* London: Verso.

—— (1998). *Democracy Realized*. London: Verso.

Valier, C. (2000). 'Looking Daggers: A Psychoanalytic Reading of the Scene of Punishment'. *Punishment and Society*, 2/4: 379–94.

Waddington, P. A. J. (1991). *The Strong Arm of the Law*. Oxford: Oxford University Press.

—— (1999). 'Police (Canteen) Sub-Culture: An Appreciation'. *British Journal of Criminology*, 39/2: 287–309.

Wainwright, J. (1967). *Shall I be a Policeman?* London: Wheatman.

Walden, K. (1982). *Visions of Order: The Canadian Mounties in Symbol and Myth*. Toronto: Butterworths.

Waldron, J. (2000). 'What is Cosmopolitan?'. *The Journal of Political Philosophy*, 8/2: 227–43.

Walker, N. (1996). 'Defining Core Police Tasks: The Neglect of the Symbolic Dimension?'. *Policing and Society*, 6/1: 53–71.

Walker, N. (1999). 'Situating Scottish Policing', in P. Duff and N. Hutton (eds.), *Criminal Justice in Scotland*. Aldershot: Dartmouth.

——(2000). *Policing in a Changing Constitutional Order*. London: Sweet & Maxwell.

——(2002). 'Policing and the Supranational'. *Policing and Society*, 12/4: 307–21.

——and Telford, M. (2000). *Designing Criminal Justice: The Northern Ireland System in Comparative Perspective*. Belfast: The Northern Ireland Office.

Walklate, S. (1998). 'Excavating the Fear of Crime: Fear, Anxiety or Trust?'. *Theoretical Criminology*, 2/4: 403–18.

Wall, D. (1998). *The Chief Constables of England and Wales: The Socio-Legal History of a Criminal Justice Elite*. Aldershot: Dartmouth.

Walzer, M. (1988). *The Company of Critics: Social Criticism and Political Commitment in the Twentieth Century*. New York: Basic Books.

Waters, I. (2000). 'Quality and Performance Monitoring', in F. Leishman, B. Loveday, and S. Savage (eds.), *Core Issues in Policing* (2nd edn.). Harlow: Longman.

Watson, S. (1999). 'Policing the Affective Society: Beyond Governmentality in the Theory of Social Control'. *Social and Legal Studies*, 8/2: 227–51.

Weatheritt, M. (1986). *Innovations in Policing*. London: Croom Helm.

Weber, M. (1948). *From Max Weber: Essays in Sociology* (ed. and trans. H. Gerth and C. Wright Mills). London: Routledge and Kegan Paul.

Weight, R. (2002). *Patriots: National Identity in Britain 1940–2000*. Basingstoke: Macmillan.

Weinberger, B. (1995). *The Best Police in the World: An Oral History of the English Police from the 1930s to the 1960s*. London: Scolar Press.

Weiner, M. (1981). *English Culture and the Decline of the Industrial Spirit*. Harmondsworth: Penguin.

Westley, W. (1970). *Violence and the Police*. Cambridge, Mass.: MIT Press.

Westmarland, L. (2001). *Gender and Policing: Sex, Power and Police Culture*. Cullompton: Willan.

Whittaker, B. (1964). *The Police*. London: Eyre and Spottiswoode.

Williams, R. (1964). *The Long Revolution*. Harmondsworth: Penguin.

——(1973). *The Country and the City*. London: Vintage.

——(1977). *Marxism and Literature*. Oxford: Oxford University Press.

——(1979). *Politics and Letters: Interviews with New Left Review*. London: New Left Books.

——(1981). *Culture*. London: Fontana.

Willis, C. (1983). *The Use, Effectiveness and Impact of Stop and Search Powers* (Home Office Research Study No. 97). London: HMSO.

Willis, P. (2000). *The Ethnographic Imagination*. Cambridge: Polity.

Wilson, C. (2000). *Cop Knowledge: Police Power and Cultural Narrative in Twentieth Century America*. Chicago, Ill.: Chicago University Press.

Wilson, J. Q. (1968). *Varieties of Police Behaviour*. Cambridge, Mass.: Harvard University Press.

Windlesham, L. (1987). *Responses to Crime*. Oxford: Clarendon.

——(1993). *Responses to Crime—Volume 2: Penal Policy in the Making*. Oxford: Clarendon.

——(1996). *Responses to Crime—Volume 3: Legislating with the Tide*. Oxford: Clarendon.

——(2001). *Responses to Crime—Volume 4: Dispensing Justice*. Oxford: Clarendon.

Wolff Olins (1990). *A Force for Change: A Report on the Corporate Identity of the Metropolitan Police*. London: Wolff Olins Corporate Identity.

Woodcock, J. (1991). 'Overturning Police Culture'. *Policing*, 7/3: 172–82.

Wouters, C. (1986). 'Formalization and Informalization: Changing Tension Balances in Civilising Processes'. *Theory, Culture and Society*, 3/2: 1–18.

——(1992). 'On Status Competition and Emotion Management: The Study of Emotions as a New Field'. *Theory, Culture and Society*, 9: 229–52.

——(1999). 'Changing Patterns of Social Controls and Self Controls: On the Rise of Crime Since the 1950s and the Sociogenesis of a ' "Third Nature" '. *British Journal of Criminology*, 39/3: 416–32.

Wright, P. (1985). *On Living in an Old Country: The National Past in Contemporary Britain*. London: Verso.

Wrong, D. (1994). *The Problem of Order: What Unites and Divides Society*. New York: Free Press.

Young, H. (1993). *One of Us: A Biography of Margaret Thatcher* (2nd edn.). London: Pan Books.

Young, J. (1999). *The Exclusive Society: Social Exclusion, Crime and Difference in Late Modernity*. London: Sage.

——(2003). 'Merton with Energy, Katz with Structure: The Sociology of Vindictiveness and the Criminology of Transgression', *Theoretical Criminology*, 7/3 (in press).

Young, M. (1991). *An Inside Job: Policing and Police Culture in Britain*. Oxford: Clarendon.

——(1993). *In the Sticks: Cultural Identity in a Rural Police Force*. Oxford: Oxford University Press.

Zolo, D. (1990). *Democracy and Complexity: A Realist Approach*. Cambridge: Polity.

Index

385 Index

380 Index

Lightning Source UK Ltd.
Milton Keynes UK
UKOW03n1900150114

224692UK00005B/42/A